PORTAVO

AN IRISH TOWNLAND AND ITS PEOPLES

PART TWO

The White Row Press

PORTAVO

AN IRISH TOWNLAND AND ITS PEOPLES

PART TWO

The White Row Press

First published 2005 by
the White Row Press
135 Cumberland Road
Dundonald, Belfast BT16 2BB
Northern Ireland

www.whiterowpress.com

The publishers would like to thank the Belfast Natural History & Philosophical Society,
the Esme Mitchell Trust, and the Northern Ireland Community Relations Council,
which aims to promote a pluralist society and encourage an acceptance and understanding
of cultural diversity, for supporting the production of this book.

Front cover: Sandy Bay, by Robert Innes.
Rear: Stockbridge Road, by Robert Innes.
The publishers extend their grateful thanks to non-fee copyright holders
for permission to use their material in this book.

ISBN 1 870132 21 1 (paperback)
ISBN 1 870132 26 2 (hardback)

Printed by Universities Press Ltd., Belfast
A catalogue record for this book is available from the British Library

Contents

'It does no harm to the mystery to understand a little bit about it'

Richard Feynman

Preface

I publish this book with trepidation. Sequels and follow-ups have a terrible track record. All too often they are embarrassing parodies of what went before, forgettable works, which rightly end up going for what sports coaches call an early bath.

Will this book escape such a fate? There are some grounds for hope that it may. The sources that it draws on are as rich as those available to its predecessor. The story it tells is at least as compelling. There is no lack of colour or incident. The time frame is tighter, and the material that forms the book is more structurally interconnected – all of which makes me cautiously optimistic that the curse of the sequel will not fall on *Portavo*.

It was never my plan to produce two volumes. When this work was commissioned, way back in 1987, in as far as such things were thought of at all, a single book seemed ample, indeed rather ambitious. I was in charge in those days. The script was mine to do with as I pleased. But it soon turned the tables, growing into what George Benn[1] called a 'baggy monster', a prodigious, ungovernable, and infinitely demanding thing, that virtually insisted on being published in two volumes.

The first of these appeared in 2003, after fifteen years of writing and research. Which makes the production of the 'sequel' just two years later seem almost indecently hasty. Not so. This book was not written in the wake of the first. It had been completed in draft when the first appeared. So the question that cuts to the heart of the matter is not, 'How did you do it so quickly?' but, 'What took you so long?'

Though both books can be viewed as free-standing, I don't see them in that way. To me, they are a single entity, a divided but indivisible whole. The experience of reading this book will be all the more satisfying if you have read the first. However, if you are coming to *Portavo* fresh, you will not, I hope, be left struggling. Familiarity with part one is not assumed.

1. Benn's *History of Belfast* (1877) also appeared in two volumes.

Jim Carr, hard at work in Ballywalter Park, 2005.

The story of the Ker (pronounced Carr) family is central to the townland's modern history. This narrative is on a par with anything in fiction. Indeed it out-fictions fiction. When the book begins in the early 1840s, the cultured, Italianate Kers were amongst the wealthiest families in Ireland. And they had yet to reach the giddy summit of their prestige and influence. By the 1870s, however, everything had gone horribly and spectacularly wrong, and the family had collapsed in a manner worthy of any of the Caesars, amidst alcoholism, incest, suicide and madness.

But the book is not just about the glamorous and dysfunctional lives of the townland's owners. The whole of the rural social pyramid is here. 'Ordinary' lives are to the fore in a way that they could not be in part one (on account of the dearth of evidence), bringing a wholeness and completeness to the tale. The book also draws heavily on the townland's oral tradition. We learn what people said to each other and about each other, and about the world around them. The spoken word, sharp and pithy, lifts every page on which it appears.

The book is also full of pictures. Many are drawn from the Ker family collection, which provides the basis of the book's illustration. But there is much else of interest besides. Gathering these pictures was a mammoth collective endeavour. They came not only from County Down, but from places like England, Scotland, the Unites States and France. One set was even couriered in by plane from Canada (thank you Ethel!), for Portavo has its own diaspora, and the families of many of the people who appear on these pages no longer live in Ireland. A lot of people have taken a lot of trouble to help illustrate this book. I think of Gilbert McCutcheon obtaining maize flour from a Belfast meal merchant so that we could illustrate the Famine chapter with a photo of 'Indian corn'; of my dad's tireless travels in pursuit of the perfect picture; of the superb watercolours Elizabeth Taggart produced at short notice for just a thank you. The number of favours I owe is past counting. My sincere thanks to everyone involved.

Writing about people who are still alive adds an additional level of sensitivity. My way of dealing with this was to send copies of the later chapters to the principal parties concerned. As you may imagine, I was heartily relieved when they gave the script a clean bill of health. I salute the individuals and families concerned. They have allowed the story to be told, warts and all. This places additional responsibilities on the author: I hope I have discharged them properly.

I am also grateful to my readers: to Alastair Browne for giving the script a general once-over; to Bill Maguire for helping with some of the finer points of landlordism and estate finance; to Jonathan Bell, Paul Bew, Gloria Siggins and Christine Kinealy for commenting helpfully on the chapters relating to their specialisms, and to the many experts and authorities who have helped with a steer on this, or a remark on that, on the way. The text is all the sounder for their contributions.

I won't repeat the fulsome set of thanks that are set out in the preface to part one, other than to say that they apply equally and in full to this second volume. I will just thank two of the project's stalwarts, Derek Tughan and David Ker. They stood by me through thick and thin. Without their unstinting backing this book would have been signally the poorer.

In 1852 Dufferin asked the Kers if he could borrow their copy of Harris's 1744 *Antient and Present State of County Down*. Anna looked everywhere, but the book could not be found, leading her to the conclusion that her husband David (then in Scotland), had put it 'in some drawer that I do not know of'. But she was able to advise Dufferin that his neighbour Ward had a copy. If he was 'in distress', he could find it there. Harris's book had entered the consciousness of the county. My hope for *Portavo* is that it will have the good fortune to do the same.

Peter Carr

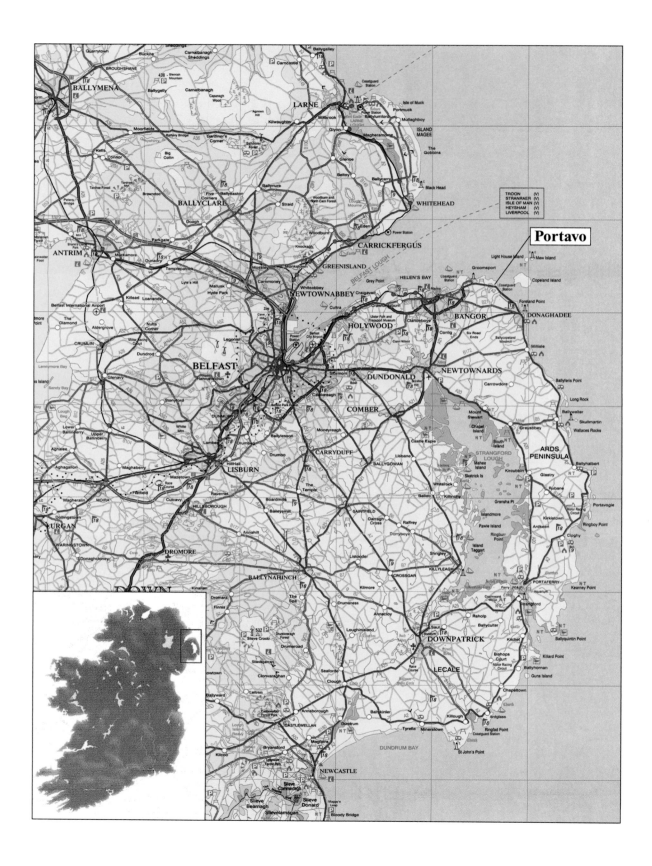

18   La belle époque

Staring into darkness

The Royal Hotel, Belfast, December 1871

Richard stared intently at the floor. It was happening again. Not in private, where it could be hidden, but in a public forum, for all the world to see. What should he do about it? What could he do about it? Nothing. Absolutely nothing.

He used to cringe when this happened. Now he was too used to it to be embarrassed, but he did feel for the first-timers, those to whom all this was new. He knew the cycle. First perplexity, then sideways glances, then the staring. First at David, then at him. At him avoiding their gaze. Occasionally there was rude, muffled laughter. Usually, though, a conspiracy formed. A conspiracy of silence. A kindly pretence that all was well. It was far from well. His poor, dear brother was as mad as a hatter, and there was nothing he could do about it.

It was not that David needed to be carted off to Bedlam. His 'madness' was not of the stark, staring kind. He wasn't foaming at the mouth. He wasn't dribbling. It was an altogether more subtle affliction. The worst kind, perhaps. A species of madness that did not let you forget what you had lost. For all his brother's fine qualities were still in there, close enough to see, close enough to reach, but not to rescue.

Richard raised his eyes to the window. He became aware of the hubbub on the street outside, the dust caught in shafts of yellow sunlight. The room seemed fusty, claustrophobic, unclean. He used at this point to have an almost irresistible urge to run away, to leap through the nearest window. But he was over that. He could sit through it now. He could stare into the darkness. And lately – God forgive him – he had even begun to see its funny side.

Who could have imagined it? David Stewart Ker, his golden, sainted brother, deranged. The estate in chaos. Their collective finances in ruins. Vast chunks of their enormous property portfolio alienated or forcibly sold.

'Few incoming landlords can have inspired such a sense of promise.' David Stewart Ker, c.1842, by W.C. Ross, watercolour on marble. (Ker family)

'Lord Montalto'

How different it had all seemed twenty-eight years before, when in 1844 at the age of twenty-seven, David Stewart Ker had formally inherited his family's great estates. Their collective future had looked so bright then. So full of promise. Yes, there was the shadow of their father's illness, the awful shock of the burning of Portavo. But for all that, it had been a wonderful time, a *belle époque,* a time of fresh and exciting departures. He had gone abroad. His dear sisters, Frances and Madalena, had married and begun new lives. And of course his brother David had taken charge of the estates.

It had been the smoothest of successions. There was no question of this heir being threatened with disinheritance, or being made to feel ashamed of his parentage. Nor was the new incumbent driven by his father's insatiable territorial hunger, or his outsider's need to belong. David Stewart Ker was born to the purple. Rank and standing were a given for him. His mother was a Londonderry. He was a pure-bred landed gentleman, the first that his mercurial family had produced.

And he looked every inch the part. The young David had a glamorous, almost princely air. Lank, elegant, doe-eyed, affable, David Stewart Ker was a gilded creature, with a proven record of commitment to the estates and the people who lived on them, people with whom he had publicly shared the great milestones of his life. His accession was greeted with satisfaction. Few incoming landlords can have inspired such a sense of promise. The Kers had come up trumps again. Cometh the hour, cometh the man.

'From the Bar of Dundrum to the town of Belfast': the Ker estates

Ker became master of a small landed empire. One in every twenty acres of County Down belonged to the family, whose territories ran 'from the Bar of Dundrum to the town of Belfast' and then beyond, through Broadisland to mid-Antrim, an area of some 35,650 acres, made up, not of barren mountain and sucking bog, but of fertile, well-tenanted agricultural land.[1] This vast domain included the villages of Clough, Whitehead and Ballycarry, the town of Ballynahinch, the county town of Downpatrick, mills, schools, two ports, slate and limestone quarries, and a borough seat in parliament that the family had made their own after a bloody contest in 1837.

Some six thousand of these verdant acres lay in County Antrim, where Ker's main presence was the 4,600 acre Red Hall or Broadisland estate, which lay between Carrickfergus and Larne. This was centred on the largely disused mansion house of Red Hall, and had been left to Ker's

Thatched cottage, Dundrum Bay, by Kenneth Webb. The bay marked the estate's southern border. (Private collection)

The Copeland Islands, viewed from the Portavo estate, 1864. (Ker family)

father by his Uncle Richard in 1822. But it had been retained only after the Kers had seen off a rival claim in a rancorous lawsuit, in which the family's dirty linen was washed in public, to the mortification of all concerned. To the north, between Ballymena and the Antrim plateau, lay another 1,200 or so scattered acres.

Ker's principal estate lay around Ballynahinch, in the thick of the County Down drumlin belt, where he held nearly 13,000 acres that were home to over 7,000 people. Here one could walk for six miles, as the crow flies, without leaving Ker's domain.[2] The Downpatrick estate, 7,300 acres with a population of nearly 8,000, came next. Then came the small fry, the 2,910 acre Clough estate, which ran from the foothills of Slieve Croob to the shores of Dundrum Bay, and the 2,585 acre Portavo estate, which bordered Belfast Lough and included the Copeland Islands. Amidst the larger rafts of land lay another 5,000 acres in a shoal of townlands dotted through the rolling countryside of mid and north Down and the Ards.

Portavo was a very small part of this mighty edifice. As a townland of some 540 acres in the sixth largest and least populous of the Ker estates, its significance should have been slight indeed. But it had been the family's original home in the county, and until its mansion house was destroyed by fire in 1844, Portavo had been the site of one of the family's favourite seats. This had given it an importance that was out of all proportion to its size.

Big as his estate was, it did not quite place Ker in the stratosphere. The Duke of Devonshire owned 61,000 acres in Ireland and enjoyed an income of £198,000 a year.[3] Ker's neighbour, the Marquis of Downshire, another of the richest landowners in the United Kingdom, had 115,000 acres and just over £70,000 per annum. The Londonderrys had an annual income of well over £100,000, making them wealthier than many European royal families.[4] That said, the Kers were not exactly anybody's poor relations. Their income placed them amongst the country's thirty wealthiest families. And though their acreage was smaller, their income was greater than that of many much larger, titled landowners.[5]

Ker managed his 'numerous estates' with confidence and aplomb. For most of the previous four years, thanks to his father's illness, he had been their *de facto* sovereign.[6] This 'regency' period had seen a revolution in the way the family's lands had been run. Farms had been re-valued. Rents had been reduced by 15-25%. Landlord-tenant communication had increased.[7] There had been a notably greater level of investment, a timely loosening of the purse strings. All this was ultimately due to David, who was instinctively comfortable with the more tenant-centred, semi-accountable forms of estate management that were then being espoused by reformers. Under his leadership, the estate had made a wholehearted commitment to modernity and reform.

The early 1840s were a period of intensive activity. New projects crowded the horizon. In 1840 Ker joined with Downshire to drain a small lake, two large bogs, 'and a vast quantity of meadow and arable land' on the frontier between their estates, a project which would employ 80-150 men over three summers.[8] Downshire had initially been uneasy about treating with Ker *fils*, but in a letter in which he contrasts his appetite for bold schemes with his invalid father's caution, David assured him that he had the authority to act for the estate.[9] The work proceeded. Mere nature was improved upon. Crops grew on erstwhile marshland. Cattle grazed where pike and perch had once played.[10]

Money was also poured into Ballynahinch. At a dinner in the newly completed Ker Arms Hotel in 1842, one old timer who had known four landlords and five agents declared approvingly that 'more improvement

Couples danced to music from a fiddler 'of the most grotesque appearance' on the completion of the joint drainage project. (Ray Elwood)

Ballynahinch Market House, restored in 2002. (Chris Halpin)

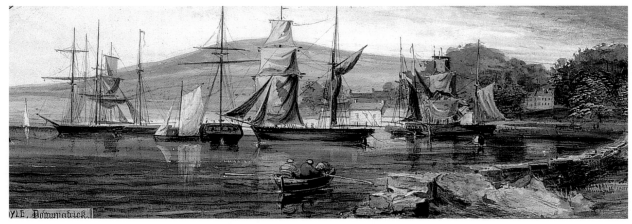

YLE, Downpatrick.

The new Quoile Quay stimulated commerce, and was a particular boon during the Famine. (Ker family)

Labyrinth without a Minotaur. The Spa and maze (bottom right) in 1864. (Ker family)

THE SPA & MAZE B·NAHINCH

had taken place [in the town] within the last 12 months than during the last 20 years'. A Literary and Scientific Society was founded in 1853, under Ker's patronage. Its inaugural lecture on 'The Pleasures and Advantages of Science' was delivered by the Rev. Henry Cooke to 'one of the largest, most respectable, and intelligent' audiences ever seen in the town.[11] The second lecture, 'The Wisdom of God as displayed in the variety of formations of the Earth's Crust' shows us the mountain that science in a small Irish town had to climb.

Ballynahinch's mood was buoyant. It was a coming town, but it was not self-sufficient. It had a good grain market, but too much value was being added elsewhere, in non-Ker breweries and distilleries, and this angered the town's burghers. There were calls for a brewery and a tanning yard to be established, and for closer trading links with their brother settlement of Downpatrick. The new quay that Ker had built on the River Quoile caused much excitement, for it was 'a great matter to have a place for shipping and receiving goods, only eight miles off.'[12] The speech communicates a wonderful sense of the estate as a single economic unit, and lets us see the county as many people saw it then, as a patchwork of little, semi-independent estates.

The Spa, just outside Ballynahinch, also struck the new regime as ripe for development. The Spa's bitter waters were held to be medicinal (they tasted so foul they had to be good for you).[13] Ker's grandfather had installed two pumps there in 1810,[14] which got the water out of the ground and into glasses, but not a lot else. David Stewart Ker followed this in 1840 with an entrepreneurial attempt to turn the Spa into a genteel tourist mecca.

He assembled an imaginative package of attractions. Assembly rooms, pump houses, pleasure grounds and an hotel were constructed. Visitors were allowed to walk within the Montalto demesne. A triangular labyrinth 'where the young can desport and the aged moralise' was laid out within the husk of a dug out bog.[15] An Anglican church was built in 1815 to cater for the spiritual needs of visitors. A Presbyterian church followed in 1872, built and paid for by a Belfast merchant for whom the Spa was a home from home.[16]

The public responded. Visitors came in droves, staying in the new hotels in the Spa and Ballynahinch, and in nearby farms, which were described as 'annually improving within a circle of a mile round the Wells.' There were no kiss-me quick hats, or sticks of rock on offer. The Spa was a polite resort, and an excellent place for hob-knobbing.

Aynesworth Pilson – ageing, health minded, comfortably off and class conscious – was just the sort of person that the Spa was intended to appeal to. And it did. Undeterred by the four-hour return journey from Downpatrick, Pilson would come for the day in his pony and trap. On arrival he quaffed several glasses of spa water (five tumblers of the wretched stuff being his absolute limit), browsed *The Times* (provided gratis), took leisurely walks, and best of all, 'conversed with… the company assembled there'. At the Spa he could be sure of meeting congenial, like-minded people, including members of the Ker family and their house guests, for the Kers themselves relaxed at the Spa, and could be numbered amongst its attractions.[17]

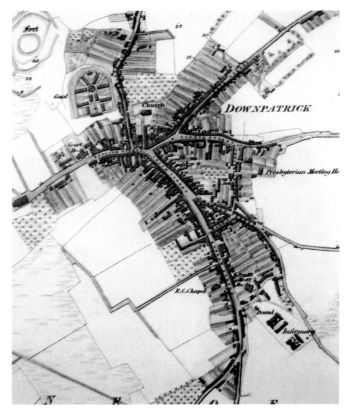

Downpatrick 1835: prim and gospel greedy? (Belfast Education & Library Board)

The town of Downpatrick did better again. Although the first harbingers of decay had already become visible,[18] Downpatrick appeared to be enjoying a golden age. Its rise had been spectacular. As one resident declared in 1847:

The progressive wealth of its inhabitants for the last fifty or sixty years, is almost incredible... in the year 1790, there were not half a-dozen individuals in this town worth more than £5,000 each. At the present time, there is one firm in it worth £200,000, and more than thirty individuals the average of whose wealth would exceed £10,000 each; making the aggregate wealth of the town, with a population under 5,000, exceed half a million, sterling![19]

a rise that the author of the Ordnance Survey Memoirs attributed to its people's religiosity and their 'love for making money'.[20] The fruits of this were everywhere apparent. In the town's dignified late-Georgian architecture. In its sky-high rental values. In the extent of its facilities, which in 1840 included two libraries, three banks, a news-room, a bookshop, an infirmary, a dispensary, a cathedral and a hospital. Baths and inside toilets had begun to appear in the wealthier houses. Pilson had a bath installed in 1835, probably for the pleasure of saying that he had one, as it was another nine months before he could be coaxed to use it. In June 1836, however, at the age of fifty-nine, he 'took a warm bath, the first in my life'.[21]

Initially, the Kers had contributed little to this prosperity. They had exploited their asset politically, but had otherwise treated Downpatrick with indifference. However, the completion of their purchase of the town in 1839 (when the wisdom was that the Kers had got a bargain[22]), was followed by an intensive programme of investment. This significantly altered Downpatrick's geography and form.[23] Marshes were drained, new streets were laid out, and the town realigned on an extended, kite-shaped north-south axis. Approach roads were improved and 'several acres of rich land' were set aside as a fair green, which hosted a busy monthly cattle market. Tenement rents were reduced by 20-30%. Fee farm leases were granted, a practice 'never... known before.'[24] Tolls worth £60 annually were commuted to encourage trade.[25] New corn, butter and pork market buildings were constructed. 'Sundry houses' within and on the edge of the town were rebuilt or otherwise improved. 'Handsome... piers and gates... shrubs and forest trees' adorned the suburbs.[26]

The market house, savaged during the 1837 election, was repaired and 'made... handsome'. The River Quoile was deepened to allow vessels of 300 tons burthen to dock at the new Quoile Quay, Downpatrick's window on the mercantile world. The quay was much improved, as was the link to it, significantly augmenting Downpatrick's capacity as a port. Ker also sought to have the dredging 'carried into the interior', with a view to reclaiming additional tracts of land.[27] It was a time of going boldly. Of

The county town of Downpatrick, jewel in the Ker estate's crown. (Ker family)

developing under-exploited assets. The bewildered citizenry hardly knew what to expect next. An entry in Aynesworth Pilson's diary, noting that Ker 'has cut a new road from the Coil Quay… to proceed across the marshes and Lord knows where', communicates one long-standing resident's sense of the audacity of the work in hand.[28]

This was the Kers at their best. As model proprietors. They didn't meddle in the day-to-day running of the town, but through judicious investment built up its infrastructure and enhanced its capacity to develop itself.[29] The estate had provided a platform for growth (one happy by-product of which was an end to contested borough elections); now, to a large extent, it was over to the citizenry themselves.

All this munificence did not pass unnoticed. David Stewart Ker's free-spending ways and aristocratic air led his political opponents to derisively christen him 'Lord Montalto'.[30] The tag, though cruelly intended, did capture something of the essence of the man. It also reflected the fact that the estate had crossed a Rubicon. The minimalism of the previous four decades had been jettisoned. A new ethos based, nominally at least, on partnership was in place. The emphasis had moved from acquisition to enjoyment, and the more intensive development of existing resources. The dizzy ascent was over. The plateau phase had begun.

Anna Dorothea Ker (nee Blackwood), c.1842, by W.C. Ross. (Ker family)

'A good match, and everybody pleased'

David also found the time to fall in love. The object of his affections was the Honourable Anna Dorothea Blackwood, youngest daughter of the third Lord Dufferin of Ballyleidy (Clandeboy). In January 1841 he confided his intention of marrying Anna to his Uncle Maxwell,[1] and confident of the outcome, urged his uncle:

to come and pay a visit to Portavo... to form yr own ideas upon the attractions of the Lady to whom I am too partial a judge to describe...[2]

Anna's effect on Uncle Maxwell is unknown. But it would have been odd if nothing in him had twitched or quickened in the presence of the comely nineteen year old. Anna was spirited, affectionate and attractive. Friends spoke of her 'sunny frankness... girlish purity [and] good true nature'.[3]

Both families heartily approved of the liaison. Helen, Lady Dufferin, summed it up as 'a good match, and everybody pleased', and hoped that the news would cheer up her fifteen year old son Frederick, who believed that Anna had missed the boat, and was sure to end up an old maid.[4] The Kers had an additional reason for contentment. David adored women, and it may have been a relief to his parents to see him settle contentedly into monogamy.[5] The news delighted the estate, where there had been fears that the bonny young heir might win a rich English bride and turn absentee. The Dufferin alliance put these fears to rest, and was seen as an affirmation of his commitment to the county.

In February 1842 the couple were married amidst 'a brilliant assemblage of... friends and relatives', with all the lavishness to be expected from 'the richest commoners in Ireland'.[6] Reporting the day's events under the heading 'Marriage In High Life', the once proud but now craven *Downpatrick Recorder* effused that:

The festivities at Portavo were of such a description for taste and elegance as have seldom if ever been exceeded in this county. The surrounding gentry far and near assembled at dinner, where all manner of choice, rare and excellent viands were in abundance. During the evening, the indefatigable attentions of Lady Selina Ker, and the amiable branches of her family were most gratifying...to all her delighted guests, who did not seem to feel a tedious moment.[7]

All seemed to be set fair. The couple were in love. They seemed well suited. Anna was intelligent and accomplished. David was genial and easy going, and had a benevolent almost chivalric side to his nature. He did not have his father's intensity and high-strung restlessness, nor his intellectual capacity, but he had all of his considerable polish. He was literate and cultured. He loved to read and draw, and at Oxford, although he did not complete his degree, David had apparently been considered a promising classicist.[8] He shot and hunted, was generous to the point of extravagance, and is remembered as being 'great fun'.[9]

Anna's father, Hans Blackwood, Third Lord Dufferin, by Richard Deighton. (Private collection)

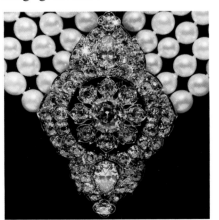

A girl's best friend: diamonds presented to Anna by the tenantry upon her marriage to David Stewart Ker. (Ker family)

After honeymooning in Paris, the couple set up home at Portavo.[10] They refurbished the house and laid out a new southerly approach road, which for the first time offered the visitor a good view of the mansion's handsome façade. This was built around a carefully contrived, but wonderfully natural-seeming *coup d'oeil*, which occurs when the vista casually opens at a bend in the road to reveal a fine three-quarter view of the house rising out of woodland, an effect which even Sutherland, the park's creator, might have approved.

But David was not content with this. He wanted not to please the eye but ravish it. Plans were drawn up to make the house half as large again, and surround its frontage with the kind of formal gardens that were then the height of fashion.[11] To ensure that the effect would be stunning, David proposed to train all this architectural firepower on that slow bend in the road. It was to become the point at which the full glory of the Ker family would be made triumphantly and ineffably apparent. The point at which awed visitors might (mentally if not physically) prostrate themselves and weep in the face of the sheer magnificence, not to say vaingloriousness of it all.[12] Given the opportunity, David would have turned the house into a palace; but the double tragedy of the fire and his father's death ensured that these ambitions came to nothing.

David's marriage to Anna placed a stable household at the centre of the estate's affairs. But not a household that was entirely based on the nuclear family unit. David and Anna lived almost communally, as David and Selina had before them. Members of the family stayed for days and sometimes weeks at a time. Weekend house parties boosted numbers further. When he was seventeen, Anna's nephew Frederick, Lord Dufferin, who would in time become Viceroy of India, attended one of the very last of these house parties, in the fateful month of January 1844.

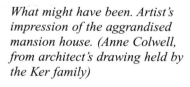

What might have been. Artist's impression of the aggrandised mansion house. (Anne Colwell, from architect's drawing held by the Ker family)

Frederick, First Marquis of Dufferin & Ava, as sketched by James Swinton, 1840s. (Private collection)

On Saturday afternoon he and his friend Cartmell entertained a 'large & crowded audience' with some chemical experiments, the first known to have taken place here since James Ross was in his prime. During their third experiment a phial exploded, driving a blizzard of glass into their startled audience. Two pieces of glass entered Anna's eye and she was fortunate not to have been blinded. Sulphuric acid also showered the onlookers. Again, amazingly, no-one was injured, but as Dufferin confessed to his mother:

Miss Ward's bonnet is covered with little red spots, which will eventually become holes. Anna's beautiful cloak of black velvet lined with fur, Lady Selina's black silk gown, Cartmell's best coat, my best coat and trousers... are all destroyed... O that the mountain would cover me!!... Could you bring them all over presents... Oh! Oh! Oh![13]

A week or so later they had rather more to contend with than the loss of Miss Ward's bonnet. The whole house had been reduced to ashes. Its remains had become a macabre tourist attraction. Friends and even sightseers called to commiserate and experience the dread spectacle of the still smoking ruins. 'What a melancholy sight Portavo is', wrote one:

Mr Ker... only expresses his thankfulness that no person was injured & that the fire broke out at the early hour that it did as the flames spread so rapidly that in all probability everyone in the upper part of the House would have been suffocated...the Plate & Pictures are saved[14]

The events of 'that terrible night' impressed themselves deeply upon the family's and the district's consciousness. It was said locally that there

Portavo by moonlight, showing the ruins of the former mansion house in 1864. (Ker family)

was 'never crow built in Portevo since the Castle was burnt'.[15] For the Kers, Portavo became a sort of abandoned Eden. 'My mother had an intense romance about the place – it was her happy home', wrote Selina Anketell, Lady Selina's granddaughter, expressing the general sentiment. All who knew it recalled it fondly. Those who didn't, wished they had; and there was frequent talk of trying 'to restore the much loved spot to its pristine beauty.'[16]

It was not just the Kers who would feel its absence. The flight of the seigneurial family changed the whole tenor of local life. One of the main drivers of the district's economy had been abruptly switched into neutral. Gardening continued, but the 'model' farm closed. The higher functions atrophied. The money stopped pumping. It was almost as if the townland had suffered a heart attack or a stroke, which left it paralysed down its left or western side. Portavo had always been self-reliant. This was just as well. From now on, it was going to have to fend for itself.

Enter the Anketells

After the burning of their home, David, Anna and their seven month old son Alfred, took refuge in Montalto, which, with over twenty-four guest bedrooms, was more than able to accommodate them.[1] They were a zestful pair, and their arrival will have done much to dispel the convalescent atmosphere that had settled on the house since the onset of David's father's illness.

Of David's brother and sisters, only Madalena was still at home, and she would be off in a few months as she was preparing to marry. Her much admired elder sister Fanny had already gone. In 1840, not withstanding 'great success in London and many chances of making a good marriage', Fanny had married Matthew Anketell of Anketell Grove in County Monaghan, heir to the 7,500 acre Anketell estate.[2]

Although Matthew was an exceedingly personable young man, the alliance was unspectacular.[3] The Anketells were the tenth largest landowners in County Monaghan, and as such were not exactly nobodies, but they were not exactly somebodies either. This was not what her

Anketell Grove from an old photograph; showing its elegant Palladian wings and Italianate bell tower, secreted behind the main dwelling house, where its impact is (some might say mercifully) lost. (Clerkin family)

parents had hoped for. Great expectations had been entertained of the 'beautiful… charming and accomplished' Fanny making a dazzling aristocratic marriage. But it was not to be. Love had beckoned and, in the eyes of the more hard-headed of her contemporaries, she had thrown herself away.

The lovers set up home in Anketell Grove, a pleasant Palladian villa, near Emyvale in County Monaghan. When they arrived, the tenantry are said to have unhitched the horses and pulled their carriage up the drive to the door, singing all the while.[4] In 1852 Fanny and Matthew added a four-storied Italianate campanile to the dwelling, a very characteristic Ker *homage*. This eccentric belfry, Matthew and Fanny's pride and joy, has not been judged kindly by posterity (one commentator called it 'freakish'), but it adds height and depth, and brings a salty incongruity to the building that may in time find favour.[5] The couple had twelve children, and lived happily here until the advent of the Famine, which dealt the estate a near mortal blow, making money a constant worry thereafter.[6]

Though the Anketells were much less extravagantly landed than the Kers, the clans were in other ways well matched. The Anketells were a cultured and liberal family, whose home boasted a fine library and a picture collection that included works by Rembrandt, Rubens and Velasquez.[7] So in terms of tone and feel, Fanny will have found much that was pleasing and familiar in her new surroundings. In terms of pedigree, the Anketells had the edge, for they were pukka gentry who had held their estates since the seventeenth century, when the Kers were hocking cloth in Ballymena.[8] Dynastically, however, there was little glory in the connection. But the amiability of the Anketells helped David and Selina to rise above this mercenary consideration and welcome their new relatives into the family.

That Fanny should have married the heir to a middle sized estate was just about alright. However, when her younger sister Madalena Selina

Miniature, thought to be of Catherine Anne Frances (Fanny) Ker, who married Matthew Anketell in 1840. (Ker family)

*Too late for regrets. Madalena
Selina Anketell (nee Ker),
photographed c.1860. (Ker family)*

started getting interested in Matthew's ambitious younger brother
William, this was definitely not alright. Madalena could not be allowed
to marry a scorpion (as younger sons were then known). In the spring of
1843 Selina whisked her daughter off to London, in the hope of
interesting her in a more eligible beau.[9]

But Madalena was not to be tempted, and in October 1844, in an
uncanny echo of the Ker-Mahon double marriage of 1812-13, Madalena
and William were wed, her parents having apparently reconciled
themselves to whatever would make her happy.[10] The couple settled in
Belfield, Ballynahinch, and had seven children. That they should live in
the bride's county of Down, as opposed to the groom's Monaghan, seems
a little unusual until we remember that the Ker estate was worth over
seven times the Anketell property. They had come to where the power
was. To where the opportunities were greater. Fortune smiled on
Anketell. In 1846 Stevenson died unexpectedly, and David offered
William the position of principal agent on the Ker estates.[11]

This left only Richard, 'the young Chevalier', and perhaps the most
capable of the four Ker children. After graduating from Oxford in 1843,
Richard joined the Diplomatic Corps, serving in Hanover (which still
enjoyed an inflated importance as the seat of the Georges) and Paris.[12] In
1847, however, at the height of the Famine, he set aside his diplomatic
career and returned to Ireland to stand for election in the Borough of
Downpatrick, i.e. to occupy the family seat in the House of Commons.[13]

Downpatrick was not being stuck with the family dunce. Richard's

The young Chevalier', Richard John Charles Rivers Gervas Ker. (Ker family)

1847 acceptance speech shows him to have been a tolerant, broadminded, and in some ways remarkably thoughtful twenty-five year old.[14] In 1851, however, after four years of 'thundering his anathemas' at the opposition benches, Richard stepped down in favour of his cousin, the Hon. Charles Stewart Hardinge, and attempted to pick up the threads of his diplomatic career.[15] This had not been damaged by his four year dalliance with politics. March 1851 found Richard en route to St. Petersburg, the glittering capital of the Russian Empire, his prospects seemingly bright.[16]

To the pyramids and beyond

In late 1845, David and Anna went abroad. Leaving Alfred (aged two) and Selina (six months) with Anna's mother, they travelled through France and Italy to Egypt and the Holy Land. This was no grand tour in the style of David's grandfather. No imperial progress. Their journey was – at times to a thoroughly alarming degree – an improvised, serendipitous affair. Nor did the young lovers follow any tourist trail. There was none to follow. They plotted their own course, and made their own impromptu travel arrangements with local captains and hauliers. With them came a single servant, Anna's intrepid Ladies Maid, 'Hughes', whose spirit of adventure deserted her after a run in with mosquitoes in Corfu. Hughes expected the three of them to end up lying in an ally with their throats cut.[1]

Leaving Florence, they crossed the Apennine Mountains on foot, then sailed down the Adriatic towards Greece. The journey proved

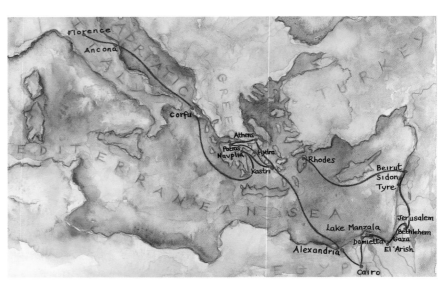

David and Anna's journey through the eastern Mediterranean. (Anne Colwell)

unexpectedly perilous, leading them into adventures which read more like tales from *The Odyssey* than passages from any modern traveller's diary. Storms forced them ashore twice, one of their landfalls being a remote island 'covered with gigantic stones… which gave it the appearance of a graveyard'. Its houses were roofless, its people were of a 'sallow unhealthy complexion' and plague was rife, forcing our anxious travellers to contemplate spending the night in a cave. Next morning they were keen to get off the island, but their captain was 'out of sorts' and refused to sail, so David, Anna and Hughes slipped off in a row boat to Hydra.

When they arrived they threw a ball to celebrate their deliverance, dressing Greek-style,[2] ordering 'bon bons… nuts… figs & plenty of wine' then throwing their doors open to the gentry of the town, a curious mixture of 'warriors & Merchants'. David entertained everyone by dancing the hornpipe. Slow and 'very graceful' Greek dances followed. Waltzes and boisterous country dances ended the evening, and they parted from their new-found friends in the early hours.[3]

From Hydra they journeyed to Patras, then travelled on horseback in saddles as 'comfortable as an Arm Chair' to Athens. These were balmy, carefree times. 'David cannot be better (nor can I)' wrote Anna. Everything seemed to be going wonderfully well.

Though Athens proved disappointing, being 'full of ugly modern buildings in the most unsatisfactory German taste', the couple found the Greek countryside enchanting. Anna was struck by the beauty of its people. David, the classicist loose in one of his spiritual homes, was moved to Byronic rapture about the peninsula's:

wild hills, her warlike plains… covered with the most varied & beautifull Vegetation – her Delightfull Climate her beautiful bays & rocks – Her Fairy Isles and their seas studded with pirate boats… and particularly the Costume[4]

From Greece the Kers sailed to Egypt, narrowly avoiding a brush with pirates. They landed at Alexandria, 'the hinge of England and India',[5] then cruised in leisurely fashion up the Nile to Cairo, which they found 'a delightful town'. There they fell in with a Colonel and Mrs Huish, and travelled with them to the pyramids, then three hours by donkey from the city. One of the most eagerly anticipated moments of their journey had arrived.

The pyramids did not disappoint. They were awesome, but not perhaps too awesome to climb. Anna and Mrs Huish 'foolishly' tried to scale the largest, the Great Pyramid of Khufu. About half way up, after they had become separated from their husbands, things got a little out of control. The ladies were commandeered against their will by three guides, who pushed and pulled them to the top, a 'very laughable but certainly disagreeable' experience.

The men folk, who of course were nowhere to be seen when they were needed, had meanwhile climbed to the Great Pyramid's summit:

and also into the inside, which feat I [Anna] attempted but when it came to crawling on hand & feet I returned it was like going into the bowels of the earth utter darkness save the light of a clip, and one was nearly smothered by the terrible dust – we had luncheon in one of the outer rooms & after it rode back, poor Mrs Huish who is rather delicate has been unable to stir almost since…[6]

Anna and Mrs Huish were rudely bundled to the top of the Great Pyramid. The pyramids at sunset, by Karl von Eckenbrecher.

Lake Manzala, the biblical 'Red' or correctly Reed Sea, which they crossed in 'a little boat... smelling terribly of fish'. (Sarah Parcak)

After recuperating, they sampled the delights of Cairo's souk, which Anna found:

the most extraordinary place, narrower than the narrowest Street or Lane in the City of London. Crammed with Camels Donkeys, horses, running footmen (Arabs) Turks & Blacks in every costume and all along the sides the shops like open boxes with the master sitting cross legged smoking his long pipe, or drinking strong coffee out of little baby cups, they look very dignified and some very handsome... you hardly ever see a man with more than one eye, they put out the left eye... not to be forced to be soldiers.[7]

The most exotic leg of their tour then followed. It began with a five day trip through the Nile delta to the ancient port of Damietta, visiting 'the Island where Pharaoh's daughter found Moses' on their way. Then they travelled east to Lake Manzala, the shallow 'Reed Sea' which the Bible says parted to allow the Children of Israel to escape from Egypt. They crossed this in 'a little boat... smelling terribly of fish'. On the far side they hoped to meet their Bedouin guides, then journey through the desert to Jerusalem.

The crossing should have taken four hours. It took three days – three windless days spent in a boat that needed swilling, in the company of a donkey that David had bought in Cairo. Anna spent her days trying not to faint or vomit. Hughes's reaction can be imagined. The journey ended abruptly two miles from the shore. Their craft could go no further. The great lake was too shallow. Porters carried the women to dry land, where, to her great relief, Anna once again filled her lungs with fresh air.[8]

But where were the Bedouins? Their guides were nowhere to be seen. Anna went for a walk and returned to find:

our Tents spread with Mats Carpets & Cushions & David most Patriarchal sitting down to a good breakfast – our… Arabs had made a large fire which they sat around half naked smoking their pipes & watching their bread baking.[9]

Three days later, the great trek began. David travelled on his donkey, stopping from time to time to gather pretty shells for Anna, who treated them 'as *great treasures*'. Anna and Hughes journeyed on chairs strapped to the steaming flanks of camels, being 'jolted continuously' for seven hours a day. Soon they turned inland, and for two weeks 'nothing but sand hills met our gaze… *one day is every day*', recalled Anna. This fortnight was spent in the care of their ferocious-looking guides, who would 'do anything for Baksiesh but nothing without it'. The wily Bedouins, who were being paid by the day, slowed their pace to a crawl in order to make as much money as possible. (There is apparently nothing

The fearless trio make their way to Jerusalem. David's 1846 drawing shows (l-r) Anna, David, and behind her bonnet, Hughes. (Bennett family)

new about fleecing tourists.) David countered by riding 'so far on ahead, that they were obliged to press up'.[10]

In the welcome cool of the evening, fires were lit, tents were pitched, stomachs filled, and the day's mendacities forgotten. Next morning the cycle began afresh, until, after a gruelling fortnight in the saddle, they reached Jerusalem. The holy city proved a profound disappointment. Anna declared it to be 'altogether the most melancholy wretched town I ever was in'. They visited Calvary, the Garden of Gethsemane, and 'the place on the Rock where the Cross stood'. They found everything prettified, and drowned in gold. A gaudy chapel stood on every sacred site. Their protestant consciences recoiled, leaving them feeling empty and bereft as they stood at the very wellsprings of their faith.

Bethlehem was as bad, but improved greatly when they were adopted by an orientalised cousin of the Batts of Purdysburn near Belfast, who lived contentedly, if less than respectably, in the town with a man half her age. They trekked on. To Samaria and Herod's palace, 'one Corner... left standing'. To Nazareth, where they narrowly avoided kidnap and possibly murder. To Tyre and Sidon, where they picked smooth stones that looked 'like sugar Almonds' on the shore.[11] They pressed on to Beirut, cosmopolitan even then, then travelled to Rhodes in a boat full of pilgrims returning from Mecca. This docked just in time to avoid 'a fearful storm', which would almost certainly have sunk their overcrowded and barely seaworthy vessel had it still been in transit.[2]

The wanderers returned to Ireland in the autumn of 1846. It was not an auspicious moment to come home. The partial failure of the potato crop in 1845 had sent the price of foodstuffs soaring, causing extensive hardship.[13] In 1846 the crop failed again. By the autumn reports of deaths from hunger were filtering in from the west. The idyll was over. As his carriage swept back through the gates of Montalto, David must, as never before, have felt the weight of his responsibilities crash down upon his shoulders.

19 The Great Famine

But should the 'tatie fail us noo,
What shall we then, pair bodies do?[1]

The triumph of theory

Until quite recently, County Down was thought to have more or less escaped the rigours of the Famine. Not so. Notwithstanding its relative wealth, the vigour of its linen industry, and the cushion provided by its plural and progressive agricultural economy, which in some ways made it more like an English or a Scottish county than an Irish one, the Famine hit County Down hard.

Initially, the system had coped. The partial failure of the potato crop in 1845 had been managed without loss of life, producing a mood of cautious optimism within government. The challenge had been met, and it was believed that public opinion within Ireland had recognised this. Some felt, perhaps wishfully, that the bond between Britain and Ireland had been strengthened, and that the Union had been given new acceptance and meaning.[2]

In June 1846 Peel's Conservative administration was replaced by a new Whig government under Lord John Russell. It inherited the understanding that food shortages were manageable, and that within this manageability tactical choices could be made. It also inherited a feeling that Ireland had perhaps been offered too much, that the state had intervened too overtly, that Irish property, Irish commerce, and in particular, the mechanisms of the market had not been allowed to play their proper part.[3] Within the treasury, which regulated the administration of relief, the belief grew up that the measures taken had come close to creating a culture of dependency, the evil that, after famine, it most urgently wanted to avoid.[4]

In June 1846, however, famine seemed an unlikely prospect. 'The whole face of the country' was described as delightful and promising.[5] A record harvest seemed to be at hand.[6] Then, to the horror of all observers,

Sir Robert Peel (Prime Minister 1841-June 1846), by George Baxter, 1853. (National Portrait Gallery)

Lord John Russell (Prime Minister June 1846-52), by G.F. Watts, c.1852. Peel's success in staving off famine encouraged Russell to believe that the 'feed them' reflex could be set aside. (National Portrait Gallery)

the potato blight recurred. North Down and the Ards had largely escaped the phytophthora infestans in 1845. This time they were not so lucky. In the fields, flourishing plants withered 'as if scorched up by fire'. Harvested potatoes blackened and 'turned to mud'.[7] On 19th August 1846 the Board of Guardians for the Poor Law Union of Newtownards (which ran from Ballygowan through Bangor to Portaferry) declared the 'total failure' of the potato crop in the region.[8]

In Lower Balloo, the townland adjacent to Portavo, the Andrews family had 'two baskets [of potatoes] from three acres', an area that might normally yield a crop of twenty tons.[9] It would have been the same in Portavo. One by one, Perry, Angus, McDowell and the rest would, with a sickening feeling, have come face to face with the unmistakable signs of blight. In places, this catastrophe was followed by a desperate scramble to replant the ground with 'anything and every thing that can supply any description of food'.[10]

But the potato crop had gone and the failure was general. Three-quarters of the crop was lost.[11] Had the government responded by replicating the measures taken in 1845-46, there might have been no Black '47. But it had bolder and more radical plans. Believing that 'the interference of the state deadens private energy', the government resolved to bring what it believed to be the most powerful weapon at its disposal to bear on the crisis: the power of the unfettered market.

The government would step aside, though this would be politically difficult, and let the market feed Ireland. It would grease the wheels by pumping money into the lower tiers of Irish society through job creation schemes facilitated by loans from the Board of Works. Private charity, and landlord-financed work schemes would compliment these. Those who needed food would acquire the power to buy it. Ireland would eat. Intervention (now a dirty word) would be avoided. The market would out.[12]

This would undoubtedly mean pain. But poor, dysfunctional Ireland needed taken in hand, and Russell's government was determined to take such measures as were necessary, and, it hoped, to ameliorate some of the country's more glaring ills in the process. So in the autumn of 1846, one of the biggest, most complex, most efficient, but in its outworkings least effective relief operations ever undertaken in western Europe got underway. The chance to steal a march on the crisis passed.

In November-December 1846, hunger began to bite in County Down. It was also wretchedly cold. Icy gales lashed the country, as one of the most baleful winters of the century got underway. Against this inclement background, relief committees were set up, tenders for public works were invited, and small job creation projects were begun.[13] In early December, Ker and his neighbour, the Rev. William Brownlow Forde, met their respective tenants. The clamour at both meetings was for drainage. This led the two men to jointly propose a drainage scheme that encompassed Ker's 13,000 acre Ballynahinch estate and the 20,000 acre Forde estate to the Board of Works. All 33,000 acres fell within the barony of Kinelarty, making 'the Kinelarty scheme' as it became known (technically at least) one of the biggest of its kind in Ireland.[14] Their application was successful, attracting a £7,120 loan.[15]

Healthy potatoes became a rare sight in the Ards. In mid-August 1846 the Poor Law Guardians declared the 'total failure' of the potato crop in the region. (Department of Agriculture)

The Rev. William Brownlow Forde of Seaforde. He and Ker met the crisis by co-sponsoring one of the biggest drainage schemes in the country. (Forde family)

The working man became 'but a labouring Pauper'. The Irish Famine by G.F. Watts (who some three years later sketched Lord John Russell). (Watts Gallery)

The press hailed the scheme as 'a model for other baronies'.[16] It was indeed innovative. It combined landholdings. It was tenant-guided. It was framed broadly to allow the widest possible access. Again (as in Downpatrick) the idea of 'enabling' comes to the fore. Ker and Forde drew down finance that their tenants could not otherwise have secured,[17] creating work for large numbers of farmers and labourers.[18] Another scheme was proposed for Downpatrick.[19] Arthur Davidson's great grandfather, a Ker labourer, is remembered as having walked seventeen miles to the Quoile Bridge to start work on this, or a similar scheme.[20]

These measures might have been expected to produce a sense of hope, a sense of the crisis being addressed, and there is an element of this in local commentaries, but it is drowned out by a rising chorus of disillusion. By the end of 1846, it was clear that the government's strategy was in trouble.[21] It was too complex. Serious problems had emerged at almost every point in the delivery chain, and not least at the chain's source, for the markets themselves had been traumatised by the transcontinental character of the shortage.[22]

Yet, for all this difficulty, trade was galvanised. *The Belfast News Letter* noted, 'an immense speculation in foreign corn... among persons who never embarked in the corn trade before'.[23] But such florescences were localised, and drew in insufficient food to drive prices down to levels that ordinary people could afford. Irish commerce, which had railed against food doles in 1846, now failed to deliver the necessary supplies. And exports continued. As Ireland's cottiers cried out to be fed, their better-off neighbours sent huge quantities of wheat, beef and dairy produce out of the country.[24] These exports were not banned. Nor did the Irish people see fit to distribute these good things among themselves. Food continued to chase the best available prices.

If the government's masterplan was going to work anywhere it should perhaps have worked here, in Portavo's Poor Law Union, the Poor Law Union of Newtownards. Located near Belfast on the eastern seaboard, with a well-developed commercial infrastructure and an agricultural economy geared towards the production of surpluses, this privileged Union was well placed to thrive within the new market-based regime. Before the Famine, local farmers had exported immense quantities of food. When the shortage struck, exports fell and imports increased, but not sufficiently to meet demand or cut prices.[25]

Nor was the cash side of the equation working. As the local economy slowed, men were laid off and went hungry. Even the working man became 'but a labouring Pauper', for his wages now bought little.[26] Few government-sponsored work schemes were started.[27] Unimpressed by the legislative requirement that such works (with the exception of drainage[28]) should be 'unproductive', the local gentry mostly went their own way. Coastal proprietors on the Ards Peninsula formed a fishing company.[29] Other local landlords began job creation schemes on their estates.[30] But these measures did not deliver the requisite cash injection, and even within this relatively affluent Union, the scheme broke down.

Soup and yellow meal cakes
In January 1847, when according to the government's calculations, the crisis should have been bottoming,[1] Lord Londonderry's agent wrote that distress in North Down was 'fearfully increasing'. Labouring families were in 'straits and difficulty':

and it is much to be feared that [the condition] of the small farmer, who is eating out of his produce, and has little to sell, will become very bad long before harvest.[2]

He was right. Hunger was creeping up the social scale. Small farmers found themselves being elbowed out of the cash and into the subsistence economy. By February 1847 such farmers in the vicinity of Bangor were described as being 'but one degree removed from complete want.'[3] On the larger farms, men were paid off because 'their meat [their meals] is of more value than their work'.[4] Left without an income, many labouring families struggled to survive.

A relief fund was begun in Donaghadee.[5] Soup kitchens were set up in Holywood, Bangor, Comber, Newtownards and Kircubbin, the diminutive 'capital' of the barony of Upper Ards. These kitchens almost certainly saved lives. In Newtownards, a reported two thousand were 'on the soup'. The Bangor soup kitchen was soon feeding six hundred, about a fifth of the town's population, and still not meeting demand.[6]

Maize flour or 'Indian meal'. Mostly used nowadays to feed cattle. (United Feeds)

The hungry countryside also had its protectors. Believing that 'Irish property should support Irish poverty', John Waring Maxwell, Lord Dufferin, 'and other neighbouring landholders' bought food from the Bangor kitchen at cost for distribution to their most indigent tenants. These 'other… landholders' are not named. But given what is known of Ker's record and character, it is almost impossible to conceive of him not being involved with his Uncle Maxwell and his nephew Dufferin in the relief effort.[7] Was soup doled out at Portavo during the Famine? Quite possibly. And the place it is most likely to have been dispensed from is the yard at Portavo House.

Ker was also active in Ballynahinch, where he set up a soup kitchen at Montalto.[8] Anna Ker took food to the cottages, and her reputation as a benefactress may date from this time.[9] A meal depot 'funded by the wealthier inhabitants' also operated in the town, distributing food 'to the extremely indigent, free of cost, and to others at a considerably reduced price.'[10] Maize flour entered the local 'cuisine'. When Arthur Davidson's great grandfather set out for the Quoile Bridge, he did so with 'three or four yella meal cakes' in his pockets.[11]

It is easy to see why this kind of intervention appealed. It was direct. It was relatively inexpensive. It ensured that food reached the hungry. But equally importantly, it was conspicuous. Many – though not all – of the county's landlords aided the famishing.[12] But most were also astute enough to appreciate, in a way that perhaps the government did not, that it was not enough to intervene. One also had to be seen to be doing so, and to be doing so with gusto. This was not just about filling stomachs, it was also about winning hearts and minds. And in this latter, greater struggle, perception was all. Hence the appeal of visible charity. Hence too its estate-based character. It was essential to be seen to be looking after one's own.

With hunger came disease. Typhus and dysentery made 'fearful devastations'.[13] In February the *Banner of Ulster* took the unusual step of sending a reporter out into the townlands to report on the condition of ordinary people. He visited rural Bangor, and the Londonderry townland of Drumhirk, four miles from Portavo.[14] Everywhere he went he found disease and hunger. In one crowded cottage the man of the house lay in 'Delerium and high fever'. He had starved himself so that his family could eat. In another he found all eight occupants weak with dysentery, and 'one poor suffering child… a living skeleton'.[15]

Conditions would have been similar in Portavo, perhaps worse, given its large number of labouring and small farming families. This latter group was in a double bind. Not only had Angus and McDowell to stave off hunger, as minor landholders they were also obliged to contribute to the cost of relief.[16] The bar had been set too low. Beggars were supporting beggars. How did they find the money? Maybe they got jobs in Donaghadee, where the Board of Works was improving the harbour's storm defences.[17] Maybe they dug drains. As one newspaper put it, 'If it were not for draining which is carried forward pretty largely in this district [the parish of Bangor], there would be nothing for it but a sure though lingering death.'[18]

February found the parish's small farmers in 'the iron grip of penury'. The weather was bitterly cold, with severe frosts and heavy snowfalls.[19] In many of the little cottages along the Stockbridge Road there was little or no food in the larder, no seed for planting, no cow in the byre, and no fire in the hearth as the 'extraordinary wetness' of the autumn had made turf difficult to obtain.[20]

On 22 February 1847 the government announced an important climb down. Horrified by the colossal expense of state work schemes, and their failure to stem the rising tide of hunger,[21] the government abandoned its huge public works programme. Out too went the one-dimensional, economic model of man that underlay it. In came food doles, which would be administered and mostly paid for by Poor Law Unions. The market had failed to deliver. The Peelite solutions that the government had scoffed at six months earlier were now hurriedly and shamefacedly embraced. It was back to square one.[22]

Not in County Down, surely? This Famine Madonna did stalk Down. The Banner of Ulster's *reporter found levels of privation similar to those shown here in mid and north Down. (Illustrated London News)*

The road to the workhouse

On March 24th, without the slightest trace of irony, the government decreed a day of fasting to 'implore from heaven a withdrawal of the present scourge'.[1] But there was to be no divine intervention. In the town of Newtownards, the six hundred bed workhouse filled to overflowing. Men and women from Herdstown, Ballymacormick, Ballymaconnell,

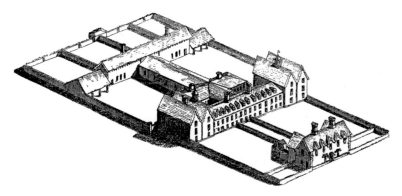

The Poor Man's Hilton, the Newtownards Workhouse.

Ballymagee, Ballyvester, Killaughy, Bangor, Donaghadee and elsewhere trooped in rags to its cold dormitories, to be separated by sex, institutionally clad, and fed on porridge.[2] In May 1847 there were 750 people in the workhouse and another hundred in the adjacent fever hospital.

How many of Portavo's people, if any, ended up here? We don't know. No record of who came here has survived. However in April 1848, in a perhaps uncharacteristic concession to the dignity of its inmates, the workhouse began to record the marriages which took place amongst its paupers, for even in the direst circumstances, it would seem that love found a way. In July 1848 the minutes record the marriage of Mary Hasley of Ballywilliam to William Angus of Portavo.

An Angus in the workhouse? Surely not. The appearance of William Angus in the workhouse records is troubling, even shocking. For William was an Angus of the Close, the son of a respectable family of small

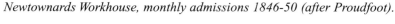

Newtownards Workhouse, monthly admissions 1846-50 (after Proudfoot).

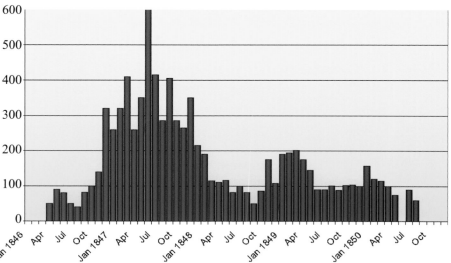

Mussels in the Mill Bay, Portavo. Did the hungry turn to the sea, as they had in 1729 and 1740-41? (See vol.1, p.98)

farmers. Mary Hasley's destitution is less statistically surprising. She was a farm hand's daughter, whose brother would shortly scandalise the neighbourhood by getting Eliza Heron of the Stockbridge Road pregnant. She had fallen one rung. He had fallen two, and his fall highlights Portavo's vulnerability. If the crisis could pick off an Angus, nearly two-thirds of the townland's population would have to be considered to have been at risk.

Who was safe? The few seasiders still connected with fishing, the two Perry families, and the Ker estate workers, whose employer's purse would have provided them with enviable security. All would have been safe or safeish. Craftsmen like Henry Small were not. His income would have fallen to nothing as people deferred their purchases and made do. For bigger producers like the Perrys, however, these were boom times. Farm produce fetched high prices, and they and other Famine 'winners' would have profited from the shortage. Did the hungry turn to the sea, as they had in 1729 and 1740-41? Did Perry stand idly by? The townland's biggest farmer was a man with a strong social conscience. It is hard to imagine him letting his neighbours suffer.[3] Which makes William Angus's descent into the workhouse even harder to understand.

Soup for Rembrandts

Trouble for an Angus could mean trouble for Ker, for the Famine ruined great estates as well as small farmers. How rigorously did it test the Ker estate? The answer to this question may well lie under the floor of the former Barnardo's thrift shop in Ballynahinch, the legendary last resting place of the bulk of the Ker estate correspondence. Were we to exhume

The hungry gather under the porch at Montalto. The Kers' response was, apparently, to remove the porch. (Ray Elwood)

the contents of this mushy pit, we might again hear the sobs of the destitute. But we do not have this luxury. We are forced to rely on secondary sources as the estate's own records have not survived.

The folklore is also scanty. And far from flattering. Two Ker famine stories have survived. One is the tale of Montalto's erstwhile Ionic porch, which 'is said to have been removed during the Great Famine because neighbouring paupers caused inconvenience to the Ker family by taking shelter under it.'[1] The story is also told of the Ker children feeding crowds of beggars 'like monkeys' from Montalto's dining room windows.[2] Both tales are damning. They positively bristle with condemnation, and read very much like authentic glimpses into the folk consciousness of an aggrieved people. The problem, however, is that these are not popular memories. They have come down to us through the Kers, the villains of the peace.

Mid-nineteenth century view of Downpatrick, showing the new Fever Hospital (r). (Private collection)

St. Johns, Ballycarry. A contrite offering to a stern creator? (Ker family)

The written record, such as it is, is more favourable, though less ghoulishly entertaining. It shows the estate responding flexibly to the crisis, and the Kers actively seeking to contain its worst effects. The bulk of the estate fell within the Downpatrick Poor Law Union, where the workhouse held '1000 paupers' in February 1847. Ker was active here too. He was chairman of the Board of Governors of the Down Fever Hospital, and in June 1847, Ker, his brother Richard and Uncle Maxwell headed the list of subscribers to a new fever hospital in the town, £5,000 being pledged at a public meeting.

The family's greatest gift to Lecale at this time, however, was probably the new Quoile Quay. In February 1847 we read of Swedish turnips and carrots from Scotland being landed here.[3] The quay was making a difference. More and larger vessels could dock here since the dredging and enlargement of the early 1840s.[4] Here we get a very local sense of commerce working as it did not perhaps work for the island as a whole. In April Ker attempted to stimulate the flow further by reducing port duties from 4d to 2d per ton.[5]

The estate's most imaginative response to the crisis, however, came at Red Hall, where Ker had a 'very pretty' new church built in Ballycarry and a new harbour constructed at Whitehead.[6] Both were in all probability relief works. The new church, the Church of St. John the Evangelist, begun in godless '47, is an eloquent declaration of faith, offered at a time when evidence for the existence of a benevolent

St. John's dog's head. Ker had his favourite dogs' heads carved in stone on either side of his private entrance to the church.

protector was particularly scarce.[7] On its completion, the Anglican liturgy was performed here for the first time since Jonathan Swift had charge of the parish in the 1690s. (Swift is said to have preached to his man-servant and horse in the ruins of the old church in order to qualify for his stipend, and reportedly never had a better audience.)

Intervention was an imperative. Self-interest, humanity, and the estate's own philosophy required it. But it had to intervene without imperilling itself. In County Monaghan, Matthew and Fanny Anketell appear to have crossed the line, for the Famine fatally wounded the Anketell estate. The Porters attributed its plight to Matthew's lack of business prowess. The Anketell family history, however, states with a certain pride that the estate's finances were crippled by the measures that Matthew undertook 'for the relief of his tenantry', measures that were 'in accordance with its tradition of treating its tenants 'as human beings and not as slaves'.[8]

The Ker estate, though larger, more removed and more resilient, was also pulled taut by the Famine. Income fell, expenditure rose. The gap was plugged by borrowing, and rather more piquantly, by the sale of books and works of art. In February 1848, sixty-eight works, 'By Italian, Flemish, Dutch, and French Masters' went under the hammer at Christies in London.[9] Rembrandts became glorified meal tickets, Van Dycks were used to plug the gap left by written-off arrears. The library – one of David's father's most notable achievements – was an even bigger casualty. Seven-day sales in 1847 and 1848, and a four-day sale in 1849, pretty well finished the collection. Rare and specimen books, some now worth millions, left the county never to return.

This hurt. These books and pictures were not just trophies, they were reference points in a mental universe, proofs of cultural identity, for this art underpinned the family's understanding of itself.[10] This was loss. Not loss as experienced in Schull or Skibbereen, and it would be grotesque to suggest so. But it was loss all the same. In this subtle and almost exquisite way, the Kers' landscape was also depopulated and emptied of friends and familiars by the Famine.

In April 1847 cheap American grain began arriving in large quantities. The corner had begun to be turned. That autumn the potato crop was healthy but small, and Newtownards workhouse admissions remained high all year. 1848, the Year of Revolutions, was another grim year, which saw a further potato failure, rent abatements (a sure sign of serious distress), and complaints in Newtownards that the local graveyard could take no more pauper dead. In 1849 the harvest was abundant, and mid and north Down at least, began to put the crisis behind them.

In 1849 Ker wrote off arrears of over £12,000 accumulated during the years of the Famine.[11] In the same year, for the second time in a decade, he cut rents on his County Down estates, an act in the spirit of Sharman

Crawford, who in 1846 had assured his tenants that in hard times he would 'not shrink from bearing my proportion of the loss'. These were humane but pragmatic moves, for most of the cancelled arrears were probably unrecoverable. As in 1843, when rents fell, or during the Napoleonic Wars, when they rose, the reductions were aimed at maintaining the landlord's share of the general wealth of the estate at a time of flux, an adjustment that was in the interests of both parties.

Grain from Gilbert McCutcheon's silo. In April 1847, American grain began arriving in large quantities. The corner had been turned.

Enter the anti-Christ

In December 1846 Ker's agent, William Stevenson, died suddenly.[1] His death removed an experienced hand from the tiller. Ker replaced Stevenson with his brother-in-law William Anketell, who had an active interest in land management and had indeed written two pamphlets on the subject.[2] Anketell's status and access to Ker made him a plenipotentiary compared to Stevenson, and the appointment may, in part, have been intended to reassure the tenantry that Montalto was taking their difficulties seriously. If it was, however, it had the opposite effect. Within months of taking office, Anketell would plunge the estate into controversy.

William Robert Anketell was no passive functionary. He had strong views, and a forceful, indeed turbulent, personality. He soon made his presence felt. In March 1847, with Ker at Westminster, sixty destitute people were refused free meal on Anketell's direction. When the rector of Ballynahinch, the Rev. Boyd, protested he was excluded from the meal store and an attempt was made to eject him from the relief committee.[3]

A Victorian villain? David Stewart Ker's brother in-law, William Anketell, appointed agent in December 1846, following Stevenson's mysterious death. (Ker family)

By the middle of the month 'upwards of 600' had been refused relief, 'the greater number destitute cases of the worst description'.[4]

Boyd was outraged, and the anger of this respected clergyman of thirty years standing gives this dispute its moral centre. Boyd fed some of the most needy at his own expense, and charged Anketell (Ballynahinch's Trevelyan?) with attempting 'to economise… at the expense of life'.[5] This was no semantic dispute. There had been deaths in the district in early March, and Boyd feared that more might follow.[6] Boyd asked Sir Randolph Routh, the Commissary-General for Relief, to order a judicial inquiry into Anketell's conduct. In the meantime, the court of public opinion passed its own verdict. Anketell became known as 'the Anti-Christ'.[7]

Was there method in Anketell's madness? In his study of the Famine in County Down, James Grant suggests that Anketell may have been seeking to clear the estate of its poorest families.[8] This is certainly possible. In his 1843 pamphlet Anketell had argued for 'the disposal of the redundant people of Ireland' through the elimination of unviable small-holdings. This was to be followed by the creation of more viable farms through amalgamation, with fair compensation being paid to the departing tenants.[9] His position had then been radical but humane. He had been at pains to distance himself from the advocates of mass clearance, and to condemn those who had ignored 'the heartrending cries of the… famishing multitude'.[10]

Now these selfsame cries went unheard. Was Anketell using the cover of the hunger to attempt to build his brave new world? If he was, he was not entirely swimming against the tide. All shades of political opinion agreed that in John O'Donovan's words, 'The present state of things must end in general destruction.'[11] The need for reform was widely accepted, leading some estates to use the crisis 'to press [the] destitute… to sell and emigrate'. The Londonderry estate evicted hundreds between 1846-51, with exactly this end in mind.[12] Such actions, however, have no parallel on the Ker estate. Its approach was informed by a Hutchesonian concern for the whole community, a concern clearly evident in November 1846, when Ker had attempted to channel two-thirds of the ditching money towards the destitute, in the face of farmer opposition.[13]

Anketell was playing with fire. His experiment was cut short, presumably by Ker, who reasserted the pre-existing ethos of the estate.[14] How this happened is unclear. But folklore may offer an insight. The crowd which besieged Montalto may provide the missing link between Boyd's protest and Ker's intervention, indeed it may have prompted that intervention,[15] or embarrassed Anketell into drawing back. This was the governmental struggle in miniature, a struggle between a reformer and a feeder, and in Ballynahinch the feeder prevailed. The core values of the estate were reinstated. Ker's doctrinally driven agent was reined in.

As far as the tenants were concerned, the Anti-Christ had been let loose on the Ker estates. (Ray Elwood)

Belfield, the home of William Anketell, from the point at which the shots were reputedly fired.

In May 1847 Anketell attempted to found a temporary fever hospital in Ballynahinch. But this does not necessarily mean that he had reformed. The establishment of local 'feeder' hospitals was part of a wider scheme aimed at spreading the burden of maintaining the Down fever hospital more evenly across the county's several Poor Law Unions, thus relieving the pressure on the ratepayers of Downpatrick and ultimately the pressure on Ker. To win support for the scheme, Anketell invoked the spectre of 'eternal disgrace' – the idea that posterity would never forgive Irish property if it let down Irish poverty at this time of crisis.[16] We might wonder at a man with Anketell's record willingly broaching such a theme. Perhaps we should just marvel at his sheer brass neck.

In time, Anketell's reputation recovered. But not everyone grew to love him. In March 1850 as he undressed for bed a shot was fired through his bedroom window. Six more followed, one bullet lodging in the bedstead.[17] Anketell escaped unhurt, but the shooting caused an outcry. A £500 reward was pledged for the capture of the would-be assassin. Who tried to shoot him, and why? Possible motives abound. It could have been the act of an aggrieved tenant. It could have been related to a contemporary outbreak of land agitation.[18] Or, of course, revenge for his conduct during the Famine. No-one got to the bottom of the matter and no culprit was ever found.[19]

But we must not let Anketell distract us. His impact was relatively superficial. The estate's underlying rhythms and procedures were unaffected by the Famine, and Anketell's experiment was not followed by clearances or mass evictions. Ker reportedly ordered fewer than a dozen evictions on his 7,300 acre Downpatrick estate between 1840-52, a period that includes the full duration of the Famine.[20]

This statistic is symptomatic of the estate's broader response to the crisis, which was substantive and geographically well spread (bar Clough and Ballymena). Though Portavo lost out because it had no resident gentry, therefore much less clout than it might otherwise have had,[21] the estate as a whole outperformed, and did so in no small part because the Famine coincided with the most dynamic and capable phase of its existence. It was solvent and in robust health. The social compact, which committed it to tenant welfare, had had time to bed in and acquire meaning. There is a personal dimension too. In a curious way, the crisis was emotionally right for Ker. He knew how to play this sort of drama. He understood the need to step forward and act. He courted popularity and gloried in giving. Had his father been in charge when the Famine struck, it is unlikely that the estate's response would have been so fulsome.

It has been wisely said that there is no such thing as an innocent account of the Famine. Nor, on a large and complex entity like the Ker estate, may there have been such a thing as an entirely philanthropic response. That said, the estate's perception that a strongly humanitarian reply was not only right, but was in its own wider interests, plus the availability of the resources to do something about it, enabled the Ker estate to come out well from the Famine. Though in March 1847 in Ballynahinch it was a close run thing, eternal disgrace was averted. Ker emerged from the Famine with his finances mauled, his reputation enhanced, and the political road before him open.

20 'That splendid ass, Montalto': the 1852 election

The Star of the County Down

The general election of 1852 was one of the most hotly contested of the century. It was also one of the most violent,[1] as radicals and conservatives clashed over the issue of 'tenant right', and the attempts of Ireland's tenant farmers to reform the conditions under which they held land. The farmers sought the 'three Fs'; fair rent, fixity of tenure and free sale, and legal recognition of the Ulster Custom. The landed establishment resisted tooth and nail. The struggle that ensued was charged and tumultuous. Both Maxwell and the Rev. Henry Cooke invoked 1798 when describing it, thanking the Almighty that this time the clash had taken place within constitutional bounds.[2]

'Wanted a cipher, and if he could get one, a slave.' Charles, Third Marquis of Londonderry, in a posthumous portrait by J.G. Middleton, 1855. (Sotheby's)

The election also marked a coming of age for the Kers, because in that year David Stewart Ker became the first member of his family to contest a county seat. Ker had not intended to put his name forward, but when his uncle, Lord Londonderry, wrote to him inviting him to take up 'the family seat', all expenses paid, the offer seemed too good to refuse.

Ker accepted, and acquainted Londonderry with his political views. This was his first mistake. Lord Londonderry was not remotely interested in his political views. Londonderry did not want a protégé, he wanted a cipher, and if he could get one, a slave. Ker recoiled. Who did Londonderry think he was? This was not 1790 or 1812. The Londonderrys were not, after Downshire, the largest proprietors in the county. The Kers had outstripped them.[3] The Fourth Marquis of Downshire's candidate, his brother Lord Edwin Hill, was already in the field. If the second seat 'belonged' to anyone, it belonged to a Ker.

Ker broke with Londonderry and stood as an independent. It was a moment of truth. An act of dynastic assertion. By it the Kers signalled that their electorate was no longer necessarily at the service of either of the county's big two political dynasties, the Downshires and the Londonderrys, who had dominated local politics for generations. The Kers were demanding to be considered a political force in their own right.

Robert Gordon of Florida Manor. Tried to persuade Ker to withdraw. (Down Hunt collection)

The Kers' emergence was at once exhilarating and deeply unsettling. Nothing quite like it had occurred since the Londonderrys themselves had erupted into the political life of the county (under a similarly independent banner) some seventy years before. Londonderry was askance, unable to believe that anyone, least of all this hitherto malleable nephew, would dare to lay claim to 'his' seat. Ker was disowned and replaced by a new and more compliant Londonderry candidate, John Vandeleur Stewart, a cousin from Donegal.

Ker's stand created consternation amongst the Tory grandees. There were now three centre-right candidates – Stewart, Ker and Hill – fighting for two seats. (County Down sent two members of parliament to Westminster until 1885.) Downshire, Maxwell and Robert Gordon of Florida Manor tried to persuade Ker to withdraw.[4] But Ker stood firm, reminding them that he was not standing as a Conservative, but as an independent. Downshire thought this 'the greatest piece of impertinence I ever heard of'.[5] But he kept a cool head. He would give his first votes to his brother, and his second to whoever seemed the stronger. The reluctant consensus was that this might be Ker.

Downshire quietly made ready to form a new junction[6] with Ker. Now the knives were out for Londonderry. His campaign had become an embarrassment. Matters got worse when the 'splenetic and overbearing marquis' tried to wound Ker by leaking carefully selected portions of their private correspondence to the press. Ker responded by publishing the full correspondence, an event which 'shocked... *everybody* in London of all sects and parties'.[7]

His name became unmentionable at the Carlton Club,[8] but in County Down the disclosure played brilliantly. Londonderry's megalomania stood exposed to the world. After more frantic diplomacy, the new fixer-in-chief, Sir Robert Bateson of Belvoir Park near Belfast, managed to persuade Londonderry that his position was hopeless. In May 1852 John Vandeleur Stewart was withdrawn. Londonderry's humiliation was 'the talk of the London clubs'.[9] Even the Prime Minister, Lord Derby, could not console him. The family seat was gone. As one balladeer had Londonderry lament:

> 'Twas won not by conquest – that Seat – or the sword –
> In its purchase was lavished the family hoard;
> Right and left the old guineas rain'd thick as the sleet
> We emptied the purse for this "Family Seat".
>
> But David the "cat has let out of the bag;"
> The secret is blabb'd – I'm the joke of each wag.
> How could you, my nephew, be thus indiscreet,
> And place in such peril the "Family Seat?"
>
> Independence has set up her back at the tale;
> "Montalto," she cries, and that cry will prevail;
> Each hour it increases: each morsel I eat,
> Is embittered with thoughts of the "Family Seat."[10]

Vowing that 'no power on earth' would induce him to give Ker a single vote, Londonderry retired from the fray.[11] However, this did not leave the way clear for Ker and Hill. There was a third candidate in the ring, the remarkable William Sharman Crawford of Crawfordsburn, a passionate advocate of land reform and a considerable landlord in his own right.[12]

The three offered electors a broad ideological choice. Hill was a copper-bottomed, right wing church and state man in the purest Downshire tradition. The thirty-five year old Ker was a pre-Disraeli, Disraelian one nation Tory. The septuagenarian Crawford, venerated by many of his supporters as a living saint,[13] was the founder of the Ulster Tenant Right Association, and had had strong links with the Land League and English Chartism. If anyone could exploit the Tories difficulties, he could.

Crawford campaigned energetically, introducing novelties like election rallies to the county. He won the endorsement of the Presbyterian General Assembly, and the backing of two influential newspapers, the liberal *Northern Whig* and the Presbyterian *Banner of Ulster*. His message also struck a chord with many voters. At last the tenant farmers had a candidate who voiced their concerns and aspirations. But in the absence of a secret ballot, would anyone dare vote for him?

Not if the *Downpatrick Recorder* could help it. The *Recorder* worked tirelessly for Ker and Hill. It rubbished Stewart and denounced Crawford

William Sharman Crawford 1780-1861, forgotten hero of Irish radicalism. (First Bangor Presbyterian Church)

as a Communist,[14] a 'visionary' (then a term of abuse, meaning dreamer), and a faint Protestant who ran 'in harness with the Pope's Brass Band', an attempt to make Crawford's Presbyterian supporters uncomfortable with the religiously mixed character of the tenant right movement.[15]

Ker got flak from both sides. The *Banner of Ulster* attacked his landlordism (until it realised that it was playing to his strongest suit). The Stewart camp lambasted him for failing to declare himself a Conservative, a Protestant, or a supporter of Scriptural Education, and for refusing to join the call to strip the Catholic seminary at Maynooth of its grant.[16] Ker also advocated modest extensions to tenant right.[17] What sort of Tory was he, wondered Downshire? An inclusive one, Ker might have replied; who sought the votes of 'moderate men' and believed that landlordism had to adapt if it was to survive.[18] At which point in this imaginary exchange, Downshire might have permitted himself a smile. Ker was trying to win an Irish election by preaching tolerance, this was priceless.

Downshire persuaded Ker to add his name to the anti-Maynooth petition,[19] a move which allowed the Orange Order to give him their backing. But soon after declaring his own candidacy, Ker stepped out of Downshire's shadow and found his own voice. This caused another flush of Tory disquiet. Ker's line was 'too liberal'. His election address was 'very milk and watery'. Downshire blamed bad advice. Bateson agreed. Ker was 'in the hands of a Radical clique who are favourable to Sharman'.[20]

Sir Robert Bateson of Belvoir, by C. Brockey, 1840. Believed Ker to be 'in the hands of a Radical clique who are favourable to Sharman'. (Bennett family)

These fears were misplaced, and show that little trust existed between the conservative 'allies'. Ker seems to have been advised by Anketell and Hardinge. His *éminence grise*, however, was the Seneschal of Downpatrick, his solicitor Hugh Wallace, an 'undisguised enemy of Lord Downshire' who was said to be 'directing all Ker's movements'.[21] All these men were cautiously progressive, but none was in any way radical. Nor was Ker, whose wife Anna dreaded a Crawford victory as much as any high Tory[22]

The landed establishment was so fearful of the tenant right movement that they saw its hand in everything. It is easy to see why they were afraid. It had been generations since they had had to face so determined a challenge, and for all its attachment to democracy, the tenant radicalism of the early 1850s had a ragged, militant edge.[23] As recently as 1850, the county had experienced a wave of incendiarism which, on the Ker estate alone, had seen the burning of evicted men's cottages, the circulation of notes inscribed with coffins and the shooting of Ker's agent.[24]

In 1852, however, the movement looked to politics to deliver change. This did not threaten Downshire. As the nearest thing that County Down had to a royal family, the Downshires were above all electoral vagaries. Their acreage was so huge, their retinue of client and affiliated gentry so extensive, their electoral machine so ruthless, that in the normal way of things, almost nothing could trouble the Marquis's candidate. For the

Downshires, elections were not so much contests as quasi-feudal coronations, elaborate affirmations of their lordship of the shire.

Ker's position was more vulnerable. A strong Crawford turnout could see him off, which made Ker's reluctance to form a junction with Downshire 'unaccountable' to most Tories.[25] The party grandees blamed Wallace's malign influence. But this overlooks the Ker family's historic attachment to independence, and Ker's need to remain distinct from Downshire if he was to be perceived as a credible independent. Ker kept his distance, allowing the Conservative press to promote a Hill-Ker ticket, while the two candidates ran separate and mutually mistrustful campaigns.[26]

The only Tory to take comfort from this was Londonderry. His deepest fear was a Ker-Downshire junction, an alliance between the county's two largest proprietors, which could consign the Londonderrys to eternal electoral darkness. He had anticipated that, free of the Stewart influence, Ker would become 'a broken reed in Lord D's hands', allowing the Downshires mastery of both county seats.[27]

But he was wrong. Ker did not snuggle up to Downshire.[28] He stood 'on his own bottom', and emerged strongly from the wreckage of Londonderry's campaign. His guts and integrity were admired. His centrist politics found a constituency. His residence and property gave his candidacy a certain fittedness. 'Ker and his lady' toured the county

Hugh Wallace, Ker's political éminence grise. A hate figure for the Downshires, Lord Edwin would quite like to have tugged his beard. (Private collection)

Laudate dominum.
Arthur Hill, Fourth
Marquis of Downshire.
(Hillsborough Castle)

'canvassing the tenants in all directions'.[29] This had its moments. On the unaligned Dufferin estates Anna ran up against a wall of pro-Crawford feeling. Converts were hard to find, but she made some inroads:

they say if Mr Crawford is safe they will give their 2nd vote to 'Kirr' but… they must see him safe first & then Kirr "will" get a lift as he has not a bad name.[30]

Things went better elsewhere. The Kers charmed the conservatives and Orangemen of Warrenpoint, and received 'unexpected encouragement' in Comber and Newtownards.[31] In Ballygowan, Ker was promised a hundred votes, leading Downshire, lip curled, to wonder if he intended 'to be returned by the tenants alone, and to throw over the gentry'.[32]

But the gentry were also assiduously courted. 'Nine tenths' of the proprietors Ker approached reportedly pledged him their votes (and voters).[33] His appeal to the county's independent tradition, or maybe the myth of it, met with a surprisingly warm response. Middling gentry like Ward of Bangor, who controlled fifty votes, and magnates like Lord Dungannon, who had 154 votes at his disposal, rallied to the cause.[34]

Did Portavo back him? The *Downpatrick Recorder* claimed that Ker's tenantry were 'with him to a man'.[35] But were they? The nearby Londonderry and Dufferin estates were hives of Crawfordism, and in 'Crawford's stronghold' of Newtownards, posters warned electors against backing Hill or Ker. The Portavo estate was of a piece with this terrain. It was natural Crawford territory.

But these places did not have a candidate standing, and this made all the difference. Ker's candidacy brought a new dynamic into play. Estate loyalty competed with, and in many cases overwhelmed class and ideological considerations. People rallied. Their man was standing. A binding collectivism kicked in. There was an excitement on the estate. There had been no contested election for twenty-one years, and this was proving a thrilling tussle.

Taking the bull by the horns, Downshire's agents canvassed Portavo. They will have plunged into a sea of red. Red was Ker's colour. Red flags will have flown from the cottages. Red rosettes will have been nailed to carts. Red banners will have fluttered from the gateposts of Portavo House. Undaunted, they went to work on the townland's eight voters, Perry, Angus, and the rest. All assured the canvassers that they would give their second votes to Lord Edwin Hill 'if M. Kerr allows them'.[36] (He did, and most of them didn't – there is evidently nothing new in telling canvassers what they want to hear!)

Downshire's canvassers were to be disappointed. The Ker estate did not push for a Hill-Ker turnout. On his own lands Ker sought 'plumpers' (votes for himself alone). With Crawford seen as Ker's main rival, Ker's managers worked hard to keep the Crawford vote low. Did they employ coercive methods? There is no evidence that they did. But then the most effective forms of coercion are often untraceable. Richard Blakiston-Houston of Orangefield, for example, was a master of the black art of invisibly knobbling voters. He worked hard:

A master of the black art of knobbling voters. Richard Blakiston-Houston. (Blakiston-Houston family)

The Hon. Charles Stewart Hardinge, later Second Viscount Hardinge. (Ker family)

to poll almost all [of his tenantry] for Lord Edwin Hill and Ker. The 5 Catholics I have will not vote at all. About 7 will vote for Sharman Crawford and Ker, but I think when the day comes most of the 7 will be taken suddenly ill…[37]

The blood was up. The campaign was reaching its climax. By now even Downshire was getting jittery. Lord Edwin made an anti-Catholic gaffe, leading Ker to present himself successfully 'as the Friend of Catholics'. Downshire felt outflanked and vulnerable. Some 2,500 of the county's 10,690 electors were Catholic.[38] Disaffection was said to be rife amongst Downshire's Catholic tenantry and Catholic voters in general, 'every one of whom' one observer predicted, 'will take the Field against Lord Edwin'.[39] With every week that passed, the result seemed more uncertain.

On July 10th 1852, twelve days before the poll, an interesting diversion took place: the Downpatrick borough election. Normally this would have been the centrepiece of the Kers' electoral year. But this time it was a sideshow.

The Downpatrick election had the character of a jamboree. Ker stood aside in favour of his cousin, the Hon. Charles Stewart Hardinge, the son of a former Governor-General of India. And to 'rapturous applause, cheering, waving of hats &c.' Hardinge was duly elected. His acceptance speech was the sort of fluent confident performance that the less than fluent Ker would have given his eye teeth to have been able to deliver.

'Deafening applause' followed, amidst which, in the immortal words of the *Downpatrick Recorder*, 'the cherished shout of "Ker for ever" was unmistakable – high above the loudest cheer'.[40] Hardinge, Ker and their entourage then drove back to Montalto, the morning's work done.

The poll was now imminent. But first the candidates had to be officially nominated. The nominations took place in Downpatrick on the morning of Monday July 21st amidst some of the 'most terrible riots that ever took place in the North of Ireland'. Several thousand people took part in these affrays,[41] which were not so much bouts of mindless brutality, as a raw, unfranchised counterpart of the poll. This was the only opportunity the voteless masses (who were as carefully marshalled as the actual electors) were going to get to have their say. And they seized it.

Advancing behind a knotted posy symbolising unity, and a huge loaf denoting plenty, Crawford's supporters stormed and held the courthouse within which the nominations were to take place. 'Stones rained like hail' during the nomination. One knocked out Crawford's proposer, the Rev. Dr. Coulter, a former Moderator of the Presbyterian General Assembly.[42] Fearful violence ensued, both inside and outside the hall:

Heads and limbs were smashed with horrible rapidity… Unfortunate wretches were reeling in all directions, pursued by assailants, who in their turn became fugitives… [many received] terrific gashes on the face and limbs; while several lay senseless on the ground, or were carried off by their friends on both sides.[43]

In spite of the best efforts of the dragoons and police, who at one point charged the mob with fixed bayonets, sporadic rioting continued until the early afternoon, by which time Ker's men had taken undisputed charge of the town. Then both sides withdrew and an eerie calm returned.

Voting was due to begin on Thursday July 24th, and last for two days. On the night before the poll, Ker and Hill's supporters reoccupied

The dragoons and police attempted to regain control. Election riot 1868-69, by 'HBL'. (National Library of Ireland).

Downpatrick, beating their drums until dawn. Early on Thursday morning, several thousand more 'Kerites' in red colours arrived and paraded round the town in bright sunshine, behind 'Hill and Ker' placards held aloft on poles. A ready supply of free beer was made available. The mood lightened to the point of becoming festive. Sometime after seven, however, an armed column of tenant right men entered the town from the direction of Saul. A savage set-to followed. 'Broken heads abounded' on both sides. Dragoons cleared the streets.[44]

It was barely eight in the morning. It was going to be a long, hot day.

At around ten, a body of several thousand Crawford supporters, 'well provided with sticks', approached the town from the south.[45] The Kerites – led by Thomas Hughes, a local butcher, whose work on Monday had earned him two choice black eyes that were just beginning to go green – advanced towards them menacingly.[46] Believing discretion to be the better part of valour, Crawford's men drew back and camped on the Gallows Hill just outside the town. A second bloody confrontation was avoided. But this withdrawal allowed Ker's supporters to turn the town into something of a lion's den for the white-ribboned Crawford voters. Many needed protection to get to the polls. Some reportedly cast their votes 'with bruised and bleeding bodies'.[47] Others were 'unceremoniously taken by the neck and thrust out to prevent them voting.'

Nonetheless, polling was brisk. A steady stream of voters began arriving from nine a.m. on. Many of them came in groups, shepherded by authority figures such as priests, agents or landlords, and looking like 'the

Red Hall, 1864. Red Hall sent a steamer full of 'troops' to County Down to back Ker's campaign. (Ker family)

REDHALL

veriest slaves'. Lord Bangor's tenants arrived accompanied by soldiers. 'Mr Ker's tenants, in great numbers, arrived on cars'. The uneasy peace held until about one p.m., when another orgy of stoning and bludgeoning erupted. One man reportedly lost his life, possibly when the dragoons, sabres drawn, attempted to regain control.[48]

Portavo voted in Newtownards, where conditions were just as volatile. On the day before the poll:

bands of hired ruffians, in hundreds, armed with prodigious clubs, and other weapons, were sent down to Newtownards from Hillsborough... while a steamer, specially engaged for that purpose, landed a similar battalion on the County Down coast [probably at or near Portavo, where local men will have joined them] from Mr Ker's Redhall estate in County Antrim.[49]

This force took possession of Newtownards. Downshire's followers had also secured Hillsborough, placing three of the county's four polling towns in the hands of the landlord interest.[50] Free beer was dispensed at all three locations, with the object of banishing 'symptoms of returning Christianity' amongst the Ker-Hill bludgeon men, a tactic seized on by Crawford's supporters as symptomatic of the wider moral bankruptcy of the right.[51]

As Crawford did not field an army in Newtownards, the Tory mob attacked Crawford's Newtownards committee room, but were repelled by police, who also ejected several 'overbearing' gentry (all JPs) from the polling booths. This unexpected official impartiality allowed Crawford's vote to come closer to reaching its potential at this station than at any other in the county.

The result was officially declared on the Monday following. It was a bitter blow for Crawford:

A second savage set-to followed on the morning of the vote. Escorting voters to the poll, 1868-69, by 'HBL'. (National Library of Ireland).

'Uncle Maxwell', John Waring Maxwell, c.1850. Thought Anna Ker 'the best canvasser in the kingdom'. The portraitist is unknown – could it have been Madalena? (Down Museum)

Hill: 4,654
Ker: 4117
Crawford: 3113

The outcome, replicated across Ulster, put paid to the tenant right movement's hope of a breakthrough in the north. In the south, Tenant League candidates triumphed, but Crawford's defeat in this flagship constituency took much of the shine off these successes. Within months, in the absence of the sort of mature parliamentary leadership that Crawford could have offered, the reformers had fallen into chaos.

For Ker, though, this was a moment of transcendence. His five month struggle had been crowned with success, but at an appalling price. In the official returns, the contest in Down is identified as the most costly in Ireland.[52] The *Northern Whig* estimated that the right had spent upwards of £20,000 on its campaign. Ker's colleagues would concede only that he had 'expended thousands', an expense that was to say the least untimely given the parlous state of his finances after the Famine.[53]

The victors celebrated with speeches and a sumptuous lunch in Downpatrick, eaten at a single table at the head of which, 'a magnificent bunch of Orange lilies raised their gorgeous... heads.'[54] Anna's contribution attracted particular praise. Maxwell called her the best canvasser in the kingdom.[55] The estate had also outperformed. Of the 485 of his tenants who voted, 465 (96%) voted for Ker. Just 39 (8%) voted for Crawford. 329 (71%) voted for Hill. Downshire's tenants reciprocated less wholeheartedly, with just 52% voting for Ker, which meant that his victory had not depended on their support, a gratifying piece of knowledge.[56]

All eight Portavo voters backed Ker. Five did so in the most flattering manner possible, by giving him the plumpers he desired, the other three voted jointly for Ker and Hill.[57] Crawford didn't pick up a single vote in Portavo, Ballyminetragh, Lower Balloo or on the Copelands (three voters, three plumpers). Ballyfotherly and Orlock were the most seditious corners of the Portavo estate. Three of Ballyfotherly's voters plumped for Ker, but four backed Ker and Crawford. This was unusual. 80% of Crawford's votes were courageous, landlord-be-damned, Crawford plumpers, which tells us much about the polarisation of the electorate. The estate had only one Crawford plumper, William McCartney of Orlock, whose family had ceased to be tenants by 1863.[58] James Aird and Andrew Agnew of Lower Balloo did not vote. They are also strongly likely to have been malcontents.[59]

How do we explain this almost totalitarian voting pattern? Enthusiasm? Deference? Bribery? Fear? Each elector will have brought his own unique mixture of these factors, and others besides, to the poll. The pattern also needs to be put in context. Votes of this order were normal, indeed expected. What is exciting about this vote is the size of the turn out, which in itself was a barometer of opinion. 72% of the county electorate voted. On the Downshire estates an impressive 77% turned out. On the Ker estates however a positively ballistic 89% did. The Ker estate as an entity was one of the most highly motivated parties to the campaign.[60]

Portavo - 1852 election scorecard			
	Hill	Ker	Crawford
William Anderson	X	X	
Alexander Angus	X	X	
Andrew Angus		X	
William Burroughs	X	X	
Thomas McBride		X	
John McConnell		X	
John McCutcheon		X	
John Pirrie		X	

Portavo townland 'voting card'. As there was no secret ballot, we can see how everyone voted. Every elector had two votes and the county returned two MPs.

This is reflected in its use of physical force. As in 1837, this was extensive and unapologetic. The estate deployed large bodies of men in ways that were inflammatory and intimidatory, and when they rampaged, called for calm, displaying an attitude to the use of force that was ambivalent, to say the least. They were not alone in doing so. This kind of tenant mobilisation was an integral part of nineteenth century electioneering.[61]

So the Kers were of their time, not ahead of it. This was not 1790. David Stewart Ker had no visionary message. Or rather, no more visionary a message than consensus, which even now has perhaps a tinge of the visionary about it. He used his power conventionally, in an unenlightened way. However, the right did not have a monopoly on the use of force. All parties fielded voteless armies. The important difference between right and left, however, was that Crawford was 'strong without money'. His support turned out for ideological reasons, while the right were alleged to have leaned on 'a hired staff'.[62]

The *Downpatrick Recorder* leapt to Ker's defence, claiming that his men took up sticks only after being routed on nomination morning.[63] This is unconvincing. As is its ingenious attempt to prove that the right was more sinned against than sinning by publishing an alternative poll of cracked skulls:

To shaving and dressing cut heads of Mr Crawford's friends (Dr Savage) £2.5.0.
To shaving and dressing cut heads of Hill & Ker's friends (Dr Mullan) £19.[64]

which tells us only that poor Crawford's friends were more likely to go untreated. For all the paper's protestations, Crawford's followers bore the brunt of the violence, which was itself only the most visible part of a wider pattern of coercion. Crawford's supporters sought to have the result annulled, arguing that Hill and Ker had won using, 'gross, extensive, systematic, and open and notorious bribery, treating and corruption.'[65] But the regulatory regime was lax, and the protest got nowhere.

The victors saw the matter differently. They believed themselves to have lived through a Homeric epic, a struggle for the soul of the north. The right's triumph was followed by a steely reassertion of conservatism in Ulster. Crawford, like Achilles, retired to his tent. The back of the reform movement was broken, and within months it had disintegrated. The stay had been pulled out of Irish politics, which for nearly two decades lost all shape and purpose. The Kers' prospects, however, could not have looked brighter. This was a moment of dynastic emergence beside which 1837 – the previous high water mark – paled. Though essentially super-middleweights who had stumbled backwards into a heavyweight contest, the Kers had come through, establishing themselves as one of County Down's great 'houses'.

met with a "complete ovation" —

head quarters / Genl Anketell / John & Sophy / Grand procession of the right
of the news / flushed with / Graham ate / sort tenants, retainers, &c
M.P. here — / victory / the letter for / route to Ballynahinch —
many rounds —

Ker's return to Ballynahinch as depicted in a pencil sketch by Charles Stewart Hardinge. (Ker family)

How times had changed. In 1797 David Stewart Ker's grandfather had counted himself lucky to sit as a Downshire nominee in the Irish parliament. In 1837 the estate had barely been able to carry the pocket borough of Downpatrick. Now a Ker had won the county, fighting in his own right, and in his own way. The man Lord Edwin Hill, with the sort of profound condescension available to few, but available to a Downshire, had dubbed 'that splendid ass, Montalto', had carried the day. The Kers now held the excessive, indeed Downshireish total of two of the four County Down seats.[66]

Ballynahinch received Ker like a conquering hero, amid scenes 'never before witnessed… even in the palmiest days of the Rawdon *regime*'. The town was brilliantly illuminated. Church bells pealed. Ker and Anketell were chaired around the town 'amidst the acclamations of… congregated thousands'.[67] A long night of merrymaking followed. Great 'shindies' were had on all the estates. Farmhouses were illuminated. Tar barrels burned on the hills. Hundreds will have rejoiced at Portavo, assisted by the usual liberal supply of beer.

What no-one realised at the time, least of all Ker, was that this was not just a high point in his own apparently charmed life, or in the life of the estate, it was the highest point in its entire existence. David was on top of the world. Let us hope that he enjoyed his time there, for it would prove to be unmercifully brief.

21

'A crow with a peacock's feather in his tail'

David Stewart Ker's coach plate. This was attached to Ker's hired coach on journeys to and from London. (Ker family)

'The Times is furious'

In the autumn of 1852 David went to Westminster not as the representative of some hole in the wall borough but as a Knight of the Shire for the great county of Down. What sort of parliamentarian was he? By all accounts, a new man. Several years previously, a friend had called at the House, seeking the member for Downpatrick:

> On business nights, with some invites,
> To dine, we sought the squire. [Ker]
> Whip Taylor says, that in that place,
> It's no use to enquire.[1]

But not now. Victory had an exhilarating effect on David. He felt plugged in. Affirmed. Connected to the world in a way he never had been before. He embraced modernity. 'The times are critical nay the Times is furious', he quipped to Dufferin as he bustled off to London on railway business.[2] These were great days in which to be alive, and David caught their speed and matched their temper.

He also evolved politically. When the Vatican restored Catholic territorial bishoprics in England in 1850, amid ill-judged statements about England's return to the Catholic fold, sections of protestant opinion were outraged.[3] The government also reacted angrily, seeing the move as an attack on its sovereignty. The 'papal aggression' was strongly denounced in County Down. In 1851 many of the county's leading landowners petitioned Parliament in support of the government's stand.[4]

Though reluctant to act in a way which might 'disturb the manes of ancient animosities', Ker took a lead in the petitioning, lending it a credibility that it would not have had, had it been championed by more obviously High Church figures like Maxwell or Downshire.[5] The campaign helped Ker electorally in 1852, but it did not turn him into the darling of the county's protestant right. At a meeting of the Down Protestant Association[6] held in 1856 to mark the 310th anniversary of the death of Luther, Ker was spoken of 'with disapprobation'. He had

The House of Commons 1854, view of the government benches. (Place of Westminster Collection)

'mistaken ideas of liberty'. He talked of moderation, 'when the history of Protestantism was traced in characters of fire and blood'.[7]

Ker shrugged off these criticisms and maintained his *via media*, becoming increasingly supportive of what he guardedly called 'measures… to satisfy the requirements of the age'. This prompted a rumour that he had turned his coat and become a Liberal.[8] Ker denied this and got on with the business of representing his constituents. By the modest standards of the time, he was a conscientious and hardworking MP. He was no meteor, even in his supercharged state, and he maintained his trappist silence in the chamber, but made up for this in committee, where he was 'an able and industrious labourer'.[9]

At home, we read that he was a 'highly enlightened and independent magistrate' and a 'zealous grand juror'. In 1841 David had served as High Sheriff of County Down, and in 1857 he became High Sheriff of County Antrim, a rare double. As well as prestige, these positions brought a fair amount of trouble and expense, which Ker accepted in a spirit of public service.

His duties were not so onerous as to prevent all pleasure. In the autumn of 1853, for instance, Anna and he toured Killarney, a place, 'beyond fancy & description as Thackery says. I don't care to own it – it is quite too handsome'. They found Cork, 'the most beautiful city in Ireland – The Buildings are of Marble brighter if possible than those of Italy or Greece – Where the Trees grow spontaneously wherever the Architect seems to want help'. They had a fine time:

perching upon Limerick darting up & down the Shannon – wading knee deep in the dirt of Tralee – the County Town of Kerry, the Sheet Anchor of the Liberator, the stronghold of Priestcraft – Thence to proselyte Dingle where the Bible was first translated into Irish – Often have we looked feet downwards on the strong sparkling foaming Atlantic when one step to the west would have separated us from the Eastern Hemisphere… I never saw such a vista in my life as that from Sybil Head embracing Brandon Head… besides the Blasquets the fairest Islands in the world.[10]

1930s tourist poster advertising Killarney. (Science & society)

KILLARNEY

IRELAND
FOR HOLIDAYS
LONDON MIDLAND AND SCOTTISH RAILWAY

Nineteenth century St. Petersburg. View of the Cathedral of Our Lady of Kazan, on Nevsky Prospect. (Kazan Cathedral)

Our man in St. Petersburg

David's brother Richard was also on the move. In 1851 he took up his post at the British Embassy in St. Petersburg, which he found 'much more Asiatic than European and one of the most picturesque towns I ever saw'.[1] Sumptuous palaces lined the banks of the Neva. Richard likened the effect to travelling for miles along the Thames and seeing only 'Greenwich Hospitals, Somerset Houses & St. Pauls with gilded Domes' on each side. He visited the Hermitage, where, as he told David, he stumbled on, 'two of your pictures, the Rubens Infant Christ & St. John with the Lamb & the Carlo Dolci head with hands crossed that used to be in the Dining Room at Portavo.'[2] These gems from the Famine sale had found a home in the imperial collection.

In St. Petersburg the policemen carried battle-axes and smoking was forbidden in public.[3] This took a bit of getting used to. The city was also extremely expensive, requiring Richard as an impecunious younger son to keep a careful eye on his roubles. The young attaché made a good impression. He worked hard, winning the regard of both his colleagues and his political masters.[4] Palmerston believed that he could rise to the top of the service.[5] Lord Randolph Churchill is said to have tipped him as a future ambassador.[6]

Some colourful reminiscences of his Russian sojourn survive. Lady Paget describes him painting a full-length portrait of Queen Victoria in her coronation robes in three days, for an embassy ball to which the Tsar was invited.[7] His grand-daughter records that when his cook fell ill on the eve of an important dinner, Richard made the meal himself, then sent up his guests by introducing each with a grandiose title.[8] (She remembers him as 'a debunker, par excellence'.) Fortunately, his guests could laugh at themselves, and he was not put on the first boat home.

It took the outbreak of the Crimean War in 1854 to blow Richard's promising career off course. The British diplomatic staff were expelled as soon as hostilities commenced. Richard ended up in Copenhagen, then was sent to Madrid, where his abilities and connections again secured him a good position. In 1856, he married Rose Calvert of Furneaux Pelham, Hertfordshire, and Quentin Castle on the Ards Peninsula.[9] Rose was one of the most dazzling beauties of her day.[10] Leighton, the artist, thought her flawless. Lady Paget agreed, calling Rose:

the most faultless beauty I have ever seen. She had the features of a Greek statue, with the colouring of Titan; fortunately she was as cold as ice, or she would have been a second Helen.[11]

In May 1856, following the Peace of Paris, Richard returned to Russia in the company of his radiant, eighteen year-old bride. He was then thirty-three. He now held the position of First Paid Attaché, the third most senior diplomat in one of the country's most important embassies.[12] They were something of a gilded couple. Everywhere they went, Rose turned heads. In St. Petersburg, she was visited by the Tsaritsa:

who had heard of her striking beauty and was curious to see her. She [Rose] had been too shy to obey the Imperial summons to court and made excuse after

Richard Ker, by Legand. The studious diplomat on the eve of an illustrious career. (Ker family)

excuse. She was found seated warming her beautiful bare feet, for she disliked shoes and discarded them whenever she could. How the Legations talked![13]

But Rose did not settle quietly into the role of diplomat's wife. Writing in the 1930s, Rose's granddaughter Lou states quite emphatically that Rose's 'intense dislike of the more prosaic facts of life ruined Richard's diplomatic career.' Whatever the truth of this assertion, Richard's career went no further. It did not get a chance to. In 1857, he resigned his position and stood for election in Downpatrick.[14]

Amidst hoots, cheers, and bemused cries of 'Here's the Rooshan',[15] Richard was returned, and represented the borough at Westminster until 1859, when his brother David 'reclaimed' the family seat. Somewhat surprisingly, perhaps, Richard did not try to relaunch his diplomatic career. Maybe Rose would not suffer it. Maybe at heart he was too much of a non-conformist to thrive in the suave world of the foreign service. The most interesting phase of his life was about to begin.

'She shines by not seeking to shine': Anna

Though she was clearly ready and able to act on a larger stage, Anna of course did not initially have any kind of public profile. Her realm was domestic, and centred on what Trollope's American muse, Kate Field, called 'sewing and babies'.

Anna had twelve children, and spent nearly half her married life carrying babies. Two were born before the couple's middle-eastern tour. By the time of the Porter sisters' arrival in 1850, the tally had risen to five (with another on the way), an unrelenting human tide which somewhat

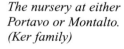

The nursery at either Portavo or Montalto. (Ker family)

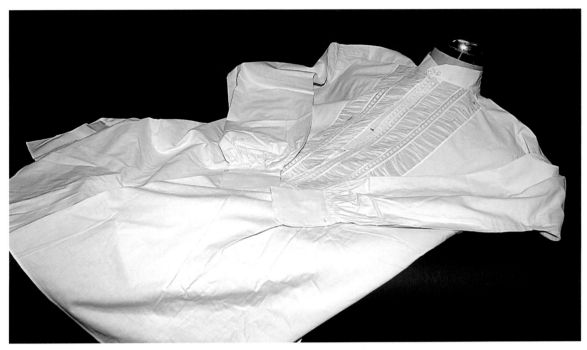

1850s hand-sewn linen shirt from County Down. (Ulster Folk & Transport Museum)

mortified the visiting spinsters. By 1852 the count was seven, with their fourth son, Henry, arriving in the middle of the election campaign. The baby was big and the delivery exhausting, but Anna seemed to have energy to burn, and days later, with Amazonian nonchalance, was 'driving about as if nothing had happened'.[1]

Anna also ran the house, serving potatoes, pork and mutton from the home farm.[2] She provided a loving environment for her children to grow up in, leading the *Downpatrick Recorder* to describe her as 'the model wife, the model mother'.[3] She was a woman of feeling and sensibility, who had all the accomplishments of the well-bred woman of her age. And her sewing and embroidery inspired poetry:

> No point is missed, from wrist to wrist,
> From collar down to skirts,
> In every part, they're works of art,
> Unequalled among shirts.[4]

a playful verse that hints at delightful relations between Anna and her friends.[5]

This was all well and good. But Anna craved more. The tireless work she put into the 1852 election campaign has already been mentioned. Another role she took on, with equal ardour, was that of 'benefactress of the poor', giving food, clothes and money to the needy. The meek and noiseless way that she went about this won her 'the prayers and blessings of the poor'.[6]

Home. The Long Gallery, Montalto. (Brown McConnell Clark)

'She shines by not seeking to shine', one contemporary put it. Anna was a sort of Diana without the cameras. She had an almost unsettling ability to empathise with suffering, an affinity that perhaps only someone who has themselves suffered can feel. Anna did not just give in the manner of a Lady Bountiful. She comforted the distressed, entering into their suffering. What ache, if any, did this answer? Anna is said to have been prone to depression. It is hard to avoid the feeling that when Anna was with those who suffered, she was in some way with her own kind.

Not that any contemporary would have seen her life as blighted. On the contrary, her existence seemed blessed. Was blessed. She had money, health, beauty, faith, standing, children, a wonderful home and an apparently contented marriage. She was liked and even loved on the estates,[7] and had every prospect of a long and happy life to come.

Ballycarry 1864. Anne Porter 'gathered a fern from the walls of the Old Church' as a memento of their 1822 visit. (Ker family)

The Porters last gambit

In 1850 Anne and Phoebe Porter returned to the north of Ireland for the first time since their ill-starred excursion of 1822.[1] After visiting their estate in Armagh, where they were a little shocked to find that their tenants' houses had clay floors, they came to stay at Montalto.[2] Although the tour was in part about reconciliation, it is clear from Anne Porter's diary that a certain amount of bad blood lingered.[3]

Anne's diary offers us one of the few glimpses we have of life at Montalto during its heyday. It conveys an impression of a life that was

Phoebe Porter, c.1820, by John Partridge. (Porter family)

Anne Porter (1801-77). Harry Porter, the family historian, describes Anne as 'a tyrant', and recounts that when the son of her heir shot her pet jackdaw, Anne lopped £80,000 off their inheritance. (Porter family)

social and congenial. There are walks in the woods, pleasant conversations, calls on each other's houses, leisurely luncheons and even more leisurely dinners.

All four Ker children turned out to greet the Porters. Mrs Forde and various Blackwoods came to stay. They visited the Perceval-Maxwells at Groomsport, and the Dowager Lady Dufferin at Ballyleidy. They inspected the ruins at Portavo and called on the Maxwells at Finnebrogue. Here, the beautifully accoutred Porter sisters received a second shock. Although she had 'a beautiful speaking voice & great culture & intelligence', Madalena 'dressed like a peasant'.[4] At her heel were some ten or so terriers and spaniels, which amused her when she was not painting, or despairing about the size of her feet (9¼ inches). After dinner, John Waring Maxwell poured his young nephews some wine and made them recite 'the Orange Toast':

To the glorious pious and immortal memory of the great & good King William – Who saved us from Popery, Knavery & Slavery – Brass Money & Wooden Shoes…[5]

Beneath the bonhomie, however, lay a settled and inexpugnable sense of unrighted wrong. A sense of wrong that time did not heal. When Madalena Maxwell died in 1873, Anne Porter sent expressions of condolence. She also sent two 'lawyers' to Ireland to quiz Madalena's servants as to whether she was compos mentis when she made her will.[6] Anne got nothing but a solicitor's bill for her trouble. Upon her death in 1877, the Ker-Porter feud was finally laid to rest.[7]

'A crow with a peacock's feather in his tail'
In the mid-1850s a new ballroom and service wing were added to Montalto, enlarging the house to nearly twice its present size. In January 1857, on the work's completion, the Kers threw a lavish ball to which eight hundred were invited. The attendance 'embraced the rank, fashion, and beauty of this part of the country'.[1] And we may imagine the anticipation-filled scrunch of iron on gravel as scores of carriages, leather polished, brass gleaming, swept along the torch-lit drive to the house.

The guest list offers us an interesting insight into both the extent and the limits of the Kers' social clout. It does not define them socially, as it was for a particular section of their broad acquaintance. But it does make clear that they were a regional power, at the same time reminding us of the huge comet's tail that filled the sky behind a resident high gentry family. This was the estate as corporation, corporately entertaining its business and social partners, neighbours and 'clients', in the form of some of its larger tenants, who were also invited to the ball.

Not everyone was impressed. To those with long memories, the Kers were still monied riff raff, 'an upstart race who 60 years ago was at the foot of the inhabitants of Belfast neighbourhood'.[2] And what of Lord Montalto? The great David Stewart Ker? 'A crow with a peacock's feather in his tail', was one farmer's stony verdict.[3] The Kers were getting above themselves.

22 The orphan townland

The orphan townland

The burning of Portavo House left a void at the centre of the townland's affairs. It was as if the generator which powered the whole mechanism had been turned off. Would the house be rebuilt? Would the Kers return? Building schemes came and went. Like Miss Haversham, Portavo waited, full of expectation, for its prince. But no prince came. And like Miss Haversham's, its finery turned to rags and dust in the meantime.

The reoriented demesne, showing the ruins of the old house (bottom), and the proposed new mansion house. (Ker family)

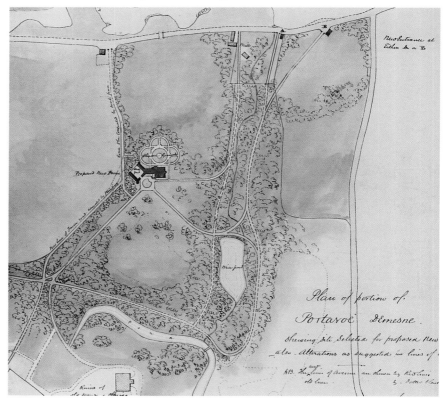

Neuschwanstein-in-Down? The proposed mansion. (Ker family)

This hope was not entirely vain. David Stewart Ker regularly dallied with the idea of a return, and in 1859 he commissioned plans from the Belfast architects Lanyon & Lynn for a new mansion at Portavo in the Scots baronial style, which had worked so well for the Clelands at Stormont Castle. Astutely realising that being commissioned by Ker was a little like being commissioned by mad King Ludwig of Bavaria, they created a fairytale castle, complete with wizard's hats and turrets, embodying in a single set of drawings all the grandeur and pretension of the Kers at the height of their powers.[1]

Lanyon and Lynn urged radical changes. They argued that the traditional site of the mansion house should be abandoned in favour of a site much closer to the sea. The long standing intimacy between house and farmyard would also end, with new farm offices being built in the far walled garden, at the end of a lane 'concealed by planting'.[2] Sutherland's Great Park, with its serpentine lake, was also to be sidelined. Its horizons were too close. Its style was too old fashioned. The new water feature would be mare nostrum – Portavo Sound. The Copeland Islands would provide the visual interest. The endless stream of merchantmen plying to and from the bustling town of Belfast would provide the requisite sense of contact with the wider world.

But the plans came to nothing. For once, common sense intervened and Portavo was left to moulder. When the Porter sisters toured the demesne in 1850, Anne Porter, with patrician disdain and perhaps a certain squalid pleasure in the Kers' misfortune, noted that 'the ruins are now only inhabited by a farmer'.[3]

Portavo 1864. Detail from illuminated address. (Ker family)

*The Portavo
Laundry, Orlock,
as it is today.*

The ruins also appear in the illuminated address presented to Alfred Ker in 1864.[4] The address depicts a range of estate landmarks, each rendered in bright colours, under blue skies. Except for Portavo, which is shown by night, in silhouette, under moonlight. A dark knuckle of buildings, some of them ruinous, sit forlorn on a hill, beyond water, remote and enigmatic, like some abandoned seat of Arthurian legend. It is a haunting, melancholy scene. The picture's message is clear. We are viewing a lost world.

The former imperial capital had become a minor province, administered with indifference from afar. Initially it was cared for, but during the 1860s, the park's budget was cut repeatedly until it became insufficient for basic maintenance. Paths grew over. Buildings decayed. The roof of the handsome laundry caved in. By 1877 most of the outbuildings were 'in ruins'. The land lost its tone.[5] Portavo 'is now', wrote one observer 'compared with what it was, a desolate place.'[6] The neglect had deepened into a kind of relinquishment. The anonymous artist of 1864 had seen further than he knew.

The post-Famine recovery
Was the destruction of the big house liberating? Did it end a culture of dependency? Most farmers would probably have scoffed at this idea, and replied that they had always been their own men. Yet there can be no denying that while 'imperial' Portavo languished, 'democratic' Portavo thrived. Indeed expanded, as the former home farm was greedily absorbed into the surrounding weave of small farms.

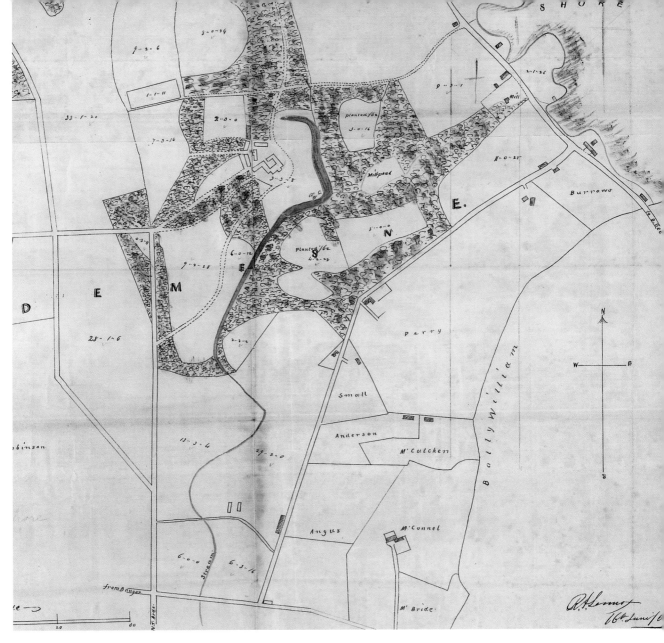

*Portavo 1862, showing the
demesne and 'independent' farms.
(Brown McConnell Clark)*

Far from creating a dead zone in the rural patchwork, its closure
created opportunities for entrepreneurial farmers, who vied with one
another to rent its fields. In the 1850s these were let out at a thumping
rental to four local farmers, Willie Burroughs of Portavo, William
Robinson of Moor Farm (Ker's election agent), Willie Aird of Orlock,
and John Robinson of Ballyminetragh.[1]

These men did well during the '50s, and particularly during the
Crimean War, when Willie Aird, Aird Lowry's grandfather, 'bought a
seven acre farm with what he got for a field of wheat during the Crimean
War'.[2] In 1850 just under half the parish was in crops. Oats, wheat,
turnips and potatoes were its main produce. Vetches, barley, peas, beans,

Boyd's farm viewed from McCutcheons, or as it would have been in the mid-19th century, Perry's from McConnells, with Small's cottage, red-roofed, left.

rye, flax, mangel wurzel, carrots, parsnips and cabbages were also planted.[3] Much of this produce was grown for the market. And the markets were buoyant. Farmers took on more labourers. New cottages were built on the Stockbridge and Warren Roads.[4]

Rents were moderate, and lower relative to income than they had been during the 1830s. Jane Small, Henry's widow, paid just under £9 a year for her seven acre holding. Her husband had paid nearly £14 for the same piece of land in 1839. The McConnell brothers paid £37 p.a. for their land, against £48 in 1839. Capital accumulated.[5] We should not wonder at the tenant right campaign losing its impetus, or that a successful farmer like John Perry could afford to invest three hundred pounds in the Ker estate, and fill his parlour with mass produced knick-knacks. Clocks, mirrors, potted plants and even carpeting became almost commonplace. The cluttered, not to say congested, Victorian parlour had arrived.

All these good things came by dint of hard work. From long hours worked six days weekly, and an inspiring tradition of communal self-help known as 'neighbouring'. Neighbouring was about sharing implements and expertise, or gathering to plant crops or save a harvest. Every farmer neighboured, from the Perrys down. It was an integral part of the townland's way of life.[6]

Neighbouring is fondly remembered not as a selfish system of favours and exchange, but as a pooling of resources, a genuine interdependence.[7] A sociologist might sum it up as a reciprocal exchange of services, a philosopher, in this dyed-in-the-wool Presbyterian townland, might note the interesting twist it gives to the idea of protestant individualism. For the people who neighboured, however, it was the only way they could get many jobs done. Born out of hard necessity, neighbouring was a tremendously plastic way of deploying labour and of matching resources with need. So the Smalls, who had no horse or rig, would give a few days labour to the Burroughs, who in return would come and plough.[8] And so on. When the map shows us eleven individual farmsteads, it is to a certain extent misleading us. We are actually viewing an interconnected whole.

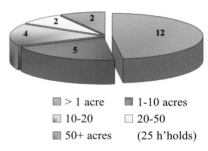

> 1 acre   ■ 1-10 acres
10-20   □ 20-50
■ 50+ acres   (25 h'holds)

Portavo: farm size & land holdings by household, 1862.

The 1860s townland

The 'Griffith Valuation' offers us a kind of anatomy of the townland as it was in 1862.[1] Its biggest component was of course the demesne, which occupied 330 or 60% of the townland's 545 acres. The remaining 215 acres were in eleven farms. John Perry's sixty-one acre holding remained the townland's 'flagship' farm. The Arnolds, a pair of young newly-weds, had recently taken over Hugh Perry's. But Stockbridge House was little to their taste, and within a year or two they had begun work on a new house in the yard.[2]

The Arnolds will have been welcomed with hansels of eggs and butter, and invitations to call. Everything will have been done to make them feel at home.[3] Had they taken on an evicted man's farm, however, the conventions of hospitality would have worked in reverse. To commit such an act was to break one of the fiercest taboos of rural life. Such newcomers were pariahs, and the feeling against them could last for decades.[4] No such transgressions are recalled in Portavo.

The Burroughs family also arrived at about this time. They were 'insiders' who came to Portavo from Ballynahinch in the 1850s on the

Minnie Connell's cottage, by D. Bond Walker in the 1930s, looking much as it did when her grandfather, William Burroughs, arrived during the 1850s. (Glendinning family)

The coal-house and kiln in Sandy Bay, c.1840. On the right are the gates of Portavo House, on the left the mill cottage (and mill gable). (Ker family)

strength of their estate connections, Willie Burroughs' brother George (a big, hale man, who played the accordion and liked his drink) being the Land Steward at Portavo. As estate people, and members of the Church of Ireland to boot, they may have been treated with some initial caution. Willie and Ellen Burroughs, their three children, and Willie's sprightly octogenarian father occupied John McDowell's old home, 'a long streak of a cottage' that was house, byre and dairy in one.[5] Their twenty-four acres lay around the foot of the Stockbridge Road, between the mill and the standing stone.

This small change was fraught with significance. McDowell was a fisherman born of a fisherman. He had been a fisherman who farmed. Willie Burroughs was a landlubber with a boat, who lobstered for pin money.[6] He didn't spit into the mouth of the first fish he caught, or cancel his trip when he met a barefoot woman. That he didn't, that no-one did, is poignant. For it tells us that we are witnessing the uncommemorated death of an archaic way of life. There were no longer any fishermen on the coast.[7] The townland ceased to be a bearer of maritime tradition. Its relationship with the sea was becoming merely aesthetic.

The mill changed hands too. Out went John Nelson, father of twenty-five children, twelve with his first wife, thirteen with his second.[8] In came his brother-in-law, James Fargie, begetter of a modest eight. Inland, there was more continuity than change. The two Angus and two McConnell families each worked their pair of split farms of thirteen and fourteen acres.[9] The remaining four farms were smaller again. Thomas McBride farmed ten acres in Portavo and Ballyfotherly. John McCutcheon, whose eldest son went to America to seek his fortune, only to find an early grave, farmed eight acres. Jane Small and William Anderson, an all guns blazing Queen and constitution man, each farmed seven.

They farmed a changing landscape. By 1860 the rolling savannah of the early plantation had been replaced by a dense maze of tiny fields. Every cow pat did not quite have a hedge around it, but things did seem to be heading that way. And the tinier the farm, the tinier the enclosures, for every farm needed a range of spaces, with William Anderson's seven acre holding being divided into four gnomic fields.

Most of the townland's other thirteen cottages and cabins were occupied by widows or labourers and their families, men like John Summers who worked for Willie Burroughs, John Patton and Robert Heron who worked for John Perry, and James McGra, who lived in the small half of Jane Small's cottage, with his wife and three children.

The bad old memories of the Famine were fading. During the 1850s wages had risen faster than the cost of living, so the position of labourers had also improved, albeit more modestly than that of farmers. A man like John Summers, for example, would have had a house, a regular wage and considerable security, which was just as well as he and his wife had just given birth to the first of their seven children. McGra would have been better off again. He seems to have worked for the estate, which paid the best wages in the district and offered employment all the year round, the dream of most labourers.

The position of others was more precarious. Especially in the 1860s, when farming again hit the doldrums. In the early 1860s the townland had some eleven labouring households.[10] Most contained two or three men and women of working age, for the last wave of pre-Famine baby boomers was then reaching maturity, creating a serious surfeit of labour.[11]

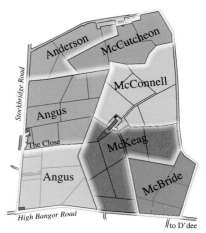

South-eastern Portavo from the 1863 Ordnance Survey map, showing its maze of tiny fields.

The flight from the land

How were these people to keep themselves? The townland could not support them. There just wasn't the work on the land, and the underlying shift from cereal growing to beef and dairy production meant that there was even less work in prospect. None of Nelson's twenty-five children remained in the townland.[1] Nor did any of Fargie's children. Nor Patton's. Nor McGra's.

People became the townland's biggest export. Many moved to the burgeoning town of Belfast, where they found relatively well paid work in its factories, engineering works and shipyards. Others went further afield again. John McCutcheon went to California. Henry Small's son Henry went to Australia, then into the outback, where he and his wife 'had the first white child in that part of the country'.[2] Willie Aird's brother Sam had a farm in Mississippi. His brother George worked 'on the railways' in the United States.[3]

Those going were almost as likely to be the children of farmers as those of labourers. Six of the Perrys' eight children left. Four of the

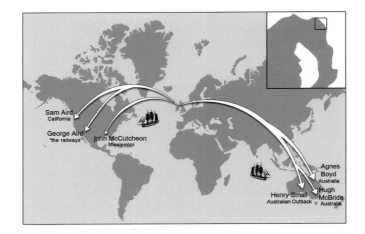

A few local emigrant destinations. Rural life offered limited opportunities. Not everyone will have left reluctantly.

McCutcheons' five children left. This did not leave the countryside in any way deserted. Far from it. In 1861 at the height of the haemorrhage, Portavo had twenty-five households with on average five people to each household. The place was still brimming. And big new families were starting. The Arnolds would have seven children. So would the Summers. The McBrides would have nine. But the trend was down. Between 1851-61 Portavo's population fell from its nineteenth century peak of 151 to 127. Over the next decade it fell again to 119, if the official figure is to be trusted.[4] Between 1851-1901 the townland's population almost halved, a fall which roughly mirrors the collapse of the population of rural Ireland as a whole.

The Malthusian separation between population and resources had occurred. The townland could not provide for its people. This was not necessarily a bad thing. Not everyone will have left reluctantly, or aspired to a life like that of their parents. Education had increased employability

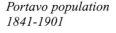

Portavo population 1841-1901

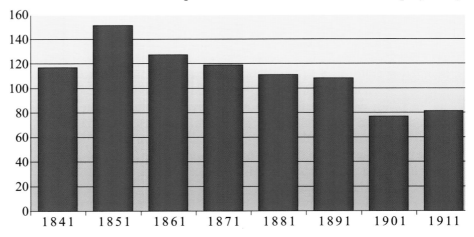

and expectations. Farmer's sons were becoming hitherto unheard of things like engineers, surveyors, and clerks.

Not everyone followed the stellar path of James Thompson, who was raised in the Ker townland of Ballymaglave South, and went on to become Professor of Mathematics at Glasgow University. His son William would discover the second law of thermodynamics and become ennobled as Lord Kelvin. But in their own quiet ways, many did something rather similar. The rural monolith was collapsing. New life choices presented themselves. Far-flung patterns of kinship created opportunities elsewhere. The adventurous left and numbers fell. Initially, this did not affect the well-being of the community. But soon the population structure began to acquire the unmistakable hallmarks of decay.

23 'Ker and Independence!': the 1857 election

'Ker and Independence!'

In March 1857, the Liberal Prime Minister, Lord Palmerston, was defeated on the issue of war with China and called a snap general election. Both Lord Edwin Hill and David Stewart Ker again stood for County Down, Hill as a Conservative, Ker as an independent. But what species of independent was Ker, all wondered? In 1852 he had stood as a supporter of the then Conservative government. Were he to do the same again, his return would have been assured, probably without a contest.

For the forty year-old Ker, however, the question of allegiance was no longer straightforward. It had never been. Ker's politics did not fit neatly into any of the available party-political pigeon holes. At heart, he was a utopian consensualist, a man whose politics, indeed whole disposition, were unsuited to the adversarial system. But he had come to terms with it, and since Richard's old boss Palmerston had taken power in 1855, Ker had mostly voted with the government. Would the hitherto inscrutable Ker now risk all, and declare himself a Liberal?

Ker was faced with an invidious choice. If he came out as a Liberal, he would risk his seat and incur the expense of a contested election. If he did not, the contradiction between his professed and actual allegiances would very quickly become impossible to live with. He made his decision. Or should we say his un-decision. Calling himself a liberal conservative[1] (for he believed that 'no Conservatism is safe that does not conceive of Liberal measures'), Ker stood as 'an Independent supporter of the present government' and issued a Liberal election address.[2]

The Conservatives reacted swiftly. Within days Colonel Forde of Seaforde had been brought forward, or in his own words 'imperatively called', to unseat Ker.[3] He was brought forward with some relish. Ker had led them a merry dance in 1852. Now the wheel had turned. It was payback time.

Lord Palmerston, by Cruikshank, c.1855. In 1857 Palmerston was invited to confer a peerage on Ker. (National Portrait Gallery)

Lt. Colonel W.B. Forde. 'Imperatively called' to unseat Ker. (Forde family)

Ker's political world turned upside down. His political friends became his enemies. Former enemies became his friends. The Tories branded him a quisling. The Liberals – who would not have fought at all had he not stood[4] – took him to their bosom, acclaiming him for having had 'the hardihood to think for himself'. Sharman Crawford emerged from his semi-retirement to endorse him.[5] The *Northern Whig* and *Banner of Ulster* put his case, denouncing Forde as a Downshire lackey. There could be no stronger proof of Ker's independence, they argued, than his courageous change of stance.[6]

'Ker and Independence!' became the rallying cry of liberal Down.[7] But was the movement that had been fatally weakened by Ker's victory in 1852 in any state to return him? Had it the strength to elect him in preference to Forde, who could depend on Downshire's votes and purse to sustain him?[8] That would depend on two things. On what sort of fire they could stoke in the belly of the ordinary tenant farmer; and on how extensive a power base they could build amongst the county's unaligned and liberal-leaning gentry.

Neither task would be straightforward. There was no burning issue waiting to be exploited, no restless mood for change. 1857 saw the debates of 1852 rehashed in a more temperate political climate. This did not suit Ker, but it did give him an opportunity to highlight the consistency of his position, as his stance on these matters[9] was unchanged.

Rowan Hamilton of Killyleagh saw the election in dynastic terms. He saw Forde as nothing more than the tool by which Downshire might

'Montaltior.' The brave but faltering Ker, with his faithful Sancho Panza, the tenant farmer. (Ray Elwood)

'obtain the long wished for object of his ambition – the second seat for the County'.[10] Most, however, saw it as a struggle between left and right, in which even important issues like free trade (which Ker supported and Hill opposed[11]) seemed to count for little. William Wallace, Ker's solicitor, characterised it as a contest between tolerance and intolerance.[12] Hill and Forde traded heavily on their Protestantism and their support for the Union. Ker refused to play any kind of constitutional or Orange card.

The versifiers took up their pens. The Tories produced a wonderful parody of Longfellow's popular poem of doomed questing, *Excelsior*, in which the poet's youthful hero was replaced by a brave but faltering Ker:

Montaltior	**Excelsior**
The month of March was waning fast,	The shades of night were falling fast,
As through the County Down there passed,	As through an Alpine village passed
An "Independent" not too nice,	A youth who bore, 'mid snow and ice,
His banner bore the strange device,	A banner with the strange device
"Montaltior"!	Excelsior!
As he walked forth they do record,	In happy homes he saw the light
The placard – "Vote For Hill & Forde",	Of household fires gleam warm & bright;
Above in spectral letters shone,	Above, the spectral glaciers shone,
And from his lips escaped a groan,	And from his lips escaped a groan,
"Montaltior"!	Excelsior!
Try not the Forde, the sage ones said,	"Try not the Pass!" the old man said:
High raised, a Hill towers overhead,	"Dark lowers the tempest overhead,
Th' opposing [stream] is deep and wide'	The roaring torrent is deep and wide!"
But still the voice of Ker replied,	And loud that clarion voice replied,
"Montaltior"![13]	Excelsior!

Forde tried to drive a wedge between Ker and the tenant farmer by impugning Ker's landlordism. He did not dare risk a frontal attack. But there were other ways of making the point. A letter from a man called McLean appeared in the papers. It insinuated that Ker had infringed the Ulster Custom by denying tenant right on a farm near Holywood.

This put Ker on the defensive, as observance of the Ulster Custom was one of the tenets of responsible landlordism. One up for Forde. But then it all began to unravel. The land in question was revealed to have been not a farm but a collection of building lots close to Belfast, upon which tenant right did not apply. The poor, downtrodden farmer was unveiled as a property speculator. The public spirited citizen who raised the issue turned out not to be a fellow farmer, but a Forde election agent, who far from being sympathetic to the speculator's position, had had the man imprisoned over debts owed to none other than Colonel Forde.[14] Attack repulsed.

But what was this public relations victory worth? Having the goodwill of the tenant farmer was one thing, getting his vote was quite another. Would farmers defy their landlords to vote for Ker? The omens were not auspicious. The mid-1850s were that rare thing, a time of agricultural contentment. The mood of the electorate was 'careless and quiescent'.[15] The lessons of 1852 were also salutary. The electorate was then highly politicised. But when it came to the crunch, few tenants on conservatively aligned estates (with the spectacular exception of the Londonderry estate) had dared to cross their landlords.

Frederick, Lord Dufferin, in an 1870 Vanity Fair *caricature. Controlled the county's fourth largest political interest. (Down Hunt collection)*

Pro-Ker advertisements from the Banner of Ulster, *April 1857. Portavo wholeheartedly endorsed Ker's new politics. (Belfast Education & Library Board)*

Archibald Rowan Hamilton of Killyleagh discounted tenant power altogether. He believed that the contest would be 'purely... between the Landlords of the County'. This, if correct, was ominous, but it did not necessarily spell disaster for Ker. Ker's conversion, and the accession of the Liberal Fourth Marquis Londonderry in 1854, had placed the second, third and fourth largest political interests in the county (those of Ker, Londonderry and Dufferin respectively) in Liberal hands.

However this did not put Ker in the clear. The next six largest estates in the county were conservative. And the Ker estate, for all its heroic political emergence, had had little time to acquire a client entourage. Only the Londonderry estate had any kind of established retinue of minor gentry, and Rowan Hamilton, ever the pessimist, despaired of Londonderry delivering the numbers required:

on his side there is no enthusiasm no organisation – as little of system or business like management as can be conceived

On the Conservative side however:

these are not wanting. Ld D. is activated by ambition so is Forde... who is himself an active man of business. The gentry with their old Tory feelings are active too... after what I have said you cannot doubt my opinion that Ker will be beaten like a hack.[16]

This view was untypical. Most observers considered the second seat hard to call. Ker campaigned strongly. Public meetings were held. Hurricane Anna again 'traversed the whole County gaining friends & bullying Foes'.[17] Parish and baronial committees urged electors to plump (vote only) for Ker, and if their landlord backed Hill and Forde, to give Hill their first vote and use their second freely.[18] 'Do not vote for Forde under any circumstances', his canvassers urged. Hill was untouchable, but Forde's challenge could be beaten. His vote had to be contained

'Oh bother the electors of Downpatrick; sure my brother owns all them niggers.'

The liberal press roundly denounced Downshire for attempting to reduce the great county of Down to 'a mere senatorial warming-pan'.[1] As it did so, the Ker estate, with velvet smoothness, was discreetly pulling very similar proprietorial levers in its own senatorial warming-pan, the borough of Downpatrick.

On March 31st 1857, ten days before the county voted, Richard Ker was elected Member of Parliament for the borough of Downpatrick. He was returned as a Liberal, and returned unopposed, providing the Ker campaign with a timely fillip. It could have been anything but. The previous borough election had taken place just seven weeks previously, following Charles Stewart Hardinge's elevation to the peerage.

Propitiously muzzled. William Johnston of Ballykilbeg. (Down Museum)

On that occasion, amid tumultuous scenes and cries of 'Away to Russia', Richard had been challenged by William Johnston of Ballykilbeg, Orange firebrand and proprietor of the *Downshire Protestant*. Scoffing at Ker's contention that 'it was wrong to keep debatable religious questions' at the forefront of politics, Johnston had characterised his opponent's attitude to the borough as, 'Oh bother the electors of Downpatrick; sure my brother owns all them niggers.'[2] Ker beat Johnston, but this was exactly the sort of publicity that the estate wanted to avoid, and Johnston's mysterious absence in April is surely testament to the growing finesse of Ker's party managers.[3]

The county votes

On April 10-11th 1857, the county went to the polls. The proceedings were peaceable and sober. No skulls were cracked. No bludgeon men ran riot.[1] It hardly seemed like an election at all. Each side concentrated on turning out its vote. But even this offered scope for skullduggery. Ker's people bought up Downshire's transport, to thwart his voters' attempts to get to the poll.[2] William Robinson of Moor Farm organised lifts to Newtownards for Portavo's voters. Ker's supporters in Knock, Dundonald and Comber came by train.[3] But it was not enough. Ker topped the poll in Newtownards, where the Portavo, Londonderry and Dufferin estates voted, but was trounced in Hillsborough and Newry, and beaten by a whisker at Downpatrick. Hill received 5,839 votes, Forde 5,341, Ker 3,735.[4] Hill and Forde were elected.

The estate was despondent. In the grieving words of the *Banner of Ulster*, Downshire's 'small-souled clique' had 'quietly garrotted' its opposition. Anketell agreed. 'Bailiff Power was too strong for us & it was

'Davy Stewart Ker, ex MP Co. Down'. (Ker family)

openly & unmercifully executed', he wrote, summarising the contest's realpolitik.[5] Ker had been evicted with less ceremony than a defaulting farmer. Parallels were drawn with the election of 1805, when the Downshires had also controlled both county seats. Ker's defeat inaugurated seventeen years of Downshire-Conservative hegemony, with Hill (later Hill-Trevor) and Forde retaining uncontested representation of the county until 1874. The clock had been turned back eighty years. The Ker and Londonderry dynastic challenges lay dead in the water. With one imperious sweep of his hand, Downshire had cleared the board of all challengers.

Ker took his defeat philosophically. Though he seemed to have been 'driven from an exalted position', the reality, he confided to Dufferin, was that he had 'escaped from considerable difficulty & troubles'.[6] Magnanimous to a fault, he renewed his friendship with Forde and Lord Edwin Hill soon after the election. They reciprocated in 1858, making Ker master of Lodge 86, the elite Masonic Lodge that served the county's gentry.[7] And so the ripples subsided. The ruling class re-formed. Would 'Montalto' fight again? Let him try, said Hill, throwing down the gauntlet. Ker left the matter open, saying only that such a course was 'not possible at present'.[8]

Dufferin's mother had no sympathy. Electoral humiliation was Ker's just dessert. But it was a disagreeable subject. She would say no more about it.[9] The Portavo estate, on the other hand, backed him to a man, unanimously giving Ker 'plumpers'. And this time, everyone who could vote, voted, raising his support from 93% in 1852 to 100% in 1857.[10] The difference is small, but it is significant, and it suggests that a new ingredient had been added to the mix: popular approval of Ker's politics.[11] The election also demonstrated the Kers' rising confidence. Thirty years before, challenging Downshire would have been unthinkable, now they had the weight to (albeit unsuccessfully) take him on.

There were disappointments too. The tenant rebellion did not materialise. It was never particularly likely. Estate voting followed predictable lines, with the Londonderry, Dufferin, Crawford and Rose-Cleland estates voting overwhelmingly for Ker, and those of Annesley, Price, Bateson, Blakiston-Houston, Montgomery and Lord Bangor backing Hill and Forde.[12] Only Maxwell had to ride out anything approaching a minor rebellion, with almost 30% of the tenantry on his

No David. The state opening of the 1857 parliament, by Joseph Nash. (Palace of Westminster Collection)

Finnebrogue estate giving their second votes to Ker, a wilfulness that may have privately delighted his liberal wife Madalena, who was also of course David's aunt.

The churches also played to form. The Church of Ireland clergy rejected Ker 'almost to a man... not withstanding his support of their Education Society and expenditure of some £5,000 in church building'.[13] The Catholic and Presbyterian clergy backed him strongly, many Presbyterian ministers being especially provoked by the aggressive caricature of Protestantism that the Conservatives had used to serve their electoral ends. 'Give that gammon to the dogs', spat one cleric, speaking for them all.[14]

It didn't save him. Landlord power, estate loyalty, and – heretical though it may be to admit it – the fact that many tenants were comfortable with the Conservative message, more than outweighed this clerical support. And for all Ker's attempts to rise above his glorious failure, there was no escaping the cold facts. This was the worst reverse the estate had suffered since the Famine. The peacock's feather had been plucked from Ker's tail. His supporters felt this keenly and argued that, in the light of the Liberal Party's national victory, the Prime Minister Lord Palmerston should:

> confer the dignity of a peerage on Mr. D.S. Ker. That gentleman owns a princely estate, and... the circumstances connected with this... important struggle against aristocratic tyranny and domination, make its hero worthy [of] any honour a British Prime Minister has the power to bestow[15]

In June 1857, the tenantry laid on a magnificent banquet for their fallen troubadour.[16] Five hundred attended, from every corner of the estate. Another hundred and fifty occupied the Ladies Gallery. Motifs like 'Live and let live' and 'Success to the house of Ker' were prominently displayed. A string band played. It was an evening of camaraderie. A time for the licking of wounds. For renewal. Ker was presented him with three splendid vases.[17] Anna received 'a gold armlet, set with brilliants', which David (populist to the end) climbed the Ladies Gallery to place on her wrist, to the accompaniment of tumultuous hooting and cheering. This courtly gesture was in keeping with the spirit of the evening. This was paternalism turned upside down. This was the estate, broad-shouldered and generous, giving succour to its disappointed child.

24 The great engine falters

To contemporaries and observers of the Ker estate, the 1857 election defeat signified little or nothing. Yes, it had been painful and humiliating, but too much should not be read into it. It was a glitch, an isolated setback in an optional area of activity, inflicted by a near irresistible power.

No-one doubted that the Kers would bounce back. As landed proprietors 'of fortune and influence', they were certain to remain powerful electoral players.[1] In addition, they now carried the hopes of the county's Liberals, who believed that the campaign of 1857 would 'have the effect of throwing Mr Ker's great weight *decidedly* into the Liberal scale at the [next] National Election'.[2] But things were not as they seemed. The estate was no longer battle-worthy. Indeed it should not have been fighting elections at all, for the heavy outgoings of the previous fifteen years had reduced its finances to a delicate condition.

This was a well-kept secret; outside a small inner circle, no-one suspected a thing. The Kers retained their blue chip reputation and their aura of having access to limitless wealth. One small proof of this came just months after the 1857 election, when Lord Dufferin (who was also beginning to drown in debt) tried to tap Ker for a 'small' loan of £50,000.[3] Even Dufferin knew nothing, and he was practically family.

Behind the gorgeous mask lay alarming levels of debt, and other more sinister kinds of corrosion. During the life of David Stewart Ker's grandfather the family's financial arrangements had been relatively straightforward. By the late 1850s, however, by dint of the family settlements of 1810, 1822 and 1842, they had assumed an almost Byzantine complexity.

David Stewart Ker's father had managed a difficult situation well. His borrowing powers had been seriously constrained by the settlement of 1810, and as a result he had spent and borrowed relatively little. By the time of his death he had largely paid off the three fortunes due to his sisters (payments of which were completed in 1851), leaving recorded debts of £176,572 on his death in 1844.[4] £39,847 of this was personal (and inherited) borrowing, £2,306 family charges, entered in the accounts as annual outgoings, £35,349 was family charges classified as capital,

Application of Ker Income, 1858

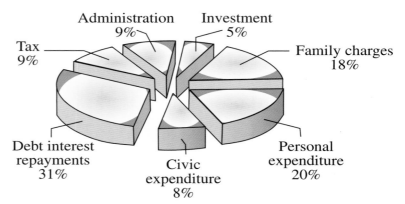

The Ker estate: estimated allocation of revenue in 1858 (from £31,600 base).

and £100,000 was 'productive debt', incurred during the purchase of Downpatrick.[5] The debt was large, but not crippling, because over half of it was income generating.[6] The 'unremunerative' family charges, when capitalised, comprised an unhealthy 37% of the total.

Family charges, then, accounted for a sizeable slice of Ker's outgoings. However the gradually reducing level of family settlements was one of the few positive features of the Kers' indebtedness. Each of David Stewart Ker's aunts was lavishly provided for. And his obligations to them did not end with the payment of their fortunes. Upon the discharge of the due £30,000, pin money of £500 Irish (£460) a year became payable to each for life. The Old Bear had looked after his girls. David Stewart Ker's brother and sisters were less well provided for, each receiving £10,000 Irish (£9230).[7] The next generation got less again, with David Stewart Ker's younger children receiving £20,000 between them.[8] By 1867 family charges had fallen to some 25% of the debt burden.

Under David Stewart Ker's more expansive regime the level of indebtedness rose. By 1850, after a turbulent decade of rent cuts, famine relief, written-off arrears and wide-ranging investments, it had risen to £225,459.[9]

The rise was undoubtedly facilitated by the ease that David had in obtaining credit. Ker had little difficulty in borrowing, and did so without fear or favour from farmers (including John Perry), doctors, ministers of religion (Church of Ireland only – neither priests nor Presbyterians seem to have had the inclination or the wherewithal to lend), merchants and gentlemen.[10]

We can see the process at work in 1851, when Richard wanted a bond for £1,000. David asked his bank to look out for a lender.[11] A lender will soon have been found. Typically, this will have been someone with a nest egg that they wished to invest in return for a reliable annual income –

which is exactly what the Ker estate provided. Loans were secured on mortgages at $4^{1}/_{2}$ or 5%. Interest payments were punctual and the capital was secured on Ker's huge land bank. This satisfied both parties. The estate was able to borrow what it needed, and construe the facility as a service. Depositors could invest in a respected local institution, which they considered to be as safe as any bank. Trollope's Miss Demolines spoke for them all when she exclaimed, 'Mama has every shilling laid out in a first class mortgage on land at four per cent. That does make one feel so secure!'[12]

There was nothing unusual or intrinsically dangerous about these transactions. All landowners juggled with debt. All estates incurred it. They were businesses. They borrowed. How much debt could an estate comfortably handle? W.A.Maguire has estimated that most could safely carry interest payments amounting to a quarter of their gross income, and could, without too much risk, encumber themselves with debts of up to eight times their annual rental. Servicing such a debt would eat up some 40% of the estate's annual income.[13]

In the late 1850s the Kers found themselves approaching this unenviable threshold. In 1858 their gross rental income was some £31,600 p.a. The payment of tithes, head rents, and taxes reduced this figure by about 9% to £28,847.[14] Interest payments on debts accounted for some £9,700 annually, or 31% of income.[15] Family charges and allowances absorbed another c.£5,600 per year (18%).[16]

Then there were the estate's social commitments. These were legion, but their cost is unclear. The best indication of their extent is to be found in the green General Account books for the Clough and Downpatrick estates. These show that in 1865-66, 'civic' expenditure accounted for 16% of the income generated by these two estates. The estate took, and

Downpatrick Cathedral: ate up money. (Down Museum)

was made to take, its civic responsibilities seriously. In Downpatrick, for instance, it employed officials such as a Town Constable, a Harbour Master and a Water Bailiff, supported hospitals, schools, almshouses and churches, including the cathedral, which devoured money. It made financial contributions to horticultural and farming societies, the cricket club, the choral society, the mechanics institute, an orphan society, and amateur bands.[17]

Here we see the landlord nourishing and underpinning an entire small society. But we should not overstate his efforts in this regard. The demands placed on this particular revenue stream are exceptional, and did not apply to the whole property. Overall, a figure of about 8% for civic expenditure is probably more realistic.

The cost of administering the estate is also unclear. On the Downshire estates, administration costs accounted for about 10% of rental income.[18] The cost of running the Ker estate, which was run in a comparable way, by a similar set of core staff, is likely to have been broadly similar, or a shade below.[19]

Money was also spent on agricultural and urban improvements. Again, in the absence of the necessary records, this expenditure is hard to quantify. Before the evolution of the social compact in the 1830s, investment was minimal. During the 1840s and early 1850s, however, it rose to approximately 5% of rental income.

Taxes and dues, investment, administration and civic expenditure, then, absorbed about 30% of income. When debts and family charges are added, some 80% of revenue is accounted for. This left Ker with maybe £6,000-6,500 per annum to meet his and his family's personal, household and demesne expenses – a sum that the 'fantastically extravagant' David had little difficulty in disposing of.

The estate then, in itself, was a hugely profitable business. Its problem was the family. Maintaining the Kers in the style to which they were accustomed consumed rather more than the odd pocketful of spare change. Unfortunately, comprehensive records of the family's personal expenditure have not survived. Occasionally, however, we are offered an insight. In 1865-66, for example, the General Account Books for the Clough and Downpatrick Estates record that personal, household and demesne expenditure amounted to 22% of income.[20] In 1871, Ker's personal expenses amounted to at least £7,700. However, as we shall see shortly, that year of disintegration does not provide us with a useful base.

In 1857, after two outrageously expensive county elections, the estate's debts stood at £264,156.[21] How much of this debt was 'estate' expenditure? How much was 'family' spending? It is impossible to say.[22] The 'virtuous' debts cannot be distinguished from the wanton. Neither can business costs ultimately be distinguished from family expenses. They continually dovetail. This points us towards an important flaw in

the structure of estate management. While business and family expenses were for the most part separately accounted, there was no clear barrier between the two. Ultimately, perhaps there could be none, for these businesses were essentially familial enterprises. The consequence was that the landowner was effectively in the position of a managing director who could, without censure, dip into the till to finance his lifestyle, a lifestyle largely defined by conspicuous consumption. It was as near a thing as could be imagined to a structural incitement to ruin.

David and Anna's reaction to the mounting debt took the form of a deep and abiding dread. They set aside the plan to rebuild Portavo and made modest retrenchments. They sold their yacht, the *Countess*, and in the late 1850s managed to live within their income for two successive years, something David had never managed before and would never manage again. But the anxiety did not resolve itself into any fundamental reorientation.

Had David drastically curtailed his personal expenditure, had he axed some of the more costly (and progressive) components of his system of estate management, and taken a harder line on rents and tolls, etc., then things might have been different. For in the late 1850s, strict austerity could have contained the problem. But he did not do this. It wasn't in him, and the window of opportunity slowly closed.

Maintaining the Kers in the style to which they were accustomed consumed rather more than spare change. Montalto by J.W. Carey. (Ker family)

David Stewart Ker, in a caricature
by Daniel Delacherois, 1861.
(Day family)

Fortunately for Ker, there were other, more radical ways of re-establishing control. In 1861 David explored the idea of selling just over half of the estate. His most immediate object in doing so was to pay off his debts.[23] But this would be more than a rescue plan. It would be a thoroughgoing restructuring, aimed at reversing the policy of nearly a century, and moving the family's wealth from land into stocks and bonds. These yielded better returns. Ker was advised that his lands could be:

disposed of upon so very advantageous terms as to produce a sum which at a moderate rate of interest will represent an annual income far beyond the Rental produced by these lands at present…[24]

This did not mean that the Kers would cease to be landowners, for under the terms of the 1810 settlement, the 'settled' estates of Portavo, Clough, Ballynahinch and the Five Towns (which yielded an income of some £16,000 p.a.) could not be alienated or sold. The other half of Ker's property was his personal estate, which he could do with as he pleased.[25] Ker was advised that if he sold this land he could clear his personal debts and turn an annual deficit of over £10,000 into an income of £3,000 per annum.

These were heretical thoughts for a landlord to think, but Ker was not alone in harbouring them. Other indebted landlords had been making similar calculations, with similarly interesting results. In 1845 the English parliamentarian Sir James Graham, who had 26,000 acres in Cumberland, worked out that if he sold up he could pay his debts, provide for his numerous children and nearly double his net income by investing the leftover cash at $3\frac{1}{2}\%$, an easy rate to obtain.[26]

But he didn't. And neither did Ker. Buying land may not have made a lot of financial sense, but then what had owning land got to do with financial logic? It was about status, standing in the community and belonging to the most exclusive club in the land. Ker was also tied by the settlement of 1810. He had hoped to sell certain of the 'settled' townlands. But this created legal problems. His counsel advised that these could be surmounted if he put lands of equivalent value under settlement. However that would require the mature consent of his heir, and Alfred would not come of age until late 1864 – three years hence.

The plan hung in the air, unamended and unacted upon. Meanwhile, the debt again began to mount. David took refuge in a mixture of *sang froid* and denial, punctuated by spasms of guilty activity. His predicament settled within him and hung about him like a fog. In public he maintained the gorgeous mask, projecting an unruffled air of business as usual. In private, his multifarious difficulties oppressed him. Slowly but surely, he began to fall apart.

Early in 1863, writhing like an eel on a skewer, Ker revisited the idea of selling land, but in a very different spirit to that of 1861. Nothing visionary was countenanced now. This would be a conventional, defensive sale to pay off debt, akin to similar sales that the Dufferins and Downshires had conducted in order to get through financial difficulties. It was not a stratagem that the privileged Kers had ever had to resort to. But desperate times required desperate measures.

David contemplated selling the Red Hall estate, but drew back. Such a sale could not be explained away as mere restructuring. Yet fresh funds had to be raised. In December 1863, Ker bit the bullet and sold 2,440 acres in the Landed Estates Court. 'The Ballymena Estate', 1,180 acres in mid-Antrim, went for £16,980, well above its anticipated sale price.[27]

The 1863 sale notice: heralded the beginning of the end. (National Archives, Dublin)

COUNTIES OF ANTRIM AND DOWN.

Sale on THURSDAY, the 17th day of DECEMBER, 1863.

In the Matter of the Estate of DAVID STEWART KER, Esq., M.P., Owner and Petitioner.

RENTAL AND PARTICULARS

OF

FEE-SIMPLE AND FEE-FARM ESTATES,

SITUATE IN

THE COUNTIES OF ANTRIM AND DOWN,

Containing in the whole 3,339 acres, or thereabouts, statute measure, and producing a net annual Rental of £2,209 10s. 1d.

TO BE SOLD BY PUBLIC AUCTION,

IN SEVERAL LOTS, AS PARTICULARIZED IN THIS RENTAL,

BY THE HONORABLE JUDGE DOBBS,

AT THE LANDED ESTATES COURT, INNS' QUAY, IN THE CITY OF DUBLIN,

On THURSDAY, the 17th day of DECEMBER, 1863, at the hour of Twelve o'clock, at Noon.

The young heir, Alfred Ker, c.1858, as painted by his Uncle Richard; a pale shy boy, possessed of 'a singularly kind and gentle disposition'. (Inglis-Jones family)

The townland of Ballyalloly near Comber, annexed with such bravura in 1831, and 835 acres in Glastry and St. John's Quarter on the Ards Peninsula were sold at the same time for an unknown sum. All monies raised were held by the Court 'towards the payment of the incumbrances.'[28]

The sale made little inroad into the debt, which in 1864 stood at £293,657, a sum requiring interest payments amounting to nearly 50% of the net annual rental. Nor was the sale accompanied by the imposition of financial discipline, or any paring down of the estate's public profile. On the contrary, the coming of age of David's heir Alfred in November 1864 was celebrated with all the lavishness and confident projection of dynastic permanence that marked David's own coming of age in 1838.

A 'Grand Ball' was held at Montalto. An exquisitely illuminated address was presented to the young heir.[29] Loyal declarations poured in from the scattered estates and towns. In Downpatrick, 'immense fires blazed... on every eminence... and there were numerous discharges of fireworks, and volleys of small arms from dark until almost midnight'. Huge bonfires raged on drumlin tops for miles around the town. In the far distance the fires of Clough could be seen. The whole countryside seemed to be aflame.

In Portavo and Ballycarry houses were illuminated, bonfires crackled on the hilltops, and the tenantry were plied with all the beer they could drink. In Ballynahinch:

Every street was illuminated... with candles of various colours, and in many places the windows inside and outside were decorated with laurels and other evergreens, and bunches of flowers hanging from the windows... some forty or fifty barrels of ale were provided, and Mr Ker's health was... drunk in flowing bumpers.[30]

Dense crowds 'thronged the streets'. Bells pealed. Flags tugged and fluttered. A band toured the town. Fireworks lit the sky. Huge bonfires blazed on the hills round the town – there were four on Windmill Hill alone – and for miles beyond, as townland vied with townland to build the biggest and brightest bonfire. The effect was overwhelming, or as the *Downpatrick Recorder* put it, 'romantic in the extreme'.[31]

As fireworks burst in arpeggios in the skies above Montalto, the irony could not have been more glaring. Unless this sort of thing stopped, there would be no great estate for the heir to be heir to. But what was the befuddled Ker to do? The revolutionary moment had passed. By late 1864 the financial picture had blackened to the extent that, had the 1861 plan been enacted, it would have amounted to little more than an old fashioned discharge of debts.

Nor were retrenchment or the limited free sale then envisaged capable of solving the problem. The initiative was passing from Ker to his creditors. For while the estate appeared to revel in its own robust good health, the unpalatable private truth was that debt had begun to choke the great wealth-generating engine that drove it. Matters were fast slipping past the point of retrieval. The Ker estate was becoming encumbered to the point of collapse.

25 'The fact is David is a complete lunatic': collapse

'Poor Mrs Ker! What Horror!'

In 1862 Anna died. She was just thirty-nine. David intended that her funeral should be private. But he did not get his wish. As a temporary grave was opened to receive her body, 'a large concourse of people… assembled… without notice or invitation' to mourn her.[1] They had not come to earn their landlord's favour. This was a spontaneous, heart felt, Diana-style outpouring of grief.[2]

'Poor Mrs Ker! What Horror!' wrote de Ros, expressing the universal feeling.[3] Anna's death caused consternation, and an astonishment that bordered on disbelief. What had killed her? David told Dufferin that she died 'from great weakness & depression'.[4] This is a most unusual cause of death for a woman of Anna's class and age. Indeed it seems almost incomprehensible that someone as bright and energetic as Anna should go in this way – a point keenly felt by her relatives and friends. What was going on?

We can only guess. No evidence remains.[5] One ready explanation of her weakness lies in the unrelenting demands of pregnancy and childbirth. Anna had twelve children. The last was born in 1861, and had she lived, more would almost certainly have followed.[6]

Oh rose, thou art sick

But there was more to this than exhaustion or post-natal depression. Anna was anxious about the way the estate was careering into debt. The letters of condolence that Dufferin received hint at another, even more intractable problem. These letters are notable for the coolness they show towards the lately bereaved husband. Dufferin's circle withholds sympathy from the widowed David in a way that seems to fall just one step short of casting blame. The question, 'What has he done to our

In the kingdom of the blind. Unable to cope, Ker turned to alcohol for help. David Stewart Ker, ivory miniature, mid-1850s. (Ker family)

Anna?' simmers unspoken within the correspondence. One writer comments reproachfully that David was 'ill adapted' to take on the responsibilities that would now fall to him.[1] Another hopes that 'the poor strange father' will deal wisely with his children.[2]

These cryptic but pointed remarks help us to make sense of much that until now has seemed merely odd or incongruous. David had not been himself for some time. His behaviour had become erratic. He had experienced panic attacks. He had been plagued by an urge to 'fly from society'.[3]

This was not like David, who had always seemed supremely at ease with himself and the world around him. Over time, however, David had been finding his customary ease increasingly hard to muster. By the early 1860s it had become a positive struggle. The gap between what he was, and what he felt he should appear to be, or to put it another way, the gap between the man and his public alter ego, Lord Montalto, had begun to become unbridgeable.

He turned to alcohol for help, and at first this was a boon, for he could drink and be the person he wanted to be, but in time it simply compounded the problem. At what point the perception of David changed from 'Yes, he can be a little odd' to 'Oh dear', is unclear. But this change took place. By 1862 David Stewart Ker had ceased to be completely *compos mentis*.

How much Anna (or anyone) could have done to alleviate his difficulties is unclear. By 1862 Anna was floundering and in need of help herself. Resentful of his inability to manage his predicament or do anything to ease her own, she would round on him in sheer frustration

(l-r) Helen, Alfred (top,) Selina (bottom), and Charles in ivory miniatures from the mid 1850s. (Ker family)

over little or nothing. It was not that they didn't love one another. It was more that neither could do the other much good.

In the end Anna lost the will to go on. Even her love for her children, profound though it was, was not enough to give her purpose. Despair overwhelmed her, and she went under, nursed to the end by her poor strange husband, the author of so much of her misfortune. Anna's death removed a strong force for stability at a time when the estate needed cool, clear heads. Her relatives looked to the future with apprehension. They were right to. With her departure, the debt, alcoholism and insanity became freer still to feed into each other. A grindingly destructive dynamic had now settled into place.

Montalto by J.W. Carey. House of horrors? (Ker family)

The worst sufferers were the children. David could be a tyrannical parent. At Montalto, according to his youngest son Hamilton, 'the whole family lived in terror of their father's violent rages and unpredictable behaviour.'[4] The inconsistency that is the antithesis of good parenting was David's hallmark. The loving efforts Anna had made to raise secure, well-balanced children were comprehensively undermined. Each child coped as best it could. Hardier creatures like David's third son Richard gave every appearance of shrugging it off. Sensitive souls like Alfred struggled.

Montalto did not produce whole, contented, resilient people; it produced frightened and in some cases damaged children. Eighteen years divided youngest from eldest, meaning that Alfred and Selina were making their way in the world while their youngest brother Hamilton was still a toddler. Selina married into the Maxwell family. Alfred joined the 12th Lancers, becoming the first head of the family to serve as a soldier.

This was in tune with the spirit of the age. Life had become oriented, as never before, towards the military and the imperial. The County Down gentry, who had once left the British Isles only to take the Grand Tour, now found themselves scattered to the four corners of the globe in the service of empire. However, it wasn't all duty. In 1857 David wrote of the family enjoying 'a perfect circle of gaiety'.[5] All had friends to visit, things to do, and dances and entertainments to attend at Hillsborough Castle, Mountstewart and elsewhere.[6]

Selina, David's eldest daughter, who married John Perceval-Maxwell in 1868. (Gavin Perceval-Maxwell)

The gorgeous mask

The invisible worm that gnawed at the heart of the estate, did so well away from public view. To all intents and purposes, the Ker estate was thriving.

The Spa and maze, from McComb's Guide to Belfast*, 1861.*

With the burning of Portavo and the letting of Red Hall,[1] Montalto now received the concentrated wealth of the estates and flourished accordingly. Its grounds were ennobled. The damage wrought during the Night of the Big Wind, when some 4,000 trees were felled, was made good.[2] Bulbs, seedlings and saplings by the thousand were bought from local nurseries.[3] Pheasants were reared. There were regular shoots.[4] The home farm competed successfully at fairs and shows, winning medals and prizes for its livestock.[5]

Visitors continued to flock to the Spa, which was kept in 'best order'. Ker did his bit to promote tourism by hosting a widely reported dinner in the Spa Assembly Rooms at which he unblushingly commended their suitability for functions.[6] He also got back into politics rather shamefacedly in 1859, when, at the eleventh hour, he put out Richard and had himself returned for the borough of Downpatrick as a Tory. Another inexplicable volte face? Ker would probably have preferred to call it another proof of his independence, which became necessary when the Liberal Party voted for electoral reform, and the abolition of boroughs such as his own.[7]

La dolce vita: the Kers at the Palazzo Barbaro

Richard took his dismissal philosophically. Parliament was expensive and his means were limited. As resuming his diplomatic career was no longer an option, he moved to where his money would go further. In the early 1860s Richard and Rose settled in Italy, joining that country's expatriate bohemian elite.

The couple's six children were mostly raised in Rome and Venice and their upbringing was far from conventional. Lady Paget remarked that

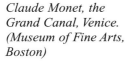

Claude Monet, the Grand Canal, Venice. (Museum of Fine Arts, Boston)

Richard Ker, 1870s, stripped to the waist and ready to take on all comers. The former First Attaché now lived as a free spirit. (Ker family)

Rose, 'did not bring up her girls, and ignored her boys', but added that 'the children were all greatly gifted and had nice natures.'[1] Richard's parenting skills were apparently no greater. On one occasion, as he was leaving a hotel in Milan, he called to his boys to hurry along. There were no porters, so they dropped their cases from the third floor into the hall, bursting the leather and ruining the contents, an incident which Lady Paget considered 'the natural consequence of their bringing up.'[2]

The early 1870s found the family in the Maroniti Palace in Rome, where they became friends with Tom and Anthony Trollope.[3] They met Garibaldi, the founder of the modern Italy, and tradition has it that one of their daughters (Nini?) sat on Garibaldi's knee.[4] Richard's new life was the antithesis of the old. The former slave to propriety and decorum now lived as a free spirit. In his own words:

after seven years of slavery "Richard at last is himself again." The frown of Power, the insolence of Seniority, and the leaden tinkling Bell, are now equally indifferent to me. Master of my own time, I follow where Inclination leads at pleasure...[5]

The chrysalis had turned into a butterfly. But a butterfly of a peculiar hue. By 1873, the suave diplomat had become, 'perfectly wild and never had any money, his hair straggled, his beard was long and forked, and his clothes [were] much neglected'.[6]

The beautiful, unfathomable Rose made him a fitting companion. Lady Paget described Rose's manner as cold, but her speech as 'terse and full of humour'. She loved books and reading and hated going out, possibly

Walburga, Lady Paget. Acute observer of expatriate life.

Gervase Ker became 'the only Englishman (sic)' to win the Gondoliers' race in Venice. In my Gondola, by Anders Zorn, 1894. (Zornsamlingarna)

because she had to put up with much unwanted attention. The pair lived restless lives. Rose's passion was arranging houses. Richard painted and sculpted, and in the words of his grand-daughter, Louise King-Hall, 'few ceilings escaped [his] frescoing hand'.[7]

In the late 1870s, the nomads settled in Venice, the home of Richard's grandmother, Madalena Guardi.[8] They lived in the Palazzo Barbaro on the Grand Canal, one of the finest renaissance palaces in the city. How they could afford to do so is unclear, as they were always short of money.[9] But live here they did, and live well, as Rose's niece discovered when she visited in 1880:

The Palazzo Barbaro, Venice. (Perceval-Maxwell family)

The Kers house is so nice… splendid rooms & pretty furniture & they all look so well in it Nini like a bit of Dresden china & Olga most picturesque. They made such a pretty group the other evening. Mrs Calvert with her white hair white cap & white lace shawl. Aunt Rose in a purple & white dress like one of the early queens & the other girls arranging roses…[10]

The gilded salon of the Palazzo Barbaro, by Ludwig Passini. The rectangular lines below the ceiling mark the minstrel's gallery. (Private collection)

Louise King-Hall rather spoils this picture of contentment by writing of the couple getting vaguer and vaguer, and of Rose leaving 'her six good-looking children to bring themselves up as best they could.'[11] This judgement seems harsh. For all their lack of parent-craft, the couple worked hard to find their boys careers that were commensurate with their standing. Rivers studied for the Bar in the Inner Temple. Rose sought Dufferin's help in getting Gervase a diplomatic posting. Richard sent Gervase to Eton and moved to England to be near him during his early years.[12]

In Venice the Kers moved in a charmed circle that included the poet Robert Browning and the painters Whistler and John Singer Sargent. The children, now growing into a precocious early adulthood, received a thoroughly cosmopolitan upbringing. As well as their Venetian neighbours, they mixed with artists, writers, and wealthy émigrés from Europe and America. Gervase mastered the gondola, becoming 'the only Englishman (sic!) who has won the Gondoliers' Race in Venice'.[13] He and his sisters Nini and Olga performed in masques and *tableaux vivants*. One evening Olga was woken and ordered to accompany Browning to the theatre. A play by Goldoni was being performed in Venetian, and the poet

Scirocco. Nini (l) and Olga Ker on the balcony of the Palazzo Barbaro, by Ralph Curtis, 1885. (Private collection)

needed an interpreter. On another occasion she is said to have asked Whistler why he wore a boot-lace for a tie, only to be told disappointingly that 'Little girls should be seen and not heard.'[14]

In 1883 the Kers vacated the Barbaro, and moved into the beautiful but ill-starred Palazzo Dario nearby.[15] A wealthy Bostonian family, the Curtises, took the Barbaro. They were shocked by what they found. The Kers had not been kind to the Barbaro. The boys had thrown cricket balls at the stucco cherubs which graced its magnificent salon, knocking off their wings and feet. Rose had covered the ceiling's gorgeous frescoes with bitumen, saying that 'she did not like faces looking down at her!!'[16]

The place was hastening to ruin. But the Curtises patiently restored its sullied glories. They were also intrigued by the Kers. Ralph Curtis likened Nini to a Botticelli, and painted her and Olga on the balcony of the Barbaro. Under the Curtises, the Barbaro became the home to a glittering literary and artistic circle that included Anders Zorn and Henry James, who finished *The Aspen Papers* in the Barbaro in 1887.[17]

By this date the Kers may have gone. 1889 found Rose and the girls in

Alexandria, where Olga met the man who would become her husband, George King-Hall, and Rose produced an Arabic-English grammar that is said to have been used in Near-Eastern schools.[18] Richard died in Wimbledon in 1890, having separated from his wife (and, it would seem, family) some years previously. In 1897 Rose returned to Quentin Castle, where she died in 1902, 'retaining her classical beauty', and her considerable enigma, to the end.[19]

Landlordism's Indian summer

At the time of the Kers departure for Italy landlord-tenant relations were good, even cordial, and they remained so during the relatively affluent 1850s and 1860s. Prosperity proved something of a social sedative. The pressure on the county's landlords eased. This gave the estate room to manouvre, but it did not try to claw back its Famine concessions.[1] Rents remained stable from the early 1850s until the advent of 'fair' or judicially determined rents in the early 1880s,[2] during which time Irish rents generally rose by 20-30%.[3]

Rents fell as a percentage of outgoings. This allowed tenants to keep a larger slice of the agricultural cake. The countryside prospered. On the estates, 'Well tilled fields and tasteful houses' greeted the eye. A culture of self-improvement took root. Tenants vied with one another to see 'who shall best educate their sons and daughters [and] exhibit the neatest and best arranged farm-steading'. In 1857, Ker's yeomen farmers declared that, 'under your fostering care, our system of agriculture has risen from the humiliation of a mere handicraft to that of a science'.[4]

The estate encouraged these advances. Its agriculturalist promoted good practice. Lime (for fertiliser) from Whitehead could be bought at a

'Well tilled fields and tasteful houses' greeted the eye. Boyd's Farm, by Robert Innes.

*The former Ker estate office in
Downpatrick, now Alexander Reid
& Frazer, on bin collection day.
The Clough and Downpatrick
estates were managed from this
office. The more northerly estates
were run from Ballynahinch.*

third below its market price. Free slates were made available in a
modernising attempt to wean tenants off thatch.[5] Interest-free loans for
fencing, at one shilling per perch, and drainage (6d per perch) were
offered.[6] By 1852, 350,000 perches or over a thousand miles of drains
had been laid at an outlay of some £8,750.[7] Take-up was particularly
strong on the Portavo estate, where Samuel McCutcheon took out
drainage loans worth over £29, and William Angus £34, subsidies that
would have financed extensive improvements.[8]

The estate also took a liberal view of tenant right.[9] The 'tenant right'
was the goodwill value of a farm, a sum which the incoming tenant paid
to the outgoing, when he or she 'sold up' and moved on. This goodwill
value was inversely related to rent, so the lower the rent, the higher the
tenant right value, or as Dufferin put it, as one went up the other went
down, 'like buckets in a well'.[10] As tenant right was ill-defined and highly
cash-sensitive, there were frequent disputes over its meaning and
application, disputes which could poison landlord-tenant relations. Ker
neutralised this potential source of grievance by allowing tenant right 'on
its broadest principle' on all his estates.[11]

All this meant that Ker tenants tended to do well in the tenant right
marketplace. In 1857 the tenant right on at will lands on the Ker estate
fetched twenty guineas an acre.[12] In 1870, it was £30-40 per acre, a sum
greater than the sale value of the land.[13] The estate had first call on this
money, and used it to reclaim loans and arrears before permitting the
transfer of a farm. On the Ker estate, advances for improvements such as
ditching and drainage, legal costs, and if applicable, arrears, were
recouped in this manner when a farm changed hands, 'according to the
custom of the estate'.[14]

RULES

TO BE OBSERVED BY

The Tenants on the Estates of D. S. KER, Esq., M.P.

1. **Division of Farms.**——Farms must not be divided by Will, or otherwise, without Landlord's assent.

2. **Sub-letting Land to Under-Tenants**——For a TERM of YEARS, or in any other way, is *strictly prohibited*; in such cases, the Under-Tenant will either be taken as a *Head Tenant*, or the Tenant who has sub-let will be charged an additional acreage rent of *Ten Shillings.*

3. **Townparks.**——EVERY HOUSEHOLDER will be accommodated with a Townpark, as far as practicable, during residence in the Town; on ceasing to reside in the Town, the Townpark must be given up to the OFFICE, and no claim for any consideration on giving up possession will be allowed.

4. **Sale of Farms.**——All Tenants wishing to sell their interest in their Farms are to give in their names at the OFFICE, and also the names of the persons desiring to purchase. If Sale is allowed, any conditions required by the Landlord must be agreed to before new Tenant can be accepted. It must be clearly understood by the purchasers that if the Landlord sees fit to raise the Rent on expiry of Leases, or transfer of Yearly Tenancies, the amount of consideration paid to outgoing Tenants will not influence the Landlord when re-adjusting the increased Rent.

5. **Houses.**——No Cottier-house is to be built without a licence from the OFFICE, under a penalty of *One Guinea per annum in each case.*

6. **Cottiers.**——No Cottiers are to be brought in without a license from the OFFICE, under a penalty of *One Guinea per annum in each case*; and all Cottiers must sign an agreement, which will be supplied on application at the OFFICE, and must be witnessed by the Bailiff.

7. **Lodgers.**——Tenants or Cottiers who make a practice of harbouring Lodgers or Strolling Persons will not be allowed to remain on the ESTATE.

8. **Watercourses.**——Any Tenant injuring WATERCOURSES, by throwing in Stuff or Stones, will be fined *Five Shillings, and be obliged to repair the damage.* Foot-sticks will be given in every case where they are required, on application at the OFFICE. When WATERCOURSES have been sunk, and all obstructions removed, those Tenants who are benefited thereby will be thereafter expected to keep them clear; and they are requested to report to the Agent any instance in which injury is done thereto.

Ker estate regulations, c.1850. (Hugh Press)

In the supremely important area of agricultural tenancies, the estate took a 'softly softly' approach. It observed the 'lying gale' and avoided socially unsettling reforms. It quietly encouraged farm amalgamation, which many reformers (including the youthful Anketell) believed would be the making of Irish agriculture.[15] 'Ejectments' did not increase in the wake of the legislative revision of 1851, which made eviction cheaper and easier.[16]

The social compact of the 1830s guided all this policy and practice. At its heart was the idea of reciprocity, what the tenantry in 1857 called the 'correlative duties' of landlord and tenant.[17] The idea is a profound one, for it implies that the basis of relations on the estate was not paternal. The perception that both sides had properly discharged these duties allowed the compact to flourish, and during the 1850s, when Ker's politics and those of the bulk of his tenantry coincided, to acquire a meaning that went well beyond the merely economic.[18]

Personality was another important ingredient in the mix. Ker was liked. Indeed, when he appeared on electoral platforms he was greeted with cries of, 'You're the best landlord in Ireland'.[19] Ker was someone the tenantry could do business with. He was accessible. He was open to argument. His mind could be changed. His credo was 'fair play' and both he and Anketell believed in the ultimate undesirability of overly favourable or one-sided deals.[20]

Though power lay with the estate, the rent cuts of 1841-43 and the Clough resistance of 1870 show that the tenantry could, *in extremis*, change its behaviour. However it is not in conflict, but in the absence of conflict, that we find the best evidence of the extent of tenant power. Conflict could have been endemic. But it was not, because the tenant voice had been *internalised* within the administration of the estate, attuning it towards behaviour which was likely to command tenant consent.[21] It should also be clearly stated that Ker's progressive regime was not his undoing. Socially responsible landlordism did not mean economic suicide. The source of the estate's hideous difficulties lay elsewhere.

The 'dripping roast'

Was the estate less well run in the 1850s-60s, as David's condition worsened? The family suspects so, but the records (such as they are) show no apparent fall-off in the meticulousness with which the estate was

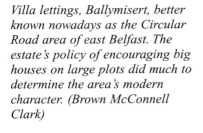

Villa lettings, Ballymisert, better known nowadays as the Circular Road area of east Belfast. The estate's policy of encouraging big houses on large plots did much to determine the area's modern character. (Brown McConnell Clark)

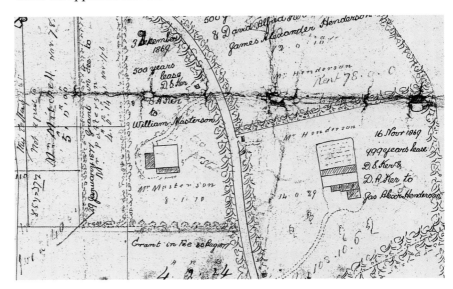

administered. At subaltern level, the line held. Strategic matters are less easily assessed. It could be convincingly argued that the estate took too small a slice of its gross wealth or 'GNP' during the period 1850-80. However, as we shall see shortly, the results of the judicial rent reviews of the 1880s suggest that in its own low-key way, the estate protected its interests well, combining a not insubstantial rental take with a reputation for socially concerned landlordism.

Nor was there any fall-off in the entrepreneurial spirit with which the estate was managed. Though the 1863 sale reduced the rental by nearly £1,400 p.a., the actual rental fell by only £450 between 1858-67, a net increase of nearly £1,000 if the sold lands are omitted from the calculation.[1] Ker appears to have achieved this increase not by increasing agricultural rents but, like the Dukes of Devonshire in Dungarvan or Downshire on the edge of Newry, by developing his towns and granting building leases.[2]

Until the 1850s these 'villa' lettings were small scale and ad hoc. In 1857, however, Ker commissioned a comprehensive assessment of the estate's building potential from Charles Lanyon. Lanyon identified a prodigious 2,400 acres on the shores of Belfast Lough, along the coast of the Portavo estate and around Ballynahinch as, 'Eligible sites for building Villas or Bathing Lodges' and predicted 'a very considerable addition to your Rental' if these sites could be let on good terms.[3] The only problem was that these lands lay within the 'settled estates', the administration of which was governed by the fiercely protective settlement of 1810.

This conferred the power to grant leases for a maximum of three lives or thirty-one years. The settlement of 1842 gave Ker the power to grant ninety-nine year leases.[4] Few could be tempted to build on such terms.[5] The situation was remedied in 1859, when the trustees of the settled estates obtained the authority to grant leases of up to five hundred years, an important breakthrough.[6] New building plots were let on these terms.

Urban expansion was seen as the way forward. With Ker's encouragement, Ballynahinch grew steadily between 1841-81, when its population rose from 911 to 1,471, against a backdrop of a falling population in the county as a whole. This was no mean achievement.[7] Would that the same could be said for Downpatrick. In 1834, Downpatrick had been bought as a flourishing town with good prospects.

Mid-nineteenth century view of Downpatrick, looking down Scotch Street towards the cathedral. (Private collection)

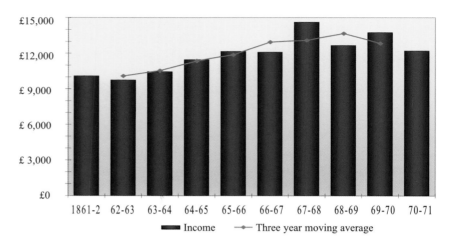

Revenue generated by the Downpatrick and Clough estates 1861-72, with three year moving average.

By the 1860s, however, the City of Downe was withering on the vine.

Local historian Hugh Press is clear as to the cause, 'The repeal of the Corn Laws ruined Downpatrick', he says.[8] Cheap American corn priced local producers out of the market. Less shipping used the Quay. It proved hard to keep or attract industry.[9] Even the building of a gasworks and the arrival of the railway failed to revive the town's fortunes.[10] During the period 1831-71, the town's population fell by nearly a quarter.[11] Hostile demographics and the northward shift in the county's centre of gravity more or less set the seal on the matter.[12] Press's assessment could not be blunter, 'Downpatrick went down the tubes'.

The town the Kers bought had been peaking, not growing, and now it was imploding. In the circumstances, one might have expected Ker's rental income to plunge or at the very least, tread water. But urban income rose substantially during the 1860s, in spite of Downpatrick's difficulties.[13]

Pilson suspected that Anketell managed the estate in his own interests.[14] Hugh Press, who in his time has been agent for the Dunleath, Annesley, Wallace and Delacherois estates, agrees. 'Ker was cleaned', he says, leafing through old estate rentals that he has worked with, off and on, for forty years. Press sees the estate as 'a dripping roast', which certain prominent local families – including the Wallaces, Keowns, Anketells and Pilsons – waxed fat on.[15] He has a point. The estate was a manager of land. It did not build. It left this to local entrepreneurs, who took plots or tenements from the estate in return for a ground rent, and developed them, keeping the profit for themselves.

Most of these entrepreneurs were close to the estate. In 1873 Ker's solicitor, William Wallace, held thirteen fee farm tenements in the town, and went on to amass a considerable property portfolio, reputedly by lending people money for mortgages then foreclosing at the earliest opportunity.[16] Anketell held fifteen tenements, Pilson had sixteen, and Keown thirty-nine.[17] Whether Ker was being 'fleeced' or advantaged by this activity must to some extent remain a matter of judgement. What cannot be doubted is the entrepreneurial vigour of the estate and those close to it during this period. It is hard to think of a time when the estate had been more creative. Or indeed, to think of a time when the need for creativity had been so great.

Armageddon and beyond

During the 1860s David's drinking increased and his mental health deteriorated. By the late 1860s he was almost certainly addicted to alcohol, and prone to violent rages. His nickname descended with him, changing from 'Lord Montalto' to 'Six-ties', a name that derived from his fondness for wearing several scarves or ties at once.[1] People became uncertain as to how to respond to him. The butler reputedly hid under the table with a poker when he visited Delacherois at Donaghadee.[2] Eva Bateson, his future daughter in law, preserved 'alarming recollections' of his behaviour, which by the late 1860s 'seems to have been quite unbridled'.[3]

As the financial noose tightened, new economies were made – economies that hit ever closer to home. The girls were forbidden to serve as bridesmaids at their cousin's wedding.[4] All but one of the boys were taken out of Eton. Ker's collection of them was a sorry affair as he had to enquire from one of the masters how many he had there, and when some boys were gathered before him, 'hardly knew who his children were'.[5] By August 1867 the debt had risen to a stupifying £371,000.[6] Outgoings

The butler hid under the table with a poker when Ker visited Delacherois at Donaghadee. (Ray Elwood)

exceeded receipts.[7] The long anticipated point of breakdown had arrived. Relations with Anketell broke down. The affairs of the estate fell into confusion. David felt unable and alone.

In his hour of need, like a contrite child, he turned for help to his Uncle Maxwell, now approaching his eightieth year.[8] Maxwell examined the accounts with a heavy heart. He was appalled by what he found. But this was no time to moralise. Maxwell was pragmatic. There was, he advised, only one course open to David. He must hand the management of the estate over to a trust, and live on an annuity.

Maxwell knew how difficult this would be. He was advising his nephew to sign away everything he had been born to, and in the most ignominious circumstances. Yet there was no halfway house. The transfer of powers had to be complete. 'Can you submit with Spirit to make the management by Trustees absolute?', he asked.[9] Ker agreed. Two trustees were lined up. There were sighs of relief all round. Richard congratulated Maxwell, adding that it was a pity that 'this wise arrangement' had not been entered into years before.[10]

But the congratulations were premature. When the moment came, David could not bring himself to sign. He went back into denial. He distracted himself with architectural pipedreams, commissioning new gate lodges for Montalto in the form of triumphal archways and a Tuscan palazzo, grandiose gateways which would have made perfect entrances to his demented realm, had he been able to afford them.[11] Unpalatable realities were ignored. Deceiving himself with extravagant valuations of the estate and unrealistic assessments of its capacity to carry additional borrowing, David saw room for manoeuvre where there was none. The

Arch and palazzo-style gate lodge designed for Montalto, 1867-68. Neither was built. (Ker family)

creation of the proposed trust was delayed.

Alternatives were mooted. The notion of selling Red Hall was revived. This had not been part of the Maxwell plan. Maxwell had sought to avoid selling land at all costs. His object had been to preserve the integrity of the estate by removing David from its stewardship and introducing rigorous financial discipline. Now, David was contemplating further liquidations.

This set the alarm bells ringing for two reasons. Firstly, it was premature. Selling land should have been a last resort, and all other remedies had not been exhausted. Secondly, it signalled David's intention of managing the financial crisis himself. This caused considerable foreboding. His son, Alfred, whose inheritance was disappearing before his eyes, begged his father to establish the trust. David refused, and the two fell out.[12]

In July 1868, however, after much persuasion and pressure David accepted a diluted version of the Maxwell plan.[13] Under its terms the estate's income, in its entirety, went directly to two trustees, Spencer Perceval and William Anketell, who were also charged with meeting all expenses, and where the opportunity arose, reducing the debt burden. The plan did not, however, give the trustees power over David's expenses, a shortcoming that would prove to be its Achilles heel.

The trustees also looked again at the idea of selling Red Hall. This caused much soul searching. Red Hall or Broad Island was the third largest Ker estate. It was a profitable and loyal province. David's father was buried there. His mother would be. He had built his only church there. For David Stewart Ker, *paterfamilias*, protector of the realm, a man whose public person was synonymous with the geography of the estate, selling Red Hall would be akin to consenting to a kind of amputation. This was the plan he had baulked at in 1863, the sale that would let the world know that the Kers had gone bad.

But these considerations were luxuries now, for the estate was no longer in control. Events had overtaken Ker, and his hand would be forced. As an unsettled estate, Red Hall had had to bear much of the weight of David's (and his father's) borrowing. By 1867-68 it had

Adieu, dear friend. The Red Hall estate, showing Ballycarry (l), and Larne Lough (r), from the Landed Estates Court sale brochure, which advertised the estate as 'one of the most picturesque in Ireland'. (National Archives, Dublin)

St. John's Church, Ballycarry, painted just five years before the sale of the estate. (Ker family)

become encumbered with debts amounting to more than half the net annual rental. This was an important milestone, for it was the point at which its creditors could require it to be sold.[14] And they did. In January 1869, after an association of almost a century, the Kers were compelled to sell the estate in the Landed Estates Court in Dublin. It fetched £114,960.[15] Ouley followed in April.[16] All proceeds passed to the estate's creditors.

At this critical juncture a new and completely unforeseen element entered the equation – Caroline Persse, eldest daughter of Parsons Persse of Castle Turvin, County Galway, and a relative of Yeats's companion, Lady Gregory.[17] In 1869 she and David were unexpectedly married. Caroline was as different from Anna as could be imagined, but David's marriage to this 'disreputable… half wild' woman from the west, an Anglo-Irish Grace O'Malley who was as 'wild as a hawk', loved hunting and 'drank like a fish' was in its own way as much a marriage for the times as his first had been.[18]

Caroline features in the Ker demonology as a bringer of chaos. A destroyer of worlds. Ker males didn't marry girls like Caroline, who fascinated and appalled the family in something approaching equal measure. As for David, when his bleary gaze fell upon her youthful form, he saw only what was fiery and desirable. He had found a kind of happiness that he had never hoped to find again. Needless to say, there was nothing temperate about their marriage. They binged regularly, argued even more, and on hunting tours out west would 'sling a case of champagne under the bed and drink themselves stupid'.[19] All thought of confronting the estate's problems was forgotten.

Back in County Down, David's family, who had come to believe themselves unshockable, reeled in the face of Caroline's edge-of-empire morality. Here was a little piece of *Castle Rackrent*, alive and well and fizzing away in their midst. The family dynamics changed utterly. What remained of Selina's influence was eclipsed.[20] The little coping strategies seemed silly now. The familial checks and balances, which had to some extent restrained David, disappeared. The throttle was full open.

For almost two years, in what should have been a period of stringent austerity, David and Caroline lived high on the hog. Expenditure went into overdrive. The trustees were assailed by a blizzard of bills.[21] Under the terms of the 1868 indenture they had no power to curb this spending. But Anketell made a most ingenious attempt to do exactly this. In October 1871 David received a summons for a small, unpaid debt. He passed it to Anketell. Anketell did nothing. In November 1871 David suffered the rude shock of being arrested in Sackville Street, Dublin, and taken to the Marshalsea, the city's debtors' prison.[22]

By good luck David managed to engineer his release later that day,[23] but it took him rather longer to get over the mortification of the arrest. He

The ballroom, Montalto c.1870. (Ker family)

had no doubt that this had been contrived by Anketell and demanded his immediate resignation.[24] Anketell refused to go, claiming that under the terms of the 1868 indenture, Ker did not have the power to sack him. Ker then took the extraordinary step of announcing that he would collect his own rents. Anketell's reply was equally unprecedented. He published a notice asserting the continuing legality of his trusteeship, and set himself up in opposition to Ker on the other side of the street, calling on the bewildered tenantry to pay their rents to him.

Ker's response was decisive. At public meetings in December 1871, he received the overwhelming backing of his tenantry. After inquiring into the legal position, he fired Anketell, effectively dissolving the trust.[25] A line had been drawn under the chaos. Might stability yet return? There was small ground for hope. Throughout these difficulties, the interest on the secured and judgement debts (the 'investment' deposits) had continued to be paid punctually, leaving most of David's creditors uneasy but quiescent.[26]

In October 1870, however, a serious default had occurred.[27] The six-monthly interest payment due to the trustees of the De Clifford estate could not be paid. There were further defaults in April and October 1871. Faced with what was fast becoming an intolerable situation, the De Clifford trustees threatened to put a receiver on the property.[28] In December 1871, jumping before he was pushed, Ker announced his intention to sell the Downpatrick estate,[29] and agreed to convene an inquisition into his finances.

Was the day of reckoning at hand? Richard came over from England in the hope that it might be. But as he wrote to Dufferin:

I spent 5 hours yesterday at the Royal Hotel in Belfast at a durbar or rather judicial inquiry upon David's affairs. It was a strange & weird scene. David has

'The fact is David is a complete lunatic'. David Stewart Ker, looking older than his sixty or so years. (Ker family)

about 8 large Despatch boxes, with which he travels about, filled with copies of correspondence & accounts, the latter he has lately taken to express in Diagrams, on a principle of his own invention. Chichester Skeffington, whom I never saw before yesterday, is by way of being guardian & porter copier etc of these various documents. He moves about like a broken down representation of the Sea King in a bad Extravaganza. From time to time David abuses him roundly for dilitariness & incapacity… David is perpetually ringing the Bell which after a good deal of mysterious knocking results in an order for a glass of sherry. I suggested it would simplify the proceedings to order up a bottle… but he only consented to change his orders to "bring me 2 glasses of sherry."

Richard despaired. The proceedings were a farce.

You may form some idea of the hopeless state of things & how impossible it is for me to do anything. Alfred & myself were… to adjudicate, but when David had stated his case, he entirely refused to admit our opinion or decision... As far as we can make out Alfred and his sisters and other members of the family are sacrificed for Mrs Ker's [Caroline's] expenses at Montalto & elsewhere. I think

Charles Ker, David Stewart Ker's second son, who fell 'desperately in love' with his step-mother. (Ker family)

I have done some good so far that Alfred has had the whole case laid before him now & also that there must be some understanding come out of it as to restraining Mrs Ker's expenses. The fact is David is a complete lunatic.[30]

Caroline's extravagance was not the only thing that required restraint. By late 1871 she had begun taking a more than maternal interest in David's second son Charley, last glimpsed sucking bon-bons in the back of his parents' carriage on their way back from Clandeboye in 1855, and now a strapping twenty-three year old, recently returned from Oxford.[31]

David had no remedy for either conundrum. He was as powerless to influence the debt problem as he was in the face of the ripening relationship between his wife and his son. This soon passed all conventional bounds. Charley fell 'desperately in love' with his stepmother.[32] Everything now passed out of David's hands. His marriage collapsed. His wife and his beloved second son fled Montalto and set up home – as social outcasts – in County Meath.

Charley was throwing his life away. Everything was in tatters. What David would not give was taken from him. In February 1872, on foot of a petition by the Northern Banking Company, David was declared a bankrupt.[33] The management of the estate passed to trustees. A receiver was appointed over the rents. David was put on an allowance of £1,000 a year and sent to live in Belfast. How could the town have contained him? How could the lord of broad acres have been accommodated in something as alien as a Belfast street? Ker in suburbia was Samson shorn. But it had to be.

The estate had pulled out of its nose-dive. The family breathed a sigh of relief. But it had all come so late, perhaps too late. In July 1872 David's debts were estimated at £296,000, £261,000 of which was secured on Ker's personal property, a total which on conservative valuations, exceeded that property's worth.[34] But even this weighty figure does not reflect the debt's true majesty. In addition to this so called 'personal debt',[35] which fell on the unsettled estates, the settled estates were liable for £55,000 in family charges, which brings the total back to £351,000 – as if the sale of Red Hall had never happened. Reviving the patient would require major surgery. The trustees, John Mulholland and the Earl of Longford, sharpened their knives.

26 Renewal? Alfred Ker and the revival

In 1872 Alfred Ker inherited the battered and indebted remains of the Ker estates. His accession was a far cry from the glittering coronation envisaged in 1864. All the usual rites of passage were missing. There had been no death of a venerated elder. No dignified moment in black over an open grave, consoled by a supportive family. No glorious moment of assumption. He was stepping into the shoes of a feckless, alcoholic father who had been turned out by his creditors. He had become head of one of the county's most conspicuously dysfunctional families. It was hardly the stuff that dreams were made of.

But it was, nonetheless, a moment of truth. Alfred had been groomed for this moment since boyhood. But here it was and it all rang hollow. The great estate that he had been born to had been hacked apart. It now comprised just 27,850 acres, 7,283 of which were being readied for sale. And what remained was not his to govern. It was managed by the trustees, Lord Longford and John Mulholland. Their authority extended into the most private realms of Ker's life, impinging even upon his bodily functions, in as much as Alfred could not install a new sewerage system at Montalto until the trustees had first given their consent.[1]

For years Alfred had watched impotently as his inheritance had been squandered. Now, trustees permitting, his salvation lay in his own hands. And there was every sign that he might rise to the challenge. He was 'upright and conscientious'. He took an active part in the management of his estates. He supported progressive measures like the attempt to bring piped water to Ballynahinch.[2] But most important of all, vowing that his family's creditors 'shall be paid off in my lifetime', he made eliminating the debt problem his main goal.[3]

There was no painless way of doing this. But Alfred set about the business with spirit. Firstly, he reassured his father's creditors that they would receive full restitution, 20/- in the pound, including the interest due on all debts including unsecured ones, over which he had the leeway to offer less.[4] A payment programme was agreed with the trustees and the

Determined to bring order from chaos: Alfred Ker. (Ker family)

creditor's assignee, and preparations went ahead for the sale of Downpatrick in the Landed Estates Court in Dublin.

And so, thirty-nine years after its de Courcyesque seizure, the half-digested estate was disgorged. Downpatrick had proved a bridge too far for the Kers. Though they had grown the rental robustly, raising it to around £11,000 per annum by 1868, the Kers never managed to turn Downpatrick into the hoped for gold mine.[5] The problem was not the income that the estate generated, but the overheads that were attached to it, and the fact that the additional income had been achieved as much by the alienation of property as by genuine urban growth.[6] When the interest payments of £5,400 due annually on the loans taken out to purchase the estate (which themselves represented only part of the purchase price), are also taken into account, the full extent of the difficulty becomes clear.[7] The long anticipated sale took place in 1873; an unfortunate piece of timing, because at this point, after years of deficit, the sums were beginning to come right. By then, of course, it was too late.

The purchaser, curiously enough, was John Mulholland, wealthy Belfast textile magnate and Ker trustee, which put Mulholland in the unusual position of being both buyer and seller, with only the auction of the estate by a third party to in any way mitigate what would appear to have been a serious conflict of interests.[8] Downpatrick welcomed its new owner, hoping (vainly as it turned out) that his wealth and business acumen might improve its fortunes.[9]

The Ker estate was done with bold civic projects. At a public meeting it explained its reasons for withdrawal. David Stewart Ker attended, and was showered with tributes and spontaneous declarations of affection.[10] What a comfort this must have been to him. As his relationships disintegrated around him, this lifelong bond with the tenantry had stayed true. Benighted, cuckolded, bankrupt, and nobody's enemy but his own, Davy Ker became a folk hero.

It was left to Alfred, the dutiful heir, whose character, like that of a coppiced oak, had been carefully shaped in order to bear the weight now being placed upon it, to pick up the pieces, or rather to help distribute the proceeds from them.[11] These proceeds were retained by the court for debt repayment. Iconic, high watermark curios like the Stradivarius violin were sold.[12] Debts to the value of £42,000, due to hoteliers, brewers, and booksellers, etc., were paid.[13] A 'sinking fund', which would not only meet interest payments on the largest outstanding debt but also whittle away or 'sink' the capital due was established.[14] This became the principal means of clearing the debt.

John Mulholland, later Baron Dunleath, the purchaser of the Downpatrick estate. (Dunleath family)

Belvoir Park in what is now south Belfast, home of Alfred's wife Eva Bateson. (C. Douglas Deane)

The situation stabilised. The figures became smaller and more manageable. Whereas his father had enjoyed a rental income of over £32,000, Alfred's income was just under £19,000,[15] some 45% of which went on debts and charges, including capital repayments. Alfred also existed within a rather narrower geographical compass. The estate no longer imperiously bestrode two counties. Between 1863-73 it had withdrawn to its 1811 boundaries, and in the process rediscovered a kind of equilibrium.

But there could be no doubting the distance the Kers had fallen. Alfred had moved into the second division of county landowners, and lived at Montalto 'as a hospitable and courteous country gentleman' rather than a grandee.[16] No-one would be calling him 'Lord Montalto', or lord anything else for that matter. The language, and even the slang, of the golden age seemed almost ludicrous now.

However, the Kers were still some way from the breadline. Though the sale of the Downpatrick estate reduced their landholding to a trifling 20,540 acres, they were nonetheless the county's fifth largest landowners.[17] And they were far from being pariahs. Surprisingly perhaps, given what we read of Victorian mores, the scandal and bankruptcy produced no lasting stigma. David Stewart Ker, now a tragic-comic figure, continued to have a profile within the county establishment.[18] Alfred's appointment as High Sheriff in 1877 was both a vote of confidence in him by his peers and a sign of the family's re-emergence from its domestic imbroglio.

The family's marriages also suggest that their social currency remained sound. In 1868, David's eldest daughter Selina married into the Maxwell (now Perceval-Maxwell) family. In the following year his third daughter, Violet, married the genial William Rose, heir to Wolston

Grange and 14,000 acres in Warwickshire.[19] And in one of those genetic hitch ups without which no generation of Ker marriages was apparently complete, David's third son Richard William Blackwood Ker married Rose's ample but attractive sister Edith.

Alfred's marriage was, of course, the most lordly. In 1871, after labyrinthine negotiations (which guaranteed his wife £2,000 a year in the event of his death), Alfred married the twenty-one year old Eva Frances Caroline de Yarburgh Bateson, the eldest daughter of Sir Thomas Bateson of Belvoir Park near Belfast, and the apple of his eye.[20]

Few of Alfred's other nine brothers and sisters conformed, and it is possible to see in some of their biographies, the ripple of difficult childhoods. Edward married a fisherman's daughter, and lived in a cottage in Cornwall, from which he contrasted 'the happiness of his present peaceful existence to the misery of their lives at Montalto'.[21] David junior took his own life in New York. Sixth son Robert 'married a Zulu and was never mentioned again'.[22] Hamilton, the youngest, became a minister in the Church of England. Fourth son Henry didn't marry. Neither did Helen or Florinda (Flossie), whom we glimpse only once, in a pair of photographs from the 1870s, in which the girls look pale and bored.

And then there was Charley, the sucker of bon bons, holed up with Caroline in their County Meath love nest. This liaison was in some ways worse than the bankruptcy, for the pain and scandal it gave rise to was too intimate and too shameful to be borne. The errant couple were outcasts. Particularly Caroline. Sir Robert Bateson only permitted his daughter to marry Alfred on condition that she would not 'ever be allowed to meet his step-mother', a creature so unclean they do not mention her by name.[23]

Edward Ker. Married a fisherman's daughter. (Ker family)

Indisposed. 1877 De Ros house party at Old Court, Strangford. The woman in the hammock is thought to be either Helen or Florinda Ker. Her sister stands beside her, pointedly avoiding the camera. (Down Museum)

*Violet Ker, in a portrait
commissioned by her doting
grandfather, Sir Thomas Bateson.
(Bennett family)*

*Daughters, only daughters. Alfred
and Eva's children, (l-r) Kathleen,
Sybil, Winifred, and Violet Ker.
(Ker family)*

Imagine the family's discomfiture, then, when bored with Meath, the fugitive couple moved to Dublin and tentatively attempted to re-enter society. No-one would receive them. Their transgression was too great. For the family's part, there could be no treating with Charley and Caroline. Charley became a non-person. His circumstances were not discussed at Montalto. They could not be. The matter was too painful.[24]

However, there were more than feelings at stake here. There was also the important matter of the succession. Charley was heir to the estates, and would remain so until Alfred and Eva produced a son. However, when Alfred and Eva produced daughters and only daughters, the dread prospect of Caroline's triumphant reinstatement as mistress of Montalto became just real enough to have to be taken seriously. Alfred cut Charley out of his will, and named Richard as his successor.[25]

Breathing a heavy sigh of relief, Montalto put the prospect of Caroline's return behind it. But the Persse era was not without its ghosts. And their cold fingers still lay on Alfred's shoulders. The estate had recovered its equilibrium. But it would take much more to put the family's lives back on an even keel. Alfred found it hard to cope. His 'singularly kind and gentle disposition' was unequal to the strains placed upon it. By the mid-1870s he was drinking to the point where it had begun to undermine his health.[26]

In February 1876 Caroline Ker, nee Persse, died.[27] Charley was bereft. He moved to digs in Kildare Street, Dublin, where, unreconciled with his family, he drank too much and dwelt morbidly on his loss. Within seven months of Caroline's death Charley too was dead. Drunken, tortured, alone, he slit his throat with a razor 'whilst in a state of temporary insanity'.[28] He was just twenty-eight years old.

His bloody, needless suicide turned the old rights and wrongs on their head. The family was now in the dock, not Charley. Their censure seemed unfeeling. Misplaced. Were they culpable? Had they blood on their hands? All the old wounds were reopened. The family's feelings of guilt and betrayal became almost unmanageable. The affair had come to the worst possible end, an end without healing or forgiveness. Publicly however, the deaths drew a line under the scandal, and whatever else Alfred felt at the news of his brother's suicide, his emotions must have included a strong element of relief.

Purse Crundle in Dorset, built for Eva and her daughters after they were 'evicted' from Montalto. (Ker family)

But the bad times were not behind them. The grim reaper had not yet done. In 1876, gout 'undermined' Alfred's 'fine constitution'. His system had had as much as it could take. In August 1877, Eva took him to Brighton in the hope that the change of air might lift him. But nothing did, not even the ministrations of the best doctors money could buy.[29] Alfred bore his ills with soldierly courage until a heart attack killed him in December 1877, at the age of thirty-four.[30] He left behind a young widow, and four daughters aged under six.

Eva was heartbroken. She wrote to Dufferin of 'her great trouble' and this acute sense of loss stayed with her, for when her father died thirteen years later, Eva described herself and her girls as 'doubly alone'.[31] She was also as good as evicted from Montalto, which became the property of the new heir, Alfred's brother Richard, and his wife Edith.

The final souls to be reaped in this bitter harvest were those of David Stewart Ker (who had been similarly evicted five years earlier), and his younger sister Madalena, the wife of William Anketell, who is said to have died 'on a heap of rags' in Quentin Castle in the spring of 1878, after 'long years of riotous living'.[32] David died that autumn, 'in the 62nd year of his age', at his daughter Selina's house in Crawfordsburn. He had been predeceased by both his wives and both his eldest sons.[33]

Few lives can have begun with such promise, and ended in such ignominy. Such at least was the verdict of his peers, now scattered to the four winds in the service of empire. 'It is sad about David Ker', one of the Prices of Saintfield wrote from Afghanistan a month later: 'What a spoilt life. With such a beginning and sad end! It couldn't last always. I mean his drinking! It is very dreadful.'[34] Tactfully glossing over his recent 'vicissitudes', his old ally the *Downpatrick Recorder* sent him off with a warm obituary, declaring that his memory would long be cherished in the county.

But it was Alfred's death that mattered. With it, power transferred again. And into altogether less sure hands. For the first time in the Kers' landed history, events had thrown up an heir who had not had a clear sense of his duties and responsibilities drummed into him since childhood. Richard was an untrained, untested, third son. He had not known how bad the bad times had been. He did not possess his brother's sense of mission. Whither now the recovery programme? Would Richard have the steel to see it through?

27 The boy can't help it: the recovery founders

The young heir, Richard William Blackwood Ker, upon whom all depended, was almost completely unprepared for the responsibilities that now fell on him. No-one had intended things to work out this way. The legal exercise which had made his succession possible had been about keeping Charley and Caroline's hands off the estates, not favouring Richard. And as Alfred was healthy and Eva had many child-bearing years ahead of her, Richard's prospects of inheriting seemed remote.

He got on with his life. As he was not considered university material, Richard went to Sandhurst, where he became a captain in the First Royal Dragoons.[1] A colourful career in the cavalry seemed to beckon, a career to which he seemed well suited, as he was a fine horseman and enjoyed the fellowship of the mess.[2]

Richard William Blackwood Ker as a young cavalry officer, 1870s. (Ker family)

Then, in December 1877, eight days after his twenty-seventh birthday, Alfred died and Richard was called to the centre of the corpse littered stage to receive the poisoned chalice.

His succession caused the profoundest apprehension. Richard was a rakish charmer, a *bon viveur* who loved hunting, women and horses. He had no head for business or administration. Were his great-grandfather still in charge, there is little doubt that Richard would have been disinherited without a second thought, for, though athletic and good-natured, the young cavalry officer was impulsive, thriftlesss, and almost completely lacking in self discipline.

Were there any chinks of light? To the extent that at twenty-seven his character was unformed, and in as far as it was impossible to predict how he would react to his new circumstances, there was hope. But few will have rested much on it. Caroline Persse had wreaked her revenge. The family battened down the hatches, said what prayers they could, and awaited the final undoing.

But it didn't come. At least not yet. Awed or maybe just stupefied by the circumstances he now found himself in, and ashen after the sight of the books and his briefings with the estate's trustees and advisors, Richard pledged himself 'to try & follow' his brother's example. The birth of his son David in 1878, amidst bonfires and rejoicing, and his appointment as High Sheriff of County Down in 1880, provided further incentives for Richard to conform.

And conform he did, presiding over a steady reduction in the estate's debts.[3] However, this triumph involved the denial of some of Richard's most basic impulses, and could only continue if he started to get an equivalent kick out of these new satisfactions. No such sublimation occurred, and as he grew less cowed, the old impulses reasserted themselves, and Richard began to spree.

He bought hunting horses at up to £200 a time, which he paid for by borrowing. He knew he couldn't afford them, but he couldn't resist. And with each purchase, his conscience pricked him. For notions of duty and service, though not deeply enough rooted to guide his behaviour, were well enough ingrained to make him ashamed of every betrayal.

Aware of the risk his behaviour posed to the recovery programme, Richard asked his agent, estate solicitor, and old family friend William Nevin Wallace to take charge of his personal finances. Wallace responded cautiously. A fastidious man in his mid-sixties, he did not need this additional burden. But he felt a fatherly affection for Richard, whom he had known since childhood, and was drawn to the idea of helping to rehabilitate this once great county family, whose fortunes had been so closely linked to those of his own.[4] When Richard agreed to follow his advice, Wallace consented, and his death by a thousand cuts began.

At this point it might be helpful to briefly remind ourselves of how the

Sir Thomas Bateson of Belvoir Park, in an 1882 Vanity Fair *caricature. Used his position to advantage his grand-daughters. (Down Hunt collection)*

bankrupt estate was managed, and who it was managed for. Although Richard lived grandly at Montalto, enjoying all the appurtenances of the head of the estate, he was in fact a straw man. For the estate was run for the benefit of its creditors, not Ker, and the contents of Montalto were no more his than the contents of 10 Downing Street are the personal property of the Prime Minister.

The creditors' interests were looked after by two trustees, John Mulholland and Lord Longford, who was replaced upon his death in 1887 by Eva's father, the mercenary Lord Deramore, formerly Sir Thomas Bateson, who promptly set about squeezing bigger allowances out of the estate for his grand-daughters.[5]

The estate was then administered in two parts. One half (the 'Trust estate', centred on Ballynahinch) was run by the trustees through their agent Marcus Gage. The other half, the 'life estate', which included the Portavo estate, was managed by Wallace on behalf of (in diminishing order of importance) the creditors, Richard's successors, and thirdly his nominal employer, Richard Ker. Richard was a life tenant and his personal interest had to be separated from, and in the event of a clash, subordinated to the interests of the estate as a whole.

Wallace, then, was far from being Richard's creature. He faced three ways, acting for the estate against Richard when Richard was being unreasonable, for the creditors when they were denied their due, and for Richard against the trustees when they went too far. Richard had limited powers, and exercised none of the informal authority that his brother had wielded. He was consulted before decisions were made. His consent was

William Nevin Wallace, Ker's solicitor, agent, and financial 'procurer'. (Private collection)

considered desirable, but it was not essential, and if he did not give it both Wallace and the trustees had the legal right to overrule him. It was not a nice position to be in. And its mixture of public privilege and private indignity cannot have been good for Richard's soul, which by 1883 was tarnishing fast.

Wallace initially believed that he could put Richard's personal finances in order, but soon realised that all hope of reforming Ker was vain.[7] Indeed the appointment seems to have freed Richard to become more spendthrift than ever.[8] It was as if Wallace had become his conscience. And an external conscience was so much easier to ignore. Unable to curb Ker's borrowing, Wallace made him agree 'to borrow no money except from or thro' myself'. By this means Wallace secured a pool of friendly lenders who, he hoped, would not rush to foreclose if things got rough.

He also worked hard to increase Ker's income. In May 1883 the estate yielded a net rental of £15,100 p.a., £11,000 of which went on family charges and debt repayment. Richard received the remaining £4,100, and received it last, so that while everyone else's portion was secure, his was prone to all life's vagaries. Late payments, politically motivated withholding, and rent failures during bad seasons reduced his actual take to well below this notional sum.[10] To add to Richard's travails, the Land Commission set up under the 1881 Land Act was poised to begin cutting rents across the estate by an unknown percentage that summer.

In the circumstances, anything that could increase income was welcome. Wallace was bullish, believing that 'if we attack the thing with energy… we might… increase the rental by £2,000 a year'.[11] He had the surplus timber at Portavo cut and sold, and the rabbits in the demesne seasonally trapped and sent to market. He attempted to interest the army in setting up camp on the Copelands, and tried to have Montalto's statuary and art collection auctioned.[12]

He tried to abolish the 'lying gale', universal on the estate but according to Wallace, virtually unknown elsewhere in the county.[13] He made the trustees invest their large cash balance at a proper rate of interest, creating additional funds which eased the pressure on Richard. He let the kennels at Montalto to the County Down Staghounds for £50 p.a. He chivvied Gage about collecting rents more promptly. And when a golf club expressed an interest in fifty acres at Carnalea at £5 or more per acre, Wallace's eyes practically watered with delight.[14]

Between 1883-86 Wallace increased Ker's net income by over £1,000. But his creativity was no match for Richard's appetite. For every wealth-creating ruse that Wallace dreamed up, Ker managed several illicit purchases, usually of horses, which were eventually paid for by Wallace and his circle at $4\frac{1}{2}$ or 5%.[16] So there was nothing investment-oriented about the borrowing.[17] It was ad hoc, and was continually chasing the spending. Wallace's job was to follow Ker with a financial poop-scoop, cleaning up the mess.

The situation became almost comical. Knowing that Wallace would disapprove of his peccadilloes, Ker told Wallace nothing, leaving Wallace to find out about each lapse maybe six months later, when, out of the blue, a solicitor's clerk would arrive in his office with a writ for the money owed. These writs – these betrayals – struck Wallace like thunderbolts. Sometimes he could pay or delay them. But often he could

Carnalea, from the illuminated address of 1864. (Ker family)

To all intents and purposes, Ker was an addict. Richard looking caddish in check. (Ker family)

not, and a mad scramble to raise the money followed.

The crises were endless, 'no sooner is one claim got rid of than another comes', and they wore Wallace down. This grubby business was anathema to him. His ways were thrifty and methodical, and Ker's high jinks kept him in a state of constant anxiety. 'This is utterly impossible and I may add unbearable', he told Ker in 1886 in a rare burst of feeling.[18] But he didn't abandon Ker. He couldn't. The man was a complete disaster area. He couldn't be let loose. God forbid! He would be eaten alive without Wallace to protect him:

The fact is this, and I state it as Captain Ker's friend – not as his professional advisor… he… has told me over and over again that he cannot control himself or avoid borrowing money. How he gets that money he does not care in the least. He pays 60% per annum without a question for it and tells me he cannot help it.[19]

To all intents and purposes Ker was an addict. But even addicts have their moments of clarity. In 1883 Richard realised that if something was not done he would destroy everything. He begged Wallace to help him.[20] Could all the monies go to the trustees for a period of, say, fifteen years during which they would pay him an allowance? This was exactly what was required, and the parallel with his father's attempt to escape his nemesis in 1861 leaps out at us. Could it be done? Wallace sought counsel's opinion, but for reasons unknown, the proposal came to nothing.

Richard was never taught and never learned how to manage money, preferring to proceed in the Micawberish belief that 'something would turn up'. The story is told that when he was young and needed money, Richard and his brother would call into the estate office in Ballynahinch.

Each would emerge with a Gladstone Bag full of cash, an exercise that led them to believe that this was where money came from.[21] In those days money equalled pleasure. Increasingly, however it became synonymous with pain. His son David could not bear to hear talk of money. When the subject came up in conversation he would raise his arms for silence and relief.

The descent continued apace. Ker's behaviour became ever more devious. He began selling things behind Wallace's back.[22] Things that weren't his to sell. To meet bills that Wallace didn't know existed. Wallace challenged Ker. Ker ignored him.

Their relationship became a game of cat and mouse. In April 1886 for example, Ker quietly sold four horses 'at Robsons' and went home congratulating himself on having outwitted his elderly minder. But he had reckoned without Wallace's spies. Word went back, and the following morning Wallace wrote to Ker asking for the £125 that Ker had made on the sale. He also kept an eye on race meetings. 'I see a horse called 'Montrose' entered at Punchestown', he observed to Ker. 'Did you by any chance sell your horse of that name?'[23]

Richard's spivishness knew no bounds. In early 1887 he attempted to sell 171 pictures advertised as 'Removed from a Mansion in Ireland', in the blithe hope, apparently, that no-one would notice their absence. (He wouldn't miss them. Why should anybody else?) But Wallace somehow obtained a copy of the catalogue and intervened to halt the sale.[24]

Richard cared little for the pictures. Tradesmen looking for payment were told to 'go upstairs and take a picture', a small one, in lieu of cash.[25] He couldn't even be bothered to pick one out for them. The Ker art collection, which had once been such an important badge of taste and identity, had become just so much uncashed booty. New values reigned, not just within the Ker family, but within the broader landed class. The elite was losing its way. Its cultural compass had become frighteningly narrow. As Standish O'Grady remonstrated in his 1886 *Address to the Landlords of Ireland*:

Christ save us all… you read nothing, know nothing. This great modern democratic world rolls on with its thunderings, lightenings, and voices, enough to make the bones of your heroic fathers turn in their graves, and you know nothing about it… Of you, as a class, as a body of men, I can entertain not the least hope; indeed who can?[26]

The landlord class was increasingly coming to resemble its hunting, shooting and fishing caricature. Being clever, literary or scientific was frowned upon. The aspiration towards taste and culture, which had been the *leitmotif* of previous generations, had been largely set aside. The landed class was becoming stagnant and less alive. The malaise was not universal, individuals continued to shine, but assailed on all sides, the

Standish O'Grady, despaired of his class.

landlord class as a body had begun to exhibit the classic signs of cultural demoralisation.

This condition was a response to complex economic, social and cultural changes. Empire was a powerful influence. This 'Junkerised' the landed class, steeping them in martial values that did not always sit well with their civil responsibilities. Everyone was a soldier now. The lifestyle that David Ker in 1791 had called 'limited and contracted' had become the formative life experience. The Grand Tour had been replaced by tours of duty that did not so much broaden the mind as hideously replicate the worst aspects of the laager mentality that many gentry faced at home.

Richard, of course, had his own kind of laager to climb out of. In 1886, out of a gross income of £17,490, Richard received £910.[27] There was no talk of recovery now. Writs arrived on a regular basis, and it became increasingly difficult to borrow to meet them. Wallace still leant money to Ker, at an uncivil 6%, but he had become reluctant to proffer lenders from his circle.

As Ker's credit worthiness deteriorated it became necessary to find new lenders, and new sources of security for them to lend against. Wallace began to look to institutions. The Northern Banking Company was good for a few hundred every now and again, but it held Ker 'very tight', and the better it got to know him, the more reluctant it became to lend. Wallace also tried to charm money out of the North British Mercantile Insurance Company, but it refused point blank as it was 'not lending any money at present in Ireland' on account of the unsettled state of the country.[28]

In 1884 Wallace negotiated a £31,600 loan from the British Empire Life Assurance Company (later Standard Life). This was a major coup. It was also the last big loan he was able to secure on a mortgage. Ker had always borrowed on mortgages, using land as security. However by the mid-1880s he had 'no estate left in him'.[29] He could no longer offer lenders anything as solid as a mortgage. He could still borrow against the incoming rents, and frequently did, but there were limits, and reducing limits, to the sums he could raise against them, as his rental income was increasingly devoured by interest charges on other borrowings.

The hunt for collateral became ever more desperate. Nothing was sacred. Ker would borrow on anything, including somewhat ghoulishly, funds due from the estates of his stepmother Caroline and late brother Charley.[30] For all that, Wallace frequently found himself in the position of having no security to offer would be lenders. His solution was to take out insurance policies on Ker's life, solely for the purpose of borrowing against them. Ker's position now was akin to that of the heroin addict who, having used up all his good veins, begins injecting through his toes. It wasn't easy to borrow against insurance policies, 'parties do not like lending upon it', but it was all Ker and Wallace had to offer. In mid-1883

Not another writ please. Wallace checks his texts. (Down Museum)

Ker held insurance policies to the value of £11,000. By mid-1885 he held policies worth £46,000.[31] The most prudent thing Richard could now do was die.

By late '85 Wallace could have been forgiven for harbouring similar sentiments. Ker's spending was out of control.[32] And the day of reckoning was at hand. It is November 1885. Ker sends Wallace a bill for £173. Wallace can't pay it. There is no money. Ker is £3,000 overdrawn against the November rents, and the creditors must 'legally and in honour' be paid first. Further bills arrive. For £300, for £245, for £176. Wallace cracks. He writes to Ker insisting that he control his spending before he ruins himself. His answer comes in the form of yet another bill. £375. A bounced cheque. It is the only answer he gets.

Wallace is at his wits' end. He is ill. Too ill to leave the house. He is in 'a state of constant worry'.[33] He cannot concentrate. He writes 'with difficulty'. He has no idea where the £375 is to come from. He scrambles to make new lettings. Another bill arrives. £410 for two more horses. Wallace has had enough of such surprises. He demands a complete list of bills. This inventory exceeds his worst expectations. £2,675 is owed.[34] Ker is abject. He professes to be eaten up with remorse.

But what use is that? The creditors are baying. Wallace begs them for more time. Most flatly refuse. One demands immediate payment as he is 'very nearly ashore himself'. The Northern Banking Company lodges an

'Good of the dog', Richard's verdict on Sir John Collier's portrait of his wife Edith, who in the 1880s appears to have been unaware of the dire state of his finances. (Ker family)

execution with the Sheriff, who threatens seizure.[35] A (false) rumour reaches Wallace that the bailiffs are at Montalto. The necessary £350 is somehow raised, and a collapse averted. But there is no relief. Another bill arrives. £500 owed to 'a noted horse dealer in Dublin'. £500 that was not on the list.

Wallace is by now too numb to react. Perhaps it is just as well. For in comes a bombshell. Ker has borrowed £768 from Thomas Joyce, the most merciless loan shark in Dublin, at a rate of interest of 90%.[36] Wallace demands that Ker immediately sell all the blood and livestock at Montalto, but the sale is a flop, leaving some fifteen of 'the best horses and sires' undisposed of. The £1,186 raised is used to pay some of the most pressing bills. But they cannot all be met. A creditor who has been passed over serves a Notice of Bankruptcy on Wallace. The sum involved is under £100. But Ker has no money. The estate is a hairsbreadth from bankruptcy. A second crash.

Wallace averts collapse by meeting the Notice out of his own pocket.

He secures another insurance policy. £2,000 this time.[37] The pressure eases. What does Ker do as all teeters on the brink? As Wallace the escapologist sweats and conjures, Ker sells horses behind his back and tries to surreptitiously pocket the proceeds. No use sending them to Wallace. Have them disappear down the bottomless pit. In spite of, rather than because of Ker, the estate staggers through till May 1886, and the merciful arrival of the rents.

But they were not out of the woods yet. Joyce's loan had not yet been repaid, and the price of repayment was increasing exponentially. Ker had borrowed £768 in February 1886. By May 1887 he owed £1,985. It is the story of the grain of wheat on the chessboard. If you put a single grain of wheat on a chessboard, and double it every time it is moved to the next square, by the time it reaches the sixty-fourth square you will have a quantity of wheat which exceeds the world's annual harvest. Joyce's loan had a similar potential. It could eat up everything. Why did Wallace not pay it more promptly? Initially, he did not have the funds. Latterly, reading between the lines, it is just possible that he was almost content to let it run. A good scare might be just what Ker needed.[38]

So the loan ran on, the figures spinning like fractions of a second on an automatic clock. Wallace tried to raise a loan to pay it, but could not attract a lender. The clock ran on. In the end it was Joyce who put Wallace out of his misery. Fearful of losing his money, Joyce served a writ on Ker. Ker did not dare tell Wallace. Weeks passed. Finally he bit the bullet, and told Wallace of the writ.

Wallace tried to stall Joyce, telling him of Longford's death, and that he can do nothing until a new trustee is appointed. But Joyce knew flannel when he heard it. He replies that he will wait six days 'and no longer' for his money. Wallace warns Ker that there is no legal obstacle that can be put in Joyce's way. If he is not paid he will get a judgement and 'sweep all before him'.[39]

An urgent sale of the stock and crops at Portavo is planned. But Richard gets in first. His idea of solidarity in time of crisis is to sell the sheep and cattle to a Belfast butcher in advance of the sale and disappear with the cash.[40] If Wallace has learned anything, he has learned not to get excited about anything as minor as a betrayal, but when he hears this he explodes. What sort of a fool is Ker? Doesn't he realise that this could be terminal?

The sheriff is hovering. He is poised to seize 'whatever he can find at Portavo'. But not on Joyce's behalf. In mid-1887, at the height of the crisis, all mention of Joyce's writ disappears from the record. What became of it is unclear. Ker had appealed to friends like Lord Arthur Hill to bail him out, and maybe one of them did.[41] But it is odd that there should be no note of this in the correspondence.

However, this settlement did not solve the crisis.

The Carlton Club, Pall Mall. Wallace has no address for Ker. His telegrams chase Ker all over London.

No sooner had Joyce's writ disappeared from view than another came forward to take its place. £500 is required post haste. Seizure is threatened. Ker is in London, ignoring Wallace's letters. Wallace telegraphs him seeking the £390 raised by the illegal livestock sale. He has no address for Ker – the relationship is close to breakdown – so his telegrams shower the London clubs – the Military & Naval, the Dover Street, the Carlton.[42] He must have the money by 4 p.m. that day.

He gets no answer. And so he lets Ker go. It is probably the most difficult thing that he has ever done. Wallace cannot beat the creditors, so he joins them, serving two writs on his former master for £400 that 'he cannot afford to lose'. Then, sick at heart, he closes his brief case and goes home.

But the bailiffs do not plunder Portavo or Montalto. A second, unrecorded intervention takes place. Ker's life seems charmed. But he cannot forgive Wallace's desertion. Wallace feels Ker's wrath. Ker refuses to have anything to do with him and attempts to take his business elsewhere. But Wallace plays hardball. He insists that existing agreements be honoured. Ker finds he cannot ditch Wallace. The two are inextricably bound. Like characters in Sartre's *Huis Clos* ('Hell is other people'), they seem destined to forever hurl through space claws locked in one another. They make up. They have no choice but to. The show gets back on the road.

For the next ten years the estate skidded on, veering close to the precipice but never quite falling over it, not withstanding recurring squalls, most notably that of 1893. Wallace died in 1895, after a valiant thirteen-year rearguard action which kept the estate solvent until the time of his death, a minor miracle that is suggestive of something close to

Richard Ker. This perhaps surprisingly reflective self-portrait dates from the 1890s. (Ker family)

genius. His son Hugh Wallace filled his shoes. Here was a new Mr Wallace to reduce to a jelly. A new set of nerve ends to frazzle.

The inevitable crash came in 1898. And the irony is that Wallace's success made the crash when it came all the more spectacular, for instead of being fuelled by five or ten years of folly, it was fuelled by a full twenty. But there is a greater irony. In 1898, the year of the second crash, the estate was due to return to solvency, and would have, had financial discipline been maintained, for in that year the sinking fund cleared the last of the inherited charges.[43]

But it was not to be. In January 1898, a century after the Widow Nelson laid her curse upon the family, Ker appeared in the Belfast Bankruptcy Court for his long postponed rendezvous with destiny. The estate was £89,000 in debt and Richard's life interest was valued at a piffling £250.[44] Though contrite, even ashamed, Richard was essentially impervious to what was going on around him. A few weeks later, he would meet Dick Blakiston-Houston in Jermyn Street, hold his hands over his face and confess that he'd been a naughty boy again.[45] It was all a game. He would fudge his way through. And however much he squandered, there would always be someone in the wings with a Gladstone Bag. Richard didn't change. If anything he got worse. He was then forty-seven. He would live to be ninety-one. There would be interesting times ahead.

28 'The gallant Nimrod'

'All cucumber and hooves'

In the spring of 1883, as he was tidying up after a particularly sharp gale, William Burroughs noticed a strange looking fish in difficulty in Sandy Bay. Burroughs put the boat out, and hauled in a ten-foot long grampus weighing half a ton, the 'first known in these waters for the last half century'.[1]

The grampus was not the only queer fish, long absent, to return to these shores at this time. In 1884-85, Richard Ker had a house built at Portavo (for £647, or in the currency he knew best, the price of three fast horses), and came to live here shortly after. The Kers were back. Richard got a better reception than the grampus, in as much as he was not gutted and

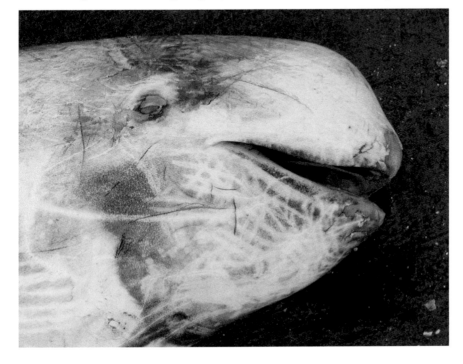

The distinctive blunt head of the grampus or Risso's Dolphin. Washed ashore in Sandy Bay in 1883. (Gary Burrows)

Ker's 'shootin' house'. This Portavo House, the fourth on the site, was built not in the grand manner of yesteryear, but as a quiet retreat by the sea. Watercolour by Robert Croft. (Tughan family)

sold on his second night here, as the poor fish was. But his arrival was only slightly less wondrous. How could the bankrupt Kers afford to build a house here? Wallace posed the same question,[2] but Richard prevailed and 'to the happiness and amusement of [their] neighbours' the Ker family returned to Portavo.[3]

It was a low-key homecoming. Their new house, the present Portavo House, has few airs and graces. It is a pleasant, unpretentious building, designed in a homely, neo-Georgian style that was intended to blend in with, and give presence to, the remains of the original Ross 'great house', which formed the return block of the new dwelling.[4]

Richard and Edith now divided their time between Portavo, Montalto and their house in Jermyn Street in London.[5] Portavo became a sporting estate. It was a fine place to shoot and ride, and Ker loved hunting. In 1881 Richard founded the County Down Staghounds, the first such hunt in the county. Richard instinctively knew the right tone to strike. Through 'great tact' and generous compensation for damage done, the Staghounds won 'the friendship of the agricultural community' at a time when many Irish hunts operated within a sullen or even hostile environment.[6]

These cordial relations caught the eye of those in high places. In the wake of the Land War the government was keen to highlight instances of co-operation between the classes, when and if it could find them. And the County Down Staghounds were clearly a beacon, a model of the way things should be. So when he made an official visit to the north of Ireland in 1887 the Lord Lieutenant, the Sixth Marquis of Londonderry, invited 'Captain Ker's famous pack' to a meet at Mountstewart. Instinctively striking the proper true blue tone, the *Newtownards Chronicle* reported that the occasion:

aroused the greatest enthusiasm among all classes… carriages and vehicles of every description… were continually arriving, whilst the members of the hunt turned out in large numbers… presenting… a brilliant appearance[7]

When all were assembled, Ker saluted the Lord Lieutenant with verses in praise of hunting:

Some traffic and trade in the city's mart,
Some travel by land and sea,
Some follow science, some cleave to art;
And some to scandal and tea;

And some for their country and their Queen,
Would fight, if the chance they had,
Good sooth, 'twere a sorry world, I ween,
If we all went galloping mad;

Yet if once we efface the joys of the chase,
From the land and outroot the Stud,
Goodbye to the Anglo-Saxon race,
Farewell to the Norman blood.[8]

*Mount Stewart, scene
of the famous 1887 meet.
(Lady Mairi Bury)*

Tally ho! The County Down Staghounds hunt against the backdrop of the Mournes. Lionel Edwards, 1936. (Private collection)

A stag was then loosed. Ker led the chase. Richard lived for moments like this. And he was magnificent in them, playing his part to perfection. Behind him came:

red coats flying in all directions, followed by an immense number of outsiders on horseback, carriages and vehicles taking along the different roads, and the people on foot through the open country.[9]

The terrified stag plunged into Strangford Lough and swam off, so a second beast was released. It 'took straight for Portavoe [i.e. home], giving the hunt a rattling ride'.[10]

Nimrod wrote up the hunts for the *Northern Whig*. One of his reports records the activities of the Staghounds over a week in 1884, when they met three times and pursued four stags. One pursuit lasted thirty-five minutes, another lasted thirty. The fates of the deer are unknown. The third animal was let loose to the north-east of Newtownards, and eluded the hunt by picking its way through the Cotton Bog then taking to the sea near Bangor, after a ten-mile chase. It was brought ashore by a boatman after a blind attempt to swim to dear knows where.[11]

The fourth, 'the invincible Luggy', also managed to throw the hunt. Out of fifty mounted riders, only Ker and three others made it from the Hillsborough demesne to Banbridge, where the four surviving horsemen plus 'five horses… with empty saddles' pursued the stag through the streets of the town. The magnificent animal then bolted for Ballynahinch, clearing a 'twelve foot wall as if it were a five-barred gate', to shake off his remaining pursuers. After a twenty-five mile chase, which involved a crossing of the Lagan and two crossings of the Bann, Luggy was found 'standing at Montalto park gates waiting for admission.'[12]

All cucumber and hooves?[15]
Richard Ker by Sir John Collier,
in a subscription portrait paid for
by members and friends of the
County Down Staghounds.
(Ker family)

Richard did not lavish all of his considerable vigour on the hunt. He had other interests. Like women. Richard was the original red-blooded male. To describe Richard as sexually active does not quite do the subject justice for Richard, in his own words, had 'a ferret in his trousers'.[13] When it came to the language of sexual signalling, he was a traffic light stuck at green. He 'had his hand up everyone's skirt', says David Ker candidly.[14] Or as the late Dick Ker put it, rather more guardedly, 'A lot of old boys round Ballynahinch used to say we [he and they] were related'.

In another story, Richard's son David was being shown around his inheritance by his agent shortly after he came of age, when they come on a young man lounging on a gate.

'Smarten yourself up', says the agent, 'This is young Mr. Ker.'

The young man is completely nonplussed.

'We're all young Mr Kers around here', he replies.[16]

Edith Ker by Sir John Everet Millais. (Ker family)

For all their closeness, Richard's wife Edith seems to have known little or nothing of his extra-marital activity, at least not in the early years of their marriage. She may have had little cause for suspicion, for she and her husband were strongly attracted to one another, and appear to have enjoyed contented sexual relations. But Richard was not made for monogamy. He could love several people simultaneously. And readers will need no reminder of the finite nature of his powers of self-control. Like a clutch that cannot hold gear, Richard slipped from liaison to liaison. By the age of thirty, he had become a seasoned voluptuary.

Richard did not confine himself to farm girls and servants, he was 'pretty famously badly behaved with all comers'.[17] Mrs Rowan-Hamilton of Killyleagh Castle is said to have sampled his charms.[18] As did his cousin Nini of Quentin Castle in the Ards, and Theresa, Lady Londonderry. Indeed Nini and Theresa used to delight in comparing notes on his quirks and foibles, and in marvelling at his Valentino-like effect on women. In one of Nini's letters to Theresa she almost gleefully recounts an unsuccessful attempt by one of the Blakiston-Houston girls to seduce him 'in a way that I would never have done, in my wildest and boldest moments'.[19]

But it was not just about sex. Or the thrill of the chase. Two of these extra-marital affairs, or rather loves, to give them their true name, were enduring. The first was his relationship with Theresa, Lady Londonderry, the wife of his friend the Sixth Marquis. The Stewarts were then at the

Theresa, Lady Londonderry (1902): sampled Richard's charms. (Victoria & Albert Museum)

height of their influence, so there will have been something Alpine about bedding a Londonderry. Not that Richard will have needed an ulterior motive. Nor Theresa, who was 'notoriously amorous, like all the Talbots', and had a taste for extravagant, good-looking men.[20]

This relationship was in full spate at the time of Londonderry's Lord Lieutenantship, meaning that while Ker publicly serenaded the marquis, he was privately courting his wife. But Theresa, 'a highwayman in a tiara', proved too much of a handful even for Richard, and his abrupt disappearance from Londonderry house party photographs in the early 1890s seems to denote the relationship's end.[21]

Both found pastures new. (Theresa's beaus allegedly included her gardener and the Prince of Wales.) Richard, who seems to have travelled through life in a state of semi-permanent sexual arousal, became besotted with his cousin Nini, the daughter of his late Uncle Richard, who had returned to Ireland with her mother Rose in the 1890s. This was as powerful a relationship as he had ever experienced. A relationship with life-making and life-wrecking potential. A frantic passion, which by 1900 was threatening to destroy his marriage.

'The gallant Nimrod' sallies forth: the 1884 election
The bravura reporting of the hunt made Ker well known throughout the county. Youths cheered the hunt when it thundered past, its riders resplendent in Hunting Pink, with the dashing Ker at their head.[1] While

William Ewart Gladstone, Liberal Prime Minister 1880-85. As sketched c.1890 by Sidney Prior Hall. (National Portrait Gallery)

there were, even then, eloquent voices raised against it, hunting as a pastime chimed well with the imperial ethos of the age, and a large audience followed the hunt's exploits in the papers, devouring news of the chases as modern audiences might follow the instalments of a weekly soap.[2]

Much of the interest focused on the hunt's charismatic master, whose 'genial disposition... made him a favourite amongst all classes'.[3] Richard was also admired by his peers, who described him as 'gallant', 'manly' and 'urbane'. And when the elevation of Lord Castlereagh to the House of Lords prompted a by-election in County Down in 1884, Richard was unexpectedly invited to stand as the Tory candidate, his name being 'the strongest that could be put forward'.[4]

The Conservatives needed a strong candidate. Although they had taken both county seats in the 1880 general election, they had won the second by a whisker, with Castlereagh beating his Liberal rival by just twenty votes. (The first seat, in time-honoured fashion, had gone to a Downshire, Lord Arthur Hill.) In the meantime Gladstone's government had passed the Land Act, which had led to wholesale rent cuts, turning the Liberal prime minister into the darling of the county's tenant farmers.[5]

To the satisfaction of Conservative party managers, Ker accepted the nomination. A path was smoothed for him. Two potential rivals, both of them prominent Orangemen, stood aside in his favour, and on November

14th 1884, Ker found himself anointed as the Tories' great white hope.[6] He was a curious choice. At a time when the Nationalist 'invasion of Ulster' and heated Orange counter-demonstrations had sent the political temperature soaring, the moment seemed ripe for a no-nonsense, ultra-conservative, right-winger. Richard was not cast in this mould. He was not a reactionary, or an Orangeman. He may not even have been a Tory. The *Northern Whig* claimed him as a lifelong Liberal, declaring ruefully that, 'The gallant Nimrod has been drawn into a false trail'.[7]

The Conservatives dismissed this claim and issued an orthodox election address on Ker's behalf, but the charge was well made. Richard Ker was an outsider, brought in by a party that did not believe that it could deliver a winner from within its own ranks. This was celebrity politics. And although he was reckoned to be 'one of the most popular men in the county', Richard was a political greenhorn.[8] How would he fare? Was he up to the job?

This question would remain unanswered. On the day before the nomination, the gallant Nimrod went stag hunting near Ardglass. His horse galloped into mud on a riverbank, where it instantly stuck fast, propelling Ker across the stream 'in brilliant style'.[9] The casualty was carted back to Finnebrogue. The Tory campaign was thrown into disarray. At first the party managers played down Ker's injury. But three days later the tone changed. A doctor's letter appeared in all the papers gravely advising Ker to do no canvassing. Beside it was printed a reply from the patient, accepting this disappointing advice.

The result was that Richard did not so much fight the election as survey it from his bed, which – sick or well – he occupied for the duration of the campaign. His injury won him not ridicule, but sympathy. It also left the potentially fraught business of sounding forth on the great issues of the day in more experienced hands than his own. We may imagine Ker's veteran agent and campaign manager, Edward Finnigan, quietly rubbing his hands in delight. Would that all callow and potentially gaffe-prone candidates could be so obliging. If recruiting Ker was the Tories' first masterstroke, their second was keeping him 'under wraps'. Things were proceeding nicely.

Ker's Liberal opponent was Arthur Sharman Crawford, a son of the great William. Once again a Ker faced a Crawford. Old stagers recalled 1852, and the epic contest of that year. Liberals also invoked 1857, denouncing Richard as an 'apostate' who had allowed himself be used by 'the party at whose hands his father had suffered the most relentless persecution'.[10]

Were we in for a re-run of the epic contests of those years? We were not. The introduction of the secret ballot (1872) and measures limiting election expenses (1883) had revolutionised Irish elections. The electorate could no longer be bribed or bullied as of old. Ireland's democracy was maturing. County elections had largely ceased to be duels between landed leviathans. They were now primarily contests between political parties, within which landlords, struggling to retain their political relevance, presented themselves not as proprietors, but as 'the natural leaders of the people'.[11]

The Crawfords had already made this transition. Decades of political commitment had turned them into one of the strongest electoral brand names in Ulster Liberalism. The Liberal difficulty in Down in 1884, however, was that they faced a temporary shortage of eligible Crawfords. Although a son of the great reformer, Arthur was a mild mannered, seventy-four year old, who stood on a moderate platform. This disappointed many tenant farmers, who were ready for a much more radical message on land reform, prompting fears that they might not come out and vote.

The Tories made great play of Crawford's age. 'Is there an idea in the county of sending a fossil to parliament?' one speaker asked, with mock incredulity.[12] Crawford was portrayed as a ghost from a bygone era. He was past it. Near his dotage.[13] Ker on the other hand represented bold modernity. There was a Kennedyesque dimension to his promotion. Ker had glamour, youth and vigour. References were even made to his swooning good looks – which drew the retort that being handsome, if anything:

ought to debar him... They wanted some long-headed [shrewd] man like the Liberal candidate. Mr Crawford had got as much in his head as the whole family of Kers. (Cheers.)[14]

And it was noted that the fossil addressed meeting after meeting, while the Tory lion lay mute in his bed. However, Ker's absence mysteriously enhanced his stature. It was as if there was something masterly about his inactivity. It was as if he was simultaneously part of and yet above the struggle. 'The gallant captain', as he was known to friend and foe alike, lay at Finnebrogue like the sleeping Barbarossa, ready when summoned to rise and save the nation.

As Richard convalesced, the Downshire-Tory election machine purred into action, undeterred, indeed positively liberated by the absence of its candidate. The 'ubiquitous' Lord Arthur Hill, MP, or 'Lord Arter' as he was known,[15] barnstormed the country making two and three speeches a day at every hole in the hedge that would have him:

No winds or no weather, could his journey debar,
Till he found a true brother, in young Captain Ker.[16]

Richard's family were also on the road. His Maxwell nieces canvassed tirelessly on his behalf. Edith appeared at (estate-based) rallies in Newry,

Finnebrogue, near Downpatrick, County Down. Ker's 'campaign headquarters'.

Gilford, Ballyhackamore, Newtownbreda (Bateson country), Finnebrogue, and Ballynahinch to 'a regular storm of cheering'.[17]

The Liberals also campaigned with gusto, but less system. Crawford proved unexpectedly puckish, forcing even the ruggedly Tory *Belfast News Letter* to concede that the fossil was betraying 'signs of life'. North and mid-Down rallied to his cause, but Crawford made limited inroads in the south of the county. Here, the canvass had to be 'left entirely in the hands of a few farmers.'[18] This should have set Liberal alarm bells ringing, for it showed that the party's message was falling on deaf ears.

Irish politics were changing. Ancient divisions were reasserting themselves in new forms. In south Down, never a Liberal stronghold, the left-right, class-based politics of land reform had, by 1884, been overtaken by the politics of ethnicity and religion.[19] The competing nationalisms of the Orange Order and the National League had captured hearts and minds. It was the shape of things to come. In 1886, with the introduction of the first Home Rule Bill, the national question would become the organising principle of Irish politics.

Yet the Tories did not play the Orange card. Although Ulster's borderlands seethed with sectarian tension, in 1884 in Down, the Conservatives offered:

no denunciation of Nationalists, no blustering about the "Invasion of Ulster," no placards calling upon "loyal Orangemen" to rise and protect the "British

Conspicuous by their absence: Fife and drums, by William Conor. (Private collection)

Constitution" and "Protestantism"... For the first time this many years Orange drums and Orange bombast played no part in the election.[20]

The Liberals were mystified but not displeased by this turn of events. The tone of the debate was rising. And about time. It was 1884, after all. But this was to prove a naive and potentially calamitous misreading of events.

Historically, to the extent that they identified with British politics at all, the county's Catholics had given their allegiance to the Liberal Party. By 1884, however, with the rise of organised nationalism under Parnell, allegiances had shifted. As Catholics numbered some 22% of the county electorate, this shift presented the Liberal Party with a serious difficulty.[21] An alliance with nationalism could have delivered a resounding Liberal victory.

But supporting Gladstone's Liberal government was the last thing on Parnell's mind. He wanted to punish the Prime Minister for forcibly repressing dissent during the 'Land War'. And he knew that he could play the king-maker in Down. But he would have to be careful as to how he went about it. Attempts to damage the Liberals in by-elections in Tyrone and Londonderry in 1881 had backfired badly, causing bitter recriminations within the Land League.[22] If he was going to get his way in Down he would have to be more subtle.

As would the Conservatives. They had to take Parnell's concerns seriously, for Parnell was not only capable of deciding the issue in Down, his Home Rule Party might well decide who next governed the United Kingdom. Tory policy was adapted to meet the needs of the moment. Cherished totems were abandoned. Parnellite policies took their place, changes that left Ulster's Tories feeling more than a little bewildered.[23] These U-turns bore fruit. By 1884, Parnell had come to believe that he could extract more from the Conservatives than Gladstone. A marriage of convenience was formed.

This kind of detente was all very well in the rarefied atmosphere of Westminster. But could it be replicated out in the townlands? The Down election showed that it could. Whether this was arranged centrally, or occurred as a result of a local initiative is unclear. All we know is that quietly, covertly, by processes unknown, the local party managers arrived at a tacit understanding. Its terms were local nationalist neutrality in return for Tory parliamentary aid, with the shared object of deposing Gladstone.

Richard (who could say things that 'proper' Tories couldn't) did his bit to develop *détente*. He condemned the use of coercive legislation. He supported calls for an inquiry into the Maamtrasna executions, a nationalist *cause celebre*.[24] And his family's long-standing anti-sectarianism leant his pronouncements credibility. Encouraged by these overtures, Father O'Hare, the parish priest of Ballynahinch, spent time 'closeted with Mr Ker in Finnebrogue House and afterwards openly avowed himself to be his supporter'.[25]

The Liberals did not grasp the significance of these manoeuvrings, and remained optimistic about winning nationalist votes. Indeed they remained hopeful of outright victory, if they could win the big debates on land and the economy. The economy would be the tough one. The early 1880s were a time of hardship. The Liberals saw free trade as the route back to prosperity, the Conservatives advocated protectionism or 'fair trade'.

This meant putting tariffs on imports, which would help hard-pressed local farmers, whose produce was being undercut by cheap imported food. But it would also increase prices. As one Liberal orator put it:

He recently met a woman who… had been in Banbridge and purchased a pound of tea for 2/6d. Now supposing her husband said he was going to vote for "Ker and fair trade" – (laughter) – and she asked what this meant, and ultimately found that it meant paying 5s instead of 2/6d for a pound of tea… and a shilling for the present sixpenny loaf, would she not exclaim "Protect me from Captain Ker's protection". (Cheers.)[26]

Charles Stewart Parnell, pictured with Birmingham and Gladstone – king-maker in Down in 1884? (National Portrait Gallery)

The point was well made, but 'fair trade' will have been a vote winner in this largely agricultural constituency.

The Liberals' strongest suit was land, 'the burning question of the day'.[27] They reminded the electorate that the Tories had been 'the bitter, uncompromising and determined enemies of the Land Acts'[28] which had been such a boon to tenant farmers, and promised further reforms. The candidates' landlordism was carefully scrutinised, leading the *Downpatrick Recorder* to claim that:

If names are to be of any account... the name of Ker... has a right to stand high or higher for landlordism than that of Crawford. When the late WILLIAM SHARMAN CRAWFORD was advocating Tenant-right... DAVID STEWART KER was practising it in all its integrity.[29]

Land was the Tories' Achilles heel. As the bidding war for Parnell's support intensified, prominent English Tories had talked openly of breaking up the great Irish estates and allowing tenants to buy out their farms. However there had been no such change of heart amongst the Tory gentry in County Down. Ker's election address had avoided all mention of the land question.[30] But the Liberals made so much capital out of this that the Conservatives were compelled to rush out an address on land three days before the poll. In this (a century after his great-grandfather had done the same) Ker declared himself in favour of tenant ownership.[31] It was a bold move, an attempt to out-radical the radicals. But there was a turkeys-voting-for-Christmas element to the proposal that led many tenant farmers to greet the announcement with an almost visceral distrust:

Ask your Nimrod Tory suitor what have his party done for you –
Did they ever pass a measure to lift you up and pull you through,

No! They spurned you from their presence - bade you labour, be content;
Doff your hat in landlord presence, bow the knee, and pay your rent!
Men of Down, the scenes are changing! In yon sky are streaks of light!
Rise and work your own redemption! Vote for Crawford! Tenant right.[32]

On Thursday November 27th 1884 the county went to the polls. Out on the Copelands, the island's five voters, three Emersons and two Cleggs, braved foul weather to cross to the mainland, after which they travelled to Bangor, to vote for Ker. At least this is what they told the man from the *Belfast News Letter*. Blissfully unaware that the estate was busily preparing to evict them, the paper held up Ker and the islanders as a model of landlord-tenant relations.[33]

Ker's friends awaited the result with 'considerable anxiety'.[34] This was the third election to take place since the introduction of the secret ballot, but arguably the first truly free vote in the county's history, for it was the first at which 'no effort was made to persuade the tenant-farmers that the

Lord Arthur Hill. As ever, the Downshire electoral machine swept all before it. (Downshire family)

ballot wasn't secret'.[35] There were still hangovers from the bad old days. Modern freedoms were exercised within the grid of the old estate voting pattern. Landlords still invigilated at polling booths. The anonymous balladeer who urged voters to:

> Seek no agent's favour
> Fear no Castle's anger;
> Plump and do not waver
> At Groomsport and Bangor.[36]

still had a point to make, as the Copeland islanders could testify.

The result was declared. Ker took 4,387 votes, Crawford 3,997. The Conservatives were jubilant:

> Long live our True voters
> Where'er they may be
> They fought like True Brittons
> Their country to free –

> From home-rule & rebels & leaguers ascore
> Now they're all left in mourning
> From mountain to Shore.[37]

That night the victors celebrated. There was a firework display on Scrabo. Around 'Donaghadee (Portavo?)... large bonfires were... kept burning briskly until far into the night'.[38] Bands played, flags were flown, and a worthy enemy was saluted:

> Now fare ye weel auld Crawford dear
> Your name we'll boast na mair
> Tho' mony a hopeful day we spent
> Bigging [building] castles in the air.[39]

On the evening of the declaration Richard arose Lazarus-like from his bed to join the celebrations at Finnebrogue and Ballynahinch, where, demonstrating that he might after all have a flair for what we now call the soundbite, Ker pledged himself to help overturn 'the present Government of funk and fumble'.[40]

The Tories portrayed Ker's victory as a slap in the face for Gladstone.[41] The Liberals were bereft. The Catholic 'defection' came particularly sore.[42] The county's Catholics had behaved like Tory lickspittles, allowing 'the nominee of Orangeism... to use them as his stepping stone'. They had betrayed their class interests, and in the words of one Liberal correspondent turned 'traitors to those who had made them freemen', an unintentionally condescending remark which helps us to understand why nationalists apparently found it so easy to go their own way. Although some 'Nationalists showed independence' and voted for Crawford:

The great majority of RC's abstained and of those who did vote nearly all owing to the influence of Father O'Hare and others supported Mr Ker.[43]

The *Northern Whig* claimed that Ker's support was strongest in Episcopalian and Catholic areas.[44] But Ker was also backed by what might be called estate-institutionalised Presbyterians, a fact that the *Whig*, which proudly claimed that 'a Tory Presbyterian is a contradiction in terms', was much more loath to face. Though some felt that the radical vote was not fully polled because Crawford was 'not advanced enough for the tenant-farmers of Down',[45] the Liberal candidate received overwhelming support in the Presbyterian heartlands. In Donaghadee, for example, he took 199 votes to Ker's nineteen. In Bangor Ker polled more strongly, suggesting that he largely retained the loyalty of the Portavo estate.[46]

James Robinson of Ballyminetragh and William Burroughs the grampus slayer led the Tory canvass here. They were supported by

staunch conservatives like William Anderson, a veteran of 1852. The estate also contained strong Liberal voices. Hugh Kinnaird and James Perry of Ballyminetragh, and Robert McCutcheon of Balloo Lower, were active in the Liberal campaign.[47] The Andrews family's votes could also be relied on.

Richard took his seat a week after the poll to 'a tremendous cheer of hearty welcome, such as only comes from the Conservative benches'.[48] Wallace spoilt the party slightly by raising the vexed question of money, ('How you are to meet the expenses naturally consequent on your attendance in… Parliament is a mystery to me!'[49]) But this and similar concerns were brushed aside. It had been a glorious victory. A personal triumph. Many also saw it as a testament to the resilience of a great county family. The Kers were a power in the land again, enjoying a prominence that they had not known for a generation.

This confident return to the public arena seemed to complete the family's rehabilitation. And to the extent that the seat had come off the back of Richard's popularity, and Alfred's re-imposition of financial discipline, there is a certain truth in this view. But it is essentially misplaced. In the 1850s the Kers had largely fought their way to the top, in the 1880s they were put there by others, not least their political enemy, Parnell.

It was the last time that the county would vote as a single constituency. In 1885 'the Yorkshire of Ireland' was divided into four. Ker stood for East Down and was returned unopposed, thanks to a secret deal in which

Andrews farmstead, c.1920. The Andrews were one of the Portavo estate's most 'advanced' Liberal families. Crawford's message may have been too watery for their taste. (Andrews family)

the Liberals agreed to stand aside in return for a free run elsewhere.[50] In the Home Rule election of 1886, Ker was returned as a Unionist, beating his nationalist opponent Henry McGrath by 5,093 votes to 2,561.[51] He represented East Down until 1890, when drowning in debt and in danger of becoming an embarrassment to his colleagues, Richard was prevailed upon to take the 'Chiltern Hundreds' and retire.

29 The world turned upside down

The miller's tale

At the end of the summer of 1882, a cart pulled up outside Portavo mill.[1] On it were two adults, several children and various sticks of furniture. Behind it were a couple of larger children, herding a reluctant cow. The cart had come from Bangor. Its driver was Willie John Boyd and he was here to take up the vacant position of miller. Boyd knew his trade, which was just as well, for he had a corn mill and a flax or scutch mill to look after. This contained parts so dangerous that Boyd would strap himself in while he worked, to avoid getting his limbs or fingers mangled by its rough wooden rollers.[2]

His wife Annabella, a miller's daughter, inspected the mill cottage. The thatch was tatty. The walls could use a whitening, and she was sure it had mice, but it was a solid old thing. She quite liked it. Claney, the land steward, showed Willie John round. He reviewed all with a seasoned eye. The mills weren't working, the dam was too low. But it wouldn't be long until autumn. His hands would soon be full.

The mill cottage, Portavo, from an old newspaper cutting. (Boyd family)

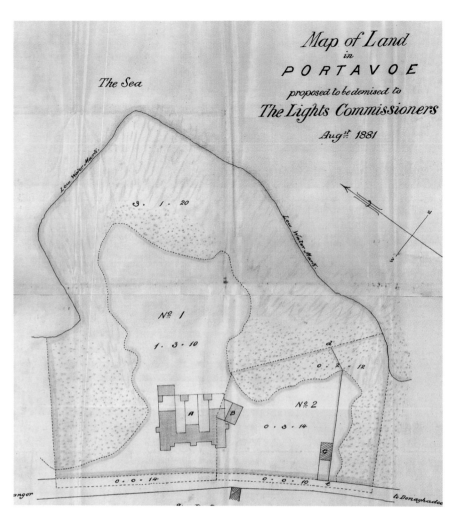

The proposed lighthouse keepers' cottages on Portavo Point. Lisa's little cottage is marked 'B'. (Brown McConnell Clark)

Their neighbour, Lisa Magee, came over to greet them. She brought a bowl of eggs in fresh straw and bade them welcome. Lisa was a kindly but eccentric spinster, whose hens were said to roost on the end of her bed.[3] She lived across the road, in a little cottage by the sea, which she had held rent free for longer than anyone could remember.[4] And she was not a happy woman, for they were trying to get rid of her.

'Who's trying to get rid of you?'

Tssch! Such a stupid question. 'The Commissioners. Hae ye no heard? They want ta toss ma hoose an get rid o'me. But ah won't go. Am tellin ye. Am no goin.'

She was quite right. The Commissioners of Irish Lights had applied to build a row of lighthouse keepers' cottages on the sea front at Portavo, demolishing Lisa's cottage in the process.[5] But would the Captain let them? Housing meant money, and Captain Ker was on his uppers. The arrival of the cottages seemed a foregone conclusion. Lisa bowed to the inevitable. Alright, she would go. But not happily, and not for less than £30.[6] A few months later, confidence rising, she dug her heels in and upped her price to £50.[7]

Lisa was not the only malcontent. The proposed cottages would leave Portavo's farmers 'shut out from the sea-weed', and denying the farmers their wrack would be like denying them their breath. No good would come of it. There was also Ker's intended return to Portavo. This gave the local aesthetics a renewed importance, meaning that nothing 'unsightly or too high' could be countenanced on the shore.[8]

Dearly as he wanted the money, Ker said no, seeing the cottages as 'a great nuisance… on account of [the] proximity of his demesne'. So the Commissioners had to take second best and build their cottages a mile down the road on the Warren, where they still stand, 'leaving for the enjoyment of Portavo the entire of the shore'.[9]

But Willie John had more pressing concerns than the fate of Lisa Magee's cottage. The harvest was almost upon them. But what sort of harvest would it be? The last few had been bad, throwing the countryside into its worst depression since the Famine. Labourers had been laid off. There was widespread hardship. Farmers struggled to meet their commitments, and the coming November would see a partial failure of the rents.[10] Every farm on the Copelands was badly in arrears. The Airds of Orlock were also in difficulty.[11]

The 'magic door', which opened onto the demesne and the mill dam.

The harvest of 1882 brought scant relief. It was by no means a bumper year. People weren't growing corn like they used to. But Willie John Boyd was busy all the same. The carts trundled in from all quarters. Corn from the Copelands was landed by boat in Lisa Magee's Bay.[12] The flax mill was busy too, for the Anguses, McBrides and Perrys grew flax, as did the Kinnairds, the McCoubreys, and the Airds, who steeped theirs in the soft ground underneath what is now Portavoe Water.[13]

There was 'powerful work' in flax. It was pulled by hand, and pulling even a small field of it took days. After every nine pulls, the stalks were tied with rush bands into 'beets', which were stacked in twelves, and then retted or rotted in cigar-shaped dams called lint holes. Nearly every farm had one, and the Anguses had two, in damp ground opposite the Close. After four to six weeks, the softened 'beets' were laid out to dry, then brought to Boyd's for scutching, the pounding which separated the fibres from the husks. The flax then went to the 'streaking shed' where the last loose ends were taken off, leaving 'lovely stuff… like long grey hair', which was baled and sold at the mill.[14]

When the day was done, Willie John went up to the dam and closed the sluice, which cut the water supply to the wheel. Water was his petrol and it didn't do to waste it. Then he went indoors to eat and hear the news of the day. Who wasn't speaking. Who had fallen in nettles. Who had found a dead bee in the well. What Sam and Minnie had learned at school that day. Each morning the pair trudged to school barefoot, clutching a turf for the fire, to learn, or in Sam's case, fidget his way through his lessons.[15]

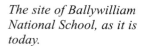

The site of Ballywilliam National School, as it is today.

Like most of Portavo's children, Sam and Minnie were educated in Ballywilliam School. In 1837, the school was thriving. By 1858 it had become a National School. But sometime after this its fortunes suffered a fatal reverse. The school closed, and in 1909 was described as having been pulled down 'years ago'.[16] By 1924 it had become a 'crumbling' object of nostalgic longing.[17] Ballywilliam is otherwise an enigma. Many former National Schools left large paper trails behind them, but nothing relating to this school seems to have survived, and all trace of the schoolhouse itself has vanished, erased as casually as chalk marks on a blackboard.[18] What became of it? Tradition is wonderfully apocalyptic on the subject, deeming it to have been 'washed away by the sea'.[19] However, a more prosaic explanation, such as its remains being used as building materials, would seem to be more likely.

Helena Williams, governess to Richard Schmidt's children. (McCallum family)

It is also unclear why it closed, but the most probable explanation is a lack of pupils. In 1841, Portavo had been awash with children. The human tide was in full spate. Between 1871-1901, however, the population shrank from 119 to 77, a fall of more than a third. By 1901, six of its twenty-seven houses lay empty. The average age had risen to thirty-five, and a third of its population was over fifty.[20] Clergy buried people where they had once baptised them. Institutionally, Portavo was more in need of an old folks' home than a school. In 1901 it had just eleven 'scholars', four of whom (the Schmidt girls) had their own governess, leaving seven.[21] Children were becoming an endangered species. And the same thing was happening right across the country.

The reasons for the fall are many and various. Changes in family structure. Rising marriage ages. The decline of tillage. The lure of the big city. The fall did not affect all groups equally. In 1862 Portavo had at least six labouring families. In 1901 it had one. A whole tier of local society had largely decamped. Its absence was most keenly felt at harvest time. Neighbouring wouldn't bring the crops in. There weren't enough neighbours. John Small would mow for Willie Burroughs, and Willie Burroughs would plough Small's four fields, but the flax and potatoes were gathered by city folk, most of whom were the sons and daughters of country people who had left the land a generation before.[22]

Two ghosts and a banshee
Of an evening, Willie John Boyd might call in at Small's on the Stockbridge Road. John Small was a farmer-blacksmith and his cottage was the local ceili house. But ceili as in chat not dancing. Small's kitchen was a place of lore and stories. A place in which local identity was shaped and forged, and individual lives were given reach and depth by being located within a rich folk tradition. Here, by a well-stacked fire, Boyd could chew the fat with the likes of Tom McBride, Hugh and Wee Willie

The cottage the banshee flew over. John Small's house, thatched in his day but otherwise little changed.

Angus, and John Small's cousin John Perry, marvelling at the changes transforming the countryside, colloguing about spats and reconciliations, or trading blood curdling tales of '98.

Stories that raised the hairs on the back of the neck were particularly welcome. Like the one about the woman in white that Jane Burrows had seen at the top of the staircase in Portavo House.[1] Or the tale of the solitary traveller who, one bad evening, had taken shelter beneath trees in Ballycopeland graveyard only to hear a sepulchral voice from behind him inquire, 'Do you think its going to rain all night?'[2] And Portavo didn't just have ghosts. It also had fairies aplenty.[3] And other creatures besides. John Small himself had heard a banshee fly over their house and, to his consternation, land on their knowe, wailing 'Och-aeo! Och-aeo!'[4] He would always put another log on the fire after telling that one.

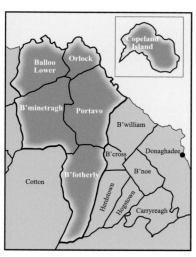

Five townlands and the Copeland Islands (inset): the Portavo estate.

The world turned upside down

In 1883, however, the talk was all of fair rents and tenant freedom. Gladstone's 1881 Land Act had transferred the power to determine rents from landlords to independent commissioners, and in June 1883, the commissioners were due to adjudicate on the rents of nineteen farms on the Portavo estate. Four of these were in Portavo itself, where John Perry, Willie Angus, Tom McBride and Small himself were contesting their rents, and if they did so successfully, more appeals would certainly follow. The hearings were on June 20th, and the sense of anticipation was intense.

The estate was defending all nineteen cases. Though bullish in public, in private it was fully aware that this would be an exercise in damage limitation, 'Of course all the tenants will get reductions', Wallace told Ker, preparing him for the worst.[1] In 1874, the estate had attempted to subvert the 1870 Land Act by encouraging tenants in Clough to sign receipts which would have denied them the full benefits of the Act, attempts that were thwarted by vigorous tenant opposition.[2] Now, it contented itself with a much more limited rearguard action, attempting merely to contain the reductions.

Wallace's prediction proved largely correct. Sixteen of the nineteen rents – including all four Portavo rents – were reduced, and we can imagine the joy around Small's hearth, when the comrades next gathered. Tom McBride had his rent reduced by two pounds to just under £12. Angus got his down from £25.9s to £21.10s. Perry's was reduced from £76 to £69. John Small's was cut from £8.13s to £7.10s, just over half of what his father had paid for the same patch of land in 1839. These victories gave the tenants a tremendous sense of empowerment. The law was on their side at last. Their chains were falling to their feet.

The reductions averaged 11%.[3] More cases followed, until even the ultra-loyal William Burroughs (*et tu Brute?*) took his case to the Commissioners, winning 30% off his rent, the largest cut achieved by anyone in the townland. By 1894 Ker's gross income had been reduced to £16,500.[4] In 1897-1902 a second round of cuts reduced the rents further. These cuts were far-reaching, abating rents by an average of 23%.[5] Ker's income plunged. Now it was the estate that felt hard done by, and in a series of appeals, heard between 1901-03, it was able to claw back some of the later reductions.

The cuts reflected the new demographics. The historically high rent levels of the 1830s had arisen when population pressure was intense and

The Angus family of the Close, who won a hefty rent cut in 1883. The balance of power was changing. (Bell family)

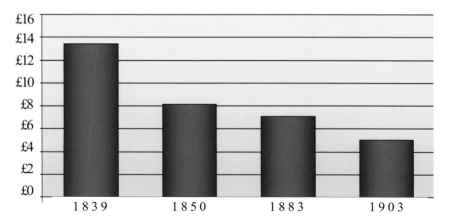

The Small family's rent 1839-1903. Between these dates, rent more than halved as a percentage of outgoings.

demand for land was almost limitless,[6] pushing the limits of cultivation far up the sides of mountains, where its melancholy tidemark can still be seen. The lower rents of the 1880s-90s were achieved against a background of rural depopulation and a relaxation of the pressure on resources, demographics which favoured the tenant. The cuts also reflected a decisive shift in the balance of power between landlord and tenant. Passed in the belief that they might bring a new stability to Irish life, the Land Acts of 1870, 1881 and 1885 swept away generations of custom and practice. The old order was turned on its head. Landlords lost the power to fix rents. Tenants acquired the right to buy their holdings.

Staggering under these body blows, landlordism drew in its horns. The expansive paternalism of the 1850s-60s was abandoned. Transactions between landlord and tenant were stripped of all nicety and grace.[7] The relationship was reduced to its brutal essence. By the mid-1880s the Ker estate, in common with estates all over Ireland, was practicing a contracted, defensive and legalistic form of estate management.

Landlordism was crumbling. Not in England, Scotland or Wales. Only in Ireland, where landlordism was more friendless, socially contentious and politically vulnerable than elsewhere. However this fact took some believing. While it is obvious to us that landlordism was reaching the end of the road, this was far from clear to many tenants at the time. The 1883 reductions were seen as victories over a beleaguered but still powerful institution, which might yet derail further reform.

The mooted 'invasion' of the Copelands

That November, the rents were paid with a smile and paid promptly, for the old 'clean receipt' ethos stayed strong here.[1] Curiously enough, the only major defaulter in the townland was Ker himself, who rented Portavo House and grounds for £30 a year, but 'never paid a shilling' for it, apparently on a point of principle. Although Wallace was 'most

Sandy Bay and the Copeland Islands, 1843. Sheep graze where the Stone House now stands. (Ker family)

unwilling… to press him for the money', he was nonetheless sufficiently provoked by Ker's behaviour to at one point consider evicting him.[2]

The Copeland islanders were another source of frustration. In the early 1880s the Copeland Island had five tenanted farms and a population of about forty-five. The depression of 1879-82 had stricken the island, leaving four of its five farms deeply and perhaps irretrievably in arrears. Something had to be done. In August 1883, Wallace summoned the various Cleggs and Emersons to his Belfast office. The sturdy and apparently guileless islanders impressed him. He was particularly struck with Robert Emerson, the rugged *rí an oileáin*, who was the sort to 'make every exertion he possibly could' to clear his debts.[3]

Convinced of the islanders willingness to pay, and of their inability to do so, Wallace left the meeting believing that the arrears were lost, and that the most pragmatic course might be to write them off.[4] But how could he? How could he wipe out their arrears and insist that others, such as the Airds of Orlock (also badly in arrears), make full restitution?[5] He would have to take a firmer course.

Arrangements were made for repayment. They fell through. Robert Emerson and another islander were evicted.[6] Emerson's eviction involved neither police nor bailiffs. It took place on paper, in Wallace's office, where his legal status was changed from that of tenant to that of caretaker. An under-sheriff served the notice on Emerson, who then entertained the man 'most hospitably' before sailing him back to the mainland.[7] Emerson continued to live on the farm, 'which is the usual course'. Wallace continued to pursue the arrears. Promises were made, promises were broken. By 1885 the islanders collectively owed £700. They were practically in open rebellion.

Then, out of the blue, in November 1885, a letter arrived in Wallace's office. It was from Robert Emerson, and he wanted to buy 'his' farm under the terms of the new Land Act.[8] Wallace saw red. They had pushed him too far. The time had come to crush the island nation. Wallace urged Ker to act:

The whole business will be a most unpleasant one. It will amount simply to this, clearing the entire Island of every person and from the situation of the Island in the sea, it will be a very difficult job... None of the boatmen in Donaghadee would go to the Island on such a mission & I see nothing else for it but to get a tug at Belfast... and let the Sheriff bring his men with him for we will have to keep possession of the holdings when we get them...[9]

But Ker balked at the military option. Permission was refused. There would be no gunboat diplomacy. Wallace turned to bribery. Each of the defaulting families was offered £50 to go.[10] This time it was the islanders who said no. The financial crisis of 1887 and subsequent breakdown in relations between Ker and Wallace for a time took the pressure off the islanders. In the early 1890s, however, the two most indebted families on the island (those of John and Robert Emerson) either left or were compelled to go. The estate was triumphant. But its triumph soon rang hollow. No new tenants could be found.

Until the 1890s, tenanting the island had never presented problems.[11] Now it did. The 1894 rental shows the former Emerson farms lying vacant.[12] Perhaps no-one would take on the evicted men's farms. But the vacancies may say something rather deeper about the viability of island life. Had the island that was once considered a little piece of Eden become unwanted marginal land?

Part of the basement storey of Portavo's burned mansion house, as it is today.

The yard, Portavo House c.1911, showing the old Ross dower house (centre). When the Kers returned the place was falling down. (Ker family)

Primus inter pares

When the Kers returned in 1885, Portavo was a sorry sight. The decades of neglect had taken their toll. The park was still beautiful, but within it lay crumbling outhouses, decaying byres and stable blocks, empty cottages and the fox-glove dotted ruins of the burnt out mansion. The Ross dower house was roofless. The drains were full of ferns. The pleasure dam had silted. The rustic bridge was unsafe. The demesne wall was unpacking. Whins engulfed the old laundry. The 'much admired' woodland was reverting to a state of nature.

It was all very post-imperial, very collapse of the landed gentry rendered in stone. However, there was stir amid the ruins. With Richard and Edith's return, something small and better suited to the times was born within the leviathan's remains. These remains were not without a certain romance. Portavo reeked of fallen grandeur. Neglect became it. And the more beggarly it got, the more enigmatic and intensely charged its atmosphere became.

Richard's house of 1884-85. Edith turned the rubble into a rock garden. The 'big house' found a new place in local life. (Brown McConnell Clark)

The big house found a new place in local life. It did not dominate it as of old. It was *primus inter pares* now. It put money into the local economy. But in a trickle this time, not a flood. Richard started farming. Edith planted flowers and converted some of the better piles of rubble into a rock garden. New gates were hung. Fresh palings appeared. Thistles were scythed, weeds weeded. A Mr and Mrs Patterson started work in the walled garden. The front gate lodge was re-thatched and lime-washed.[1]

Claney the Land Stewart ran the farm. But it had hardly got going before the financial crisis of 1887 brought it to its knees and its carts and livestock were forcibly sold at 'absurdly low' prices.[2] Claney's position became untenable. He begged Wallace for help. In a letter that positively bristles with unstated accusation, Wallace informed Ker that:

the grass at Portavo is going to loss; the hay and potatoes will be immediately ready for sale, but without instruction he [Claney] cannot know what to do... he has no money in hand to meet current expenses, or pay the labourers...[3]

He got no answers. There were no answers. The farm collapsed. The woods were also decimated. In August 1887 Richard culled many of the park's most distinguished trees, wreaking 'sad havoc' in the demesne.[4] The woods regenerated in an ad hoc, bargain basement fashion, but farming did not revive.[5] The demesne was let.

Wallace would have liked to have seen the house let too. Or better still, both houses, for it was 'perfectly ridiculous… that a man on the edge of bankruptcy is to be keeping up these places'.[6] Montalto in particular was completely beyond them.[7] It was a vanity. A white elephant. A relic of the glory days, retained because to sell it would be too humbling. Who wanted to keep it? Edith blamed Richard. Wallace blamed Edith, for as he saw it, poor Richard was 'completely in her hands & must do as she tells him'.[8]

In 1893 Wallace – sort of – got his wish. The Kers moved to Cheshire. There they replicated their County Down lifestyle, right down to Richard becoming master of the Wirral Harriers and the Wye Valley Otter Hounds, positions he could no more afford there than here.[9] The Pattersons were left in charge of the house and garden. No sooner had the Kers gone, however, than the Pattersons apparently started taking advantage. Wallace dismissed them and reclaimed the house, not knowing 'what is in it… or what ought to be in it.'[10] Portavo would be let. Edith asked if they might make any money from the letting, prompting Wallace to reply, with ungentlemanly relish, that 'Anything to be made [from] it… will not be made for you'.[11]

The circle widens

Sometime around 1890, after nearly a century in the townland, the Anderson family left Portavo. They did not go because they were evicted. Their departure was an act of free will.[1] Horizons were widening. Seven acres were no longer enough. 'Anyone leaving got a bonfire', Jim and Sarah George recalled,[2] and we may imagine the leave-taking of such a

Bittersweet farewell. Artist's impression of the leaving bonfire. (Emma Bayliss)

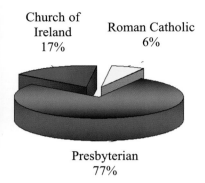

Church of
Ireland
17%

Roman Catholic
6%

Presbyterian
77%

*Portavo, population by religion,
1901.*

long established family being a memorable affair. But who would get the farm? Hugh Angus and Willie McCutcheon both wanted it. In the old days, the estate would have arbitrated. But now things were less cut and dried. The citizenry took more of a role in the management of their own affairs. And on this occasion they managed them in a very civilised fashion. Angus transferred three of his fields to McCutcheon, who let Angus take on the vacant farm.

Conflict was avoided. It had to be avoided. Everyone was too inter-dependant, too interrelated. Angus and McCutcheon were both brothers-in-law of John Perry. Had Perry leant a helping hand? He may have, for as an elder in First Donaghadee, as his father had been before him, he was a man of considerable local stature and influence. His neighbour Willie McCutcheon was ten years younger, and a promising member of the congregation, who may well have been receptive to any pastoral advice given.

The informal hand of the Kirk may have been at work here. If it were, it should not surprise us. Sixteen of Portavo's twenty-one households were Presbyterian in 1901. Four of these families attended First Donaghadee,[3] supplying the church with no less than two of its eight elders, John Perry and Thomas McBride.[4] Twelve families attended Shore Street, a group that included Lisa Magee, whose mite added four shillings a year to the minister's stipend.

But the circle was widening. And Willie John Boyd helped to widen it. In the 1890s he took on Paddy Fitzsimmons as a flax scutcher. From now on he would simply dress the flax, leaving the sore work of scutching to his son Robert and Paddy. Willie John was a freemason and an Orangeman. Paddy was a Catholic, and as such, a stranger in a strange land. The presence of Paddy Fitzsimmons and his three boys, and Catherine Kelly, a servant of the Schmidts, brought the townland's Catholic population to a mighty five, its highest level in at least a century.[5]

The social mix was changing in other ways too. In 1901 the population included a butcher (John Herron) and a retired train driver (John Campbell). Three heads of households worked in flax. Three were widows. Eleven heads of households were farmers. But just one, sixty-eight year-old James Patton, was a labourer, as was his son James, who like his father worked for Perry.[6]

The Census also hints (but no more than hints) at the important part that women played in the local economy. Four farmers depended entirely on female labour. The townland also contained a dressmaker (Sarah McCutcheon), two embroiderers (Lisa Magee and Agnes Patton), and a seamstress – Willie John Boyd's wife Annabella, who sewed all her life and 'could thread a needle without her glasses at ninety-six'.[7] Annabella was a feisty woman. When she was in her nineties, her grandson asked

The Boyd family, c.1910, (l-r)
Minnie, Willie John, Annabella,
and one of the Lightbody girls.
(Boyd family)

her when women stopped being interested in men. 'You'll have to ask someone older than me, Sidney', came Annabella's coy reply.[8]

As they saluted the new century, if they did, she and Willie John are unlikely to have regretted their move here, eighteen years before. Or even thought about it. Why would they? They were part of the furniture now. Old timers almost, with their own roots and milestones like their son Robert's marriage, the re-thatching of the cottage, the dreadful deaths of their daughter and grand-daughter in the typhoid epidemic of 1898, and the closure of the corn mill, which gave Willie John the melancholy distinction of being Portavo's last miller.[9]

The world around them was changing too. In 1884, an 189,500 candlepower light, one of the most powerful in the United Kingdom, was installed on Mew Island.[10] In 1899 North Down Trams attempted to build a tramline between Bangor and Donaghadee. The farmers were all for it. Johnny Aird said it would be the making of the place. Maxwell of Groomsport supported the plan, as did Sir Daniel Dixon of Balloo House (later the Adelboden), who envisaged a building boom on his land. But Ker said no, because the company wanted to bypass Orlock Hill by running the tramline through the Portavo demesne, and Ker would not have his property despoiled.[11]

A second proposal was brought forward. This time the line would just clip the corner of the demesne.[12] Ker agreed. The trustees agreed. But now Maxwell had second thoughts. Ker tried twice to change his brother-in-law's mind. But Maxwell was adamant, and the new century brought no transport revolution. Maybe it was just as well. The tramway would

have linked Portavo with Bangor and Donaghadee, and through them
Belfast, triggering a building free-for-all. Dozens, maybe hundreds of red
brick Edwardian villas would almost certainly have descended. As it was,
the coast remained pristine. It was a merciful reprieve.

30 Going, going, gone!

Going, going, gone! – the estates are sold.

Richard's second bankruptcy scarcely caused him to break his stride. At fifty he was beyond shame or reform, and on his return to Montalto in 1900 he rumbustiously resumed his old ways. But he did not quite have the freedom of old. New minders were in place around him. Hedging him in now were Wallace's son Robert, as creditors agent, and Edith's brother William Molyneux Rose, who acted on behalf of the trustees.[1]

This quartet, Rose, Wallace, Richard and Edith, all got to know each other so well that they became able to almost intuitively understand one another's thinking and behaviour. Wallace was the youngest of the four. After graduating from Oxford and being called to the Bar, he had set his legal career aside to serve, with distinction, in the Boer War (which he dubbed 'a comedy of errors'[2]), rising to the rank of colonel. He also rose to the top of the Orange Order, becoming Grand President of the Grand Orange Council of the World. He was keenly interested in politics. By the time of the Home Rule crisis Wallace had become a confidante of Craig and Carson, and key figure within Unionism, which used his legal and military skills to the full.[3]

William Rose (whose brother Admiral Harry Rose commanded the royal yacht, and was a friend of the Prince of Wales[4]) was another important new ingredient in the mix. Good humoured, pragmatic, and as wily as Richard, Rose was as committed and resourceful a trustee as the estate would get. He backed Wallace, as opposed to undermining him in the way that Bateson had undermined his father.

This new positive was, however, offset by a new negative – the change that had overcome Edith. In the early years of their marriage Richard had apparently shielded Edith from all knowledge of his clandestine dealings. And ignorance had been bliss. Edith's life had been contented and secure. By 1900, however, this age of innocence was over. Edith had been drawn into the quagmire, and become corrupted and undermined by the impossible situation she found herself in.

Now she was as bad as him. Worse than him. She had almost had to become so. She loved Richard and wanted to share her life with him. And

Robert Hugh Wallace. Wallace's Blimpish appearance belied a jovial and gregarious nature, and a love of poetry and song. (Private collection)

Edith's brother, William Molyneux Rose. Brought an unaccustomed sanity to the estate's proceedings. (Ker family)

Edith's pet cemetery. (Ker family)

this is what sharing one's life with Richard meant. Covering for him, lying for him, unending dissembling, 'Continually trying to go behind [her brother's] back'.[5]

Becoming Richard's accomplice cost Edith dear. Deviousness sat lightly on him, but it turned Edith into a jelly. She fretted, she seethed, she despaired. But she had her consolations. Her Cairn terriers, at least, gave her unconditional affection, and she returned it in the most lavish fashion, clothing them in little outfits when they were alive, and burying them under engraved headstones in a small pet cemetery overlooking the lake at Portavo when they died.

Richard's bankruptcy had made matters worse, for it left Edith – very reluctantly – holding the purse strings. Had she been a stronger person, this might have given her the whip handle. As it was, it just gave her responsibility without power, further aggravating her sense of helplessness and entrapment. She couldn't check his spending. There were ferocious rows. When, in the fury of argument, Richard shot one of her Cairns, Edith's wails 'could be heard in Donaghadee'.[6]

Edith was also given the distasteful job of raising money. Within months of their return she tried to borrow £500 from Fox, the trustees' solicitor, as:

Our expenses have been very heavy & Mr Ker would start everything at once… I unfortunately am paymaster & have to order everything that Mr Ker wishes for & am too weak to refuse him.[7]

Nor could their former income be relied on. In 1901 the 'Fair Rents' of the mid-1880s were under review, and the Land Commissioners were

David Ker followed his father to Sandhurst. The family then purchased him a commission in the 6th Dragoon Guards. (Ker family)

cutting the old rental to pieces. On the Portavo estate, reductions of one quarter to one-third were commonplace, cuts that Edith described as 'a *stunning* blow'.[8] By 1903 the rental had fallen to £9,777, just over half of what the same lands had yielded in 1879.[9] Edith admitted that they were 'now in a very desperate hole.' Richard carried on regardless, 'throwing money about like there was no tomorrow'. He bought more horses. He mustered a new pack of hounds. He ran Montalto like 'a free hotel'.[10] He gave his son David, then serving with the 6th Dragoon Guards in South Africa, an allowance of £500 a year.[11]

Rose despaired: 'The whole thing is *Insanity*', he declared, hardly knowing whether to laugh or cry.[12] The only way to save the Kers, he believed, would be to persuade them to sell Montalto ('A Belfast ship-builder is the man to look for!'), and have them live on a weekly allowance. But Rose had no power to compel, only to advise. And when it came to Richard and Edith, 'advice is always useless and generally *offensive*!'[13]

In 1903, however everything changed. In that year parliament passed Wyndham's Land Act. This was the fourth attempt to encourage tenants to buy out their farms, and to induce landlords to sell them. But it was the first to really work, and it worked because it offered irresistible sweeteners to both sides. Landlords who agreed to sell the whole of the agricultural part of their estates got a 12% bonus. Tenants got a 20% discount on the purchase price and had their legal fees paid. It was almost too good to be true. There was a mad rush to subscribe.

Edith with Cairns, Portavo, c.1920. (Ker family)

It is easy to understand why the Act appealed to landlords. Thirty years of hostile legislation had taken its toll. Their power had been broken, their incomes had been slashed, and their prospects looked bleak. Now the government was offering to buy them out at just under twenty-five times the rental. Richard was wary, believing that some dark plot was afoot. Wallace advised acceptance. Edith agreed:

I quite see this – that if we hold out until a compulsory Bill comes at perhaps 18 years purchase [18 times the rental] or that these tenants go in for a 3rd reduction – we are simply done for…[14]

So in 1905, after Richard had been convinced that he was 'talking rot', Wallace and the tenants' representatives began to parley. Terms were agreed in 1905-07.[15] Similar agreements were reached all over Ireland. The land was passing to the many from the few. It was a great endeavour. A massive social, legal, financial, and even moral undertaking which would take years to bring to fruition. A model of peaceful and far-reaching social change. There was also an element of decolonisation about the transfer. The imperial power, through those seen as its proxies, was pulling out.

Estate-supported local institutions, like the National Schools at the Burren, Magheraknock, and Glassdrummond passed into local management.[16] Estate offices closed. Estate traditions died. The last vestiges of the old estate ethos disappeared, and to the extent that it had been internalised, that equivalent tier of personal identity vanished. The camaraderie and collectivism of the tenanted era had no direct equivalent in the brave new world of owner-occupation. Farmers were individuals now. And most were more than ready to be so.

Across the country, estates liquidated themselves, indeed queued up to be liquidated, for only so much money was made available for estate purchase in any given financial year. There was even some unseemly jostling in the queue as, for example, the Ker estate was urged to get in before the Downshire, which was so huge that by itself it would swallow up half a year's funds.[17]

Who would get the lakes? The shooting and fishing rights? The rights to sand and gravel? What discount would the tenants accept? What would happen to arrears? Could the estate get potential building land excluded from the sale? The negotiations ground on, enlivened occasionally by spats of brinkmanship, as first one side and then the other threatened to pull out. Both sides were constantly looking over their shoulders, ever ready to exploit favourable precedents set elsewhere.

The Downshire estate, which had seven times the value of the remains of the Ker estate, was particularly important in this regard. And when it offered to treat the current year's rent as part of the purchase price the Ker estate was compelled to follow suit, or it would be 'hopeless to expect the sale to go through'.[18] This gaffe led to a closing of landlord ranks. Estates liaised, and came up with a common approach to shared concerns, like the surprisingly vexed question of sporting rights.

In the case of the Ker estate, it was 1911 before all was finally ratified and the last of the money was handed over. The agricultural part of the estate (five-sixths of the total) was sold for £247,000. The Portavo estate, excluding the Copeland Islands,[19] which Ker partly retained, made up £57,400 or just over one fifth of this sum.[20]

The Portavo demesne at the time of the sale. (Brown McConnell Clark)

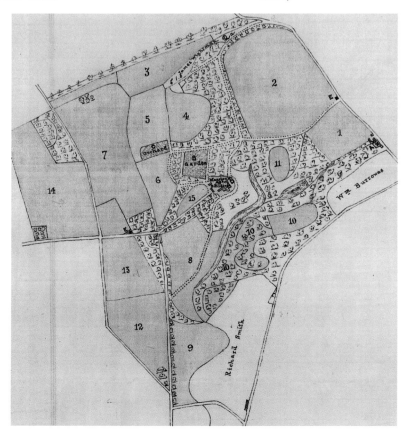

The estate was now awash with money. But the inflow was in the nature of a flash flood. It was no sooner here than it was gone. The purchase money went to the trustees, who used it to pay off debts and buy out family settlements dating back to the 1840s. The rest was invested in a wide variety of stocks and bonds, including Chilean, Egyptian, and Russian Government Bonds, which by October 1917 were looking rather less than the sure thing that they had seemed in 1912.

These funds generated an income of about £4,000 per annum. The non-agricultural rump of the estate[21] brought in another £3,500 annually, which after deductions left the Kers with some £1,800 per year.[22] Or rather, it would have done, were it not for the bonus, the fabled bonus, the landlord's delight. In the case of the Ker estate this amounted to nearly £30,000. And it was almost all Richard's, to spend as he pleased.[23] Never in his life had he had so much to squander. Bit by bit, to Edith's horror, this nigh inexhaustible sum was frittered away:

I am nearly heartbroken to find out what Dick's wild extravagance has come to… He is simply hopeless, he does not want to know what he is spending that is why he has these awful running accounts … he will go thro all his Bonus – What can be done – He at this moment [has] got 14 horses in the stable & 9 others in the fields…[24]

This *cri de coeur* left Wallace torn. He felt real sympathy for Edith. She was on the rack. But on the other hand she was an awful bloody nuisance. Edith had no idea of how to go about things and had a genius for antagonising people.[25] When she was not begging for his help, she was berating him, or complaining to her brother that he was neglecting their affairs. And she would have stabbed him in the back without a

Mind map? Letter from Edith to Wallace, 1912. (PRONI)

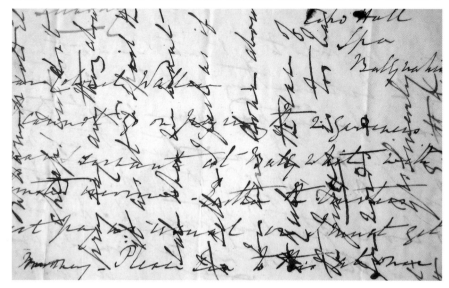

Last lingering look.
Montalto was sold in 1912.
(Brown McConnell Clark)

him feel sick in the pit of his stomach. When it all got too much he would send a distress call to Rose, who would insist that his sister retract her claws, and let the leader of twenty thousand Orangemen 'possess [his] soul in peace'.[27]

Edith had more than money worries. She had man trouble too. Her husband's affair with his cousin Nini had not fizzled out. It had grown to the point where by the early 1900s Nini had become a serious rival. Aware that her marriage had become a little crowded, Edith put her foot down. In 1903, she threatened to leave if the affair did not end. Richard thought she was bluffing. But she was in deadly earnest. And when the lovers did not cool it, Edith carried out her threat and left.[28] Richard's response was perhaps surprising. He did not set up home with Nini. He needed Edie. He wanted her back. By 1905 she had been persuaded to return.

Did Edith get the fresh start that she must have hoped for? We can only guess. She did however secure one concession long wished for, Richard's agreement that they should sell Montalto. This delighted Wallace. Rose too was cock-a-hoop. Even young David was pleased, for the house was patently unaffordable.[29] But it was a humbling and unpalatable act. Another milestone in the dynastic retreat. It was also the family home. Wallace tried to sweeten the pill by pointing out that the family's ancestral seat was Portavo, not Montalto, but this helped little. The significance of the abandonment of Montalto was clear to all.

Edith Ker, from a 1909 newspaper cutting, looking for all the world like the missing third member of Hinge and Bracket. But her complexion is smooth, her features are neat, her expression is determined, and there is not a dowager's jowl in sight.
(Newtownards Chronicle)

Richard Ker c.1905
(Ker family)

Richard's brothers and sisters were galled and saddened by the news of the intended sale, and their views were important, because the consent of each was required for the transaction to go through. Edward's irritation boiled over. He flatly refused to countenance the sale of his 'dear old Home'. But a buyer had been found, and Edward was not going to be allowed to obstruct the sale. The trustees informed him that if he did not reconsider he would be sued to within an inch of his life and bankrupted by the award of costs against him. Uncomfortably aware of how little his veto was worth, Edward backed down.[30]

The path was now clear. The would-be buyer, Ker's friend and neighbour the Earl of Clanwilliam, was keen to get in as soon as possible. His bride had refused to live in the family mansion at Gill Hall on the grounds that it was 'unduly infested with ghosts'.[31] So in 1912, after lengthy legal searches and some last minute haggling, the house and demesne were sold to the earl for £20,000.[32] Amidst what Richard's tricycle-riding sister Flossie called 'a free robbery… of plants & vegetables' from the gardens, Ballynahinch's Ker century came to an end.[33]

Richard and Edith prepared to move to Portavo. There was much to do. The house was 'alive with rats' and in dire need of refurbishment. Rose wanted to see some of the sale money used to give the house an imposing new frontage.[34] Wallace approved:

If Montalto is sold Portavo becomes the Mansion house at least we will endeavour to make it so… It is the old Ker Mansion in the Co. Down & could be made a lovely place. You have glorious timber & judiciously thinned I don't mean by experts, but by those who love the place… you would break out pretty views & alter the whole appearance in 18 months…[35]

They would need somewhere to live in the meantime.[36] Richard wanted to buy a house called Abbots Mount in Ballywhite, near Portaferry. Edith said no and begged Wallace to rid him of:

this folly about buying Ballywhite. That neighbourhood is more than distasteful to me, also it seems the height of unreasonableness to burden ourselves with 2 places again after having by wonderful luck got rid of this [Montalto]…[37]

But Richard prevailed, and off they went, down the Ards peninsula to a damp, leaky house in what to Edith seemed the back of beyond. What could have induced them to live here?[38] The only possible answer is Nini. Ballywhite is less than four miles from Quentin Castle, which Nini had inherited in 1902. There is much here to marvel at. How could Richard have had the temerity to move them to his mistress's doorstep? How could Edith agree? Her sense of self-worth must by this stage have been virtually non-existent.

Richard and Nini's relationship flourished during his four or more years at Ballywhite. It had never quite ended. Edith's return had stalled things, but when the pressure eased, the relationship resumed and in time Edith came to know of its resumption. She was 'absolutely mortified' but did not leave again.[39] She could not. Her courage had gone. She had not

Quentin Castle, which Rose Ker left to Nini in 1902. (Elizabeth O'Hara)

The coffin recess from the 'black magic room' at Quentin Castle. (Elizabeth O'Hara)

become reconciled to sharing her husband, she simply lived with it, uneasily.

Nini was stiff competition. Not only was she younger than Edith and very good-looking, she was unconventional and independent, a romantic free spirit whose Italian upbringing had given her a sophistication that Edith could never hope to equal. She may also have been drawn to spiritualism, then very much in vogue. Quentin Castle's infamous 'black-magic' room, which has a coffin recess in the ceiling and the zodiac painted on the floor, could well be Rose or Nini's creation.[40]

Richard doted on Nini. Her pet name for him was 'Bravo'. Their nickname for Edith was 'Martello Towers', an unflattering reference to her more than ample legs, based on information faithlessly supplied by Richard, who was now apparently repulsed by her physical form. (Her opinion of Richard's fast deteriorating physique has not survived.) Edith was a figure of fun to the lovers. And they could be scathing. As Nini wrote to Theresa, Lady Londonderry:

He [Richard]... Does nothing but think of the Princesses [Herself and Lady Londonderry] day and night... the Princesses are like beautiful lilies resting on a moonlit pond compared to the beefy Martello Towers he is overcrowded with and loathes – [he] can only breathe, and write, because Martello Towers had waddled off to church.[41]

But they did not spend their days maligning Edith. They had something very precious of their own. As Nini told Lady Londonderry in 1914:

You who are versed in Love lore Do you know why I love my Bravo more at this moment of my life than ever before? We are both getting old, and I have always read, and heard, that lovers are less loving and loved – in middle age. It is the reverse with me, and when I show him that I love him, which I have never done much (not because I did not dearly love him, but from a share of "Stewart aloofness") his innocent joy is so great that it never ceases to amaze me...[42]

As her husband and his cousin discovered new intimacies, Edith lunched. Anything to get out of the house, which was 'poisoned' by gas leaks and became 'a dripping well' in winter. Edith attributed this to the use of sea sand in the mortar, a fact she asked Wallace to keep under his hat, 'as it w^d spoil [things] when we want to sell'.[43]

Down here she was a big fish in a small pool. Everyone wanted to make her acquaintance. Edith had never been so much in demand, and she loved it. 'I have too many luncheons & Teas!' she confessed to Wallace, basking in the unaccustomed attention. The barrage of tray bakes did nothing for her hippopotamine proportions. But it was the price of popularity. It simply had to be paid.[44] And they would not be here for ever. By 1916-17, amid fears that the old place was being seriously mismanaged, the talk was of a return to Portavo.

31 Guns & freedom 1900–1914

Smiths and smugglers

The collapse of the Bangor-Donaghadee tramway project put the townland's future on hold. No horde of suburbanites descended. The clink of cocktail glasses rang unheard. Portavo remained obstinately rural. In some ways this was a relief, for the place needed rural regeneration, not a suburban overlay. In other ways, it was unfortunate, for new life was desperately needed. In 1901, after fifty years of steady decline, Portavo was inhabited by just seventy-seven people, its lowest population count since records began.[1]

This fall – which was replicated across rural Ireland – took the wind out of the townland's sails. As the population aged and dwindled, many small businesses closed. A lighter and more widely dispersed infrastructure formed. Portavo lost its corn mill, and when John Small hung up his bellows, it lost its part-time smith. This was a shock to the system. As a manorial townland, Portavo had historically been a provider of services. Now it depended on other places to supply its basic needs.

John McCready of Kinnaird's Crossroads on the High Bangor Road, a man with a terrible temper, became the townland's nearest smith. He

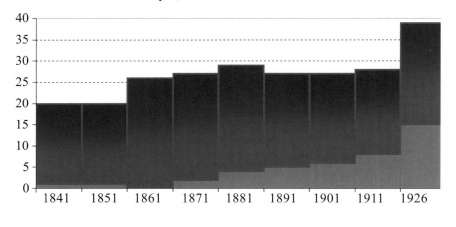

As the demographics soured, the housing stock became increasingly under-utilised. Portavo: inhabited and uninhabited houses, 1841-1926.

Animal husbandry was the thing now. Everybody had livestock. Inquisitive heifer in what were once John Perry's fields.

'kept the place goin', and it didn't do to fall out with him, for the next smithy was miles away on the Gransha Road.[2] Older and creakier now, Willie John Boyd still ran the flax mill, but his days of employing others had gone. His son Robert worked as a breadman, and dear knows what had become of Paddy Fitzsimmons and his boys. The old team was no more.[3]

Animal husbandry was the thing now. Everyone had livestock.[4] In 1901 the Perrys and the Anguses raised sturdy beef cattle. Most of the other farms had small dairy herds, or a mixture of beef and dairy cattle. Annabella Boyd had a couple of cows and her own fresh milk and butter.

By 1911 the orientation had changed again. The emphasis was on beef, and just three farms were dairying.[5] You had to be flexible. Follow the market. Most of the farms had geese, hens and a rooster or two, and most people's days began around dawn, with the rooster's endless squalling. It was a long day, and you could be up at all hours. At midnight with a calving cow. At two a.m. to take the new potatoes into Belfast, a four hour journey, stopping for breakfast at a bar in Holywood on the way.

Pigs were another staple.[6] In 1901, fourteen of Portavo's twenty-one households had piggeries. Not everyone's pigs, however, were treated as royally as Johnny Aird's. When a holidaying neighbour left his pony with Johnny for safe keeping, he came back to find that Johnny had shot and boiled it and fed it to his sows.[7] Maybe there was a reason. Maybe it got injured and had to be put down. But then maybe there wasn't. You never quite knew with Johnny Aird.[8]

Not Sir Roger Casement. Johnny Aird, cutting a fine figure on the Copeland Island, c.1900. The former lighthouse is faintly visible in the background. (Anderson family)

He wheeled and dealed round the country, and what he wasn't in, wasn't worth getting into. His name is also linked with smuggling, and large quantities of contraband were reputedly landed on his farm. These landings were conducted with military precision. At night, the boats lay offshore until Johnny's neighbour Billy McCartney put a light in his rear window. This signalled that the coast was clear, and allowed the job of landing or exhuming the goods to begin. An obliging 'ghost', a man in a white sheet, was ready by the road in case a stranger passed. There was no need to worry about the locals. Seasiders like the Boyds and Johnny's niece, Minnie Burroughs, all knew to look the other way.[9]

Off-limits to smugglers? Lisa Magee's cottage & bay from an old postcard. (James Harding Watson)

These manoeuvres took place under the very noses of the coastguard. I ask Aird Lowry why no-one was arrested. My naivety would seem to be endearing. He allows himself a wry smile, 'The coastguards were in on it', he replies. He savours the impact his revelation is having, then goes on to explain that George Batten, the Head Coastguard at Orlock, had 'gone native' and married Johnny's sister, Aird Lowry's great aunt, a union that did much to open the local seas to smuggling. Indeed, made them all the safer for being thought to be intensively policed.

Sometimes the smugglers used Sandy Bay and Lisa Magee's little harbour.[10] But they did so unwillingly, for Lisa could be unpredictable and she strongly disapproved. So much so that when a coal boat ran aground one night, she chased its luckless crew from her door, telling them to 'Take yer oul' boat away er' that. There's nobody allowed in here but Sammy Murdock'.[11] In the end, the coal was thrown off so the boat could be re-floated. This opportunity was too good to pass over: 'the neighbours helped themselves'.[12]

Hanging by a thread: the Copelands
Legitimate traffic to the Copeland Islands also sailed from Lisa Magee's bay. Island cattle were landed here. Minnie Burroughs sent out cows. Johnny Aird sent pigs, seed, and his bull.[1] There was a small, steady trade. But how long could it last? According to some experts, the islanders were already living on borrowed time. The battle between centrifugal and centripetal forces had been lost. Its small community should have been collapsing, like island communities all round Ireland.

But the demographic imperative had been roundly defied. Against all the odds, the island was thriving. It had shrugged off the half-tenanted uncertainty of the mid-1890s.[2] In 1901 its five farms were lived in, and lived in to bursting. (David Clegg's three-roomed croft held fifteen.) The land was worked. Its cottages were pristine, its gardens well tended.[3]

Officialdom had embraced it. The Royal Mail cemented a shiny red

Poste restante. *The Copeland Island postbox. (Reid family)*

Nineteenth century view of Lighthouse Island from Orlock. (Ker family)

post box into a stone mount near Chapel Bay, wishfully inscribing it, 'Next collection 3.00, weather permitting.' Its arrival caused amusement and much quiet satisfaction. This was a vote of confidence from on high in the future of the island community, a lipstick kiss which the island wore with a flush of irrational pride.

The island had a youthful population. In 1901, 29 of its 41 inhabitants were under thirty. It had a schoolhouse and a young schoolmaster, who lived with the Cleggs, seven of whom were his pupils. Their young lives were far from carefree. On these hard shores, work was esteemed above learning, and play came in a poor third. As young James Clegg recalled ruefully:

Boyhood fun was not for me or any of the youngsters on the island as it is a very hard life... I remember ploughing when less than 12 years of age, starting at 8.30 a.m. and ending at 6.30 p.m.[4]

On summer evenings the islanders caught blocken and lythe, which were cured with salt and dried in the sun, then roasted and eaten with butter in winter. They trapped several thousand rabbits annually, and sold them on the mainland. They grew their own grain, baked their own bread, churned their own butter and cured their own bacon. Growing grain on an island that teemed with rabbits might seem at the very least foolhardy. But the islanders prided themselves on building 'the best fences in the county', and these – mostly – kept the bunnies at bay.[5]

This activity was lit not by the brilliance of noon, but by the glow of an almost radiant sunset. By 1911, two of the island's five farmsteads had fallen vacant. There were just twenty-five people left.[6] But there were grounds for hope. Half of this number were in their twenties or early

An island funeral.
(Reid family)

thirties. Between 1911 and 1926, however, just one new household formed and the population fell to a worrisome nineteen.[7] Meanwhile, the steady flight continued.[8] One islander left to become a teacher, another became 'a Coldstream Guard', a third went into service in Ballyholme, but came back because she was 'too lonely'.[9] Those that stayed put, stayed single. The breeding stock was there, but it did not pair and mate.

This was odd in a people, if we may describe the islanders as such, whose survival instincts were otherwise so well honed. Could the islanders' legendary self-sufficiency in some sense have been their undoing? We can only guess. As the years passed, the pulse beat more weakly. It became increasingly difficult to cope. But the islanders were resilient. When young James Clegg's uncle died, for instance:

owing to the very bad weather the minister could not get across to perform the burial ceremony, and we had… to perform the rather gruesome task ourselves. Luckily we were able, after some searching, to discover a Bible, and after much perusing, we were able to complete the ceremony with all due respect to my uncle.[10]

The bible had to be searched for. The correct text stumbled upon. The islanders had lost their religiosity. To those of us weaned on stories of pious islanders sailing to Donaghadee for church on a Sunday, it comes as a bit of a shock to learn how occasional these trips were. And to learn that souls were polished up not on a weekly but on an annual basis:

by a clergyman who used to come over once a year, and sometimes not at all. We held a service which was usually very well attended by us all... The minister would never come over at his own expense... we had to bring him across in our boats.[11]

The island lay on the rim of the church, which gives an interesting twist to the joke about the missionary who went out to save the islanders: 'All they found was the heels of his boots'. The story about the visiting minister who asked: 'Are there any Christians on this island?' to be told, 'No, only Cleggs and Emersons', is another gem, in the same vein, from the same period.[12] The islanders had come to be seen as a people apart.[13]

Which was fine, as far as Peter Halpin was concerned. Maybe even a plus point. Halpin was a Belfast auctioneer, and in 1909 he took a farm on the Copelands which he allowed to go to rack and ruin, a circumstance which mortally affronted the frugal islanders, who had an inbred horror of waste.

Halpin was not interested in farming. Or weekending. Or the islanders' ethos. He was interested in bringing over day-trippers and the more the better. He turned his cottage into a 'Refreshment House', and let the trippers roam over the farm. The problem was that the trippers went everywhere, and during the summer, 'hundreds' of high-spirited factory workers from Belfast arrived daily, 'causing great annoyance and damage'.[14]

The shy and introspective islanders, like the Amish, found themselves the abashed objects of a puerile and gawping attention. They had become exhibits in a human zoo. Overwhelmed, they turned to the estate for help. They got a sympathetic hearing. Wallace threatened the Donaghadee boatmen with proceedings for trespass. Two carriers promptly backed out. Only Halpin's partner, Bunting, the owner of the *Seagull*, sailed on. So the estate threw the book at them. This was too much even for Halpin. Peace was restored.[15]

The farmers lose their awe

By the war's eve, the Copeland Island was just about the only agricultural part of the estate not to have attained its 'freedom'.[1] Portavo's tenant farmers had become owner-occupiers seven or eight years before, after protracted negotiations in which the estate had sought to deal with tenants individually, in the hope that some would strike disadvantageous pathfinder deals, which would bring 'the rest... to their senses'.[2] But its attempt to divide and rule failed. It was not dealing with greenhorns. The fair rent hearings had familiarised the tenantry with quasi-legal processes, and shown them that they could take on the estate and win.

In 1903 the farmers 'had their tails up'. In the 1897-1902 round of judicial rent reviews the estate had been routed and the rental decimated. John Perry had won a 31% rent cut, Hugh Angus 25%, and Tom McBride

34%.[3] These were stunning successes. Tenant self-confidence surged to the extent that in 1901 'wee Willie Angus', Perry and McBride appealed their reductions. They were champing at the bit. They wanted more. Angus got 2% more, but Perry and McBride got bloody noses – rent increases and a nasty bill for costs.[4]

The farmers had lost their awe. And in December 1903, when the estate offered to sell them their farms at 26¼ years purchase, the offer was unanimously rejected by the tenant body, speaking through a legally represented Association that formed its policy at public meetings.[5] The Portavo tenantry wanted 24 years purchase.[6] Extreme sensitivity also attached to anything that bore on the 'sovereignty' of the would-be independent farms. Shooting rights were a particular bone of contention. Farmers were not buying out their land so that strangers could shoot all over it on their former landlord's say-so. Strictly limited access was agreed.

A settlement was reached in 1907, and its terms, 24⅔ times the rental (less the 20% provided for in the Act), show how tough the negotiations were and what competent negotiators the tenants' representatives proved to be. Portavo's farmers became freeholders. Three hundred years of landlordism came to an end.

The big house in its park now stood naked in the landscape, stripped of the hinterland that had formerly sustained it. What place had such houses in a democratised countryside? Some flourished, enjoying a wonderful Indian summer. On the back of the biggest liquidation of assets in Irish history, their owners had money aplenty, more money than most of these houses had seen since the day of their foundation. Roofs were repaired, rooms refitted, electric light and even heating were installed during this period of what Bence-Jones has called 'false prosperity'.[7]

Portavo House missed out on this boom. In 1906 it was let to Sir Robert McConnell, a former Lord Mayor of Belfast who had made his fortune building streets of kitchen houses along the Falls and Shankill Roads, and constructing 'some of the prettiest villas that have been erected since Noah left the Ark' in the suburbs of Cliftonville, Knock and Malone.[8] McConnell was equally well known as the plaintiff in a sensational divorce case, taken after his young second wife was discovered *in flagrante*. In 1911 the house was occupied by a prosperous linen manufacturer, Thomas Somerset, and his family.[9]

Somerset and McConnell did not live here as country gentlemen. They lived amongst fields full of other peoples' animals, and woods that were akin to a glorified stage set. Portavo had ceased to be an entity. It had been let in pieces to half a dozen people, and all functional coherence had disappeared. It was as if killing landlordism had not been enough. It was as though its physical form had also had to be dismembered, to ensure that it would not return, Frankenstein-like, from the grave.

In 1906, Sir Robert McConnell, one of Belfast's biggest house builders, came to live at Portavo. (Belfast Education & Library Board)

The Perry farmhouse, from an old photograph held by the Boyds. (Boyd family)

But landlordism would not be coming back. The world had moved on. However it took a while for some landlords to appreciate this, as the following small incidents make clear. One occurred when, without a by-your-leave, Lady Dufferin and her friends blocked Johnny Aird's narrow yard with their cars in the course of an excursion. Aird filled the cars with clocking hens, which did their business all over Lady Dufferin's upholstery.[10]

On another never-to-be-forgotten occasion Hugh Andrews took a pitchfork to Sir Daniel Dixon (another former Lord Mayor of Belfast) when the latter shot on his land without permission, a red-letter day indeed! He also lit on Perceval-Maxwell of Groomsport after a row about sheep, prophesying darkly that the day would come when 'the grass will grow around the landlords' doors'.[11]

Such liberties would have been unimaginable a few short years before. Times were changing. Even one's club was no longer a sanctuary. Ker entered the Ulster Club one day to find it full of linen barons and factory owners. 'Open the windows, I smell flax', he wheezed, asserting the pre-eminence of old money, and forgetting his own roots at the same time.[12]

Ker himself was confronted at the hunt by 'ould Robbie Baxter' from the Six Road Ends, who had sold him corn two years previously and had never been paid. Ker fended him off.[13] But it was embarrassing. And symptomatic, not only of the boldness of the emancipated tenantry, but of the diminished standing of the Kers. Gone were the days when their name was synonymous with Mediterranean culture, limitless wealth and

David Ker (standing, third from right) with the officers of the 6th Dragoon Guards, the Carabineers, 1903, 'the grandest regiment that could have been afforded at the time'. (Gloria Siggins)

enlightened landlordism. Now, thanks largely to Richard, the Kers were seen as a hopeless lost cause.

Wallace pinned his hopes on David. David could restore the family's reputation if he were not corrupted by his parents' devious ways. Rose feared that he may already have become tainted, but hoped not. It was bad enough dealing with the devious duo. 'If we have to deal with a conspiracy of three… we are in for a pretty time of it.'[14]

They were right to be concerned. David was stagnating. He had served in the cavalry during the South African War, spending much of his time rounding up Boers for delivery to Kitchener's new 'concentration camps'.[15] On the war's end he had been transferred to India. But he had been dogged by health problems, and in 1904, anaemic, rheumatic and afflicted with gonorrhoea and thread worms, the twenty-five year old was pronounced unfit for service and sent home.[16] He put in his papers shortly afterwards, his hoped-for military career in tatters. This took a bit of getting over. A new role or challenge might have helped, but none emerged and David fell into the limbo of the uncalled heir.[17]

This took its toll. David had always been 'quite reliable in a steady sort of way.'[18] But under-utilised, he began to go stale. He cultivated a taste for the bloodier 'field sports'. Cock fighting and hare coursing became his *metier*.[19] Then came the 'Affaire David', in which he lost money dealing in horses. Rose got Wallace to bail him out, lest he be driven into 'the hands of Jews' and a life like his father's.[20] The incident pulled Rose and Wallace up short. It seemed so out of character. David was sensible and trustworthy. Wasn't he?

They would soon find out. In 1911, urged on by Lord Londonderry, Richard decided to make a few pounds by felling trees in the Montalto demesne. It would soon be gone, so what the hell. As the trees were not his, he proceeded in his most clandestine manner, getting David to identify the seven hundred that were to be cut so lightly that they seemed to have been 'scratched only as if with [a] stray pin'. But he was not discreet enough. Richard's sister Flossie rumbled him, and wrote to Rose, who insisted that the intended felling stop forthwith. Edith denied everything. Rose was undeterred. Richard must be stopped:

or he… will put his tongue in his cheek & perhaps plan something else trusting to succeeding again… This wd be simply fatal. Remember Dick is a very clever man in spite of his recklessness & he is absolutely lawless![21]

Rose knew his man. Ker was completely unabashed, and within a few months was at it again. This time the target was Portavo. Again David did the marking. Nine hundred trees were to go. But this time Richard encountered a timber merchant who was as devious as he was. The 'bad scraggy storm tossed trees' that David had marked for destruction were ignored. This merchant wanted the cream of the crop. Now it was the Kers turn to raise howls of protest.[22]

The trustees intervened and the woods were saved. But David's reputation took a beating as he had conducted the illicit negotiation.[23] Wallace was crestfallen. He should have known better than to get his hopes up. As he confessed to a friend, 'These Kers are quite too fond of doing things behind back & Mr David is only carrying on the family tradition.'[24]

The imbroglio was symptomatic of a wider neglect. Portavo was going to the dogs. Poachers tramped the woods at night. Farmers' carts had rutted the avenue. 'Umteen loads of gravel' had been drawn illegally from the shore.[26] Edith blamed their agent, William Wellwood, asking Wallace somewhat rhetorically if he thought 'that poor old Wellwood is fit at his age <u>89</u> to cope with such strenuous work'?[27]

When Richard complained that 'Everything is going wrong at Portavo',[25] Wallace took a stand. (Brown McConnell Clark)

NOTICE.

ANY PERSON OR PERSONS FOUND TAKING AWAY SAND OR GRAVEL FROM PORTAVO FORESHORE WITHOUT FIRST OBTAINING PERMISSION FROM THE KER ESTATE OFFICE, 45 VICTORIA STREET, BELFAST, WILL BE PROSECUTED ACCORDING TO LAW.

J. Nicholson, Printer, 26 Church Lane.

Robert H. Wallace,
(Agent of the Ker Estate),

Robert Wallace, stick in hand, cigarette in mouth, deep in conversation with Carson. (Private collection)

Portavo needed taken in hand, so David was sent down to put the place in order. With him came loyal retainers like the Gillespies, the Lillys, the Watsons and the Bells, who had been displaced by the sale of Montalto. Like the *Grande Armée* retreating from Moscow, this faithful Old Guard followed the estate as it shrank back to its point of origin. If anyone could lick the place into shape, they could. All that was needed now was leadership.

'We live in Wonderful Times': the Home Rule crisis

Before an Empire's eyes,
The traitor claims his price.
What need of further lies?
We are the sacrifice.[1]

In 1912 to shouts of 'Traitor!' and 'Resign!' Asquith attempted to push the third Home Rule Bill through the House of Commons. Reactions in Ireland were equally intense. Nationalists broadly welcomed the Bill, seeing it as offering a long overdue measure of national self-determination. Unionists feared it, anticipating subjugation within a narrowly Catholic and Gaelic state.

Wallace found himself in the eye of the storm. He was in the forefront of Unionist resistance to Home Rule, and deeply involved in the political and military planning that anticipated the state of Northern Ireland. He sat

Carson raises the sacred standard aloft, October 1912. Wallace is on his right, wielding a Union Jack. This scene is depicted on the base of Carson's statue at Stormont. (The Graphic)

Unionist propaganda postcard depicting Carson, Craig & Wallace, c. 1912.

on the commission of five which prepared a constitution for the Provisional Government of Ulster. He sat on the secret committee of the Ulster Unionist Council which masterminded the importation of arms, secretly testing illegally imported rifles with Fred Crawford. In January 1912 he obtained authority for Orangemen to drill using guns, a legal breakthrough which paved the way for the formation of the Ulster Volunteer Force.[2]

In September 1912, at a tumultuous rally in Belfast on the eve of 'Ulster Day', it fell to Wallace to present Sir Edward Carson with a frail, silk banner that had allegedly been carried before King William at the Battle of the Boyne.[3] Thrusting the timeworn standard aloft, Carson identified their cause with the Glorious Revolution, claiming that its ideals of civil and religious liberty were their objectives too. It was a thrilling, almost ecstatic moment, a moment to send shivers down the spine. The struggle had been consecrated, the ancestral ghosts invoked, the reckless adventure blessed.

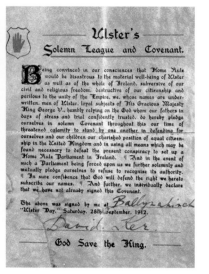

David Ker's copy of the Ulster Covenant. (Ker family)

On the following day, in an attempt to exercise some control over their political destiny, tens of thousands signed the Solemn League and Covenant and the associated Women's Declaration. Seventeen from Portavo signed, one in five of the population. Most did so in Donaghadee, but Jane McKeag and Maggie Moderate signed in the Woburn Hall in Carrowdore. Lizzie Bell and Nellie Angus went in together. Sarah Campbell got a lift in with the Agnews of Ballyfotherly. Margaret Small's husband, John Muckle, went in with Wee Willie Angus. Robert Boyd went in with John Perry, and when his eighth son was born a week later, named him Edward Carson Boyd, in the great man's honour.[4]

'Political matters is looking very serious. We live in Wonderful Times', Richard exclaimed to Wallace in March 1914.[5] His remarks were prescient. In April 1914, as Unionism moved towards armed rebellion, guns were landed at Donaghadee. David Ker almost missed the landing. He had intended to go to the Grand National, but his neighbour Delacherois tipped him off and he stayed at home.[6] James Craig, an

Landing the guns at Donaghadee. (PRONI)

erstwhile Ker tenant and one of the architects of the importation, was in charge of the landing at Donaghadee.[7] Was he the right man for the job? Nini had her doubts. Craig had just given up alcohol, and was reportedly struggling with serious withdrawal problems. Nini kept Lady Londonderry *au fait*:

It is said that James Craig is "not himself", they think on the verge of a breakdown. His knocking off the drink has been too much for him, report is – that he paces his room all night – in a state of agitation, and everyone notices how changed he is...[8]

But Craig passed muster. Whatever demons allegedly assailed him, the picture he presented to the world on that nerve-jangling night was of capable and unflappable calm. And while the chief coastguard, Lieutenant Ducat, slept off the after-effects of a Delacherois bridge party (officialdom was well entertained that night) the *Innismurray* discharged some 6,000 Vetterli and Mauser rifles and an unknown quantity of ammunition at the quay. This was whisked off to bolt holes 'all over the country', including Portavo, where rifles are said to have been stashed in the tunnels.[9]

This arsenal was never used in anger, as over the next few months the volunteers did not get beyond playing at being soldiers. In August 1914, however, all that changed.

Wallace by William Conor. Conor painted the colonel four times. All four pictures are practically identical. (Private collection)

32   'Past talking about': World War One

In 1914 the Muckles celebrated the birth of their eighth child, a daughter, who they named Willamina in honour of John Muckle's kindly German employer Richard Schmidt.[1] It was one of the few pieces of détente going that year. In August 1914 Britain and Germany went to war.

The war threw the local economy into overdrive. Huge quantities of crops and vegetables were grown. Grassland and gardens were planted or ploughed. No-one could remember the land being so intensively tilled.[2] Thousands of trees in the demesne were felled to meet the endless demand for timber.[3] Flax too came into its own, and Willie John Boyd's little scutch mill was busy the war long making linen 'for Zeppelins', tents, rucksacks, uniforms and after 1916, aircraft fuselages.[4]

The bloody object of all this activity, however, could not be forgotten. This was a vast conflict. It filled the papers, and consumed the thoughts of all whose loved ones had enlisted. The pressure to join up was intense. Florence Mary Wilson did her bit with her poem, *The Portavo Poachers*, in which two leery Ulster-Scotsmen, Big Andy Logan and the narrator, habitual poachers in the woods of Portavo, are shamed into enlisting by an underage boy from Athy, i.e. *a southern fenian*. It was provocative stuff, which made its point by turning the perception that southern Catholics were shiftless and disloyal, and northern Presbyterians patriotic, on its head:

> Big Andy Logan looked at me, an' I couldn't meet his eye
> But he stood up bold fornent me, gripped his gun as sojers do;
> Sed he: "I've larnt my lesson off this wee lad from Athy,
> So, if Kitchener bes willin' here is me," said he, "here's you."[5]

Four men from Portavo joined up – one in four of the eligible male population, providing powerful witness, at townland level, of the mass enlistment of the folklore. But the extent of the recruitment should not be exaggerated. Just three of the townland's twenty households had someone in the services.[6] And none of its nine farming families sent anyone to war. The rural middle class held back. What was a war in Europe? Or an interplanetary collision, for that matter. The farm came first. Here

1915 Irish recruiting poster. (Trinity College collection)

at least, it was the cottages and the big house that sent their sons.[7]

Two of the four joined the army, and in keeping with the townland's maritime tradition, two served in the navy. Willie Boyd, old Willie John's sixteen year old grandson, who had signed the Covenant at the age of fourteen, served with the 13th Battalion of the Royal Irish Rifles, a unit of the 36th (Ulster) Division, and was wounded on the first day of the Battle of the Somme, during the assault on Grandcourt, to the north of the

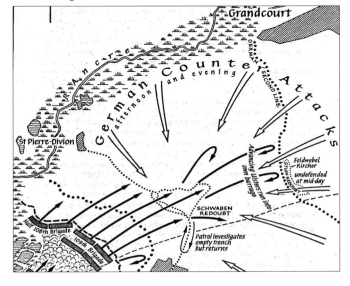

The first day of the Somme. Boyd's Battalion was part of the 108th Brigade. Its men 'were shot down like dogs'[9] by intense machine gun fire from St.Pierre Divion. 578 of the Battalion's 800 men were killed or wounded in the attack.

Charge of the 36th (Ulster) Division on the first day of the Battle of the Somme, by James Prinsep Beadle. (Belfast City Council)

Schwaben Redoubt. (He got a bullet through the ear, and wore a piece of cotton wool in the hole for the rest of his life.) His elder brother Tommy became a gunner on the super-dreadnought battleship *HMS Valiant*, one of the finest ships in the Grand Fleet, and fought at the Battle of Jutland. So did his Uncle Sammy, a seaman on the *Valiant's* sister ship, the *Warspite*.[8]

The *Warspite* was in the thick of the fighting, which Tommy Boyd described as 'very rough'.[10] After a tetchy encounter with Hipper's battlecruisers, the *Warspite* helped to repel a German torpedo-boat attack, then saw action again in the late afternoon scoring several hits on the battleship *Konig*, which made her glow 'like a burning haystack'.[11] At just after six in the evening, however, its luck ran out. Its helm locked, causing it to circle helplessly under the guns of the advancing High Seas

The cruiser Warrior *(l) and the battleship* Warspite *are pounded by the guns of the German High Seas Fleet. (Ewart Oakeshott).*

Fleet. The lashing it received was so merciless that, as one crewman recalled, 'Everybody thought we had gone… and ceased firing.'[12] The *Warspite* limped to safety. But her troubles were not over. No sooner had she returned to the main body of the fleet than her helm jammed again, sending the stricken ship careering off on a second death ride.

Again, the seas around her erupted. A second blizzard of shells rained down. Deep in the bowels of the ship, Sammy Boyd must have wondered if his time had come. He would have stood no chance if the *Warspite* had gone under. But the *Warspite* was one of the finest fighting ships of her day. She survived everything the enemy could throw at her and when her steering gear re-engaged (thanks, it is thought, to the impact of a German shell), she once more managed to steam out of trouble. Incapable of further action, the wounded battleship was ordered to return to Rosyth. On the way it was twice attacked by U-boats, but again, quite astonishingly, it survived.

Grainy photograph of the British Grand Fleet at seat, guns trained and ready.

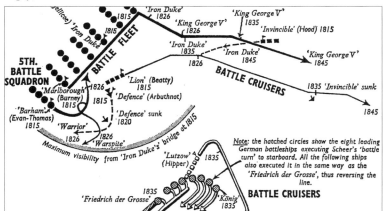

Jutland 6.30pm, showing the positions of the British Grand Fleet (black) and German High Seas Fleet (hatched) at the time of the Warspite's potentially suicidal turn.

David Ker at the head of his squadron of the North Irish Horse, 1914. (Ker family)

The fourth of our volunteers, David Ker, served as a captain in the North Irish Horse, part of the First Army Corps of the British Expeditionary Force. He embarked for France on August 17th 1914, accompanied by two grooms from Ballynahinch.[13] September 1914 found Ker just behind the front line in Flanders. He was thrilled to be there, feeling that it was 'a grand thing to see a bit of active service'.[14]

The relatives mobilised too, sending him socks, mittens, mufflers, food parcels, and more letters than he could keep up with. Richard sent copies of the *Field*.[15] Edith sent jerseys, buckskin boots and 'aunt nelly mufflers'. Out too went cheese, biscuits, ginger cake, chocolate, blackcurrant and damson jam (his favourite), false teeth with which to eat these delicacies and toilet roll to deal with the end product. (Every stage of the digestive process was catered for.) Mysterious hampers arrived from Jacksons of Picadilly, benefactor unknown. Within no time David had accumulated enough food to withstand 'a month's siege'.[16] He gave most of it to his men, particularly after his unit was attached to the General Headquarters (GHQ) of the British Expeditionary Force, where he noted with some distaste that HQ staff lived off 'the fat of the land'.[17]

David found himself at the nerve centre of British operations, rubbing shoulders with generals like Allenby, French and Haig. To many, this would have been a dream posting, an intoxicating dalliance with power. But not David. He was a doer not a planner, a man of action who could inspire those under him, an almost swashbuckling figure with a rebellious streak which the army never quite harnessed and which regularly got him into trouble. There was more than a touch of the Blair Mayne about his character, and charismatic presence. Standing 6'4" tall, Ker was a good shot and a fine horseman. He had movie star looks, dash and verve in abundance, despised silly bravado and was totally fearless.

In time he would be mentioned in despatches, and receive a Belgian 'Criox de Guerre' for his role in the conflict.[18] But his initial placement proved impossibly frustrating. At headquarters we do nothing but groom horses and polish buttons, he lamented, chafing to do 'some little good in furthering the end of this desperate War'.[19] Within days his prayers were answered. The First Army Corps engaged the Germans at the First Battle of Ypres. The fighting was 'desperate... the slaughter... awful'. David wrote that First Corps bore 'the brunt of all the big fighting', and were pitted against the crack Prussian Guards:

Kaiser Bill said they must break through at all costs 12000 attacked & they did drive us back but did not break through... we have stuck it out wonderfully[20]

The Germans were fought to a standstill, but at an appalling price. As David had previously confessed to his mother:

the whole business is past talking about the number of good kind friends gone & many left the most repulsive sights imaginable from dreadful shell wounds hardly any face left...[21]

His words read like an epitaph to a bloody conflict. It is sobering to think that they were written when the war was not yet three months old, and Passchendaele, Verdun and the Somme had yet to come. David feared for the future. The allies were not making the most of the good autumn weather, and as he observed prophetically, 'when the bad weather comes & the armies dig themselves in trenches, it seems to me neither party can... dislodge one another any how'.[22]

But David had more than 'sausages' (Germans) on his mind. He was also in love. In 1913 he had become engaged to the beautiful Anna Pollock of Mountainstown, Navan, County Meath. She and David were temperamentally well suited, and David's willingness to make sacrifices (which he hid from Anna, as she would 'feel it frightfully') in order to afford marriage gratified the trustees. This was the David of old. Wallace's confidence in Ker made a comeback.

Not everyone was thrilled, however. Dynastic marriages were also mergers, and the Pollocks had little to merge. 'She brings nothing', sighed Edith, with terrible resignation.[23] Nini was also thoroughly nonplussed:

David brought his fiancé to see me last time he was on leave, sorry to say I didn't think much of her, quite uninteresting. Dick does not care for her and we are in hopes it may be broken off, they [Anna's mother and the Pollock trustees] have been behaving in an arduous way about Settlements! I don't think the girl (who has no money, looks, or family – cares for him, she is willing to marry him, if he really is going to be as well off as is said but not otherwise. I am sure they have heard tales of Bravo having gone through everything and they want to make sure

*'There was a wee fellow called Dave,
who did the fair Anna enslave,
The boys said 'Begorrah!'
We'll see you tomorrow,
And call you no fool but a knave.'*

Anna Ker, nee Pollock. (Ker family)

the dollars are really there. I sincerely hope their greed will be the undoing of them...[24]

But Richard and Edith were won over, and in February 1915, with his parents' blessing, David travelled to Mountainstown to propose:

Dearest Ma, I have been & gone & done & this time properly so hope you will be pleased. She is just the sweetest little "Colleen" in the world to me & I do love her better than anything... she realy is in love with me too, so if we both are spared every thing should be alright...[25]

In December 1915 the star-crossed couple were married. Anna got what she had dreaded – a war wedding, with young widowhood the spectre at the feast.[27] Then it was back to the front. To a war that, in David's case becomes a bit of a blur. We know that in November 1915 he was promoted to the rank of major, ending the war as Horse Master to the 17th Corps, but very little else.[28] No further letters have survived, just some reminiscence, which in the way of so much First World War reminiscence, avoids with iron reticence all reference to fighting and what that fighting may have entailed.[29] A terrible silence hangs over the conflict, a silence that wards one away. What are we being shepherded away from? Shame? Guilt? Morality abandoned? Tales too obscene to be told? Recollections which, to preserve the teller's sanity, must *perforce* be locked away?

The lore deemed fit for retail is determinedly colourful. The Ker family folklore has David travelling to France with a pack of hounds. Johnston Kyle, who served under him, informs us that Ker arrived with a pair of hounds and some fighting cocks, and soon had the cavalry out chasing hares, in wild early morning gallops. He was also arrested by the Belgian police for fighting mains. 'Tell no lies except the lies I tell you to tell', he instructed his batman, Flanaghan, upon their seizure.[30] He had no trouble in obtaining Flanaghan's loyalty. 'The men all thought he was wonderful', Kyle's son-in-law recalls.[31]

Nini (the donor of the Jackson's hampers?) also had a colourful war. Her service included a stint with the War Office Censors, where she spent her day, 'reading every single love letter, every child's letter "to darling daddy" – etc. to the bitter end – never missing a word!'[32] The office, alas, was almost entirely staffed by women and offered her no opportunity to deploy what she rather coyly described as her 'knowledge of men, & matters!' but it was fascinating nonetheless.[33] 'I have learnt more in these 3 weeks', she told Lady Londonderry, 'than in all my 50 years of life, and I thought I knew a thing or two!' It was an education in other ways too. The classes were mixing, affording Nini the novel experience of sharing an office with 'nothing but trained workers!'

Lady Paget came to fetch me yesterday at the office and was horrified by the look of the crowd that passed from the door[34]

Lady Paget's alarm, however, was not caused by the dubious company her friend was keeping. It had a patriotic origin:

She said she saw several unmistakable Germans & I can well believe it – they are all foreigners, I don't believe there [is] a genuine english woman in the place (English people do not know many languages)[35]

Hugh Andrews, c.1980. Hugh remembers his father standing helplessly by the burning barn, pails of water in his hands. (Andrews family)

Lady Paget was not alone. Everyone was seeing Germans. On a moonless night in 1917 at the height of the German submarine offensive, someone set fire to Hugh Andrews' hayshed. That same night, a merchantman was reportedly sunk in Belfast Lough. Putting two and two together, local opinion decided that the blaze had been started deliberately in order to guide the U-boat in. Two strangers, certain Germans, had apparently slunk through the yard that day. This was seen as the clinching piece of evidence.[36] Seventy years after the incident, Hugh Andrews' son, also Hugh, who had witnessed the fire as a boy, and still remembers his father standing helplessly by the barn, pails of water in his hands, vividly recounts the story, then eyes me from the back of his armchair, giving me a pointed look that seems to say, 'Can't you see this fits together?'

But what need have we of phantom Germans when we have a *bone fide* Prussian in the frame? How did Richard Schmidt get through the

Clogger's Yard, behind Portavo House. Tom Connell had his workshop here by a walnut tree, now gone.

war? What became of his family? By 1918 the Schmidts had left the townland. No-one is clear when or why. Some believe that they went during the war, or were perhaps detained as enemy aliens. However, the Census records show that they had gone by 1911, at least three years too early for Stockbridge House to have had its windows smashed by patriots.

This must have been a testing time for the Schmidts, wherever they were. The good neighbours had become krauts, sausages, huns. Home was now the Home Front; all things German were reviled. The Saxe-Coburgs became the Windsors. Willamina Muckle became Mina, and stayed Mina for the rest of her days. There were recruitment posters on the walls, off duty soldiers in the shops. Women knitted gloves and Balaclavas for soldiers and seamen.[37] The high price of leather revived the wearing of clogs, which were made of beech or ash cut from the woods of Portavo, and fashioned into clogs by Tom Connell, 'the best of cloggers'.[38] But the war did not alter everything. Some conventions were immutable. In November 1916, a man found the body of a one or maybe two day-old baby that had been deliberately drowned in Sandy Bay.[39]

Edith stopped travelling to London for fear of U-boats (which led David to ask, with heavy irony, if there was now a U-boat base on the Copelands).[40] Belfast Lough was protected. Dirigibles crossed it, frightening the children, who were unused to seeing things hanging in the sky.[41] A manned sentry box appeared at the junction of the Groomsport and Kylestone Roads, at which passers by were asked for their papers.

Johnny Aird was challenged so regularly that he stopped treating the sentries seriously:

'Who goes there?'
'The Devil.'
'Pass on.'[42]

One did so at one's peril. In 1914, a passing car did not stop when hailed. The driver's daughter was shot dead. In 1918, another over-zealous sentry shot a butler on a bicycle.[43] His fate is unknown.

When Germany surrendered on November 11th 1918, Marcus Monaghan the postman was first with the news, telling 'everyone round the country the war was over.'[44] Work stopped. Church bells pealed. There was a universal sense of relief and elation. Sammy McCully's father put on his suit and went into town. 'They were going mad in Belfast' and he went mad with them.[45]

And so it ended. How is it to be summed up? Uncomfortable as it may be to do so, it is hard to avoid the conclusion that the conflict's impact was essentially positive. Put bluntly, Portavo experienced the gain without the pain. It had seventeen men of fighting age; and as one in eight men of military age died in the conflict, in bald statistical terms alone, it might have expected to experience two deaths.[46] However none of its combatants was killed or seriously injured. Not everyone was so fortunate. Miss Angus from the Cotton (who would later make her home in Portavo) lost three brothers at the Somme.[47] Her mother is said to have died of a broken heart.

Most people here, however, experienced the war not as a conflict but as a high in the economic cycle. And a giddy high at that. There was work for all, on the land and in the mills, shipyards, factories and foundries. Farmers enjoyed a prosperity that many had never known before. Labourers' wages rose faster than the cost of living. The townland basked in an unaccustomed affluence. Its new owner-occupiers did particularly well. Wartime inflation more than halved the real cost of purchasing their farms. People 'ate butter, and went back to margarine after the war'.[48] The townland's hard-headed farmers contemplated the peace with apprehension.

33   Through a golden glow – the 20s & 30s

'John.'

No answer

'John.'

A bright-faced boy with dirty, bare feet appeared at the door. His mother pressed a penny into his hand.

'Away up to Mrs Boyd's and get me a turnip.'

Off he went to Boyds, the farm that used to be Perrys, a fact that he is too young to remember.

Ellen Boyd was in the yard. She took his penny, and brought him not one but three turnips. Could he manage them alright?

'Yes Missus,' he replied, eyes wide. Three turnips! Something within him surged. He could just picture his mother's delight when he arrived back with these trophies.[1]

All three turnips went into the pot. There was no shortage of hungry mouths at home, as Ellen Boyd knew well. John was the youngest of nine, all boys, most of them still at home. Meaning that John got humoured and tortured in equal measure. As he had been since the age of two, when he was dunked in the water barrel by the door for crying too loudly.[2]

This was the sort of thing that happened when you had eight older brothers. And a father of fifty-five, going on fifteen. On one occasion Robert his father and Tom Connell the clogger, who hadn't done a day's work since he married Minnie Burroughs, had dressed up a doll to look like a baby and drowned it in the sea. They were careful to play out the whole pantomime of Robert trying to drown the baby and Tom Connell trying to save it under Lisa Magee's watchful gaze.[3]

Lisa saw everything. Every gruesome detail. It was murder. Murder most foul.

She couldn't stop it. Man dear, she was over eighty. But she could tell the polis, and see that justice was done. So when the coast was clear, she slipped off to do her duty. But to Lisa's chagrin, no prosecution followed.

Ellen Boyd of 'The Hill' 1930s. (Boyd family)

The sash our nine sons wore. The Boyds of the Mill in their Orange regalia. Back Row (l-r): Walker, Sidney, Billy, Carson, Tommy, Sam. Front Row: Bob, Irvine, Ethel & Robert, John. (Boyd family)

That Robert Boyd could wriggle out of anything, what with him being a mason. One funny handshake and away he went.

The Boyds of the Mill were a very loyal family. Three of them had fought in the war. All nine of Robert's sons became Orangemen. John too, when he was old enough to put away the things of childhood, followed his brothers into LOL 781 in Donaghadee, and helped raise the Orange arch on the Warren Road each summer.

Everyone helped with this. Even the Naughton boys. And the arch was a sight to see. It was brightly painted, hung with portraits, and adorned with lilies from Minnie Connell's garden, orange lilies grown specially for the purpose. It stood opposite Minnie Connell's cottage at the foot of the Stockbridge Road, and every time Minnie looked out at it, it did her heart good. For Minnie was also very loyal, like all the Burroughs before her, and the Finlays before them, way back in 1798.

What, no flag? Joe Gillespie, Orangeman, mason, and land steward at Portavo was renowned for flying the flag. This photograph shows his home, the Warren Road gate lodge, after a whitening. (James Harding Watson)

*Early car silhouetted
as it arrives at
Portavo. (Ker family)*

Minnie gave dancing classes, held ceilis in her little barn and was reckoned a great turn on the dance floor. And she kept her ear to the ground. When it came to knowing other people's business she was 'better than a newspaper'. 'Here's the *Telegraph*', Samuel John Boyd would remark, with his usual sarcasm, when he saw her coming.[4]

Young Willie Bell saw Minnie quite differently. Willie Bell grew up in the labourers' cottages on the Stockbridge Road without tuppence to rub together, and as far as he was concerned, Minnie Connell had it all. A bit of land. A few cows. A fine cottage, a big, scrubbed table and a well-stocked dresser, and two bedrooms, one of them *spare*, she'd got so much it was almost criminal.[5]

Then there was her monkey. Minnie and Tom had two pets, a cat and a monkey, both given to them by sailors. But the two did not get on, and one day the monkey put the cat into a pot of boiling water, and at a stroke got rid of its rival.[6] It took a lot to get Tom out of his chair. But that did.

Marriage had made Tom lazy. He did a bit, but never took to farmwork. After all, he was a skilled man. An artisan. So he sat by the fire with three coats on, complaining about the draught, while Minnie ploughed and harrowed, using a horse for sense and a bullock for muscle.[7] The couple kept a dishcloth as a communal handkerchief. John Boyd, who did not know this custom, can still remember the shock he felt when Minnie first used it to wipe her nose.[8]

It is a fine day in early summer. Robert Boyd and his friend Sammy Moderate are out in their rowboat, hauling in their creels. There is a lobster in each, sometimes two.[9] The breeze barely ruffles the water. Someone is fishing off the Point. 'You could catch your dinner very nicely off the rocks' in those days.[10] The days of dry toilets. The days before the sea was full of sewage.

A charabanc passes. Minnie cranes through the window. Is it the *Pioneer* or the *Coaster*? From this angle it's hard to tell. Then she recognises young Nelson. It was the *Coaster*. Jamesy Smith, Groomsport's Mr Big, had put the *Coaster* on the road a few years previously. He'd done well, carrying people between Groomsport and Bangor, then Bangor and Donaghadee. Excursions to Portrush and the Glens of Antrim followed, day trips from which everyone returned squiffy, including the driver.

Jamesy Smith did so well that Jacob O'Neill set up against him. A ruthless price war followed, a war that ended up with the red *Pioneer* driving the brown *Coaster* off the road. There's been no peace on the roads since they'd come out with these motors. Johnny Aird had the right idea. He drove his cart down the middle of the road and let the motorists honk all they liked.[11]

Johnny Aird was not the only local to resist the horseless carriage. Richard disliked them, and stuck to his barouche. Edith hated them, particularly after a nasty accident in 1924.[12] But the old guard would have to get used to the car. And much else besides. The early 1920s were a time of change and upheaval. Ireland was partitioned. The state of Northern

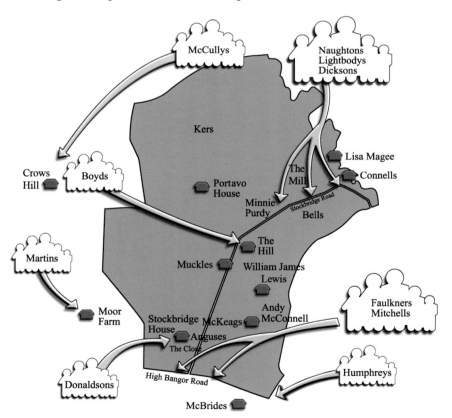

All change. Old families depart and new ones arrive in the early 1920s.

'Cramp' & Mrs Faulkner outside their picture postcard cottage. See also vol.1, p.261. (Bell family)

Ireland was founded. An IRA campaign, a state clampdown, and a southern boycott of goods made in Belfast followed. Sectarian feeling heightened. Protestants were driven out of the new Irish Free State. There was anti-Catholic rioting in Belfast.

The Church of Ireland Humphreys family settled in Ballyfotherly, after being driven from their farm in County Longford.[13] The Perrys died out, the Arnolds emigrated, creating vacancies in the townland's two biggest farms. In 1924 the Donaldsons from Movilla near Newtownards replaced the Arnolds at Stockbridge House.[14] The Boyds (of three turnip fame) supplanted the Perrys on the Hill. The McCullys took on their old farm in Ballyminetragh. The Martins moved into Moor Farm.

The townland's working class – almost extinct in 1900 – was also reborn. Mr and Mrs Mitchell, a plasterer and a seamstress, arrived from the Lake District. They were followed by Mrs Mitchell's brother, 'Cramp' Faulkner, a war veteran with a clubbed foot, who moved into a nearby thatched cottage on the High Bangor Road. Labouring families like the Catholic Naughtons, the Lightbodys and the Dicksons settled alongside the Boyds, the Bells and Minnie Purdie around the raggedy foot of the Stockbridge Road. Here, in a clachan of cottages and rustic looking council houses (much sought after because they had luxuries like cold running water), a poor but close-knit community formed, a community that is still remembered with affection.[15]

Money was tight in all these households, but the Naughtons and Bells had it worst. Mrs Naughton, 'a fine lookin woman', and Mrs Sarah Bell were widows. Both their husbands had worked for the Kers at Montalto. Mrs Naughton's husband had been a groom. Mrs Bell's had been a gardener, who had died in the flu epidemic of 1919, leaving her with five children. It was a constant struggle to make ends meet.

The other households had male breadwinners. Jimmy Lightbody gardened and his son, also Jimmy, worked for Minnie Connell. Alec Dickson chauffeured and gardened at one of the big houses on the Warren Road. Robert Boyd had worked as a breadman before succeeding his father at the mill. His run took him down the peninsula, and when the Big Snow of 1923 struck, he and his cart were in Ballyhalbert, fourteen miles from home.

Like Mary Angelique Montgomery's walk to see Miss Ross in 1729, Robert Boyd's journey home from Ballyhalbert leaps out at us from the townland's history. The blizzard was terrifying. The snow was so thick he could hardly see. The north wind chilled him to the marrow. How would he get back? His horse could barely breathe. Indeed, it found the going so slippy he had to call at a smith's and have it unshod. Then it was back into the teeth of the gale. They inched forwards, wading through snow that had reached the bread cart's axle by the time he got to Donaghadee. At Portavo, the drifts spilled over the demesne wall. He arrived home numb and exhausted. It was six weeks before the cart could go on the road again.[16] But his children had the time of their lives. Snow rarely lies on this famously mild shore, and here it was in mountains.

The local children made their own fun. They played hounds and hares on what is now Stockbridge Park. They played with clay marbles on the roads. They spun hoops with cleeks, and whipped pirries. They played hopscotch, kick the can, rounders, and hide and seek. They collected willicks and cribbins (edible crabs) from the rocks, and sold or ate them.

Minnie Purdie's cottage as it is today.

No warmer then! Boys from the 10th Belfast Scout Troop swimming in Sandeel Bay. (Andrew Totten)

They played football and hit golf balls, swam in Sandy Bay, and dived at the New Kea, where a tourist family called Glendinning had a springboard.[17]

Older boys caddied at Donaghadee Golf Club for sixpence a round.[18] In the Bell household these sixpences were treated as income, and Willie Bell gave the money to his mother.[19] The Club had no shortage of caddies. Demographically, the 1920s-30s were in some ways akin to the 1820s-30s, with the difference that this generation grew up not to famine, but to war. Numbers mushroomed to such an amazing extent that Portavo started its own football team, the Glenburnie Swifts, which played in the Bangor League.[20]

After the closure of Ballywilliam, children went to school in Donaghadee. It had five schools: one Methodist, one Catholic, one Presbyterian, and two belonging to the Church of Ireland: the Admiral Leslie and the Mount Alexander. Here 'Bull' Adair held sway. Adair is remembered as a strict disciplinarian. He was also a big Franco fan, who visited Spain in summer 'for the bullfights', and caned his children with

Billy Boyd, John Bell, and John Boyd (r), with Lisa Magee by her cottage door. (Boyd family)

split rods, to make sure that when he punished them they got nipped as well as bruised.[21]

The long walk to school was not the only legacy of the previous century's demographic breakdown. Another was a surfeit of spinsters and bachelors, particularly amongst the more longstanding farming families. But it was the small farmers whose predicament was the most serious. Economically unviable, strategically adrift, and incapable of renewing itself by attracting in new blood or money, this once vigorous class was on the road to nowhere. By the 1920s-30s, in Portavo at least, many formerly respectable small farming families were in a state of disintegration.

How does something as vast and as complex as the collapse of a class play itself out in individual lives? The answer is here to be seen. Tragically. Poignantly. In phenomena that appear diffuse and unconnected, but in their origins can be traced back to the deeper malaise. The situation of the Anguses is a case in point. Old Mr Angus was no longer with them. He had committed suicide by walking off the end of Donaghadee pier.[22] Mary Jane Angus was 'away with the fairies'. She had stopped taking care of herself, and stood at her front door, ranting at strangers.[23]

On the hill in front of her lived Andy McConnell, scion of another once eminently respectable small farming family. Andy, the last of the McConnells, rarely washed either and is remembered as being as 'dirty as coal and never sober'. He grew spuds and rhubarb, which he traded for drink in Donaghadee. He also laboured to many of the farmers round about, working hard for a few extra shillings, which he got in his hand that evening, and spent that night in the bar. He smoked butts in his pipe, and ate his boiled eggs out of a hole in the table. When done he would hit the shell with a slap, which despatched it to the floor, where it joined its predecessors.[24]

He could also be thran and awkward. On one occasion Willie Boyd needed help on the farm, so he sent a boy to ask McConnell to come over. Knowing that Andy could be cussed when it suited him, he told the boy to: 'Be sure and get McConnell, and if you can't get McConnell get two men.' This did the trick. When Andy heard these words he felt ten feet tall, and not only came and did the job, but lived on the story for years afterwards.[25]

Andy's loves were Guinness and football. But when he played he never passed and always stuck out his elbows so that no-one could tackle him. If he scored, he 'bummed and blowed' for hours. There was no-one to equal McConnell the Great. And no end to his ego. One day a letter arrived from the Soviet Union, in what was believed to be Russian, inviting him to Moscow to play darts. Andy was quite unfazed, indeed scarcely surprised. His fame had reached the Russias. About time. Travel

Andy's sentiments exactly.
1930s Guinness advert. (Guinness)

The Oceanic. Didn't look complete without Andy McConnell's bicycle outside it. (Elizabeth Taggart)

arrangements were investigated, boat time-tables scrutinised. It was weeks before the fact that he had been hoodwinked finally dawned.[26]

As the years went by, Andy McConnell drank more and farmed less. The fourteen acre farm went to the dogs. His sisters didn't like to visit. They didn't know what they might find. When drunk he was full of self pity. When sober he was argumentative and rude. He was throwing his life away, and there was nothing they could do about it. He had their hearts broken.

The once pristine McConnell farmstead, home to the family for four generations, went to rack and ruin. One day Harry Humphreys called to find water coming in the back door and going out the front. Andy was unconcerned. He had tied a brick to the sole of each boot and was getting about just fine.[27] When the roof started to leak, McConnell slept under an eiderdown made of two sheets of corrugated iron, and consoled himself by drinking the molasses used to sweeten silage. When the roof caved in and the briars grew through it, he retreated to an old 6'x12" caravan in the yard.[28]

This didn't bother him unduly, for he was never exactly a housebird. His homes from home were the Moat and the Oceanic in Donaghadee, a hole-in-the-wall bar that did not look complete without Andy's bike ('no brakes, no lights, no nothing!') propped up outside it.[29] This was where Andy spent his finest hours, giving out on every subject under the sun. On one unforgettable occasion, a Glasgow Rangers first team player was lured into the bar. The regulars mobbed him, crowding round to shake his hand and buy him drinks. Andy McConnell insisted on dribbling a matchbox around him, to show the whippersnapper who was boss.[30]

*Sandy McKeag with horses
and dog. (Bell family)*

Andy McConnell shared a yard with three other stars from the local
gene pool, Sandy, Willie and Rabbie McKeag, three droll old bachelor
brothers whose family had farmed here since at least the 1850s.[31] They
too worked fourteen acres, growing potatoes, wheat and barley. They
kept a few calves and an old milk cow, and in season drew wrack from
the shore. All talked broad Scots and 'dressed very plain and old
fashioned. You never seen a collar on them.'[32]

Sandy was 'small, with a big deep voice and a wee fat pony'. All three
of these rough, upright men were considered characters, Rabbie being the
most renowned. The McKeags rubbed along well enough with Andy
McConnell. When McConnell stole their eggs and sold them for beer
money in the Oceanic, Sandy McKeag left out rotten ones in their place.
The egg trade ended. There was never a dull moment. The brothers kept
McConnell in check, but at times it took all three of them to do it.[33]

These stories evoke a world now gone, a world filled with colourful
'characters', who individualised themselves with amazing ease, and scant
regard for convention. We can take them at face value, and enjoy them as
entertaining recollections of the rough and tumble of country life. But
there are messages here too. The trained eye would find these stories
replete with symptoms of social decay.[34]

The decay was not always terminal. The fallen could be redeemed.
Take the case of William James Lewis, another wayward bachelor who
lived a few fields away from the McKeags and McConnell, at the end of
his own loanin', which was 'all humps and hollows like the rocky road to
Dublin'. William James was a nephew of the Misses McCutcheon, the
last of the McCutcheons, another sturdy family of small farmers. He had
twelve acres, on which he grew spuds, corn and thistles.

William James's corn was alive with thistles. Homogenised, pest-
controlled agri-produce this was not. 'Ah say, ah say, you're hellish
feared of a thistle', he would inform the squeamish, a puzzled look on his
face. He never felt them. Couldn't understand the fuss. He also grew
potatoes, and is remembered as taking two or three hampers of them into
Bangor twice a week, and 'coming out happy as Larry'.[35]

Boyd family of the Hill, with scarecrow. (l-r) Ellen, Maggie, Edwin, Ginnie, unknown; (front) John Boyd (of the Mill), Bob Boyd. (Boyd family)

Until he found true love, that is. One fateful night in John Muckle's kitchen, William James met Agnes, a cousin of the Smalls, and within a few months he was a bachelor no longer. The wedding, at Ballygilbert, was a rare old do. 'All the countryside' was at it – from idle curiosity if no other reason, for he was pushing sixty and she was not much younger. That morning, the Boyds and Muckles took the wheels off his cart, his nuptial carriage, put it in an outhouse, then put the wheels back on, so he couldn't get it out the door. Then they put a sack over the chimney and smoked him out of the house.[36]

It was a day to remember. Like the day his thatch went on fire. The blaze had neighbours scampering over the fields and up his rocky lane to carry buckets of water, in relays, from the well. One stood on a ladder, throwing the water onto the pyre. Others carried out his few belongings. It was a hopeless task. In the end they could do no more than watch the place burn. But they were determined not to let this beat them. A collection was got up. William James would get a new cottage.

The collectors even had what seemed to be a stroke of luck. The chimney of the old Donaghadee brickworks was demolished. Some of the bricks were bought as salvage, and carted back to Portavo. They weren't great bricks. In fact they turned out to be hopeless bricks, but William James didn't seem to mind. It was powerful. The whole thing was powerful. And so 'the greatest oul' sowl there ever was' got a (nearly) new cottage, and the townland got a monument to neighbourliness forby.[37]

The Boyds and Donaldsons met with similar kindness. When Edwin and Ellen Boyd arrived, 'on a spring cart with a big goose on it… all the neighbours came over with a pair of horses and did a day's ploughing'. It was a handsome welcome. A welcome which introduced them to the townland's communal ways. And they soon felt at home. Indeed Edwin, who liked a drink, showed every sign of fitting in too well. On market days he would drink himself to a standstill and let the horse bring him home. Whereon his young wife Ellen tipped him from the cart and let him sleep where he lay. The horse and the horse alone got stabled.[38]

Ellen may have been 'a raw one', who 'would have cuffed your lugs right n' quick', but she drove the business of the farm forward at a tremendous pace. She baked, cooked toffee, and made all her children's clothes. She whitewashed the house and roofed the outhouses with corrugated iron. She carried a hammer and nails in her apron, fixing and mending as she went, and is said to have worked 'as well as any man' in the fields. Once, for pure devilment, she shot up Johnny Aird's pigeons. Ellen had a wild streak, 'you wouldn't know what she'd be up to'.[39]

Her boys, Willie, Bob, and young Edwin were put to work on the farm at an early age and their talents helped to transform it. In the early 1920s, the Boyds got a tractor, a new fangled machine then virtually unknown in the country. Then they got another and began doing contract work. Then they got a combine harvester, reputedly the first in Northern Ireland, and did the same with that. Most of this was down to Willie, who was barely fifteen when the Boyds got their first machine.[40]

Willie Boyd was wasted as a farmer. He was a natural mechanic who 'could take a tractor to bits and put it back again', and he was a genius with cars. But he farmed, alongside the rest of the family, growing potatoes that were 'famed for quality and taste' for McVeigh & Arnold in Belfast, who each year sent down a squad of pickers that slept rough in the barn for the week of the picking.[41]

Until the depression. The economic downturn destroyed the price of potatoes. Alec Martin remembers nearly a hundred tons of potatoes being picked at Moor Farm. They were then bagged and stacked for the lorries, but the lorries never came. The wholesale price had fallen to the point at which it wasn't worth the trouble of collecting them. Some were fed to animals, but 'tons and of tons' were dumped on the shore.[42]

Studio 'portrait' of Willie Boyd mid-1920s. (Boyd family)

Willie Boyd in the Bean Field with an International Junior tractor, 1924. The Hill is in the background. (Boyd family)

*Old clay Millar's jam pot.
Was it once filled with fruit
from Portavo? (Ulster Folk &
Transport Museum)*

Fortunately, while the money was missed, no-one, not even the most backward of Portavo's farmers, was any longer dependent on potatoes. A variety of produce was grown, including blackcurrants, strawberries, and gooseberries, which made their way by the hundredweight from the Muckles' seven acres to the Millar's jam factory in Belfast.[43]

In 1924 the Donaldsons arrived to find Stockbridge Farm 'laid out in White Clover' and awaiting them like a bride.[44] As there was work enough for four, the newly-married Donaldsons hired Lizzie Lewis (Mary Jane Angus and William James Lewis's love child) to help round the house, and Hugh Moore to help on the farm. He got eighteen shillings a week and his food, including 'a big fried egg and a piece of soda bread' every morning.[45]

Willie Donaldson grew corn, wheat and barley, and kept fifteen cows and 'a wheen a' sheep'. Martha Donaldson baked three times a week. She and Lizzie washed everything by hand, airing the clothes on a pulley line in the kitchen on the days when there was no drying. The dirtiest items were scrubbed on the scrubbing board or steeped in the bath, then starched and smoothed with a flat iron, warmed on the range.

Although Portavo looked to Belfast for almost everything, the Donaldsons held fast to their native Newtownards. All the farm's produce went to 'Newtown'. All their tools – barrows, shovels, grapes, nails, spades and so on, came from Wardens of Newtownards, the Harrods of the peninsula. The Donaldsons and Boyds were young and progressive. But they did not entirely turn their backs on the old ways. Willie Donaldson carted wrack from the shore. He also turned an Austin Sixteen into a 'tractor' by taking the back end off and connecting it to the binder. The experiment worked brilliantly. Machine gelled with machine to create an instrument that could cut and harrow at speeds that were almost frightening.[46]

The district's farmers were looked after by an extraordinarily wide range of people. Commercial representatives called, as did tradesmen and peddlers like Tinker Johnston, who made milk churns, and reportedly sired children all over north Down, Stevie Thorpe the saddler, who mended harnesses, and Dick Pogue (properly Dick Pollock) the thatcher, who could have worked wonders with Andy McConnell's roof, had he accepted payment in money-back bottles. There was Robert Mitchell, 'a droll, comic sort of a boy' who clipped sheep and sold scobes, the stick pins used in thatching. Children collected the sticks, which he scraped and pointed and then sold in bundles of fifty or a hundred.[47]

Two pig butchers served the district – Pedie Keag from Carrowdore, a big, fat, jolly man who arrived on a pony and trap; and James McClelland from the Cotton, a turf cutter and travelling butcher, who came on a bicycle, with only the hammer and the big knife in his belt to betray his deadly purpose. The Bell children hated his visits. They always kept one or two pigs, and each got named and petted. By the time the butcher called, the beasts were almost part of the family. But what must be, must be. McClelland was shown into the pigsty. The children were taken indoors. Thump. Squeals. Thump. Silence. The pig was dead. Its body was then 'dressed' – bled, slit, gutted, then cleaned out with boiling water. The hair was taken off and the carcass was hung.

Stockbridge Farm, home of the Donaldson family since 1924.

Tea in the fields, 1930s. (l-r) Willie Boyd, John Boyd, unknown, Bob and Edwin Boyd. (Boyd family)

Within forty-five minutes of his arrival, McClelland was on his way, with half a crown in his pocket and a clutch of sobbing children left behind him. Their four-legged friend was no more. Within a day the carcass had browned and become 'as hard as wood'. The liver would be shared round the neighbours, and 'haddock' would be made with the bladder, oatmeal and onion.[48]

Along came meal reps. and lime men, gypsies and beggars like William Mooney, who toured the houses with a button-keyed accordion, playing for his food and a few drinks. He would have been invited in to eat with the family. There was Johnny Whitley the stone mason, 'a desperate character, dirty and bad, who chewed tobacco and drank what he earned.' He lived in a dirty, smoke filled cottage near Kinnaird's Corner with his half brother Jimmy Henderson. On Saturday nights, he got poor Jimmy to do handstands till the 'simple crather's' money lay all over the floor, whereon he gathered it and drank it in Groomsport. The next morning he could be found 'lying on a bank, full as a lord', his bicycle somewhere beside him.[49]

Pedlars like John Gaw from Newtownards hawked clothes. Fowl dealers bought up old hens. Respectable traders like Joe and Henry McNarry sold ling three feet in length, which were hung from the ceiling with the hams. They sold eggs in waterglass, and crocks of salt herrings, which kept all winter.[50] Honor Rudnitsky, who holidayed in Ballywilliam during the 1920s, remembers all sorts of huxters calling, the most stylish being Jinny the fowlwoman:

On her feet she wore men's boots; on her head she wore a hat known as a sailor hat… of shiny black straw, turned up all round and secured with two murderous hat pins. And on each arm she carried an enormous basket full of chickens beautifully plucked, trussed with a wooden skewer, their giblets tucked into their wings as you never get them nowadays and each basket covered with a snowy white tea cloth... "Now there's a fine pair of birds for you ma'am. Three shillings each I'm asking, but I'll give the pair for five", and she would beam a smile at me.[51]

Fresh herrings were delivered with even more pizzazz. Two Donaghadee fishmongers vied with each other to sell them round the country, so when the catch arrived, it triggered:

a chariot race between [the] two rival fishmongers with the ponies going at full gallop and the boys standing up on the flat carts shouting "Herrins alive, herrins alive, Ardglass herrins".[52]

The boys sold herrings like their lives depended on it:

If anyone signalled that they wanted some, the poor pony would be reined back on its haunches, the boy would jump down, degut the herrings with a speed that had to be seen to be believed and then, as his rival had now got ahead, would be off again at full gallop.[53]

The herring boys did a good trade at the foot of the Stockbridge Road, where Jinny's chickens were an unaffordable luxury. In the mid-1930s a labourer earned maybe thirty shillings (twenty if he got his food) for a fifty-eight hour week, less in winter, for there was no electric light, even at Ker's, and the men were sent home when darkness fell.

The nights were then their own, and they were not wasted. Willie Donaldson's son David remembers 'manys a gather up with a fiddle or an accordion on the farm here', and dancing in the drawing room. There was visiting, music making and singing. Aird Lowry recalled a liveliness about the country 'that you just don't get today'. John McCoubrey agrees. 'Before the war people socialised more. You would have gone to their house and they to yours.'[54]

At harvest the Kers had a bash for the men, to which the wider neighbourhood was invited. Young and old danced the hornpipe, the lancer and the highland fling to the sound of the gramophone or someone playing the melodeon. Singers would be coaxed to sing. Mrs Naughton would deliver a note perfect version of The Rose of Tralee. Mrs Ker called in. David helped with a barrel of cider, said his hellos, then made a tactful withdrawal. There was a supper of sandwiches and pastries, then the dancing recommenced with even more gusto than before. People also attended the sixpenny tea dance in Donaghadee Orange Hall, or went for a movie and chips in Donaghadee. The more socially confident sampled the bars and bright lights of Bangor, now a well-established seaside resort.

'The bees knees'. The Rev. David Watson, of First Donaghadee. (First Donaghadee Presbyterian Church)

Which brings us finally to sin, and its management. The rather daunting job of keeping Portavo on the straight and narrow fell primarily to the Rev. Watson of First Donaghadee and the Rev. Andrews of Shore Street. As we have seen, their efforts met with only mixed success, thanks in no small part to the challenging nature of the raw material they had to work with. There were many moralities in the townland, and many moralities within each person in it.

The clergy did their rounds. The Rev. Watson came on his pony and trap, the Rev. Andrews arrived on a bicycle, a difference that was seen as sure proof that Shore Street was for the 'plainer people' and First Donaghadee had 'more snobs'. Andrews, known as 'the black knight' on account of his sober attire, was an amiable man and a kindly pastor who baptised children at home. He had lost four fingers on one hand but could still ride his bike and play golf with six fingers, which was considered a regular marvel given that most people can hardly manage with ten.

If the Rev. Andrews had too much water in his make up, the Rev. Watson had perhaps too much fire. He was severe and straight laced. Eloquent and masterful in the pulpit, he inspired all the crackling awe traditionally associated with the black-frocked Presbyterian divine. In the kirk, he led from the front, 'calling the tune in no uncertain manner'. Topical issues were pronounced upon. Miscreants were denounced by name from the pulpit, in the presence of their peers.

Watson's home visits were the nearest thing the families got to entertaining royalty. Every member of First – the Boyds, McBrides, Donaldsons and William James Lewis – received regular calls. These encounters were usually pleasantly superficial, but if someone wanted to talk they could range deep into peoples' lives. The Rev. Watson got a particularly warm welcome at the McBrides. But then everyone did. There was nothing Hugh and Maggie, a bachelor and spinster couple, liked better than a bit of company and a good yarn after tea. Hugh would get out his pipe, use most of a box of matches trying to light it, and everyone would enjoy themselves mightily.

Hugh and Maggie were the last of the McBrides of Portavo.[55] Their home was a neat, tin-lidded, thatched cottage, clad with money Hugh sent home from Australia, where he had worked as a young man. Around the cottage lay the nine ancestral acres, laid out in five fields. Though small farmers, the McBrides had escaped the malaise and lived solid, respectable lives.

One reason for this was undoubtedly religion. Hugh and Maggie 'lived for the church', and had a wonderfully life-affirming relationship with the Rev. Watson, who was every inch their idea of what a Presbyterian minister should be.[56] 'They thought he was the bee's knees', Fred McCutcheon recalls. And when he was with them, he was amongst his people. They were the audience that never disappointed, the people from

The McBride family 1934. Hugh and his sister Maggie (r) with Mrs McCutcheon (l) & her grandson Max, who died in a tragic accident on Hugh's farm shortly after this photograph was taken.

whom he drew his formidable strength.[57]

Watson's end seemed to come out of nothing. He stubbed his toe on a gate, but carried on regardless. When he finally had it seen to the doctor unexpectedly diagnosed gangrene. The toe had to come off. But the gangrene had spread. The minister had to have his leg off. But even this did not rid his body of infection. Watson carried on, showing surpassing courage. He continued to preach, struggling into the pulpit on crutches which he had not had time to learn how to use properly, a sight that is remembered as heartbreaking. Upon his death, the last of the old-style Presbyterian ministers to govern Portavo passed away.[58]

34 'Bankrupt to the hilt & knee deep in bills'

Richard and Edith returned from Ballywhite in 1917, bringing all their old bad habits with them. Back too came the contents of Montalto, and as Montalto was six or seven times the size of Portavo, their new home bulged at the seams.[1] Richard created some extra space by adding an extra storey to the return block of the house. The Northern Bank helped out by sending the Kers a safe for their valuables (which in itself tells a story – in the good old days they had needed two). But 'many hundreds of articles', some of them very fine, ended up 'rotting in the yard'.[2]

The home farm wheezed to life then collapsed again, with Richard complaining that the trustees would not advance him the capital needed to run it, and that he could not 'make gold out of stones'.[3] He couldn't make it, but he still knew how to spend it. At the time of his return, Richard was busy going through his second fortune.[4] Most of the wealth of the estate now lay in stocks and bonds, and these did well during the 1920s.[5] Richard's life insurance policies matured at the right time too, paying well beyond their anticipated bonuses.

This money went to the trustees, who provided Richard and Edith with separate allowances, which should have been enough to allow both to live very comfortably. However, words like 'live within' and 'allowance' meant nothing to Richard. He spent as he pleased and the trustees picked up the bill, allocating an ever-increasing proportion of the revenue to debt repayment. David's allowance shrank from £500 to £131 p.a.[6] It was business as usual. Richard spent, Edith fretted, *plus ca change*.

Though Richard was incorrigible, 'everybody liked him', with the exception of his elder brother's widow, Eva Ker. When these dreadnoughts met it was said to be, 'as good as a play to watch my Aunt looking down her nose at Captain Ker!'[7] Richard's dress was every bit as flamboyant as his personality. A visitor to Portavo around 1930 encountered him in green stockings and bright orange tweed plus fours.[8] Gavin Perceval-Maxwell recalled that by then, 'Dick Ker had the reputation of being so much of a "card" that no-one was surprised at anything he did or said'.[9]

Though he had long ceased riding, Richard kept 'a stable full of hunters' at Portavo. Edith did not approve, so he tried to hide the horses from her, employing a boy with a flag to keep them out of view. Occasionally, the trustees put their collective feet down and insisted that some go. However, the story of Ker taking three horses to England to sell them and coming back with six, just about sums up the success of their endeavours.[10]

Richard and Edith grew old together. He became deaf and gouty. She became crippled with arthritis. But they had each other, and when she hadn't him, she had her beloved Cairns. It was no idyll, of course. And Nini's unexpected death in 1922 was a time of particular turbulence. All the difficult emotions Edith preferred not to confront ran riot. Richard was inconsolable. He is said to have cleared her house (Quentin Castle) in the aftermath of her death, the prerogative of the next of kin, and therefore his right and duty.[11] It was months before things got back onto an even keel.

As Richard aged, there was talk of David taking over, but as ever, nothing happened. Richard stayed in charge, running everything 'in his usual upside down way'. The demesne went virtually unmanaged.[12] Its rental value fell, until it was 'let out at a trifle for grazing' and Portavo turned in a loss each year.[13] Whins and rushes multiplied. The place became overrun with rabbits. Joe Gillespie, Richard's redoubtable land steward, got away with doing very little.[14]

Richard was by now more interested in disposing of Portavo than maintaining it. Various get-rich-quick schemes were mooted. One of

Sticks and spats. Richard & Edith at Portavo, c.1920. The sticks are Edith's. The flamboyance of Richard's attire can be imagined. (Ker family)

these envisaged half of the demesne becoming a golf course, and the other half going for housing. Pound signs jiggled in Richard's eyes. A two-hundred dwelling suburb took shape in his head. It was left to Wallace to keep the Kers in their ancestral seat by vetoing the housing proposal, advising the would-be vendors that the time was 'not ripe'.[15]

So Richard and Edith stayed put. And they did so with a certain ersatz magnificence. Both were wonderfully, impossibly, anachronistically grand. Edith is remembered as dripping with furs and 'very aristocratic, you wouldn't have got to know her'.[16] Richard was a *bone fide* Knight of the Shire, driving around in a barouche with a blanket on his knees, 'looking like Hindenburg'.[17]

By the 1920s Richard and Edith had become creatures from another age. It is true that they could be obtained by telephone, on *Groomsport 29*, but in most important respects they were by their own choice fairly ex-directory. The world had become such an incomprehensible place. Richard now had 'little faith in anyone', believing most people to be 'Sinn Feiners (all for themselves)'.[18] But one had to live amongst them. The couple tried to do a little more for themselves.

Occasionally, they even went shopping. But not shopping as we know it. Sammy McCully remembers the pair food shopping in Bangor in the mid-1920s. Their gig, with its piebald pony and gleaming rig, pulls up

Richard and Edith in old age. (Ker family)

Indomitable at eighty.
Richard Ker at Portavo.
(Ker family)

outside Robinson's the butchers. Edith is in her furs. She wears a heavy broad rimmed hat that makes her head seem at least three times its natural size. She is stroking a Cairn terrier. Neither goes inside. Indeed neither moves. Emporia of this kind are no place for gentlefolk. But then, they did need some meat for dinner.

One of them calls the butcher. Out comes Tommy Robinson, smiling and doffing. The articles they want are brought to them. It is the same at the grocer's, and so on, all the way down the street. Silver service at every door. At nearly every door. Outside one shop they are kept waiting. Mrs Ker becomes impatient. Is there a little too much on the tab, perhaps? This thing can work both ways. Outside the milliners, Edith apparently tries to pay her bill but Richard doesn't let her.[19]

Young Sammy McCully from Crow's Hill, Ballyminetragh, watches the whole thing open-mouthed. The sixteen year-old is at once fascinated and appalled. These people thought they were so high and mighty. What were the shopkeepers doing dancing attendance on them? Everyone knew they 'hadn't tuppence'. That Ker was 'bankrupt to the hilt and knee deep in bills'.[20] McCully did not appreciate what a huge compromise it was for the Kers to go shopping at all. Or pick up on the extent to which the old pair were being humoured. When he saw the Kers he saw how ill-divid the world was. The *ancien regime* may have been dead, but it had not gone. And young McCully would soon feel its wrath.

At the end of 1925 he and his friend Tom Brown decided to 'shoot the New Year in and the old year out'. They were after rabbits. And Portavo

Joe Gillespie with dog and gun. Joe, 'a hell of a wild man', gave poachers 'the hot lead'. (Ker family)

was teeming with them. But they didn't dare trespass on the demesne. Joe Gillespie liked nothing better than giving poachers 'the hot lead', and they were as likely to get it on New Year's eve as any other night of the year. Not that this stopped people trying. Florence Mary Wilson's poem *The Portavoe Poachers* hints at the illicit excitement of these midnight excursions:

It was rabbits we were after in Portavoe that night,
Lyin' snug between the whins there, up on the Warren Hill,
A red moon rose behind us that made the dark lake bright,
An' you'd almost been afeart to breathe, the trees they stud that still.[21]

That Saturday night Sammy McCully and his friend went out with their lamps and guns. It was just after midnight. They had done well, bagging fifteen rabbits, when all of a sudden they found themselves surrounded by men with guns, among them a constable from Donaghadee. Joe Gillespie had snared them. Their rabbits were confiscated and they were accused of shooting on the Portavo estate.

The boys maintained that they hadn't been. That you didn't need to enter Portavo to bag rabbits. Rabbits regularly foraged in the fields beyond the demesne. The neighbouring farmers were plagued with them. So when word of the case spread, all the local farmers – Willie Donaldson, Johnny Martin, Sammy Angus, and the rest – willingly produced affadavits giving Sammy McCully and his friend permission to shoot any rabbits that entered their fields.

The case had ceased to be about poaching and become a test of the rights of farmers. It tapped deep, atavistic suspicions on both sides. The fact that Joe Gillespie's ambush had taken place not on demesne land, but on a right of way between the estate and Donaldson's also fuelled a sense

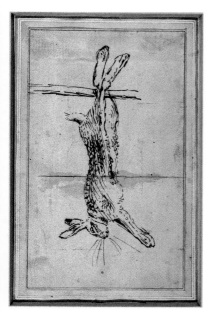

Hare by James Seymour. (Ker family)

of popular injustice. Gillespie was a shrewd operator, and if the best he could do was nab them on neutral ground, then maybe the boys weren't lying. Before long, Brown and McCully had become 'the Portavo Two'.

When the big day arrived, the courthouse was packed. On the bench sat Ker's friend Delacherois, and big farmers like McIntosh, a Resident Magistrate from the Cotton. The Kers did not enter the courthouse. They sat outside in the same gig that young McCully had so admired the year before, behind the same piebald pony. She was drowning in furs, he was at his most colossally imperious. All of a sudden there was a cheer from inside. McCully came out, shook the rabbits in Ker's face, and disappeared, borne away in the surge of the crowd. He had won.

Sammy McCully breaks off as he finishes the story. He has relived it, nearly seventy years on, and he is almost in tears as the emotion of the occasion comes back to him. Only now that the story is over do I begin to get any sense of what losing might have done to this, the mildest of men. He had given the estate a bloody nose. It was as well that the McCullys were no longer tenants.

By the late 1920s Richard and Edith's regime was in its twilight years. David was keen to take over. The old couple talked of moving to the late Miss Wellwood's house, which would soon be coming up for sale. Had the big moment finally arrived? Not on your nellie. Richard wouldn't budge, and so David remained in limbo.

David and Anna had had a trying time. He had been demobbed in 1919. However, as Europe demilitarised, Ireland went in the opposite direction, and when the Ulster Special Constabulary was formed in 1920, Ker was appointed County Down Commandant of the 'B Specials', a part-time, volunteer constabulary that was used to back up the police. He led this force of some 3,500 men through the Troubles of 1920-22, receiving an OBE in 1923 for his services.

Ker's position made him a prominent IRA target, and his decision to live in the busy end of his constituency, in Newcastle, Seaforde Lodge

The 1920-22 Troubles. David Ker with his bodyguard, Charlie McClurg (l), who is believed to cradle a revolver in his pocket. (Ker family).

*Novels by Magdalen King-Hall. One,*The Wicked Lady*, became a Holywood movie, starring Margaret Lockwood and Robert Mason. It was remade in 1983. Magdalen's sister Lou also wrote four books, and her brother Stephen became a well-known author, broadcaster and playwright.*

and then Church Hill near Castlewellan, did nothing to increase his or his family's safety. But David was 'totally fearless'.[22] The threat of assassination left him unmoved. Not so Anna, whose cousin Winnie Barrington had been murdered by the IRA in 1921.[23] She was on eighty Woodbine a day, and sent their children, Rosemary and Richard, to England.[24] This proved wise. In May 1922 the IRA attacked the Ker's house in Seaforde. But their intelligence was poor. Anna and her cook were alone in the house. Half a dozen or so B Specials were on guard outside. A sporadic, three-hour gun battle ensued, during which the water tank in the attic was holed, leading a ceiling to fall in.[25]

Theirs was not the only house to be attacked. In May 1922 Old Court in Strangford was burned to the ground. David posted guards of ten B Specials at all the district's big houses. He called at Quentin Castle to see if his cousins the King-Halls, wanted to have it protected. They and the Nugents of Portaferry declined the offer, preferring to put their trust in the goodwill of the local population. (This trust was repaid. Neither house was attacked.)

The IRA stepped up its offensive, attacking Killyleagh Castle, Ballywalter Park, Castleward and Myra Castle. Though all these assaults were beaten off, they left the gentry badly shaken.[26] Anna was completely beside herself. On the morning after the attack on her home she had fled to Finnebrogue for safety. That night it too was attacked.[27] 'Many bullets entered the house' leaving Anna, 'quite unnerved poor thing' and very fearful for David. Nini's brother-in-law, George King-Hall wrote of:

Anna Ker: left dreading the sound of the door bell. (Ker family)

a determined attempt to get at David who is in charge of Specials and Constabulary in Down. Poor Anna dreads the sound of the door bell, expecting any day David may be carried in shot by these murderers.[28]

In 1931 the couple's limbo ended. Edith died. David and Anna moved into Portavo, ostensibly to look after Richard as he entered his ninth decade. But Richard was not to be taken for granted on this or any other matter. In 1933 he surprised all and sundry by announcing that he intended to re-marry. His bride-to-be was Rowena Manley of Prospect House, Donaghadee, a child-like creature who 'wasn't of the world at all', and whose chief pleasure was said to be her weekly cup of tea with the rector. David and Anna disapproved, but love had its way:

Yesterday 14th Aug Dick Ker and Miss Manley were married! He is 83! And I think she must be nearly 58 at least. Old enough to have more sense. Mary did all she could to put her off. I think she will soon be a nurse. The wedding was in Prospect Ho.[29]

After sandwiches and champagne, they drove to Rostrevor, with Richard, now stone deaf and frighteningly loud, hollering the immortal words, 'She's not much, but she'll do me' to his driver. Brutal as this

Prospect House, Donaghadee, scene of belated domestic bliss. (Elizabeth Taggart)

Dick Ker at Eton. Lived on a small allowance as his parents struggled to manage the fees. (Ker family)

assessment sounds, these were lover's words. In spite of the rumour that they married because he thought she had money and she thought he had, there was a real affection between them. 'He calls his new wife "Baby"', Anna reported with a giggle. The couple lived together in Prospect House until Richard's death nine years later.[30]

Richard's tuxedoed departure gave David a free hand at Portavo. But the new broom did not sweep clean. By the time the fifty-three year old took over, he had run out of reforming zeal. There was no renaissance. There was no renewal of farming. Money remained a continuing problem.[31] The family's finances were mauled in the stock market crash of 1929, and though their investments recovered, they never regained their former buoyancy. It became hard enough to manage the children's school fees, never mind roll back nature.

David got comfortable with the place as it was. Indeed, it is quite possible that it overwhelmed him, as it overwhelmed the antiquarian H.C. Lawlor, who in 1942 described Portavo as 'remarkable for the ruinous remains of huge accommodation for horses and carriages, barns, cattle and farm stock'.[32] David had two men clear the ruins of the 'old castle', but made few other inroads.[33] All notion of improvement fell by the wayside. The would-be reformers cleared themselves a nest in the midden, and made themselves at home.

David and Anna were very different kinds of people, but were compatible 'in a funny sort of way'. Anna is remembered as a good natured, easy-going woman who dressed as she pleased and had 'no pride about her'. David was 'a big lath of a man', 6'4" to her 5'2", good looking, and most usually seen in tweeds, flat cap, and plus-fours; the dress of the slightly down at heel, toff-in-the-country. He was laid back

John Bell, Head Gardner, 1930s. Thoughtful and conscientious, Bell was as much a friend of the family as an employee. (Ker family)

and unflappable, a bit of a loner, a socially timid only child who stuttered and found new people difficult. Willie Bell, who saw the best in everyone, remembers him as 'happy go lucky… all for nature', adding that he 'never bothered the workers much'.[34]

That was Joe Gillespie's job, and as there was no farm, he didn't have too many workers to bother. The walled garden was still cultivated, but Joe had no authority there. This was John Bell's kingdom. Three worked in the garden in summer, Bob and Jimmy Muckle, and of course Bell himself, who rejoiced in the now slightly Ruritanian title of Head Gardener.

Under Bell's inspired direction the walled garden flourished. Somehow it avoided the general malaise, becoming the one small arena in which standards did not slip. Grapes and peaches waxed fat in the vine house. Gravel paths, set off by neat box hedges, led to flower beds and all manner of fruit and vegetable patches, apple, pear, and plum trees, and 'row upon row of the loveliest strawberries'. Black and red currents, gooseberry, loganberry and raspberry plants also decked its buttressed walls.[35]

These good things attracted great interest. The rabbits couldn't raid it, the walls were too high. But the demesne was full of red squirrels, and 'these cheeky wee boys were the devil for the strawberries'. They cut the nets and thieved the fruit, then climbed onto the walls and chittered and raged at everyone who rebuked them. A big hawk also visited. And people came in droves. Jimmy Muckle recalls that the garden was 'often packed… an awful crowd used to come' to buy fresh fruit and vegetables. Honor Rudnitsky used to come with a flock of housewives from Ballywilliam. Hawkers bought strawberries 'wholesale' to sell to hotels

*'Guilty as charged'. David
Ker with fighting cock and
dog. (Ker family)*

in Donaghadee. A van toured Donaghadee and Groomsport three times a
week, selling the garden's produce.[36]

While John Bell and Joe Gillespie looked after the great outdoors,
Anna managed the house, and its staff of cook, maid, and butler. Nobody
was driven very hard, but nobody was trusted. Anna expected servants to
steal, so everything was locked up, including the maid, who was locked
away in the dining room whenever she cleaned the silver. Rooms were
locked on a regular basis, while Anna toured the house 'like a jailer',
accompanied by a giant bunch of keys.[37]

Though he had resigned from the B Specials in order to devote himself
to the reform of Portavo, David never became essential to its running.
This freed him to pursue his 'sporting' interests. In the early 1920s he and
his father set up a coursing club, which met on Shore Hill. He shot and
hunted.[38] He bred hounds, and was regularly seen on the roads on his
bicycle with ten or twelve dogs scurrying behind him. He hunted otters.
He bred fighting cocks, and would go as far as County Monaghan for a
cockfight, carrying his mains in a false compartment in 'his beat-up
Austin Twelve'.[39]

He also fought them at a pit 'hidden in the woods' of Portavo, betting heavily on the outcome.[40] Animals were pitted against each other in gladiatorial combat. The cocks were kept in pens in the yard and fed on beans to put fighting spirit in them. Then Ker and his cronies gathered at daybreak (to avoid the police), put the spurs on their birds, and watched them hack and gash each other to pieces.[41]

David photographed his champions. This proud bird ruled the roost in 1926. (Ker family)

If he caught a badger, he would lock it in the barn then throw in the dogs. The 'yapping and yelping' is said to have been awful. When nature could not keep up with him, he supplied himself, breeding foxes in 'the Orchard', the far walled garden. It didn't matter what was pitched against what, Ker wasn't fussy. If he had a terrier after a rat he was happy, and if he had a bet on it so much the better, for 'he would have bet on two flies crawling up a wall'.[42]

All this made people uneasy. As did Ker's strange fearlessness. David possessed immense *sang froid*. He did things that sensible people wouldn't dream of, like putting his hand in a foxhole to pull out a fox. The Major was strange alright, no question.[43]

The heads shook. But there was no rush to judgement. It was a matter for sorrow. There was a great pragmatism about the country. A great urge to include people and rub along regardless. There was good in the Major. There were a few good people around him. And it didn't do to get worked up about your neighbours' little foibles. The War had done terrible things to people. At least Ker didn't take it out on humans.

Some may also have considered the bigger negative that lay behind this; the ruination of Ker's class. For the land purchase money wasn't just running out at Portavo. It was running out in big houses all over Ireland. Ker and his small farmer neighbours were in some ways on a parallel road. Both belonged to classes that had lost their economic relevance. The social differences between them were as wide as is conceivable, but irony knows no boundaries. The gentry and their economic opposite numbers the small farmers were going to hell in a handcart, together.

35 Toffs and tourists

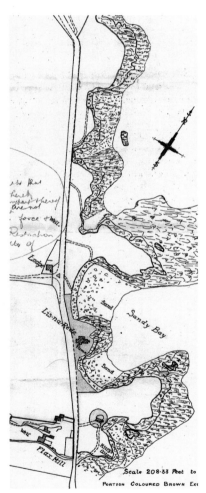

Virgin territory. The largely unbuilt shore, c.1920. (Brown McConnell Clark)

Toffs and tourists

By the 1920s the scenic coast of northern County Down was enjoying an annual tourist invasion. This tourism was of a kind no longer seen, a kind that involved very large numbers of people travelling very small distances. Most of the visitors came from Belfast, and they came by bicycle, charabanc, car, and train. Sandy Bay became popular with bathers. People picnicked on the sward upon which the Stone House now stands.

A gaily-painted wooden Tea Room, Dunns, opened on the shore, funded out of 'the pittance' Mr Dunn, an ex-soldier, had received 'for his services in the Great War'.[1] Visitors flocked to it, as did locals. The atmosphere was free and easy. Mrs Dunn would serve up a pot of tea, and 'not mind if you brought your own piece of soda'. It sold ice cream, lemonade and buns, and on good days tables and chairs were set up outdoors. Occasionally there were even dances.[2]

Johnny Aird was equally quick off the mark. He built Orlock's first wooden tourist bungalow on his best field in 1921. Brick and mortar summer houses followed in 1928, and before long a regular shanty town had grown up on the north side of Orlock Hill.[3] The family showed great entrepreneurial spirit. But this spirit had a rather hard edge. In 1935 the Airds, who fifty years before had themselves faced eviction, evicted Dunn so that they could take his land for building.[4] The Tea Room was unceremoniously closed.

Letting rooms and even one's home to tourists was another giant moneyspinner. In Donaghadee, families let out their houses to tourists and moved into shacks and sheds at the bottom of the garden. If they had nowhere to go, they made do with letting rooms. In Portavo, Mrs Bell let rooms, and most of the Close was rented out during the summer.

The demand was terrific. Minnie Connell built two cheerfully painted wooden bungalows in one of her rockier fields. A pair of swanky, semi-detached houses was speculatively built in Ballywilliam with the tourist trade in mind. They were filled every year. Even the genteel Miss Wellwood got in on the act, renting her home in summer to friends of the family, called Erskine, from Holywood.[5]

Girlfriends galore! Couples on the Stockbridge Road, c.1930 (l-r) Davy Muckle, Belfast girl, Walker Boyd, Willie Bell, Belfast girl, Tommy Boyd, Belfast girl,Myra Bailey, mystery boy, with his arms over Myra and Kitty, Kitty Fletcher, Carson Boyd, Belfast girl, John Boyd, Jimmy Lightbody. (Boyd family)

All classes came. The Atkinsons, who took one of the rather lordly Ballywilliam semis, arrived with their cook and maid, and stayed the whole summer. Arthur Atkinson, a senior partner in a firm of Belfast accountants, swam every morning, played golf in the evenings and went to work as usual during the day. He was driven to Donaghadee station each morning, and went to the office by train.

As the menfolk toiled, the womenfolk mingled, getting to know the locals. Servants attended Minnie Connell's soirées. One thing led to another and before the Atkinsons knew it, Susan their lively, hare-lipped cook had married young Jimmy Lightbody and moved into a cottage on the Stockbridge Road.[6]

If tourism meant money to the grown ups, to the young men of the district it meant girls. Lots of them. 'A new girl every month', as John Boyd puts it, with a blasé wave of the hand. On Sundays, they would arrive in Donaghadee by train, then walk out to Dunns or Boyds. Some managed the three miles in high heels, John Boyd remembers.[7] The male youth of the place turned into gigolos. Or so they would have us believe. And why not? Tourism may indeed have brought with it a certain amount of sexual and emotional freedom, even to Presbyterian Portavo.

Some of the visitors wanted to settle. In the late 1920s two parties approached the estate seeking building land. The estate had hitherto largely resisted attempts to clutter up the shore. Only two houses, Lis-na-rede, and Glenburnie, a special concession to the daughter of a trusted retainer, had been built on the Ker shoreline in a hundred years.

On the face of it refusals seemed likely. However these were no ordinary solicitations. The first was from a tea merchant and decorated war veteran, Walter (later Sir Walter) Smiles, grandson of Samuel Smiles, the author of *Self Help*, the nineteenth century bible of self improvement.

Portavo Point, built for Sir Walter Smiles in 1929.

Smiles' lineage did not end here. He was also grand nephew of the famous cook, Mrs Beeton, and son of one of the founders of the Belfast Ropeworks, formerly the largest in the world.[8]

Richard was impressed. Smiles was just the sort of neighbour he could warm to. The fellow might even be good for a loan. And his new villa would be charming. Smiles planned to erect a two storied summer house 'at a cost of about £2000' on Portavo Point. He did not want anything cheap or nasty built around him, and before signing obtained a guarantee that 'no smaller houses than Miss Wellwood's' would be permitted nearby.[9]

So up went 'Portavo Point', cool and pleasant, but after all this huffing and puffing, something of an anticlimax. Hard on its heels came the Stone House, built for John (later Sir John) Johnston from Fallowfields near Lurgan, a wealthy linen baron and a newly elected Stormont MP.[10] This was the real thing. Where Smiles faffed, Johnston delivered, building a fine Arts & Crafts Revival house on the northern promontory of Sandy Bay in 1929, at a reputed cost of £10,000.[11]

'The Stone House' set a new architectural standard. Sitting alone on the point, with just the sea and sky for company, it offers us a seductive vision of man and nature living in harmony.[12] However, this utopia is an illusion. The Stone House subordinates nature as completely as Ker's mansion house did in 1820. But it doesn't *seem* that way. On the contrary, the house appears to surrender to its surroundings and become as one with the things around it. The garden emphasises this sense of integration. Almost everything in it looks as though it could have been

The Stone House is at its most chameleon-like in this aerial view from the 1940s. (Mrs Thompson)

growing there before the house arrived. Even the lichens that garnish its Westmoreland slate roof conspire to enhance it.

The house works wonderfully well. Though extravagant it is tasteful, though showy, it seems almost meek, asserting itself so quietly that its perfectly well-built neighbours look cheap and attention-seeking by comparison. Johnston, who 'looked like Mr Punch' and had a strict, Edwardian manner, lived here during the summer with his wife and eight children. A large staff danced attendance on the family. Fresh flowers and vegetables arrived each week from Fallowfields.[13] Portavo had not seen style like this since the destruction of Ker's 'castle'.

Three 'great big mansions' also rose on the landward side of the road.[14] The earliest was Kilcoroon, built on a corner of Minnie Connell's farm for another linen magnate, Saville Hardy. Its glory was its garden. Hardy was a passionate gardener who, with a little help, turned a rough whin field behind the house into something approaching a fairytale garden. Six gardeners, including Alec Dickson and Jimmy Lightbody, worked here all year round under the amiable direction of Robert Boyd, who came here after giving up the mill, and rose to the position of Head Gardener.[15]

Once every year, a marquee was put up, catering staff were hired, the gardeners put on their Sunday best, and the garden was opened to the public (all proceeds going to the Boys Brigade), while proud bachelor Hardy, his bachelor brothers and spinster sister, fluttered from grove to grove, basking in the universal praise.

Kilcoroon's neighbour, Stramore Lodge (none of these houses was known by anything as vulgar as a number), was built in or around 1930,

The effervescent Stramore Lodge,
built for Sir Samuel Kelly.

at the height of the mansion building boom.[16] It is an exuberant white
house with a tower, a long vaguely boat-shaped footprint, proud, prow-
like gables and funnel-like chimneys, an effect the Ulster Architectural
Heritage Society rather sniffily described as owing as much to Disney as
Lutyens.[17] But it surely owed as much to the long whitewashed cottages
around it. It is a sort of playful, stretched limo version of a traditional
Ulster cottage. Were it a wine it would be light and sparkling, were it an
actress, it would be Marilyn Monroe, its prows her dress rising in the
warm New York subway air. Stramore Lodge was built for Sir Samuel
Kelly, a coal importer and shipping contractor, hence its nautical theme.[18]

The villas rained down. Tigh-na-Mara (gallic for House by the Sea), a
tall, handsome, even haughty Mr Darcy-ish affair, appeared to the north
of Kilcoroon in 1930. Hip-roofed, four chimneyed, with herringbone
brickwork and mock stone facings, it is mindful of order, propriety,
tradition, but at the same time prepared to be tastefully flash. It was built
for A.M. Hamilton, the owner of a coastal shipping company based in
Belfast.

All these magnates. It was getting out of hand. There were more 'Sirs'
in Portavo than ordinary people.[19] Or so it seemed. In three short years
Portavo's down-at-heel shoreline had become Millionaire's Row. Great
swathes of the shore had been privatised. Favourite picnic and fishing
spots had gone. Three distinct and not particularly compatible groups
now shared the terrain; the farming community, the estate (sadly reduced
to the condition of burnt out superpower), and the lotus-eating
newcomers who had colonised the shore.

The newcomers lost no time in asserting their values. They saw the
shore aesthetically, and loved its picturesqueness. And there was no place
in their vision for sweaty farmers forking seaweed. Had the farmers been
a little more charmingly rustic, had the womenfolk danced in folk

Effortlessly classy. The Stone House by D. Bond Walker. (Mrs Thompson)

costume to the sound of tambourines while their menfolk gathered, then the custom might have had their blessing. But Portavo's farmers were the wrong kind of quaint. The bays were fenced to stop the farmers from gathering wrack.

But the farmers would not be denied their seaweed, their shingle or their sand. Trouble flared. Smiles's fences were torn down. The gates on the Corbies were thrown into the sea. Sir John Johnston put a gate on the Blocken Hole and tried to stop Willie Matear of Ballyfotherly from taking sand. Matear protested that he had gathered sand here all his life. Johnston threatened to take him to the House of Lords.[20]

But a crisis was averted. A kind of acceptance dawned. There were no more threats or fences. Indeed, links between the townland and the colony grew. Farmers took hay off the grounds of the big houses. The interior provided the shore with maids and gardeners. Pearl Gillespie stoked the Johnstons' boiler. Mrs Bell cooked for the Smiles. The shore provided the labouring community on the Stockbridge Road with a new economic base.[21] But there was no wider integration and it is unrealistic to expect it. In as far as they were part of any broader grouping, the newcomers belonged to the community of blow-ins that lived on Donaghadee's golden mile, the affluent Warren Road.

The Warren Road grew steadily during the 1920s. In 1833, at the time of the first Ordnance Survey, the town had not quite reached the Road and there was very little on it. In 1858, the year of the first revision, the Road was still fairly bare.[22] The arrival of the railway in 1861 did not turn Donaghadee into a boom town. Between 1861-91 its population fell by nearly 30%.[23] It took decades for it to become a minor watering resort for Belfast. When it did, towards the end of the century, settlement struck out northwards, under the careful direction of the Delacherois estate, which encouraged the development of large, gracious dwellings.

By 1900, a line of rather wonderful, slightly elephantine villas had arisen on the landward side of the road. By 1939, the brick and mortar procession had arrived at the golf course. It then leapfrogged the golf links, and spilled onto the Warren, which filled, infilled, and then had its infills infilled, to create the agreeable chaos we see today. The mansions at Portavo were not quite part of this. They were about going somewhere lovely and unspoilt, but not too far out of the way. So Portavo was just right for them. In 1927, on the eve of the Jazz Age building boom, there were only two clusters of seaside houses to the north of the golf course. Their independence was shortlived. By 1930, the road had found them, and drawn them into its suburban embrace. Then everything stopped as the Great Depression brought the building boom to an end.

Water, water everywhere...

By 1931 it had become all too clear that Donaghadee's infrastructure had not kept pace with its expansion. Water was a particular problem. Things were fine in winter, but 'during the summer months it was almost impossible to get a supply'.[1] Something would have to be done. But by whom? During most of the 1920s, Donaghadee and its hinterland (which ran north to Orlock), had been governed by an Urban District Council. In 1929, however, this factious and incompetent body had been suspended. A Major Sam Brush had been appointed Town Commissioner, and given the invidious task of 'ruling' in its place.

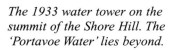

The 1933 water tower on the summit of the Shore Hill. The 'Portavoe Water' lies beyond.

Brush moved in a hostile environment. Many of the aggrieved former councillors bitterly disliked him, and had a strong vested interest in seeing him fail. They hated him all the more when he tried to tackle the water problem, which they had done little about for years. When Brush sought advice he was told that Donaghadee had two options. It could draw on the Belfast mains supply at the prohibitive cost of £40,000, or it could build its own reservoir, at a cost of £25,000.[2] Only one place in the town's low-lying and almost riverless hinterland could accommodate such a reservoir: the low-lying land on Portavo's northern border.

Brush's advisors included W.J.E. Binnie of London, the Consulting Engineer on the Silent Valley Reservoir, and 'one of the greatest authorities on water in the world'. And Binnie was bullish. His studies had convinced him that this damp, almost boggy land would make 'an excellent site for a dam'.[3] The locals were rather more sceptical, but no-one came up with an affordable alternative. The project went ahead. The land was bought.[4] About a hundred men, most of them local, spent about a year and a half cutting the hull of the new reservoir, building the dam, and raising a fifty-two foot water tower on Shore Hill. The work came at the height of the Great Depression, providing a tremendous fillip for the local economy.[5]

By the summer of 1933, Portavo's northern border had been transformed.[6] The cow's graveyard[7] had become the Portavoe Water, a shimmering 31½ acre lake containing fifty-four million gallons of water. This was working water, which was pumped to the top of Shore Hill, where it was held in a 100,000 gallon steel tank and then piped to nearly every corner of the Urban District Council area. The sublime nectar was drunk in the Stone House and the cottages. It flushed the toilets and made the tea. By special arrangement, Portavo House received its own direct supply.[8]

The 'Portavoe Water', opened in October 1933, at the height of the Great Depression.

But all was not as it should have been. Although the new water was much softer than the old supply, it was 'not considered a treat' in Donaghadee. It was said to be 'Good to drink, but useless for washing, as it needs lots of soap.'[9] There were complaints about its curious, indeterminate taste and smell. Embarrassed officials put this down to teething troubles. But they didn't go away and as time passed, the wails became bitter.[10] The blows rained down on poor Major Brush. The scheme's critics had a field day:

We have a sturdy football team, and... girls who cannot be beaten in Ulster for physique, but after a few years of Portavoe bog muck we will have a troupe of contortionists and a bevy of bow-legged lassies[11]

The project came to be regarded as a disaster. In winter the water was merely aromatic and curious tasting. In spring, however, it came to life. By summer it had matured into an ecologically rich brew that stained baths and turned washing brown. At times it ran out altogether. In dry summers following dry winters people had to resort to wells and standpipes.[12] Water lorries toured the streets.

Many blamed the farmers. The reservoir drew its water from farmland, and when the use of artificial fertilisers became widespread, these additives were carried into the water supply producing copious amounts of algae in dry years. The farmers blamed the designers. The catchment area was too small. There were no good feeder streams. The reservoir collected all 'the auld shuck water'.[13] Another problem may have been the way the supply was used. Binnie had intended the reservoir to be seventeen feet deep, with only the top ten feet being drawn.[14] Had the water service been tempted to go deeper, in order to maintain a supply?

Remedial action was taken. A pipe was run in from the Glenburnie Burn. A new water tank was fitted around the old. A ring of sixteen stanchions was added to the water tower, making it look 'like Stonehenge'.[15] But the improvements made little difference. Matters came to a head in the early 1970s, when some fifty angry townswomen besieged the Town Hall, waving their streaky washing at the by now reinstated councillors.[16] The southern half of the town was capable of being supplied by the Silent Valley Reservoir, and they demanded to be connected. Pronto.

The council hesitated. This went right against the grain. They could not have the working classes drinking pure Mourne water, while the Warren Road drank mud. That would be turning the natural order on its head. To which the protesters, hearing of the Warren Road's plight, supposedly retorted, 'Let them drink gin.'[17] The council was swept away in the local government reforms of 1974. The Mourne water arrived soon after, whereon the Portavoe Water, the eighth largest lake in County Down, began a new life as a trout fishery.[18]

Farewell to the island

In 1931 the Great Copeland Island had eleven inhabitants. It had one young family, that of Jim Emerson, and while the Emersons remained there was some hope that the island might have a future. But when his children reached school age Emerson left, feeling like a Judas. He had had little choice. If he had stayed, the children would not have received an education. It was no longer possible to raise a family on the island. The course was set. Now it was just a matter of time.

In 1935 there were just six people on the island, most of them in their late fifties, all of them lifelong islanders. That Easter, however, they were joined by a pair of idealistic newly-weds, the Campbells, who had fallen in love with the island during the previous summer, when they had honeymooned there. The couple bought twenty acres, which they

Mew (r) and Lighthouse Island from the Great Copeland Island, 1934, by J.W. Carey. (Tughan family)

Clegg and Emerson (both r) landing coal on the Copeland Island, 1930s. Note the clog wheeled cart. All the island's fuel had to be imported. (Reid family)

David Emerson (l), Freddie Clegg (r), and an unknown guest pictured outside the Cleggs cottage, 1930s. (Reid family)

intended to farm. Philip Campbell was an unemployed teacher, so had he arrived a couple of years earlier, who knows what might have been. Had the island won a reprieve? A faint hope stirred.

But it was not to be. Six months later, with winter closing in, the Campbells fled the island. In 1948, when the island had ceased to be permanently inhabited and the way of life of centuries had come to an end, Philip Campbell's wife (known to us only as M.H.) wrote a short account of their time there.[1] It is an unsentimental but affectionate final glimpse of island life.

We meet John Emerson with his sweet tooth, Freddie Clegg, who seems far too chatty to have been an islander, and David Emerson, his half-deaf friend. We get to know David's sister, Mary Jane Emerson, who lived on bread, potatoes and tea, and when she needed to clean her hands to make butter, scalded them with near boiling water.[2] Mrs Campbell was taken aback. These islanders were tough, and hardworking. The Emersons got up so early they had their dinner at eleven.

Though not so much as a word was spoken, the islanders were thrilled by the Campbells' arrival, and did all they could to make them feel at home. The Campbells, in turn, discovered a less complicated and, they felt, more authentic way of life. The island 'purged life of the unessential'. There was a profundity in the simplicity of their lives there and something uplifting about the communal character of island life. The term that summed it up best, Mrs Campbell felt, was the old English word 'halig', meaning 'hale' or 'holy':

There is little of Celtic imagination in the folk there, little of song or poetry as the Hebridean Islands know it; the Copeland Islanders know themselves in a downright un-imaginative, common-sensible sort of way and they accept

The auction of David Emerson's farm, 1944, from an old newspaper cutting. The Emersons sat in the kitchen while the auction took place outside.

themselves and all human nature just as they accept tide and weather, sun and cold, age and sickness. And this acceptance... gives to them and to the land they farm a sense of harmony and peacefulness...[3]

But this was not enough to keep them. Island life proved too authentic, and maybe too damn hard. Did Mrs Campbell idealise island life? Of course she did. She could not have done less – she was writing its obituary. And she had her guilt to live with too. The classic Copelands guilt, the guilt of leaving.

'You'll no like it over there', David Emerson had remarked, when he heard that they were going. By the island's laconic standards Emerson had as good as beseeched them to stay. Did the islanders feel abandoned when the Campbells departed? Ach no, there was too much to be getting on with. And there would be more visitors along next spring.

Island life went on. But its pace got slower. No new generation pushed through to let the tired bodies rest. The island wound down. But all stayed fair until John Emerson, the island boatman, died in 1943. Life was tough without John. Jobs that had been shared three ways now had to be shared two. In the following year, David Emerson turned seventy. His position was the most exposed. His thirty-nine acre farm was three times the size of Freddie Clegg's, and he had just one sister to help him. The hard fact had to be faced. The farm was too much for him. It had probably been too much for him for years. The Emersons made their decision. It was time to go.

The auction of the farm was a melancholy occasion. The Emersons sat by the fire as everything they owned was sold in the yard outside. David Ker bought the farm, as he had bought John Emerson's the year before, and Jim Emerson's a few years previously. The estate was reclaiming the island.[4]

And now they were three. Three in one household. The compulsively chatty Freddie Clegg and his sisters Eliza and Essie (Isa) spent the winter of 1944-45 on the island. But David Emerson's decision to go was a decision made for them all. Island life had become 'too lonely'. In 1947, the Cleggs moved to East Street in Donaghadee, where they encountered their first flush toilet. 'C'mere Lisa, there's a well in the house', being Freddie Clegg's – perfectly logical – reaction to the sight of this new-fangled mod-con.[5]

The island had no literary afterlife. No Peig Sayers or Tomas O'Crohan stepped forward from amongst the islanders ranks to, 'preserve from forgetfulness those days that I have seen against the time [when] there will be none... to remember them'.[6] Only Mrs Campbell took up her pen to record its latter days. The island way of life passed into history. The Great Copeland was left to the curlews and the rabbits, to seasonal visitors, and to David Emerson's old horse thresher, which still sits there rusting in what was once his back field.[7]

36 World War Two

When Britain and Germany went to war in September 1939 there was little expectation that Northern Ireland might become a Luftwaffe target. Lady Londonderry's view was typical. Talk of bombing was 'rot'. Air raid precautions were absurd, 'Air raid wardens and blackouts! As if anyone cared or wished to bomb Belfast'.[1]

The fall of France made no dent in this complacency. The war was something that was happening 'over there'. In December 1940, a visitor described Belfast as 'a fools paradise'. In early 1941 a senior civil servant wrote of widespread 'disbelief in the... possibility of air raids'.[2] Then in March 1941, Clydeside was bombed. And on the night of Easter Tuesday, April 15-16th 1941, the unthinkable happened. Belfast was bombed. And so was Portavo.

It is 11pm on the night of Easter Tuesday, and no-one is in any doubt that trouble is coming. The air raid sirens have gone off in Belfast. A distant, ominous hum could be heard. The Muckles were gathered in the kitchen, away from the windows. The Martins of Moor Farm were under the kitchen table. Suddenly, flares illuminated the night sky. The sheer intensity of the light was staggering. 'You could have read the smallest print by it', Alec Martin recalls.[3] It was brighter than day. But this light was very different from daylight. It sought people out. It mocked their illusions of safety. It found them under their kitchen tables. It left them feeling foolish and horribly exposed.

But surely it would go no further than this. This was not Belfast or London. This was the middle of nowhere. There was nothing here to bomb.

But suddenly, unaccountably, bombs fell. A landmine exploded about 150 metres from Moor Farm, ripping its roof off. A wall collapsed onto a bed, driving its legs through the kitchen ceiling.[4] Bombs screamed. The house quaked. The Martins cowered. High explosives and incendiaries followed. A bomb sent 'a stone the size of a wheelbarrow' through Willie Boyd's hay shed.[5]

An incendiary bomb struck 'the Kennel' in Ballyfotherly. Thankfully the house was empty. Its occupants, the Hannas, had fled on hearing the

Take cover! A flight of German Dornier bombers approaches. No-one here expected to be bombed.

drone of approaching planes. In the confusion, Mrs Hanna had left the lights on, and for years afterwards tortured herself with the mistaken belief that those lights had attracted the bombers.[6] The neighbours and an off-duty soldier fought the blaze, saving one room and a lean to, which the Hannas lived in for the rest of the war.[7]

High explosives fell singly and in small clusters. They were thinly spread, so that to be hit or even hurt by one would have been very bad luck indeed. The incendiaries were a different matter. They positively rained down, and the risk of fire was considerable. The incendiaries were delivered in a most ingenious manner. They fell in their own wicker dispenser, known as a 'Molotov bread basket', because it was filled with bombs placed tail downwards, making their plump heads look like so many grey baps. The wicker pan was attached to a parachute to ensure that it fell slowly. After a pre-set time this started to spin, sowing its dragon's teeth in an ever-decreasing spiral pattern.

It was these that fell on Portavo, Ballyfotherly and Ballyminetragh on that never-to-be-forgotten night. And they fell in droves. Mina Muckle remembers incendiaries 'dropping everywhere. It was very frightening.'[8] Dozens ignited in the fields. Small, persistent blazes started. Everyone who lived under thatch – the Muckles, Faulkners, Campbells and Bells – had their nerves stretched to breaking point. The McCullys of Crow's Hill spent the night in a dry shuck wrapped in blankets.[9] The Humphreys spent it in the hay shed, hiding amongst the bales.[10]

A troop of soldiers was on exercise on the Kylestone Road when the bombing started. They flung themselves to the ground, and stayed there.

A woman living opposite came out to offer them shelter. 'Get back inside' their officer shouted. Then added, 'Don't worry, we'll look after you,' in best Captain Mainwaring fashion. [11]

In the morning there was much to wonder at. There were people and animals to check on, anxieties to be assuaged. Moor Farm had been worst hit. Its front door had been blown in, sucked through the roof and left lying in a field. Fifty metres in front of the house, a crater ten metres wide and five metres deep straddled the lane. It was a chilling spectacle, particularly when it is remembered that the soil cover here is less than a metre deep. But it was not a unique one. Alec Martin estimates that maybe fifteen large and small high explosive bombs fell locally that night, seven of them on Moor Farm.[12]

Unexploded incendiaries littered the fields. That Wednesday the military authorities made safe over three hundred, most of them collected from the southern Portavo-Ballyminetragh border. Farmers gathered some and kept them as curios.[13] In the Moor Field, the Martins discovered the author of much of the previous evening's mayhem, an almost intact Molotov bread basket, complete with fins, swivel and parachute, surrounded by unexploded incendiary bombs, some of them just six metres apart. This trophy was kept as a souvenir. The delicate parachute silk is said to have kept Mrs Martin in 'smalls' for years after.[14]

The raid left the Martins homeless. For three weeks they lived with the Donaldsons, while the War Damage Commission fixed the house. (The

Deadly visitor. The casing of one of the incendiary bombs that fell on Portavo. (Ker family)

Home on leave. Carson Boyd with his niece Ethel in Saville Hardy's garden. (Boyd family)

repairs were botched, and had to be redone when mushrooms started growing out of the walls.) The neighbours rallied round. That Thursday, a fleet of carts and tractors filled the crater that lay across the lane with gravel and stones from the Orlock foreshore. Within a few months the Martins were back on their feet, and the farm was again a going concern.[15]

The damage to Belfast was not so easily made good. Nine hundred died in the April 15th-16th raid. The city was horribly scarred. Refugees poured into the countryside. 'All the wee places along the Stockbridge Road' were rented to city folk.[16] Farms took in evacuees to the delight of the local youngsters. All of a sudden they had twice as many friends, and enough footballers for two teams. Many of the visitors stayed until (and in some cases, beyond) the war's end, and went to school in Donaghadee.[17]

The biggest influx, however, was military. An anti-aircraft battery was stationed at Groomsport.[18] A coastal battery was set up at Orlock, where large bore anti-shipping guns defended Belfast Lough.[19] A three-acre army camp was set up in a corner of the Portavo demesne, on what is now the site of the Stockbridge Road sawmill. British and later American units were stationed here. The British are remembered as well-behaved. The Yanks are remembered for shooting all the deer.[20]

The Americans created quite a sensation. Patricia Smiles and Jacqueline Delacherois imperilled their reputations by fraternising with the visitors (officers, not other ranks, of course).[21] The local girls were just as keen, and the G.I.s did not want for company. Soldiers looking for 'a good time' did not always have to resort to the fleshpots of Belfast and Bangor. Some basic services were available locally. On Saturday and Sunday afternoons, a woman from the Springwell Road entertained yankee soldiers at half a crown a time in Fanny's Meadow, in the Dark Wood in Portavo demesne. She was kept busy. Another from the Cotton also made her rather riper charms available. The units 'were always changing', and they did a roaring trade.[22]

Portavo had more to offer the allied war machine than personal services. As in World War One, its main contribution was food. Farming boomed. 'There was a market for everything', Alec Martin remembers. 'We all had to put our hands to the plough', says David Donaldson, recalling compulsory wartime tillage. Lacking Clydesdales, the Kers ploughed with high tempered hunters, which opened nearly an acre a day ('the men could hardly keep up with them'). Joe Gillespie outraged local Sabbatarians by ploughing on Sundays.[23] The walled garden came into its own. Strawberries, gooseberries, and even lettuce and cucumber became sought after delicacies. Everything it produced was promptly sold.[24]

Flax growing revived. Huge amounts of grain were grown. The land was pushed hard. Maybe too hard. In 1942 yields faltered and were

Farming boomed during the war, 'There was a market for everything'. (HMSO)

maintained only through the copious use of fertilisers. 'Places that were not fit to be ploughed' were brought into cultivation.[25] Food prices rose. Farm incomes rose. Farm labourers' wages more than doubled.[26]

Grants and loan schemes encouraged mechanisation. The Donaldsons got their first tractor, a Fordson, in 1942.[27] The Kers got a Fordson and an old binder.[28] The Boyds, ahead of the game as ever, upgraded to an 'International' in 1941. Farmers got extra petrol rations and some sold the petrol.[29] Even time changed. 'Double summer time' was introduced to boost productivity. This meant that in June, 'it was broad daylight until after midnight. They got a day and a half's work out of us every day'.[30]

The other staple Portavo could offer was people. It offered these sparingly. As in World War One, the farm came first. Few labouring men were tempted to join up. Enlistment was modest. Most of the inter-war glut of young men were now in their thirties, and perhaps a little long in the tooth for campaigning.

But there were notable and even distinguished exceptions. Two men with Portavo connections served on the battlecruiser, *HMS Hood*,

The HMS Hood being refitted in Glasgow. (Scottish Record Office)

William Campbell from the Close and Jackie Erskine, who as a boy had spent carefree summers at Glenburnie.[31] By an amazing stroke of luck, Campbell was not on board when the *Hood* intercepted the mighty German battleship, *Bismark*. Jack Erskine was not so lucky. The duel lasted just eight minutes. The *Bismark's* gunnery was uncannily accurate. After just three or four salvoes, one of her shells struck the *Hood's* munitions, and the huge British battlecruiser was blown apart. 1,419 crewed the vessel. Just three men survived.

Tommy Muckle, John Muckle's youngest son, joined the Royal Air Force and was shot down and taken prisoner by the Japanese. He did not survive captivity.[32] Jack Erskine's brother Basil was shot down and killed on his first bombing mission over Germany.[33] Carson Boyd joined the RAF as an airport fireman. He had 'many close scrapes' in Cyprus and North Africa, during Luftwaffe attacks on allied airstrips.[34]

David's son, Richard (Dick) Ker, also served in the desert. When war broke out, he joined the Royal Ulster Rifles, but later moved to the

Coldstream Guards, attaining the rank of major.[35] Ker fought in the Western Desert, where he proved a courageous soldier. In 1942 he was awarded the Military Cross for pressing home an attack on a heavily defended Afrika Corps position, in the face of withering mortar and machine gun fire. Six months later, just after the Salerno landing, Ker was wounded in both legs during an attack on a hilltop redoubt. An anti-personnel mine had exploded beneath him. He couldn't move and he couldn't be retrieved; there were too many snipers. But Ker had had the presence of mind to get himself wounded in a vineyard. For twenty-four hours he lay injured on the battlefield, living on grapes picked for him by his dutiful sergeant, Charlie Smy.[36]

Dick Ker, wounded at Salerno. (Ker family)

It took him two years to recover from his wounds.[37] Indeed he never fully recovered, and in later years, his legs periodically leeched little filaments of metal.[38] He would see no more fighting. By the time he had recovered, Hitler was dead, victory had been secured, and the Labour Party had won its famous post-war landslide. A new era was at hand.

37   The new brooms

In 1948 David Ker fell ill and his son Dick came back to take over. With him came his new wife Virginia, whom he had married that July, after a whirlwind romance.

The couple had met on the royal estate at Sandringham, where Dick had been learning farm management. Virginia Howard's parents lived at Anmer Hall, a couple of miles away. She worked in London, but came home most weekends, and it was on one of these weekends that they met. They got married 'four or five months' later and moved into a little flat on the estate. Dick was offered a job at Wokey Hole. A life lived among English place names, to English rhythms, seemed to beckon.

Then, out of the blue, in grey November, he was called back to Ireland. It was all new to Virginia (known to all as Bidger). A new place. Unintelligible accents. Strange people. And motherhood too, for she was then two months pregnant with her daughter Caroline.

Nothing had prepared her for the circumstances she now found herself in. She had been brought up 'in a very strict English way' in an autocratic but smoothly run household. Her father, the Hon. James Howard, was a younger son of the 18th Earl of Suffolk. Her mother was Nancy Lubbock, granddaughter of Sir John Lubbock, the first Lord Avebury, a banker, philanthropist and parliamentarian, and the 'inventor' of the Bank Holiday.[1]

In their day, Bidger's mother and her two sisters, had been tremendous heiresses, owning twenty-five percent of Whitbreads Brewery, among other assets.[2] Although most of this fabulous wealth had gone long before her marriage, Bidger was used to money, order and propriety. To servants in starched linen. To instructing staff, not negotiating with them. To a certain level of efficiency.

She was also used to being part of a viable social group. The English gentry in the 1940s were still a going concern. They had held onto their estates and maintained their standing. The Irish gentry, on the other hand, were for the most part in a state of disarray, and their down at heel, never-mind-the-quality-feel-the-width ways came as a profound shock to the system.

Bidger (Virginia Ker) with son David, London 1953. (Ker family)

Bidger hated it in Northern Ireland. She was cold, miserable, and sick every morning. She wanted to go home. But her father wouldn't hear of it. She had married Ker and must stick with him. That was the end of it. So she sought continuity. Like-minded people. These people were not exactly numerous, but they could be found. People like Joyce Byers, Lady Clanwilliam (her best friend), and Patsy King, daughter of Lord Annally, and wife of estate agent Ossie King. This little coterie of English girls in Ireland found one another out and stuck together.

Her new home was uninviting. Everything at Portavo seemed 'primitive' and throughother.[3] The house was freezing. The grounds were a shambles. Whins 'as thick as trees and as high' covered half of Shore Hill.[4] Twelve acres of rushes surrounded the pleasure dam.[5] Fences were rotten, drains were tramped, goats grazed where wheat had once grown.[6]

The place needed taken in hand. Dick sold prints, pictures, furniture,

Erin Lodge, Donaghadee. Furnished with bric-a-brac from the yard at Portavo. This bric-a-brac was highly exotic. David Ker remembers stumbling on a head by Canova in a byre here in the 1960s. (Elizabeth Taggart)

books and silver. He sold land at Sydenham. He got £3,000 for a set of Canaletto engravings. The money went into restoring Portavo.[7] 'Thousands and thousands' of rabbits were trapped.[8] The wetlands were drained and ploughed. Beech, larch and fir trees were planted.[9] Superannuated retainers, including 'the butler with the food down his front', were let go. The house was refurbished. The ivy was cut. David and Anna moved aside. They bought Millbrook Lodge in Ballynahinch, but never got round to living there. In 1954 David died, and Anna moved into Erin Lodge, furnishing the house from the bric-a-brac stored in the yard.

Dick Ker set up a sawmill in the old Army Camp. It made pit props for coal mines, and 'every bloody light in the country' went out when its big horizontal saw was turned on.[10] Frank Lynch, a Catholic from Enniskillen, managed the mill. The idea of a Catholic managing Protestants ruffled feathers. Two anonymous letters of protest were sent to Ker.[11]

Ker pressed on. He revived the farm, breeding pigs, growing grain and fattening beef cattle. A state-of-the-art cattle shed was built.[12] The farm employed about eight people, including John Bell, Pearl Gillespie (Joe

Gillespie's daughter, who became gamekeeper after her father's death in the 1940s), and the Muckle brothers from the Close. In January 1953, a week before the sinking of the *Princess Victoria*, they were joined by Joe Clarke from Carlingford, one of several displaced Protestants from the border counties to find work here.[13]

Lawrence Willoughby became Ker's farm manager and land steward. As Willoughby had been the land steward at Carrowdore Castle, Ker felt lucky to have secured his services. The new land steward was a commanding figure, 'a big strong man of about eighteen stone', who wore a collar and tie on all occasions. But he was a hard taskmaster, and a hard man to get on with. Soon everyone was afraid of him, including his employers.[14]

Willoughby now drove the renewal forward. Drains were laid, fences mended. Extra staff were hired and war was declared on the Shore Hill whins in 1953. Whins 'the size of houses' bit the dust. Joe Clarke pulled their roots out using the tractor. Others hacked at their trunks with bill-hooks. But the campaign went badly. One worker sliced off two of another's fingers. Shortly afterwards, Willoughby and a boy were grinding corn when the machine stalled. The boy who was ordered to clean it lost two fingers. Then a man at the sawmill lost a finger. Pearl Gillespie was not surprised. Fairy thorns had been cut in the clearance. Pearl had warned that trouble would follow, but no-one had listened. Small wonder the fingers were flying. It was as clear as day. The fairies were wreaking their revenge.

The clearance resumed. In time, another fairy thorn came to light. The men eyed it warily. Their bill-hooks hung limp by their sides. Everyone was waiting to see what Joe Clarke would do. Joe offered a Socratic

Jimmy Muckle (l) and Joe Clarke. (Caroline Fellowes)

solution. 'We'll pull it out', he said, 'when its turn comes.' So that was that. Its fate had been decided. But somehow its turn never came. The men worked round and then beyond it. The lonely thorn survived. The re-conquest regained momentum. The lost province was reclaimed.[15]

Ker entered pastures new. He raised the £70,000 necessary to buy himself into a high-powered insurance syndicate and became a Lloyds 'name'. Energetic, thoughtful, and above all good with people, Ker was eminently employable. Businesses tried to head-hunt him, and several good opportunities to work in the city were passed over. Ossie King offered Ker a partnership in his estate agency, Osborne King & Megran, but Anna thought Ossie was 'sharp', so that went nowhere.

Ker also became interested in politics, and was 'asked endlessly' by the Ulster Unionists to stand for the safe Westminster seat of North Down. This time it was Bidger who exercised her veto. Ker had something of a roving eye. There was no way she was going to let him loose in London. So Ker did his politicking locally. He served on Down County Council, and in 1954 became chairman of the North Down Imperial Unionist Association. But his first taste of local politics was so off-putting that he very nearly did not get involved at all.[16]

This occurred in an Orange Hall in Donaghadee, at a meeting convened to introduce the new Stormont MP, Maurice May, to his constituents. Sir Walter Smiles sat on the platform and Dick Ker stood at the back of the hall, while May did his best to ingratiate himself by telling his audience that, as far as he was concerned, the only good Catholic was a dead one. At this point the atmosphere could have been cut with a knife. People could not believe what they had heard. Some got up to leave. Ker, the newcomer, lit on May. Sir Walter Smiles followed.[17]

Ker next heard May speak in Ballywalter. This time the bloodthirsty Ards backwoodsmen got a slightly different message. In Ballywalter May took great pains to tell his audience that, irrespective of class or creed, he was their MP and he would serve them. May went on to become Minister of Finance and then Education, and something of a liberal by Ulster standards. Ker liked to think that he helped him on his way, and was much saddened by his early death.[18]

Ker never got a 'proper job', a decision now considered a serious misjudgement, both financially and in terms of personal growth. But it didn't seem so at the time. He and Bidger began breeding horses. With the breeding came racing. The Kers raced their stock all over Britain and Ireland, and Dick Ker in particular became a familiar sight at courses on both islands, 'ever on the lookout for a betting coup'.[19] Ker was just as interested in the science of breeding as the thrill of racing. In an effort to raise standards, he founded a Northern Ireland branch of the Irish Bloodstock Breeder's Association.[20] The stud had some startling early

'Ever on the lookout for a betting coup', Dick Ker at the races. (Ker family)

Portavo stud. Horses graze by the pleasure dam. (Brown McConnell Clark)

successes. One of his foals fetched 4,000 guineas at Goff's, a huge sum in the mid-1950s.[21]

Portavo again became a hive of activity.[22] The walled garden and stud turned in modest profits. The sawmill held its own. Lawrence Willoughby's stewardship of the farm, however, was proving problematic. Incident followed incident. Good men left, or were got rid of. One man got his cards for being ten minutes late on his first day; he had spent too long taking his daughter to school. Joe Clarke also felt Willoughby's wrath. One Saturday morning soon after he arrived he brought in a load of turnips. The tractor tore up the yard as he braked. In an instant, Willoughby was down on him.

'You might have torn the yard up where you came from, but you'll not do it here.'

Clarke snapped.

'I'll not indeed. Away and get me my cards, I'm leaving.'

Willoughby had not been expecting this. To Joe Clarke's surprise, the big man 'was all over' him, and after that left Clarke alone.[23] The Kers did not get involved. They knew that Willoughby had a temper, but did not believe it was their place to interfere. Nor did they like to. The older man was far too formidable. The men knew it too. There was little point in appealing to the Captain, Willoughby ruled Portavo.[24]

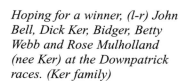

Hoping for a winner, (l-r) John Bell, Dick Ker, Bidger, Betty Webb and Rose Mulholland (nee Ker) at the Downpatrick races. (Ker family)

But Willoughby's days were numbered. The farm had twenty-seven beef cattle, which grazed together as a herd under Willoughby's supervision. One day Willoughby fell ill, and Ker was required to check his own cattle. He counted thirty beasts in the field. He counted them again. And again. And every time the number came to thirty.

Willoughby's health deteriorated and he was admitted to hospital. In his absence the farm ledgers went to Ker, who made the unsettling discovery that the estate had purchased three cows which had not been entered in the books. Lawrence Willoughby, tormented by his wife, tormentor of his men, was 'for the high jump'. But before any action could be taken, Willoughby had a fatal heart attack.[25] What had begun as an imprecation had become a full-blown tragedy. Young David Ker brought snowdrops to his grave.[26]

David M'Wha, 'a big fine rattlin' goin' man', became the new farm manager, and his wife began working in the dairy. The Captain got more involved with the farm, 'throwing off his coat and working with the men at harvest time…never asking them to do anything that he wouldn't do himself'.[27] At the marts, the farmers would crowd round him, looking for tips. He would have a laugh and a joke with them all, naming three or four runners he fancied: someone would win.

Bidger spent her time with the horses and became master of the East Down Fox Hounds.[28] She was also 'dying about dogs'. A small posse followed her everywhere and she was 'always bringing animals home'.[29] Ker shot regularly and was considered 'an outstanding shot'.[30] They 'were great people for entertaining'. Dick in particular was very gregarious and liked nothing more than having people round.[31] Who did they have? 'Who did they not have?' replies Freda Jamison, the children's former nanny. Alec Martin of Moor Farm recalls bumping into Princess Margaretha of Sweden in the yard.[32] Brookeborough and Terence O'Neill were close friends. The Blakiston-Houstons, Montgomerys, Dufferins, Clanwilliams, Dunleaths and Rowan-Hamiltons dined regularly;

'You never knew who you would bump into'. Camilla Ker with Enoch Powell at Portavo, c.1967. (Ker family)

discussing century old events as though they had happened the week before.

The family grew. The arrival of a second child, David, in 1951, was celebrated in time-honoured fashion with a bonfire on Shore Hill, prepared by Pearl Gillespie, one of the small band who were still mindful of the rites and observances due on the birth of an heir. A third child, Camilla, followed, without fanfare, in 1959.

The children were neither seen nor heard. Dick and Bidger had a 'hands off' approach to parenting. They raised their children as they had been raised themselves; i.e. they left the job to nanny. And when the children reached school age they employed a governess. The children's first governess was Miss Boyle, whom they adored.

Then came Miss Weir, ex-governess to the Abercorns, a 'lunatic woman' who controlled the children with a whistle. Though 'loathed by everyone in the household' she brought a certain discipline, and more than a little eccentricity to proceedings. For Caroline, David and Juliana Brooke, who lived here during term time, long walks through the park in all weathers became the rule, along with sugar and brown bread sandwiches. Life revolved around the schoolroom and the nursery. The children were six or seven before they really 'came downstairs'.[33]

When they did, however, they made their presence felt. Arguments and fisticuffs were the order of the day, over toys, over friends, over anything. David and Caroline quarrelled incessantly. They were too much alike, and too competitive to rub along quietly, so 'there was always someone

The Ker children, by Joan Wanklyn, c.1964, showing (l-r) David, Caroline, and Camilla, with the Portavoe Water and Belfast Lough in the background. (Ker family)

Caroline Ker on Squirrel Nutkin.
(Caroline Fellowes)

separating them'.[34] Dick and Bidger's relationship could also be pretty volatile. Bidger was the 'sharp' one. She tackled problems. Dick was so easy going that she had to be tough just to get things done.

Dick was the procrastinator. The reality avoider. The dyed-in-the-wool hater of conflict. If there was a hard fact to face, it was left to her to face it, or push Dick into facing it by giving him the rough edge of her tongue. But when there were rows, 'she'd shut up when he started'. The relationship was committed but abrasive. Explosive rows were part of the cycle. But ultimately they seem to have been about clearing the air, and letting affection back in. And there was plenty of affection.[35] Freda Jamison remembers Portavo as 'the happiest house I was ever in'.[36]

With the children it was typically Caroline in charge and David challenging. When the family went to Montalto to play with the Clanwilliam girls, he wanted to join in and be included. She didn't want him. Younger brothers were a pest. Which left David feeling left out and frustrated. When they became too old for governesses, the children went to Miss Biddle's private school in Holywood. At nine, David was sent to boarding school in England. He was desperately homesick. While Caroline flourished, spending her time painting and riding her pony, David became wilful, disruptive and inattentive. He struggled at school, and spent his holidays 'getting up to every sort of innocent criminal activity that was available'.[37]

David was not conforming. Unable to wholly embrace his big house upbringing, he instead experienced one of its classic variations, the upstairs-downstairs double life. On the one hand he became comfortable with privilege and all that went with it, and on the other he roamed the demesne with Joe Clarke's son, Winston Churchill Clarke, looking for mischief.[38] They found it. In 1961 they broke the horizontal saw, the pride of the sawmill. David was becoming a handful.

38 Farmers, fairies and the 'Karpet King'

In 1947, the year of the Big Snow,[1] Isobel Martin married Willie Boyd and came to live at the Hill. Two children, Rosemary and Martin, followed in 1949 and 1951. Willie Donaldson's eldest son David married in 1953. He and his 'townie' wife Anne also had two children, William and John. In the old days, a mother of two would hardly have been getting off the starting blocks, but families here were smaller now, and fives and sevens unheard of.

The Boyds and Donaldsons were by now the mainstay of Portavo's farming community. Both families had had their troubles. In 1942 the Donaldsons lost their only daughter Grace in a freak accident on the farm. The tragedy cast a long shadow. Willie Donaldson was never really himself afterwards and in the 1950s had a nervous breakdown. Heart attacks and poor health left him unable to do heavy work. His eldest son David took over the farm.[2]

David kept cattle and 'grew a bit of this and a bit of that' so that if one crop failed or fetched a poor price, another would hopefully cover it. In

David Donaldson, with helper, in his herringbone milking parlour. (Donaldson family)

*Feeding the binder. Boyd's farm,
late 1940s. (Boyd family)*

1951, he had twenty-five milking Friesians, grew ten tons of hay, three
hundred tons of silage, five acres of oats and five of barley, besides an
acre of potatoes. Anne kept two hundred hens in cages and another
hundred in deep litter. These were good times. David grew what he
pleased, following the best prices. Another godsend was the help of his
brother James; until James married, and their father bought him his own
forty-five acre farm beside the home farm on the Kylestone Road.

The Boyds too had their ups and downs. When Edwin Boyd died in
1940, a cortege 'at least a mile long' followed him to his last resting place
in Bangor Abbey. It was a long time since Portavo had seen such a
funeral.[3] But what of the succession? Both of his sons, Willie and young
Edwin, dearly wanted to farm. Ellen Boyd's dilemma was the same as
Willie Donaldson's, and so was her solution. The family dug deep, and
bought Edwin his own farm in Ballywilliam. Edwin moved into
Ballywilliam House, the former residence of no less a figure than James
Arbuckle, scourge of the United Irishmen.[4]

Willie Boyd got the home farm. He married, and there were high hopes
that children would follow. But it was not to be. Suddenly and
unexpectedly, not long after their marriage, his wife Peggy died in her
sleep. It was a devastating blow and for some years life was lonely, until
he met Isobel Martin at a do in Ballygrainey, and the idea of sharing his
life with someone seemed possible again.

Agriculturally, the trailblazing continued. In the mid 1940s Boyd got a
combine harvester. In 1959 he got a self-propelled machine, believed to
have been the first or second in the county. This mechanisation involved
no sacrifice of independence. If Willie Boyd needed a tractor, he didn't

Still smoking. Willie Boyd on his runabout, early 1960s. (Boyd family)

buy one, he made one. If a machine needed a part, he would make it, or fish it out of one of the wrecks that lay behind the hedge. He would spend hours on end in his workshop 'cobblin' as Ellen put it, a cigarette hanging on his lip, with half an inch of ash on it.[5]

The place was agreed, Willie Boyd was a genius, or the nearest thing to it that anyone here would ever see. And moody with it. Temperamental. 'There were days he wouldn't a' spoken to you, you had to talk to make him talk.'[6] Not that this seemed to put people off. Friends called to talk Rudges and New Imperials. Cars and especially motorbikes were religion on the Hill. Willie Boyd raced, and liked nothing better than careering round the barn at full throttle, cigarette clenched between his teeth, having first thrown water on the ground 'to make things interesting'.[7]

Willie also mended things. Anything mechanical that got broken came here to be fixed.[8] The mending got fitted in with the farm work, the contract work, and after the war, the electrical work, for Willie Boyd was also up to his neck in that other great enterprise of the post-war years, the electrification of the countryside.[9] Johnny Martin of Moor Farm was the first here to get mains electricity. The Donaldsons were connected up in 1947.[10] The Kers received a supply by pretending to be a dairy farm. About half the farms did not electrify, could not electrify, for the costs involved were beyond them. These small farms, many of them in their death throes, fell even further behind.

The death of the little farms

The post-war years were a time of enormous change on the land. The little farms, the subsistence farms that had been the mainstay of life here since the seventeenth century became unviable and were swept away. Between 1940-70 seven of Portavo's eleven farms disappeared.

A whole class disappeared with them, and it disappeared without dignity or resistance, its spirit having long been broken and its condition

When farming mechanised, the Boyds of the Hill were to the fore. Garvie Mill in the Harrow Park, Portavo, late 1940s. (Boyd family)

reduced to that of landowning poor. Anketell's 1840s dream was realised. Rural life was re-ordered, but re-ordered in a way that left people feeling less secure. Everyone moved down a notch. The Boyds and Donaldsons fell from the upper middle to the lower middle reaches of the farming pyramid. Equally disorienting, they went from being the leaders of a numerically large local farming community to becoming that community's entire extent.

The nature of farming changed too. Working horses disappeared. Everything became mechanised. This took some getting used to, as the story of Will Patton of Ballywilliam careering round his fields saying 'Woa, boy' to his new tractor reminds us. In the post-war world, the tractor was king and, 'what you can't do with a tractor, you don't do'.[1]

Although they had always run mixed farms, the Boyds and the Donaldsons found themselves compelled to specialise.[2] Both moved into dairying as it was much less labour-intensive. Men were laid off as mechanisation cut the need for labour. As farms individualised 'neighbouring' dwindled. Men who had regularly come looking for a day's or a week's work stopped calling.[3] Most of the peddlers stopped calling too. The ancient rural service sector shrivelled up and died.

A new one took its place. Hughie Hamill the grocer visited the Boyds on Monday. The butcher called on Tuesday. And although Isobel Boyd baked religiously – turning out a steady stream of sodas, wheatens and traybakes – bread vans called regularly. Bains came on Monday and Friday, the Co-Op called on Tuesday and Thursday, Inglis on Wednesday and Kennedy on Saturday. And just in case anything needed topped up, Sid Elliott the grocer came between nine and ten on a Saturday evening, arriving even later at Christmas, full to bursting with seasonal cheer.[4]

Frights and fairies

When the small farms folded, a whole galaxy of local legends disappeared. The three McKeag brothers, Hugh and Maggie McBride, Tom and Minnie Connell, Joe and Pearl Gillespie, McConnell the Great, and good old William James Lewis had all passed away by the mid-1960s. And though no-one could exactly say what, everyone was clear that something remarkable had gone with them. Their like would not be seen again. 'There wasn't a character left in the country.'[1]

Gilbert McCutcheon from Ballyminetragh took over the McBride, McKeag and McConnell holdings, turning three subsistence farms into a more viable thirty-six acre unit.[2] Bob Best, a townie with a dream, and a shoe shop on Belfast's Woodstock Road, bought William James Lewis's place in 1965. He re-christened it the *Ponderosa*, after the Cartwright ranch in *Bonanza*, as TV westerns were all the rage and Bob was a sucker for cowboy stuff. This was as near as Bob could get to Nevada and still mind the shop, and so the *Ponderosa* was born.

Bob Best was a dab hand at selling shoes, but never got on top of the loaded economics of small farms. After a catalogue of disasters, he threw in the towel in 1972-73. This was considered a great shame, for this easy going, larger than life figure with a penchant for drink and cigars, had naturalised well, and had been considered a worthy successor to William James Lewis.[3]

Minnie Connell's son George was another square peg in a round hole. He was a successful music hall and boxing promoter who, as Minnie Connell's son, had come into the farm. He managed his inheritance unsentimentally, keeping on the family home as a rooming house for fighters in training and variety artists from England.[4] The fields his mother had toiled in, however, had become highly sought-after building sites, which soon sprouted bungalows and houses.

Six new dwellings, on large plots, were built between the Stockbridge Road and Miss Wellwood's old house at Glenburnie. Two were inspired by the Stone House and have a vaguely Arts & Crafts feel. The other four are pro-forma buildings that, sadly, bear no trace of inspiration at all. Two stark, *avant garde*, red brick sixties rectangles, and a pretty, nubile bungalow with massive bays were built to the south of these at around the same time. These nine houses filled the gap between Kilcoroon and Glenburnie. A suburban community, that is to say a community that was not a community, took shape along the shore.

The older families were pushed toward the margins. Dark-clad, elderly and poor, the proud bearers of what had once been the townland's mainstream culture now shuffled about like the undead. Minnie and her brother Samuel John Boyd were amongst the last old timers to retain a footing on the shore. They still lived in the mill cottage, he in one half,

Gilbert McCutcheon. Heir to three of the old small farms. (McCutcheon family)

Minnie & Samuel John Boyd in front of the Mill Cottage. (Boyd family)

she in the other. Neither had married. Minnie had stayed at home to look after her parents, which everyone declared an awful waste, for she was a fine looking woman, with long, fair hair that tumbled to her waist.[5]

When they died, she looked after her brother, 'an old sailor man', back home from the sea. He was solitary for rather different reasons. There was some talk of a mystery woman and a broken heart way back in his past. But so far as most people knew, the only woman Samuel John had ever had any time for was his mother. The rest were 'whores and bitches'. Apart from Minnie, who was just his sister, and didn't count.[6]

Sammy Boyd was 'a desperate character' who rarely washed or had a good word for anyone. Poor Minnie, how did she stick him? No-one knew. Yet she bore up through all, washing and cleaning, keeping the chickens, collecting mussels in the Mill Bay which she boiled for their dinner, and most important of all, keeping Sammy in bottles of stout.

This 'wild swearing man' drank his pension as soon as it came in, then sang 'Round Cape Horn in a Row Boat', accompanying himself on the melodeon, 'slabbers flyin' everywhere' as he sang. Then he would march about the house all night, unable to sleep for fairies playing in the garden. These creatures were both feared and hated: 'Them bitches was out dancin' again. Ah couldn't get sleepin' for them.'[7]

He was not the only one to believe in fairies.[8] Pearl Gillespie was a firm believer. So was Andy McConnell. He had fairies on his lane, including an 'aul black one' he particularly dreaded.[9] Having fairies was like having rats, only worse. Samuel John Boyd had Andy McConnell's every sympathy. At least McConnell's fairies stayed in the fields, where they belonged. Sammy Boyd's were trying to get into the house.

When Minnie died, Sammy Boyd became reclusive. The blinds came down hours before nightfall. 'Them bitches' could dance all they liked, he wasn't going to watch them. Most people despaired of Boyd, or had as little to do with him as possible. But he wasn't completely ostracised.

Willie Bell called in most days on his way to work, and on one of these calls found the old sailor lying dead behind the door.[10] The Jutland veteran had apparently died at his post, fighting off his phantoms. His cottage was flattened a few years later, to make way for the new Warren Road.

Suburbanisation

In the mid-1960s, the road between Donaghadee and Groomsport was widened. Down came the mill cottage. Down came the pretty, thatched gate lodge.[1] Houses lost the bottoms of their gardens. The demesne lost part of its wall. Department of the Environment walls described by the late Roy Neill as 'not so much stone masonry, as crazy paving on its side' were built on the new boundaries. Amputated sections of the old road festooned the new carriageway, like ox-bow lakes or swirls of grace notes. A slew of granite boulders shored up the road where it crossed Sandy Bay.[2]

Completed in 1968, the new carriageway transformed the shore. The suburban villas looked comfortable beside it. They were 'at home' in a way they had not been previously. But it made the cottages look quaint

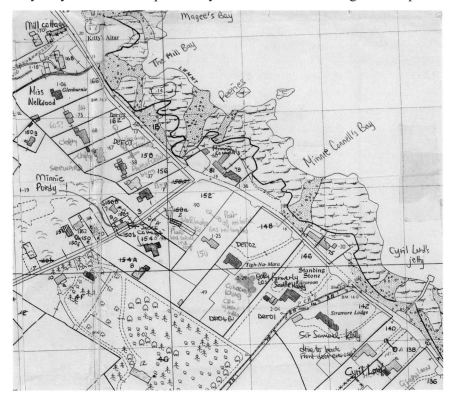

The Portavo shore, 1962, showing the suburbanised coastline.

and out of place. The road improved links with Belfast's commuter-land, and drew Portavo closer to suburban Donaghadee. The tenor of life was changing. The suburban grip was tightening. The demographic balance was tipping to the point at which farmers were becoming something of an endangered species. Their language, once the townland's *lingua franca*, was reduced to the status of an incomprehensible minority tongue. And every time a tractor dared to venture onto the road, it was set on by a gang of impatient cars.

The suburban community became 'the community'. Their wishes were now the commonweal. The middle class burgeoned. The townland's inhabitants became surgeons, stockbrokers, builders, bankers, estate agents, professors, and successful businessmen.[3] Mores changed. The place acquired a prosperity that it had never known before. But it lost its salty regionality on the way. Its working class were priced out. Its rustic vocabulary and the Scots grain of its speech both largely disappeared, as did its craggy Presbyterian character. As the place acquired a new and interesting cosmopolitanism, its 'native' culture died.

'Keep the old trap shut': the Smiles

The leading lights in this new community were probably the Smiles family of Portavo Point. In 1945, Sir Walter Smiles became the local Westminster MP.[1] He was by then a seasoned parliamentarian, having represented Blackburn since 1931, the year after his return from India.[2] After the war, however, in an attempt to simplify his life, Smiles had abandoned his seat in England and stood for County Down.[3] He was

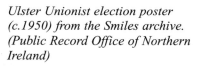

Ulster Unionist election poster (c.1950) from the Smiles archive. (Public Record Office of Northern Ireland)

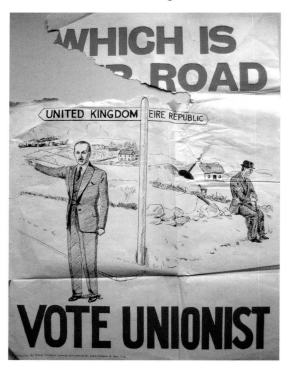

The foundering of the Princess Victoria *in January 1953, by Norman Whitla. (Colourpoint Books)*

returned with a thumping majority.[4] The move saved his political career. In 1945, Blackburn had resoundingly rejected the Tories and elected Labour 'firebrand' Barbara Castle in his place.[5]

Smiles began a new life as an Ulster Unionist, a life guided by little cues and maxims such as, 'Shake hands with everyone but the horses', which saw him through many successful election campaigns. 'Keep the old Trap Shut', also served him well. 'What would old man Jesus Christ have done?' was a sage question he turned to in moments of difficulty.[6] Smiles was not perhaps a natural politician. He had no taste for glad-handing. But his 'tact, ability... and breadth of outlook' won him many friends, and on the retirement of Sir Hugh O'Neill, he was elected leader of the Parliamentary Party at Westminster.[7]

In 1950 Smiles was returned for the new division of North Down with a majority of 31,000, one of the largest in the United Kingdom. In 1951, using a ten, and maybe a twenty year old photograph of himself on his election literature, he was returned, unopposed with an even larger majority. Then disaster struck. Smiles usually flew from London to Belfast, however in January 1953 he took the ferry, the *Princess Victoria* from Stranraer. The boat foundered in stormy seas. His travelling companion, the Northern Ireland Minister of Finance, Maynard Sinclair, jumped off the stricken ferry, but Smiles was too weak and too ill to follow. Resigned to death, he went down with the ship.[8]

In a poignant coda to these events, Harry Humphreys recalls meeting Lady Smiles on the road that morning. She was on her way to Larne to collect her husband, apparently unaware that anything was amiss.[9] The local folklore holds that Smiles drowned within sight of his home.[10]

In the by-election which followed, his thirty-one year old daughter, Patricia Ford took the seat, becoming one of only nineteen women MPs

Patricia Ford, Barbara Castle and comrades present the 680,000 signature 'Equal Pay for Women' petition in 1954, from a rather battle-scarred newspaper cutting. The petition was gathered in support of a private member's bill promoting equal pay.

in the House of Commons. Tall, good looking, and accomplished (she was fluent in four languages, and had been educated in Florence and Lausanne), Patricia Ford brought an unaccustomed pizzazz to the Unionist benches.[11] As well as championing the local farming, fishing and linen industries, she was keen to advance the position of women, and in 1954, Ford and Barbara Castle presented the Chancellor with a 680,000 signature petition, calling for equal pay.

Her parliamentary career ended in 1955, the year of the General Election. By that point she was having a relationship with Tory MP Nigel Fisher. Had this leaked out there would undoubtedly have been a scandal, which would have left her reputation in tatters, and perhaps set back the

Lady Fisher with broadcaster Sean Rafferty. (Caroline Fellowes)

cause of women in parliament by years. Mindful of these dangers, Dick Ker persuaded her not to stand again. To the bafflement of her electorate, George Curry went forward in her place.[12]

In 1956 Patricia Ford and Nigel Fisher married and moved to England. Portavo Point became a summer watering hole for members of the political elite, a place where polished, successful people mingled. Leading Ulster Unionists, and Tory luminaries such as Pensions minister Richard Wood and Ian McLeod (whom David Ker took fly fishing on Portavoe Water), befriended one another in the sun, on the back of the Smiles-Ker connection.[13]

The 'Karpet King'

In 1957, the peace of the Warren Road was shattered by the arrival of Cyril Lord, working class Lancashire lad made good. Lord was loud, flash, and loaded. And in 1957, three years after making his first million, he founded the largest carpet factory in Europe in Donaghadee, and settled on the Warren Road.

Lord didn't buy a house, he bought two. Two adjacent bungalows, on large plots by the sea. In came the architects, who turned them into arrestingly contemporary buildings – brutal, boxy, glassy, pink-painted evocations of 1950s cool.[1] One was for Lord and his wife, the other (linked to the main house by a covered walkway) was for their house guests. Cyril Lord wasn't one to live quietly. He liked to entertain.

And entertain he did. Lavishly. Continuously. Errol Flynn stayed here. So did Gracie Fields, along with favoured clients, financiers, TV personalities, and stars of stage and screen. One guest, a Holywood producer, paid Lord the compliment of casting him in a cameo role in *Batman*. Lord played himself a.k.a. 'The Karpet King of Europe', managing, without really trying, to be as dayglo as any of the weird and wonderful fictional characters around him.[2]

Lord was 'a little turkey-cock of a man'. He was a showman. An impresario. A barrow boy. He was charming, compelling and obnoxious by turns. He loved mixing business and entertainment, money and glamour. He revelled in publicity. He starred in his own advertisements and featured in other people's. He had public spats with rivals, union leaders, uncompliant politicians.

He believed in creating a frisson. In 1965, for instance, the Lord Group won an order for some 9,000 room-sized squares of carpet from the Soviet Union. Never one to miss an opportunity, Lord had the carpets sent to the Belfast docks in a fleet of lorries emblazoned with the message, 'Cyril Lord carpets for Russia', in an operation which was both dazzling and kitschy at the same time. Rather like its author. Lord did nothing quietly. Everything about the man was bold and brash and – in the view of his patrician neighbours, whose relations with him were characterised by a steely condescension – in the worst possible taste.

Lord's alleged offences against good taste were legion. The most obvious were his toys, the helicopter, the twin prop Riva speedboat named the 'Sea Lord', the cavalier way he drove it (spray everywhere), the fast cars, the five garages, the Bentley, registration CL1.

Nor were the *haute bourgeois* of the Warren Road impressed by his manner ('he thought he was God'), his endless cigars, his habit of drenching himself in perfume ('he smelt like a sweet pea'), or his dumping of his wife of twenty-three years for a pretty journalist half his age.[3] His house was also considered a little too pink and shocking for its tweedy surroundings. Lavishly furnished with eccentric *objets trouvés* and pink carpets, neighbours left dizzy with sensory overload after their first privileged glimpse of the indoors.

Much as he wanted to stand out, Cyril Lord also wanted to fit in. This proved rather more difficult. His impatience was legendary. He honked at cattle as they were herded along lanes. He took up shooting and nearly killed Dick Ker. But there were positives too, such as his surprising friendship with his farming neighbour, Will Patton (the same Will Patton who missed his horses so much that he talked to his tractor),[4] and his offer to build the Donaghadee golfers a new clubhouse, an offer they declined from 'pure snobbery'. He had an electric effect on Donaghadee. The place 'came alive' during the Lord era. By the early 1960s, the factory was working round the clock, and producing some sixty miles of carpet per year. 'Processions' of lorries roared up and down the High Bangor Road. There had never been so much work, or so much money in the town.[5]

Carpet was just one of a myriad of business interests. But it was the big one, and the most successful. In the early 1950s Europe was climbing out

Lifting the lawn for Cyril Lord's swimming pool, (l-r) John Boyd, Irvine Boyd, Lex McMullan, man from Bangor. (Boyd family)

Cyril Lord, with trademark cigar, 1960s. (National Portrait Gallery)

of austerity. Aspirations were rising. There was a huge appetite for the good life. Enter Lord, the man whose mission was to bring carpet to the ordinary man and woman. Acting on gut feeling, Lord caught the mood and produced a product that matched it. It was a classic case of the right product at the right price at the right time. Lord was one of the entrepreneurs who led luxury-starved Europe back into the consumerist temple after the war, paving its way not with palm fronds but rubber-backed carpet.

Having cracked carpet, Lord took up the idea of creating a small, affordable 'people's car'. Prototypes were tested. Negotiations were begun with Short & Harland of Belfast who were to manufacture the vehicle. But these ended acrimoniously. Which may have been as well, for the Mini appeared shortly afterwards, and cornered the small car market. Some analysts believed Lord had a narrow escape, and that the early end of his attempt to build a three-wheeled 'bubble car' probably saved him millions.[6]

There was no standing still with Lord. He was constantly innovating. This inevitably meant failures, and there were quite a number. Imitation astrakhan, synthetic fur coats, and artificial grass called Cyrilawn (which was not dyed sufficiently permanently, causing it to turn a shade of blue) all ended badly. However, the core business continued to thrive. At least it did until 1967, when the Group over-reached itself, aggressively acquiring an additional one hundred and fifty outlets in England. This proved a step too far. The shops lost money, and could not be turned round, and in the following year the Group collapsed with debts of over seven million pounds. The adventure was over.[7]

But there was no Lord in the wreckage. The bird had flown. The crash found Lord in Carolina, recovering from a heart attack. He had been 'compulsorily' retired on health grounds some months before. His business empire was dismembered. Viyella took over the Donaghadee plant, but only a fraction of the jobs could be saved. Lord moved to the Bahamas, where he lived quietly, shunning the media. Shirley Lord, his second wife, moved to the United States, where she married a former editor of the *New York Times*. The house, with its phone in every room, including the toilets, found a new use too. It became a convalescent home for Baptist stroke victims. An unaccustomed quiet fell on Millionaire's Row.[8]

39 'This auld place wouldn't be for sale, would it?'

'This auld place wouldn't be for sale, would it?'

In his memoirs, George Best recalls returning to his hotel in Bloomsbury after a night on the town, and ordering a bottle of champagne. When the porter duly arrived nursing a bottle of Dom Perignon (it was nothing but the best in those days), he found Best, a former Miss World in a negligee, and £15,000 in casino winnings strewn across the bed. Recognising the footballer, the porter fixed him with a pained expression and asked, 'Mr Best, where did it all go wrong?'[1]

It was a little like this at Portavo. Beneath the healthy, even glitzy looking surface, things had begun to go awry. In 1961 the saw-mill had been compelled to close, priced out by cheap timber imports. In the mid-1960s agricultural wages rose, making the farm less viable. In a more disciplined business environment this would have meant redundancies, but Ker was loath to sack long-serving staff, and the farm became as over-manned as a Soviet factory.[2]

Ker responded not by changing tack, but by attempting to run the same regime more cheaply. Expenses were pared and pared again, but expenditure still exceeded income. The estate drew on its reserves. Ker 'borrowed on a dripping overdraft', selling assets when the bank got restive. These borrowings were made to cover current expenses. Ker rarely borrowed to invest, and it would never have occurred to him to borrow enough to, for example, set up a good dairy unit.[3] When something wore out, there was a flurry of plugging and patching, which Ker oversaw with a cheerful smile and a 'That'll do *pro tem*.'[4]

By now Ker had to a large extent lost interest in farming. Breeding and racing horses had become his all-consuming passion. Antiques were another big interest. 'Dad always saw himself as a bit of a Steptoe,' his son David recalls. The yard was still an Aladdin's Cave, and the old Ross dower house was stacked with pictures. Dick sold everything, charging what he thought was top dollar, but 'getting ripped off every time'.[5]

Looking lost. John Bell delivers strawberries to the house. (Ker family)

The walled garden, reduced to a paddock; a border of strawberry plants remains. (Brown McConnell Clark)

Freda Jamison, the children's nanny, with her husband Charles. (Caroline Fellowes)

As the Troubles bit, Ker became less actively involved in politics, but remained a liberal unionist. Aware that he was privileged, and should 'give something back', he devoted much time to working with charities and good causes. Camps and fetes were held in the park, and in 1967 Ker gave Lighthouse Island to the National Trust, for a rent of one peppercorn, if demanded.

Staff departures (there were no such things as sackings) helped to ease the financial pressures. The family's 'sensational' cook Vida Woodhouse left in 1964. Frank Lynch retired in 1965. This saved four salaries, as each took their partner with them.[6] No-one was replaced. To John Bell's consternation, the walled garden was turned into a paddock. Jimmy Muckle swapped his spade for a dandy brush, and began to work with yearlings.[7]

Camilla, the baby of the family, also felt the wind of change. She became the first Ker in centuries not to have a governess. No Madame Sabonadiere stood at her elbow. Not even a Miss Weir. But she was not neglected. Caroline and David's nanny, Freda Jamison, 'a wonderfully kind woman', who loved the children 'as if they were my own', was coaxed back from England to look after her.[8] Freda returned to a much more *laissez faire* regime. Camilla was not confined to the nursery. She had the run of the house, and spent a lot more time with her parents.[9]

This liberalisation came too late for Caroline and David. Their lives followed more time-honoured paths. In 1963 Caroline was sent to Tudor Hall in Banbury. David was sent to his father's prep school, St. Aubins, and then at thirteen to Eton. He found both a great struggle. He wasn't sporty. Academically, he was written off as a duffer until about the age of sixteen when he suddenly grew into himself, became much more able to cope, and made the amazing discovery that he could to some extent shape his own life.[10]

Hiram Winterbotham, Caroline Fellowes (nee Ker) and Lynn Chadwick, Joucas, France. (Caroline Fellowes)

He also worked out that if he was ever going to enjoy Eton, he was going to have to get himself elected to POP, Eton's schoolboy elite. He succeeded, and in his final term was elected chairman, which made him the second most senior boy in the school, a position of considerable influence and prestige.[11] This all came as a welcome surprise to his bemused parents, who had been revising down their expectations for their son for nearly a decade.

After school Caroline studied art history. She married at nineteen. It was too early. The relationship did not last. In 1975 she moved to Provence, where she and her partner, sculptor Lynn Chadwick, built a solar house near Joucas. She studied with the surrealist Julien Levy, and painted and exhibited widely.

David passed over the option of a short service commission in the Coldstream Guards ('not my thing'), and a chance to go to Oxford (a tutor offered to 'fix it for him'). He and two friends took to the road. They drove a landrover across Europe and Asia to Australia, grew beards, worked on farms, drank beer, and looked for hippy chicks to hang out with. The parents went back into worried mode.

They needn't have. When he got back in 1970, David got a job with an estate agent. A more resounding return to conformity would be hard to imagine. Crucially, he decided not to come home, but to get a job in London. In 1972, David met and two years later married the glamorous receptionist at Knight, Frank & Rutley. Cue another wave of parental anxiety, which also turned out to be misplaced. His new wife, 'Twinks', Alexandra Watson, was the Fourth Sea Lord's daughter, which gave her the right to be married in the King Henry VII Chapel at Westminster, where the knot was tied in June 1974.

Back door Portavo, sunny day, by Caroline Fellowes. (Caroline Fellowes)

The contrast between the cut-throat, margin-oriented world David now moved in and the lax, even slap-happy regime that prevailed at Portavo was glaring.[12] David saw the old place with fresh eyes. He urged his father to close the farm and let the land. Dick refused. The youngster didn't understand. The estate owed obligations to its men. They couldn't shut the farm. It was inconceivable.

But the old regime no longer rested upon secure foundations. The Trust Fund that had seen the Kers through the 1950s had gone. The stud – the estate's one success story – was also coming under pressure. The arrival of wealthy Arab owners inflated prices and made life difficult for small

Party or wake? The leaving party, 1980, (l-r) Margaret & John Bell, Bidger, unknown, Mrs McWha. (Caroline Fellowes)

owner-breeders. Income consistently fell short of expenditure. The overdraft rose to an alarming £80,000.[13]

England beckoned. David urged his parents to sell up and come over. Bidger, who had never really put down roots here, also favoured going. Dick resisted. Filled with a sense of history, keenly aware of his family's place in the county, Dick Ker would not budge. But his resistance was worn down, and his resolve was undermined by the gathering sense of financial crisis. The day of reckoning was coming. Should he sit and wait for it to arrive, or cut and run? His land was rising in value. English property was at a discount.[14] Dick began to think the unthinkable. He began to think of leaving Portavo.

It is the autumn of 1979. A chilly, grey day. There are just three men left on the farm, Joe Clarke and the two Muckle brothers. Had the workforce been scaled down to match the remunerative work available? Not likely. One employee would have done. But there were three. And on this particular morning, all three were together in the yard when they spied a dapper stranger. He seemed to be sizing the place up. Joe Clarke approached him. The man was an estate agent.

'This auld place wouldn't be for sale, would it?'

'Oh, no.' the agent assured him. But Clarke's doubts were not assuaged. The rest of the morning passed slowly. Infinitely slowly. At dinner time the men were too restive to stay silent. Bob Muckle put it up to Mrs Ker. Was the old place for sale? Her reply was plain. Maybe even defiant. 'It was,' she said, 'and it'll be sold too.' He could not have had a

A penny for your thoughts? Dick Ker in the improvised auction room, surrounded by his worldly possessions. (Caroline Fellowes)

*The lorry at the door. The Kers'
bantams travelled with them,
laying eggs on the boat to
Liverpool. The next morning, in
Lynn Chadwick's house, the
travellers ate the bantam's eggs.
(Caroline Fellowes)*

clearer answer. 'There wasn't a sharper woman in Ireland,' Joe Clarke
remembers. No-one had any room for doubt now.[15]

The decision to sell was followed by a period of high emotion and
intense confusion. In December David was diagnosed with cancer and
went into hospital for emergency surgery. For months he lingered. No-
one knew which way it would go. As David lay gravely ill in a London
hospital, his wife by his side, their four month old son David Edward and
his nanny came to Portavo. He was well looked after. Doted on even. One
mild March day he was taken out to have his nap in the garden. When his
nanny went to check him, he was dead. The shock was stupefying, the
feeling of helplessness overwhelming. The helplessness of those at the
scene. The helplessness of his parents, far away. Everyone felt wretched.
These were very dark days.

Numbly, as though through a fog, the sale proceeded. The farm sale
cleared the overdraft. The house and land went for over half a million
pounds. The furnishings went under the hammer in April 1980, and so the
last vestiges of two once great interiors were scattered to the winds.[16] The
move was made. Caroline helped her parents pack. Patricia Fisher
burnished the silver. Dick and Bidger loaded what remained of the
family's two hundred and fifteen year tenure into the back of the lorry
that usually carried the horses, and drove off for the last time. 'I don't
know how Captain Ker packed that lorry and shut that door' Joe Clarke
recalled. Nor did Ker, but he did. Having snuffed out the sacred flame,
the Kers drove down the drive, and disappeared into history.[17]

New owners arrived. Two families ended up acquiring the estate, the
Tughans, who bought the house and park in 1980, and their relatives, the
Cannons, who three years later bought about sixty acres in
Ballyminetragh that Ker had held onto. For good measure, another
Tughan settled in the old estate laundry in Orlock.

The Tughans were a Bangor family with a background in the law, property development and local politics. Fred Tughan, the new owner's father, had virtually single-handedly established the family's fortunes, transforming the Tughans from a comfortably off legal family to local magnates with wide business interests.

It could all have been very different. When Fred Tughan was a boy, his father had drowned off Ballyholme beach, in mysterious circumstances. His widow struggled to bring up the children. Times were hard. Tughan's break came when his uncle offered him a job as an articled clerk in the family law firm. He ended up running it, but made his money in property, building 'houses for the people' by the hundred after the war. In the 1960s he was one of the first people in Northern Ireland to develop unwardened fold accommodation for the elderly. Then, ever restless, he promoted social housing, becoming one of the founding fathers of the Housing Association movement.[18]

In his early years he had even burrowed into the disintegrating Ker estate, buying building land at Sydenham from the Kers in the 1930s, little imagining in his wildest dreams that he would live to see one of his children take their place at Portavo.

But this is exactly what happened. At thirty-eight, Derek Tughan, his wife Tina, and their three children, moved from suburban Bangor into the vacant ex-imperial seat.[19] The couple were euphoric. They had fallen in love with the place as soon as they had seen it, and could scarcely believe it was now theirs. But there was so much to do. They had the house refurbished from top to bottom, living in a cottage in the grounds while the work was done.

Disused cowsheds, Portavo, by Robert Innes.

The Tughans brought the estate what it most needed: money. However, this money did not come off the back of inherited wealth. In an act reminiscent of David Ker's will of 1810, Fred Tughan divided his wealth equally amongst his five children, leaving each well-off but not rich. In order to buy Portavo, Derek Tughan had had to make his own fortune, which he did, courtesy of some astute property deals in the mid and late 1970s. Even so, the purchase left him seriously stretched, and had his business not continued to thrive, his tenure would have been brief.[20]

But things worked out. The Tughan occupancy came into its own. Tughan spent a fortune on the house and grounds. He spent another on stock and machinery. The plan was that while Derek looked after the ever more diverse Tughan business interests, his brother-in-law Geoff Cannon would manage the revived and hopefully resurgent home farm.

It seemed like the perfect arrangement. Cannon loved the outdoors and had farming in his blood. African farming. His family had previously grown tobacco and maize in Rhodesia, now Zimbabwe. However in 1977, with the political situation deteriorating, and Cannon 'fed up going to bed with an automatic rifle by my side', his family joined the white exodus, trading the parched soils of Mashonaland for the demerara loams of Portavo.[21]

The new arrivals made a big and not entirely favourable impression. To their neighbours, long accustomed to the Kers' indulgent gentry ways, the Cannons and Tughans seemed almost unbearably *nouveau riche*. They were uppity. Abrupt. High handed. All sorts of people, from the Fishers and their dogs, to David Donaldson and his cattle, had enjoyed a certain amount of access to the estate. There had been fetes, fairs, Boy Scout and Girl Guide camps. But precedents set by the Kers did not bind the Tughans. The jollification stopped.

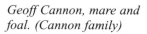

Geoff Cannon, mare and foal. (Cannon family)

Sheep grazing on the home farm, 1989.

Mrs Stone (nee Delacherois) disapproved strongly. She believed that the big house should be a part of the community. Tughan was unmoved. He focussed on renewing the demesne, planting softwoods, breeding pheasants and holding shoots.[22] The farm again took wings. Dick Ker's once state-of-the-art, but now antique byre was converted to house three times as many cattle. Two new silos were built. Stone outbuildings were renovated. Fields were drained, and six or seven miles of fencing were re-laid. With the aid of generous government grants, the farm was thoroughly mechanised for the first time in its history. The aim was to become self sufficient. Not to need contractors. To enable Geoff Cannon and two men to do more or less every job themselves.[23]

And so it was. Three men and their machines did what would have been the work of fifteen a century before, running the home farm and the Cannon holding as a single unit. They grew about 150 acres of cereals (oats, wheat and barley) and kept a flock of some 350 breeding ewes. In time they got into beef cattle. But in 1993-94, after selling the fattened herd for £103,000 while working up £101,000 in costs, Geoff decided that the cattle had to go. The profits had become as lean as the meat. Six years later, it was the core operation that was in trouble. Markets were flat or collapsing. Geoff could not get decent prices for his produce. In 1999 the farm closed, a victim of agriculture's millennial crisis.[24]

This was hard on the men. And hard on Geoff, who had loved the place, and 'felt blessed' to have farmed it.[25] When Cannon had first arrived he had not been welcomed. Some felt that he had brought a certain amount of Rhodesian baggage with him, and saw the locals as the white Rhodesians had seen the blacks. But he had mellowed. He had become well-liked. Where once there had been distrust, there was sympathy. At fifty, Cannon left to start anew.

The song of the earth
With the best-resourced farm in the townland foundering, what hope was there for the rest? Funnily enough, their prospects were in many ways

David and Anne Donaldson, Stockbridge Farm, 2005.

better. They were not subject to the business discipline that had governed the home farm. As family farms, they worked to an altogether fuzzier and more inscrutable logic.

This made them hardy, which was just as well, for there would be testing times ahead. By 1990 the pressure to consolidate had become so compelling that there were just three other farms left in the townland, Boyds, Donaldsons and McCutcheons. David Donaldson dairied. Martin Boyd both dairied and raised beef cattle. Gilbert McCutcheon mostly grew vegetables, but hedged his bets by trying 'a little of everything'. This was not the done thing. The experts recommended specialisation. But where did specialisation get you? David Donaldson specialised in dairying. He preserved margins and achieved economies of scale by adding the fourteen acre 'Strad' field to the farm when the Kers sold up in 1980, increasing his holding to sixty-nine acres.

Yet in 1995-96, not withstanding a gratifying spike in the milk price, the farm went under, one of some 1,200 dairy farms in Northern Ireland to do so between 1993-2001.[1] For sixty years Donaldsons' farm had been one of Portavo's success stories. It had won awards. It was lauded in the

*The fourteen acre 'Strad',
which the Donaldsons bought
from the Kers in 1980,
photographed with bails.*

farming press. It featured in advertisements for dairy products. Now it
had gone. David's son William, who had intended to farm, became a
storeman in Wellworths. David Donaldson shakes his head, but remains
philosophic. He is sad that there is no longer a Donaldson working the
land, but almost relieved when he thinks of the grief the family avoided
by getting out when it did.[2]

The land did not go to waste. These 1,200 closures were part of a wider
cycle of change and renewal. Robert Gray of the Moor Farm rented
Donaldsons. He also rented a sizeable portion of the defunct estate farm.
But who was Robert Gray? And didn't the Moor Farm belong to the
Martins? It did until 1994, when the Moor Farm too came a cropper. In
that year, ground down by old age and poor prices, Alec Martin sold the
farm. It was a vexed decision. A painful business. But what was the
alternative? The man he employed had earned more than him for two
years running. His son did not want to farm. And who could blame him,
given the risk-reward balance on offer?[3]

But was it really that bad? And aren't grumbling farmers as much a
fact of life as rain, death and taxes? Maybe. But it is probably a long time
since they have had so much to grumble about. Alec Martin thinks the last
decade has been the worst since the 1930s. Cringing at the perfection of
his timing, Geoff Cannon believes that farming has been on a downslope
since the early 1980s.[4]

Gilbert McCutcheon agrees. 'We've had to run harder just to stand
still', he says. He's been through the ringer too. His eighties were nearly
as difficult as his nineties. But he believes that expanding the size of his
farm (he now rents the old Aird farm in Orlock) and doing a little bit of

everything saw him through. If he and his wife Nessa had a bad year with the sprouts or the potatoes, they had the turkeys by way of insurance. Something would come good, and if they had 'one good year in three' they would be fine. In the mid-1980s they didn't get even that. 1983 was bad. 1985 was a washout, a year of rotting crops and hardship payments. '86 and '87 were indifferent, and the rogue year of 1988, in Nessa's words, 'just about put our light out'.[5]

That year saw the arrival of Bovine Spongiform Encephalopathy or BSE. Over half of the McCutcheon's eighty-five cattle were slaughtered and burned.[6] The Boyds also lost stock, again, not to the disease, but to the cull intended to contain it. These were trying times. Willie Boyd's son Martin now ran the Boyd's farm, a responsibility he inherited at just seventeen, after a heart attack carried off his father. The farm weathered the BSE crisis, for it was robust and capable of handling difficulty. Martin grew it from 51 to 80 acres (nobody here counts in hectares) by buying ground that marched Will Patton's in Ballywilliam. He rented the Bell's, Muckles' and Miss Angus's land, which hoovered up another thirty acres. This enabled him to double the size of his dairy herd, achieving the sort of critical mass necessary for the farm to stay afloat.[7]

But planning only takes you so far. On Easter Tuesday 1987, out of the blue, Martin Boyd felt a thumping pain in his chest. He had to lie down. He was sure it was a heart attack. The doctor diagnosed ME, and told him to slow down. Which was not easy when all the work of the farm fell to

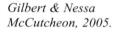

*Gilbert & Nessa
McCutcheon, 2005.*

Martin and his mother. Poor prices, bureaucracy, and health concerns may have turned farming into an uphill struggle, but they have not quite killed Martin's sense of humour. 'Have you ever thought of quitting?' I ask.

Martin Boyd and Millie, at the Hill, 2005.

'Every morning', comes the reply.

Sixty years ago there were eleven farms here. In 1990 there were four. Now there are two. Robert Gray, the biggest farmer in the townland doesn't even live here. Do we chalk this up to progress? Not according to Sammy McCully. He ran his farm traditionally, drawing wrack from the shore till the mid-1980s, the last local farmer to do so. He has no truck with intensive farming. 'Food's poisoned now', he says, 'Why, you can't even taste it'. If this is progress, it is not for him. McCully is equally angered by the cull of farms. 'Many a good man's gone to the wall', he declares, smarting from the injustice of it all.[8]

Where is the whole thing going? No-one knows. And locally, fewer and fewer people care. Farming has become a marginal activity, practised by a small and ageing fraction of the population.[9] Few on the coast even knew of the hinterland's agonies. Contact is accidental, haphazard. People do not meet or talk. In days gone by, nearly everyone was wired into the same circuit, and when something happened, every kitchen buzzed with the news. Even in the 1930s and 40s there was a kind of upstairs-downstairs relationship between the townland's various sub-cultures. But all this went. By the 1980s, the townland's component populations were living in largely separate worlds.

Thesis, antithesis, synthesis

The outbreak of the Troubles in 1969 made Northern Ireland headline news across the world. Decades of conflict followed. However, the direct impact of the Troubles was slight. Some 'Portavo says No' grafitti appeared in the wake of the 1985 Anglo-Irish agreement. Cyril Lord's neighbour, Sir Ivan Neill, the last Speaker of the Northern Ireland parliament, lost his seat and his job in 1973.[1] But no other families are known to have been personally affected by the Troubles. No police estate formed here. No searches, arrests or outrages took place.

Few will perhaps be surprised by this. Portavo lies within the 'apathy belt'. Its new arrivals were the people who famously opted out of politics during the Troubles. This opting out is often described pejoratively, but it could also be seen as a slipping of the noose, a refusal to take part in a zero-sum game. When this group is taken out of the equation, who is left? Almost no-one. The district's working class Orangeism, which during the 1920s-30s appeared unshakably deep rooted, had melted away with gentrification. Seventy years ago, the townland's people built an Orange arch at the foot of the Stockbridge Road. The idea of them doing so today is the stuff of fantasy.

Not that its people were spectators to the conflict. They voted, mostly for the Ulster Unionist or Alliance parties. But few became members. There is no pride in political activism here. No status or glory attaching to it. Yet for all this apparent disengagement, Portavo was viscerally connected to the Troubles, and lived through the emotional roller-coaster they provided. What has twenty-five years of often harrowing conflict done to hearts and minds? What, indeed, has it done to peoples' souls? These intangibles are much harder to assess. We must leave the question hanging.

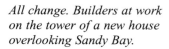

All change. Builders at work on the tower of a new house overlooking Sandy Bay.

Deep in the private heart of the townland. Back gate lodge, Portavo, by Peter Jamieson, c.1980. (Ker family)

During 1970s-80s, as the Troubles raged, the bourgeoisie completed its conquest of the Portavo coast. With the estate in introspective mood and the farmers on the ropes, the shoreside commuterland became the prime generator of the townland's identity. It also sought more land. In 1989 it began to colonise the interior, founding an anonymous cul-de-sac called Stockbridge Park on the last of Minnie Connell's fields.

This inward march was checked by the creation of the Belfast green belt in 1990, which set (as yet unbreached) limits to the shore's expansion. There have been provocations – such as the building on Saville Hardy's garden – but by and large the line has held, leading, over the last decade, to what might be called an intensification of settlement, rather than expansion. The inward movement created two tiers of coastal settlement: 'Broadway' – which offers the all-singing, all-dancing seaside experience – and 'off Broadway', along the Stockbridge Road, where the housing has more of an 'off the shelf' feel, and the sense of seaside living is more muted.[2]

Muted is not the first word that comes to mind when one thinks of the shore, however. It is still a catwalk. A hothouse. An architectural Easter parade. Here houses have pizzaz, élan, their own individual postcodes.[3] In the 1960s-70s the shore's housing took a worrisome lurch in the direction of affordability, with the building of houses that might, at a stretch, be within the purchasing power of the common man. By the 1990s, however, to the relief of all right-thinking people, filthy lucre was back in charge. In 1997, Lis-na-rede on Sandy Bay (site value £250,000) was replaced by a stylish house with a ground plan resembling a banana.

Derek Tughan exploring the 'Roman Bath' with Tim and Pam Fogg.

Within the last year or so, another three large houses have been razed with something similar in mind. The world waits agape to see what will replace them.

It's a jungle out there. One day your face doesn't fit and – bam! – you're gone. In the heart of the townland, things are quieter. Here, the biggest innovation has been the establishment of the Donaghadee Garden Centre, the twenty-first century heir to the eighteenth century walled garden, which welled up through a chink in the planning legislation in 1990, and now employs nearly sixty and covers three acres.[4] Here you can buy everything from seeds to statuary, and in the cafe sample scrumptious home-made lemon meringues and apple pies.

Customers come in droves. Cars scuttle to and fro, doing little for the townland's formerly blissful sense of repose.[5] But there is still a charm about the place, the faintest dusting of enchantment. Inland, there has been no cull of older houses. The homes of Minnie Connell, Minnie Purdie and John Small still stand. Even Cramp Faulkner's picture postcard cottage can still be seen. The Tughans have also largely left well alone. There have been mishaps. The removal of Edith Ker's pet cemetery, and the demolition of the walled garden's elliptical potting shed are regrettable *faux pas*. But they must be seen in context. Portavo has not become a conference centre. It has remained a home. New woods have been planted, new vistas laid, a new lake, adorned with orchids, has been created.

As their horizons lengthened, the Tughans turned from softwoods to hardwoods. Some 30,000 new trees, mostly native oak and ash, have been planted in the last seven years. This was followed by an interesting ecological experiment, which has no name but could perhaps be called benign neglect. The idea is simple. In the past when a tree fell it was cut up and sold or used as firewood. Now when a tree falls, it lies. It rots. It becomes a habitat. The insects move in. The birds move in, and soon the whole locality is working in a higher eco-gear. Derek Tughan, the original hard-headed businessman, going eco with a touch of zen – who would have thought it? It is wonderful what a place can do to a person, if they are prepared to give themselves to it.

But what of the Tughans' predecessors? What of the Kers? Dick and Bidger used the proceeds from Portavo to buy a Wiltshire mansion, where they lived well for nearly seven years. Then they moved to Aldworth, in the Berkshire Downs, a delightful village with a flint walled church, which lies within striking distance of four first class racecourses, Newbury, Salisbury, Bath and Wincanton. Dick Ker, incorrigible as ever, became a steward and enthusiastic participant in the life of all four, living 'in a permanent state of denial' about his gambling. This was compulsive, but tightly controlled, and so well managed that it never seriously dented his finances.

But dented they would be. More than dented. Since 1948 Ker had been a Lloyds 'name', a part of an insurance syndicate whose members accepted unlimited personal liability for the policies the syndicates accepted. For years this had been a lucrative connection, and never more so than in the 1980s, when profits broke all records.

David Ker, reclining with pug and Havana. (Ker family)

Between 1988-92 however, Lloyds in general and Ker's syndicate in particular were hit by a string of huge claims. Ker lost everything. The remains of the money he had had from the sale of Portavo, all his Lloyds gains, his half of the house in Aldworth, just under three million pounds in all.[6] Desperate attempts were made to protect some small portion of his assets. But the claims consumed all. Ker was left without a penny, and thrown into a state of acute depression. He entered the Lloyds hardship scheme, becoming a bankrupt in all but name.

Fortunately, by this stage, David was in a position to support his parents. He had shrugged off his cancer, quit property, and gone into business, selling paintings and antiques. One thing led to another and in 1993, after securing financial backing from a Saudi prince, he and a director of Christie's set up Simon C. Dickinson Ltd. Within seven years the company had became the biggest art dealership in Britain, handling everything from canvasses by fifteenth century Italian masters to the work of Van Gogh and Picasso.[7]

Kers spending money, yes. But a Ker making money? Can such things be? Apparently, so. Thesis, antithesis, synthesis. We have arrived at a kind of equilibrium. Taking the long view, one could describe David as having squared the Ker circle by bringing the family back to its mercantile roots, while maintaining its gentry air and connections. Indeed, the one has been brought fruitfully to bear on the other.

A considerable feat. The girls flourish too. Camilla practices alternative therapy. Caroline has become a respected portraitist, religious painter and graphic designer.[8] Bidger fusses over her dogs. David and his

Sandy Bay, by Robert Innes.

family still come to Northern Ireland. As visitors now. The move freed them, but it took something from them at the same time. The weight of history is no longer in them. At least not in the way that it was. Removed from the land of their amazing florescence, taken out of the society that once, metaphorically, trembled beneath them, the Kers have become mere mortals, individuals whose lives have solely personal significance. The Irish connection is weakening and will, in time, be gone.

Not that nature notices or cares. Indifferent to all, the waves break over Sandy Bay. The plovers circle overhead. The fishscale glint of light off water rouses our driver from his reverie. How long has it been? Minutes? Hours? From the corner of his eye he glimpses shadowy woodland, in front of it the old 'famine' wall. Around him are stylish houses, prima donnas every one. It's time to go. His friends are ready. So why the hesitation? Why the last lingering look? And why does everything feel so familiar? It's been good, but it's time to move on.

Ker family of Portavo

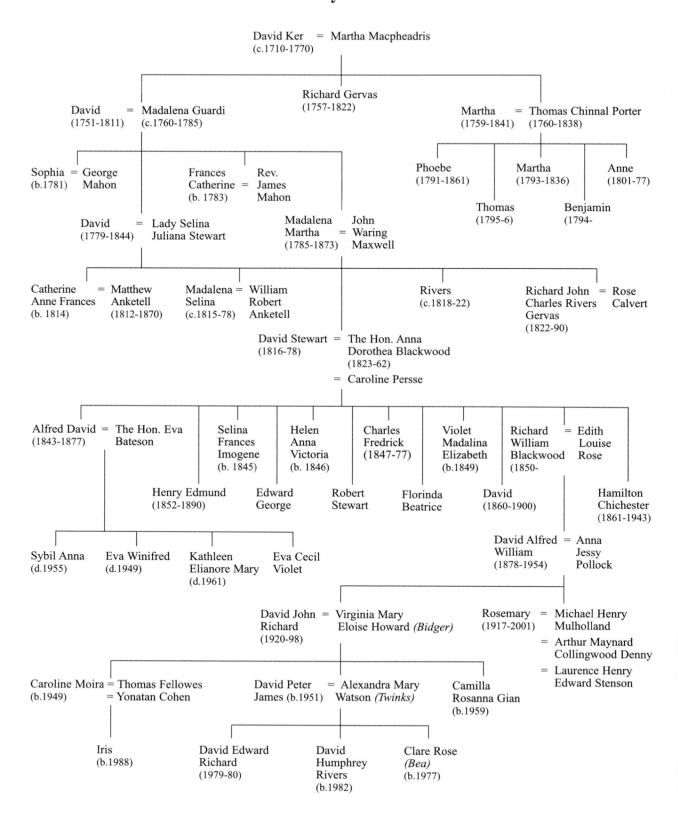

Appendix 1

County Down top thirty. This list of the county's most powerful landowners, with the number of their voters, was prepared for the Marquis of Downshire in or around 1852.

1. Marquis of Downshire, Hillsborough — 1554
2. David Stewart Ker, Montalto — 543
3. Marquis of Londonderry, Mountstewart — 503
4. Lord Dufferin, Ballyleidy — 377
5. Trustees Earl of Kilmorey — 372

6. Colonel Forde, Seaforde — 269
7. Lord Annesley, Castlewellan — 235
8. J.C. Price, Saintfield — 188
9. A.R. Stewart, Dunfanaghy — 171
10. Sir Robert Bateson, Belvoir — 164

11. Hon. Robert Meade (dead) — 158
12. Viscount Dungannon, Brynknolt Castle — 154
13. William Hampson, Newry (erased) — 151
14. General Meade (dead) — 150
15. W. Sharman Crawford, Crawfordsburn — 145

16. John Waring Maxwell, Finnebrogue — 142
17. Charles Douglas, Lurgan — 133
18. Viscount Bangor, Castleward — 125
19. Earl of Clanwilliam, L. — 122
20. Mrs Eliza Cleland, Stormont — 110

21. Hertford, Marquis of — 100
22. Blakiston-Houston, R. Orangefield — 98
23. Forde, Lady H, Hollymount — 95
24. Innes, Arthur, Dromantine, Loughb. — 93
25. Beauclerk, Mrs. Ardglass — 92

26. Miss Delacherois, Donaghadee — 88
27. Harrison, John, Marton Hall, Belfast — 83
28. Gordon, Robert, Florida Manor — 81
29. Heron, J. Holywood — 80
30. Hunter, Captain John, Warwickshire — 78

The 1852 Hill townland poll book puts Ker's vote at 563.
Compiled from the Downshire Papers, PRONI D/671/O/2/4.

Notes

18 La belle époque

'From the Bar of Dundrum to the town of Belfast': the Ker estates

1. *Belfast News Letter* 16 Jan.1838. The words are those of William Stevenson, Ker's much respected land agent.
2. The old Ballynahinch and Five Towns estates.
3. From his combined Irish and English estates. (Proudfoot, *IESH*, p.35, 40.)
4. McCavery, p.112.
5. For example, the Conolly estate in County Donegal, which extended to 150,000 acres, but generated a rental income of £15,000. (*House of Commons Sessional Papers* 1872 vol.11, p.147.)
6. During the period 1838-44 the triumvirate of David, his father, and their progressive land agent Stevenson had been at the centre of decision making.
7. Ker is said to have moved 'freely' amongst his tenants. (*Downpatrick Recorder* 12 Oct.1878.)
8. The scheme cost over £1,500, and was described as 'more extensive than any [then underway] in the North of Ireland'. (*Downpatrick Recorder* 9 Sept.1843.)
9. As his father was 'unable to attend to these matters'. (PRONI D/671/C/143/7 Ker to Downshire 24 Nov.1840.)
10. The scheme was privately financed, not withstanding the 1842 Drainage Act, which provided Board of Works loans for drainage. (Black, p.184.) Reclamation was highly profitable. Investors could expect a return on their money within three, or at most seven years, by letting out the reclaimed land at £1 per acre.
11. *Downpatrick Recorder* 22 Jan 1853, 12 Feb.1853. Ker was the Society's patron, Anketell its president; its office holders and committee included four ministers of religion and Ker's agriculturalist, Stafford.
12. *Downpatrick Recorder* 5 Mar.1842.
13. Pilson records that a sample from one spring was analysed and found to be 'nothing more than ordinary water'. (Pilson, 'Historical Illustrations', p.128-29.) He did not let this deter him.
14. The pumps were made by J. Braham of London, the inventor of the flushing lavatory. (Brett *Mid Down*, p.43.)
15. J.A. Pilson 'Historic & Topographic Illustrations of the County of Down' (1850-53) The maze was said to have been laid out after a fall of snow, and was planted with rhododendron and laurel hedges. These stood seven foot high, took six weeks to trim in summer and, like the Forth Road Bridge, had to begun again as soon as they were completed. (Arthur Davidson, Spa, pers. comm. 1998. One of Arthur's ancestors helped

to plant the maze.) According to the folklore, the paths were seven miles long, an estimate that seems to have more to do with the difficulty of finding the exit than their physical length! (*Belfast News Letter* 6 Oct.1979.)

16.   James Robert McQuiston.
17.   A. Pilson Diary vol.2 18 July 1838, 3 July 1838, 6 July 1838, 7 July 1838, 20 Apr.1855; PRONI D1167/10/1
18.   Buchanan & Wilson, p.7.
19.   *Downpatrick Recorder* 9 Jan.1847.
20.   Day & McWilliams, *Down IV*, vol. 17, p.46.
21.   Pilson's diary, quoted in Wilson, p.161.
22.   A Pilson, A Downpatrick Diary, Vol.1, 17 Oct.1840, records that 'The purchase at £205,000 [£183,000, plus £22,000 for additional townlands not apparently considered part of the estate] is considered cheap', an assessment that is all the more interesting for having been made at a time of agricultural recession.
23.   A. Pilson Diary vol.2 various; Buchanan & Wilson, p.6.
24.   *Downpatrick Recorder* 15 May 1852.
25.   Ibid., 27 June 1857.
26.   Ibid.
27.   By the Board of Works in Dublin in c.1851. Ker lobbied (unsuccessfully) to have 'the navigation' extended for several decades. See also *Downpatrick Recorder* 13 June 1868.
28.   A. Pilson Diary vol.1, 13 May 1839.
29.   Ker's name, unlike John Waring Maxwell's, rarely features on the various boards which administered the town's main institutions.
30.   PRONI D/3244/G/1/230 Hill to Maxwell 5 Aug.1852.

'A good match, and everybody pleased'
1.   David enjoyed cordial relations with his Uncle Maxwell all his life, in spite of their political differences.
2.   PRONI D3244/F/7/5 David Stewart Ker to John Waring Maxwell, Portavo, 17 Jan.1841.
3.   PRONI D1071/F/E2/2 Caroline Norton (grand-daughter of the playwright Richard Brinsley Sheridan) to Mrs Hamilton Ward, 8 Jan.1863, upon hearing of Anna's death.
4.   PRONI D1071/F/A1/3/1 Helen, Lady Dufferin, Rome, to her son Frederick 28 Feb.1842.
5.   One of David's first public pronouncements, at his majority dinner in 1838, was a paean to 'the loveliness of creation' arrayed in the Ladies Gallery. (*Downpatrick Recorder* 13 Jan.1838.)
6.   Mrs Stone, the Manor House, Donaghadee, pers comm. 1988. In his 1864 coming of age address David Stewart Ker's eldest son Alfred was described as heir to 'the largest estates possessed by any commoner in Ireland'.
7.   *Downpatrick Recorder* 5 Mar.1842, p.3. Anna brought a dowry of £11,558 (over twice the sum Lady Selina brought with her in 1814), which will have done nothing to dim her welcome. (PRONI, unclassified box B42270.) Dynastically, this was a marriage of equals.
8.   Christ Church College, Collection Records 1835-39, p.459; *Downpatrick Recorder* 12 Oct.1878.
9.   David Ker, pers comm. 1999.
10.   PRONI D/1071/F/A1/1.
11.   Jupp, *Heritage Gardens*, introduction. (See bib. under websites.)
12.   Unlike his father, David was not reaching for the sublime. He was quite happy to settle for majesty.
13. PRONI D/1071/F/B1/1 Frederick to Helen, Lady Dufferin, 'Portavoe Monday 1844'.

14. Elizabeth Leahe to George Dunbar, Belfast, 15 Jan.1844. Undeposited Ker family papers. Fortunately the house was insured with the Royal Exchange.
15. Sammy McCully, Crows Hill, Ballyminetragh, pers. comm. 1995. The folklore also has it that 'black people' who had been smuggled through the tunnels into the catacombs of the house perished in the fire. John McCoubrey, Ballyfotherly, pers. comm. 1998. Mr McCoubrey had this from his uncle.
16. PRONI D2651/5/31 Selina S. Anketell to Eva Ker, 29 Sept.1917.

Enter the Anketells
1. Red Hall may have been too peripheral to make a suitable home for this active heir.
2. Elizabeth Inglis-Jones, Memoir. Matthew's mother Sarah was John Waring Maxwell's sister. The couple may have met at Finnebrogue. U.H. Hussey de Burgh (1878) quoted in Collins, p.4.
3. The family genealogy describes Matthew (1812-70) as 'refined, and cultured, with a charm of voice and manner possessed by few; sympathetic, amiable, genial, and generous, he was beloved and respected by all... No finer specimen of a landlord, gentleman, and patriot can be found in the pages of Irish history.' (*Anketell Family*, p.55). Bateson (1878) cites the rental value of the Anketell estate as £4,300.
4. Matthew D. Anketell (Port Elizabeth) to Dick Ker, 27 Jan.1964.
5. The tower, a romantic, Pre-Raphaelite invocation of antiquity, is intended to suggest that the house may have its origins in some now razed religious foundation, or medieval tower house.
6. Upon his death in 1870, Matthew was succeeded by his eldest son, also Matthew (b.1841), an accomplished Egyptologist. His brother, Henry (b.1855) joined the Land Restoration League and (unsuccessfully) attempted to persuade Matthew to 'return' the family estates. He afterwards moved to South Africa, where he worked with Ghandi on behalf of Cape Indians.
7. From material supplied by Laurence Clerkin, the present owner of Anketell Grove.
8. P.J. Duffy, quoted in Collins, p.2-3. The Anketell family history states that Oliver Anketell received his Monaghan lands in 1636.
9. Elizabeth Inglis-Jones, Memoir; undeposited document held by Ker family.
10. They were married in St.Georges, Hanover Square, London, on 8 October 1844. (D2651/1/31).
11. PRONI D/1167/10/2. Anketell received 4% of the rents. As the standard cut for agents was 5%, one could say that he got no favours. On large estates, however, agents were often salaried, and he could be said to have been fortunate to be on a percentage at all. Harrell, the agent for the Clough and Downpatrick estates, was also on 4%. (PRONI D/2651/5/36.) Though aware of his brother-in-law's interest in estate management, Ker appears to have had no prior intention of giving Anketell employment. (PRONI D/2651/5/35.)
12. PRO Kew. Foreign Office List, 1858, p.70. Before Richard left, Downshire got a him a commission in the North Down Militia, so that he would have a uniform to wear at court. (PRONI D/671/C/815 & 845.)
13. Richard was elected twice, serving between 1847-51 and 1857-59.
14. *Downpatrick Recorder* 7 Aug.1847. Richard's youthful internationalisation evidently stood him in good stead.
15. PRONI MIC 22/2/36 Richard Ker to Frederick, Lord Dufferin 14 Jan.1850. It is not clear why Richard stood down. The position of MP was unpaid and financially demanding. Richard may not have been able to afford to continue. His uncle, Henry, Viscount Hardinge, a former Chief Secretary for Ireland and Governor General of India may have used his influence to obtain a post for Richard; putting his able son Charles into parliament was the least the Kers could do in return. (See also PRONI D/2651/5/19 for

Hardinge's support for Richard's career.)
16. PRO Kew. Foreign Office List, 1858, p.70.

To the pyramids and beyond
1. Though she admitted that, 'The musquitoes torment me & Hughes to Death', Anna wrote that, 'If I ever travel again I shall never bring an English maid as they are perfectly miserable not speaking any language except English & not caring for the scenery, the very life her mistress thinks most delightful they think quite horrible'. PRONI D/2651/5/35, Anna to Lady Selina, Patras, 24 Dec.1845.
2. Ibid. David found this 'anything but agreeable having about twenty stay laces bound so tight around my waist I could barely sit'. PRONI D/2651/5/35 David Ker, Syra, to his mother Lady Selina, 29 Dec.1845.
3. Ibid.
4. PRONI D/2651/5/35 David Ker, Athens, to his sister Madalena Anketell, 26 Dec. 1845.
5. A hinge that 'wants oiling', as the British diplomatic presence compared poorly with that of the other major European powers, particularly France, 'which has quite got the ear of the Pasha'. PRONI D/2651/5/35 David to Richard, Alexandria, 7 Jan.1846.
6. Ibid. Anna to her mother, Cairo, '16 Dec.1845'.
7. Ibid.
8. Anna to her mother, Smyrna, 14 Mar.1846. 'How we got through it I do not know, but we did.'
9. Ibid.
10. Ibid. After sending '100,000 kisses to our beloved children', Anna signed the letter 'Kar', then corrected it to Ker, as though unused to the spelling of her new surname.
11. Anna to her mother, Smyrna, 16 March 1846.
12. Anna to her mother, Smyrna, 14 & 16 March 1846.
13. The price of oats rose by one third, and the price of potatoes more than doubled in Newtownards market in April 1846. Grant (1997, p.354) writes that 'the normal export of potatoes had been abandoned, farmers 'throwing' them into the home market and eating them while they were still sound'.

19   The Great Famine

The triumph of theory
1. From 'New taties – corn laws' (1840s) by County Antrim bard, Thomas Beggs (1789-1847), quoted by B.M. Walker in Gray & McCann, p.135.
2. Kinealy, *Calamity*, p.52, 69.
3. Irish merchants lobbied against further government imports of food, arguing that these had threatened their profits and livelihoods. Kinealy, p.73-74.
4. Ibid., p.53, 70.
5. *Belfast News Letter* 9 June 1846, quoting *Downpatrick Recorder*.
6. Ibid.
7. O'Grada (p.200) recounts a discovery tale from County Galway in which a man: 'went out to the garden for potatoes for a meal. He stuck the spade in the pit, and the spade was swallowed. The potatoes turned to mud inside. He shrieked and shrieked. The whole town came out. All the potatoes were in the same way.'
8. PRONI BG 25/A/1/p.63. The farmers did not need to be told. When the Ards Farming Society met in Kircubbin on August 10th, the consensus was that the blight had 'completely destroyed' the potato crop in the Ards. (*Belfast News Letter* 14 Aug.1846.)
9. Hugh Andrews, pers. comm. 1987. Yields: O'Grada, p.17.

10. *Belfast News Letter* 31 July 1846.

11. Connolly, p.238.

12. Or would it? In his pamphlet of 1843 Anketell cautioned that market forces would not work in a subsistence economy, 'for the simple reason, that the poverty of people will prevent them from being consumers of any food, except potatoes, or wearers of any apparel, except rags.' (Anketell, *Absenteeism*, p.36.)

13. Grant, p.360-68; *Belfast News Letter* 5 Nov.1846; *Downpatrick Recorder* 26 Dec.1846; McCavery, 'The Famine in County Down', p.104, in Kinealy & Parkhill. The reminiscences McCavery cites are especially valuable, as the small schemes instanced are the sort that are all too easily missed by the regular documentary 'radar'.

14. Ker and Forde owned 55 of the barony of Kinelarty's 63 townlands. (Frey, ch. 1. Frey's total of 54 omits the Ker townland of Creeghduff.) When the countryside gathered to discuss public works, the call was always for drainage. (Grant, in Proudfoot, *Down*, p.356.)

15. *House of Commons Sessional Papers* 1847, vol.50, p.512. This grant was authorised under the terms of the Labouchere letter sometime during the period 10 Dec. 1846-8 Jan 1847. Ker and Forde subsequently reapplied for the scheme under the Treasury Minute of 1 Dec.1846, which offered more favourable terms (Ibid., p.491.) See also Grant, in Proudfoot, *Down*, p.359.

16. *Downpatrick Recorder* 19 Dec.1846. The scheme did not involve the drainage of 33,000 acres, but approved farm-by-farm drainage works, which could take place within the area applied for. It was, notwithstanding this, a very considerable scheme, which given the rates of aid then prevailing is likely to have involved the drainage of over 1,000 acres.

17. Ker and Forde stood as guarantors for the £7,120, each underwriting approximately half the sum. They hoped to recoup most of this via a levy on participating farmers of 4/- per £1 of Poor Law Valuation. Ultimately, agreement between landlord and tenant would determine what each participant paid, with commissioners arbitrating in the event of disagreement. (*Downpatrick Recorder* 19 Dec.1846.)

18. These labouring jobs were open to any destitute male of working age from the barony, whose property had a Poor Law Valuation of under £6. The scheme was administered by relief committees in Ballynahinch and Seaforde. (*Downpatrick Recorder* 19 Dec.1846.) Farmers who wanted their lands drained applied to Ker and Forde, who lent them the sum due at 5%, to be repaid over ten years. (*Belfast News Letter* 15 Dec.1846.) Labourers who wanted work applied to their respective relief committee, as opposed to Ker or Forde, neither of whom seems to have used (or been able to use) the scheme to exercise overt patronage.

19. Downshire, who was indefatigable during the crisis, announced his intention of draining bogland in the vicinity of Downpatrick 'in conjunction with other proprietors' in the spring. (*Downpatrick Recorder* 12 Dec.1846.) As we have seen, Downshire and Ker had successfully conducted a joint scheme of this kind in the early 1840s.

20. Arthur Davidson, Spa, pers. comm. 1998. If this was the 'Downshire scheme' (and Quoile drainage schemes were then a perennial of Downpatrick life), it would have been a private scheme, giving Downshire, Ker, and other participating landlords control over who was employed, hence Arthur Davidson's great-grandfather's possible involvement.

21. Kinealy, *Calamity*, p.80-81.

22. Ibid. Trevelyan wrote of the whole world being 'ransacked for supplies'.

23. *Belfast News Letter* 15 Dec.1846.

24. Some of this produce was diverted to domestic markets. Wheat would have helped to feed the hungry, but the other items were luxuries. Unaffordable even in good times.

25. Andrews to Londonderry 10 Jan.1847, quoted in McCavery p.122.

26. PRONI BG/25/A/1, p.291-94 Resignation letter of Robert Nicholson of Balloo,

Newtownards Poor Law Guardian. Nicholson, a descendent of the Nicholson who had torn strips off Ker when they met on the road on the eve of the 1798 rebellion, was very much the conscience of the Board.

27. The returns for June 1847 showed 114 employed on public work schemes in County Down, against 2,103 in Antrim and 8,710 in Galway. (*Downpatrick Recorder* 7 Aug. 1847.)

28. Exempted under the Labouchere letter of 5 October 1846. This stipulation was intended to push landlords towards self-financed schemes, and to prevent them from advantaging their estates at public expense. Downshire and Roden financed large schemes out of their own pockets. (Grant, p.359.) Many smaller works did not become a matter of record, making their number and extent extremely difficult to discern.

29. The Ards Fishing Company, formed in November 1846, was both a response to 'the present trying crisis' and a longer term attempt to develop the peninsular fishing industry. All the major proprietors (including Ker) subscribed, providing the company with capital of £5,000. (*Downpatrick Recorder* 9 & 23 Jan.1847.)

30. At a meeting in Kircubbin in December 1846, Ward, Nugent, Montgomery, Blakiston-Houston and other Upper Ards proprietors resolved to create work for unemployed labourers on their estates. (*Belfast News Letter* 22 Dec.1846.)

Soup and yellow meal cakes

1. Kinealy, p.78, 81.

2. Thomas Andrews quoted in McCavery, p.122.

3. *Banner of Ulster* 26 Feb.1847. Article on distress in Portavo's home parish of Bangor.

4. Ibid. There are accounts from mid (*Banner of Ulster* 19 Feb.1847) and south Down (Grant, p.357) of men seeking work (on the railways) in Scotland and England.

5. *Banner of Ulster* 12 Feb.1847. It was administered by the Rev. John McAuley, minister of First Donaghadee.

6. *Banner of Ulster* 23 Feb.1847.

7. On 15 & 22 May 1847, in its coverage of fundraising for the Down Fever Hospital, the *Downpatrick Recorder* took the unusual (and unfair) step of comparing Dufferin's generosity unfavourably with that of Ker.

8. *Banner of Ulster* 19 Feb.1847. The outlying townlands were not forgotten. In February 1847 Ker gave £5 to the relief committee in Killinchy-in-the-Woods. William Anketell added a further £1. Both donations were widely reported.

9. Fanny Anketell played a similar role on the Anketell estates in County Monaghan.

10. This was also largely funded by the Kers, with David contributing £100, Anna £10, Lady Selina £10, and William Anketell £20 of the Ballynahinch Relief Committee's £202.17.0 budget. In late December the Committee bought ten tons of Indian corn, which saw them through to early February, when the Government supplied matching funding of £202.

11. Arthur Davidson, pers. comm. 1998.

12. *House of Commons Sessional Papers* 1847, vol.52, p.91. Brereton's Journal, week ending 9 Jan.1847, Barony of Mourne. Brereton very properly takes the absentee General Meade to task for authorising his agent 'to give but sparingly to his famishing tenantry', but omits to mention that in November 1846 Meade reduced his rents by 10-20%. (*Belfast News Letter* 13 Nov.1846.)

13. *Banner of Ulster* 19 Feb.1847.

14. Though he later contributed to them, Lord Londonderry had initially spoken out against the formation of relief committees, so the *Banner* may have sent its man to Drumhirk to make a political point. *The Vindicator*, 22 Apr.1846, cited in Killen, p.60.

15. *Banner of Ulster* 5 & 26 Feb.1847. Journalistic licence not withstanding, the reports are a powerful testament to the extent of local sickness and hunger. Saintfield was

described as 'in an extremely bad state'; Newtownards and Donaghadee as 'still more deplorable'. (*Banner of Ulster* 12 Feb.1847.)

16. Farmers with rateable values of over £4 (most of Portavo's farmers had rateable values of between £4-10) were required to pay the Poor Rate. Rates varied between Unions, and between electoral districts within the same Union. In the Newtownards Union the rate was levied in May and November 1847. In the Bangor Electoral District the rate stayed the same, at 10d in the £1. In Donaghadee the rate nearly trebled, rising from 7 1/2d in May to 1s/8d in the £1 in December. The rates were collected; arrears were rarely written off. (PRONI BG/25/A/1, p.327, p.388.) These sums were as nothing to those levied in some western Unions where, with the advent of 'outdoor relief', rates 'were struck on an unprecedented scale'. Forty-two of Ireland's 130 Poor Law Unions went bankrupt attempting to raise the money necessary to fund relief. (Grant, p.376-77.)

17. *House of Commons Sessional Papers* 1847, vol.17, 14th Annual Report Board of Public Works; vol.52, p.197. This scheme almost certainly had a relief dimension. The payment of £19.10.8 in wages in February 1847 suggests something like sixty men employed for five weeks. This would have been heavy, difficult work.

18. *Banner of Ulster* 26 Feb.1847.

19. *Downpatrick Recorder* 13 Feb.1847.

20. *Banner of Ulster* 19 Feb.1847. *The Banner* records that, in spite of their difficulties, people 'struggled on hopefully', bearing their lot with great courage. (Ibid. 26 Feb.1847.)

21. In February 1847, although 625,000 people were employed on public works schemes at a cost of nearly a million pounds, the number of destitute was increasing at the rate of 20,000 per week. (Treasury minute of 10 Mar.1847, *House of Commons Sessional Papers*, 1847, vol.17, p.3-5.) The minute is remarkably candid, stating that, 'all effectual control of the number of persons employed, and over the manner in which the work is executed by them, has for the present, been lost.'

22. During the 1846-47 financial year the government spent £2 million on 'Irish distress', out of an estimated expenditure of £51.5 million, a figure of 3.9%. This figure can be looked at in many ways. In terms of modern expenditure, based on 2002-03 figures, it represents a sum of over £16 billion, that is £1,950 for every man woman and child then living in Ireland, a sum scarcely compatible with a strategy of genocide by starvation. Equally, it could be forcibly argued that £1,950 will not go far if a pint of milk costs £5 or £10. The gross sum spent per person was about 5/-, which for a labourer was about a week's wages. Famine expenditure is often unfavourably contrasted with the amount spent on the Crimean War. The most interesting parallel the Crimean War offers, however, is probably the government's inability to feed its own troops at Sebastopol during the winter of 1854-55, during which thousands died.

The road to the workhouse
1. A. Pilson, 'A Downpatrick Diary', vol.1, 24 Mar.1847.
2. PRONI BG 25/A/1. List derived from marriage notices.
3. Perry would have been able to help out of his own pocket, or through the Donaghadee relief fund, administered by his good friend, the Rev. McAuley, of First Donaghadee. The Anguses belonged to Shore Street.

Soup for Rembrandts
1. Brett, *Mid Down*, p.37.
2. Dick Ker, pers. comm. 1988, relating a story told to him by his grandfather Richard William Blackwood Ker (b.1850), who spoke of a crowd of some seventy beggars gathering round the dining room window. He also told of the children giving a beggar money to scare and chase them. The porch story focuses plausibly on the importance of shelter during a bleak winter. The monkeys story is problematic in that the Ker children

were three, two and one year old at the time of greatest scarcity.

3.   *Banner of Ulster* 12 Feb. 1847.

4.   The capacity of vessels that could use the quay was tripled to vessels of 300 tons burthen, opening the quay to traffic from much further afield.

5.   *Downpatrick Recorder* 3 Apr.1847.

6.   H&WRO BA 3940/64 Anne Porter's diary 11 Sept.1850. Local tradition has it that the masons divided their time between the two according to tide and weather. John McClintock, Red Hall, pers. comm. 1998.

7.   The Church of St. John the Evangelist was consecrated in 1847; the keystone bears the date 1848. God, widely understood to be, for his own good reasons, the ultimate author of the Famine, was then felt to be both very distant and very close.

8.   Anon, *Anketell Family*. The truth is almost certainly more complex. Monaghan was one of the worst affected Ulster counties, so the Anketell estate is as likely to have been crippled by the temporary break down of the socio-economic structure it existed within as any action of its owners. Fanny is said to have been Matthew's 'ready helper in every good work'.

9.   Christie & Manson, *Catalogue*, sale of 19 May 1848. The works included two purported Rembrandt self portraits, interiors by Teniers and Jan Steen, devotional works by Rubens, Murillo, Veronese and Caravaggio, landscapes attributed to Claude and Titian, and Napoleon in his Robes by Gerard. These pictures, removed from Ker's residence in Upper Grosvenor Street, comprised some 20% of the collection.

10. In 1845 David described to his mother a card game in which the 'cards and their accompanying excitement were dealt around as Skillfull as in Paris, and as quietly as in a picture of Teniers'. That he would feel this, and his mother would understand it, hints at the place of the family's art in its every day consciousness. (PRONI D/2651/5/35 David to Lady Selina, Athens, 23 Dec.1845; Richard to David 'St.Petersburg Feb.18'.)

11. *Downpatrick Recorder* 15 May 1852.

Enter the anti-Christ

1.   Stevenson's death shocked all who knew him 'as he appeared to possess unusual bodily strength'. Stevenson was a Giles Winterbourne figure, a solid, dependable man with a farming background, who related well to farmers and owed his position to his abilities. (PRONI D1255/3/32A.)

2.   *The effects of absenteeism briefly considered (1843)* and *The Conduct of the resident landlords of Ireland* (1844). Ker appointed Anketell as his 'agent and man of business', a wider remit than Stevenson had enjoyed.

3.   Boyd to Routh 10 Mar. & 16 Mar.1847, NAI Relief Commission Papers (County Down) 1A/50/45/n.14075 & n.14382 (with thanks to James Grant).

4.   Ibid. One of the sixty died 'of exhaustion' the following day. (Anketell is perhaps fortunate that the poor were too weak to riot.) Boyd's letters make clear that the arrival of this powerful outsider (he describes Anketell as 'a mere stranger') upset an established way of doing things, putting a new and harsher dynamic in place.

5.   Ibid. Boyd complained that Anketell (who 'rules the committee in a very arbitrary manner'), had interpreted the regulations too narrowly.

6.   Work on a new church had recently been abandoned as the builders were too weak to labour. (Arthur Davidson, pers. comm. 2004.) This was Third Ballynahinch. Its congregation was not only starving, it was so impoverished that it could not pay its mortgage, causing its bank to foreclose. The minister, the Rev. Davis, sailed to America, returning two years later with enough money to pay off the loan. (Reid, *Ballynahinch*, p.8.) The story recounted may be the folklore's *coloratura* take on the foreclosure.

7.   Arthur Davidson, pers. comm. 2004, who had it from his neighbour Arthur McCoubrey. No inquiry appears to have taken place.

8.   James Grant in Proudfoot, p.366. This is logical in that the group hit hardest by this action would have been tenants' tenants, people over whom the estate otherwise had no direct control.

9.   Anketell, *Absenteeism*, p.30-32.

10.   Anketell, *Conduct*, p.11.

11.   O'Donovan *Ordnance Survey Letters*, Co. Donegal, quoted in Kinealy & Parkhill, p.170.

12.   Thomas Andrews to Londonderry 2 Feb.1847, quoted in McCavery, 'The Famine in County Down', in Kinealy & Parkhill, p.120.

13.   *Downpatrick Recorder* 19 Dec.1847. Francis Hutcheson, born in 1694 in the townland of Drumalig, near Carryduff, County Down, was one of the catalysts of the Scottish Enlightenment. His view was that 'the end of all civil polity [was] the common interest of the people'. (Barkley, *Hutcheson*, p.11.)

14.   It is unclear that it would have been in Ker's interest to remove small farmers. Vaughan has suggested that small farms perforce tended to be more productive than large farms. (*Landlord & Tenant*, p.86.) The 1838-39 Ker estate rentals show small farmers paying their rent as punctually as larger holders. (PRONI D/500/173 & 174.)

15.   A nuance the Ker children, the bearers of the tale, would have been unaware of. Ker may have backed Anketell and then taken cold feet. But his defence of the claims of labourers in Nov.1846 makes this scenario unlikely.

16.   *Downpatrick Recorder* 15 May 1847.

17.   *Downpatrick Recorder* 2 & 9 Mar.1850; Arthur Davidson, pers. comm. 2004. Arthur McCoubrey, Arthur Davidson's neighbour, always used to smile when he told this story. No love lost there, it would seem.

18.   *Downpatrick Recorder* 23 Feb & 2 Mar.1850.

19.   The Anketells moved out, returning in January 1851, amidst cheers of welcome from 'a large body of the tenantry', who walked to the house to greet him and his family. (*Downpatrick Recorder* 23 Jan.1851.)

20.   *Downpatrick Recorder* 8 May 1852.

21.   Hence no Ker representative on the Newtownards Board of Guardians, etc.

20   'That splendid ass, Montalto': the 1852 election

The Star of the County Down

1.   Hoppen (p.397.)

2.   *Downpatrick Recorder* 31 July 1852. County Down largely escaped the agrarian and sectarian strife that tainted much electioneering elsewhere.

3.   The last contested county election had occurred in 1831, prior to David Ker's purchase of Downpatrick. This acquisition gave the Kers the second largest voting bloc in the county (see Appendix 2). In the late 1830s-early 1840s the Kers' energies had gone into stamping their authority on Downpatrick, and establishing uncontested control of its Westminster borough seat. The contested election of 1852 provided the Kers with their first opportunity to assert their new standing.

4.   PRONI D/3244/G/1/121 Maxwell to Ker 13 Feb.1852.

5.   PRONI D/3324/G/1/224 Downshire to John Waring Maxwell 10 June 1852.

6.   Political alliance between two families, such as that effected by the Londonderrys and Downshires in 1812 (see Part 1, p.223).

7.   PRONI D/3244/G/1/178 Bateson to Maxwell 19 May 1852.

8.   PRONI D/3324/G/1/183 Thomas Greg to Maxwell 21 May 1852.

9.   PRONI D/3324/G/1/200 Bateson to Maxwell 24 May 1852.

10.   From *The Family Seat, a Lament, by V[ane] L[ondonderry]*, a printed election squib

held by the Ker family.

11. PRONI D/3324/G/1/129 Londonderry to Maxwell 19 Mar.1852. Londonderry called on his tenants to plump (vote exclusively) for Hill (/179 Bateson to Maxwell 20 May 1852). The main advantages Ker derived from this brief dalliance was perhaps the chance to copy Londonderry's poll books.

12. William Sharman Crawford, MP for Dundalk 1835-37, and Liberal MP for Rochdale 1841-52, passed over the chance of being returned for Rochdale in order to contest Down. In 1875 Bateman listed the Crawfords as owners of 5,750 acres.

13. The novelist William Carleton urged that he be persuaded to sit for a sculptor. (PRONI D/856/F/59 Carleton to Crawford Apr. 1855)

14. It is interesting to see this term in use in County Down five years after the publication of the Communist Manifesto. It was used exclusively by the right with the object of inspiring fear. *Downpatrick Recorder* 12 June 1852; PRONI D/3324/G/1/163 Downshire to Maxwell 29 Apr.1852.

15. *Downpatrick Recorder* 12 June 1852.

16. *Downpatrick Recorder* 8 May 1852; PRONI D/3244/G/1/122 Price to Maxwell 25 Feb.1852.

17. *Downpatrick Recorder* 27 Mar.1852.

18. PRONI D/3244/G/1/121A David Stewart Ker to Maxwell 23 Feb.1852.

19. PRONI D/3244/G/1/122 Price to Maxwell 28 Feb.1852.

20. PRONI D/3244/G/1/134 Downshire to Maxwell 28 Mar.1852; /220 Bateson to Maxwell 5 June 1852.

21. PRONI D/654/N2/31 Andrews to John Vandeleur Stewart 27 June 1852. Downshire agreed, declaring that, 'The devil that is Wallace shows unmistakably in all Ker's conduct.' (PRONI D/3244/G/1/224 Downshire to Maxwell 10 June 1852.)

22. D2223//21/7 Ker to Londonderry 3 Mar.1852; PRONI MIC/22/3/26 Anna Ker to Dufferin 31 May 1852.

23. The more reflective of the county's landlords may have taken comfort from the fact that they were, in the main, facing open, democratic protest. Eighty years before, this level of disaffection might have produced a violent secret society like the Hearts of Steel.

24. *Downpatrick Recorder* 16 Feb., 23 Feb., 2 Mar.1850. The arson attacks took place in Killinchy Woods. In Clough, 'respectable' tenants were told to withhold their rent. The authorities responded by increasing the police presence, which Ker and Maxwell felt was likely only to exacerbate the problem. Ker unsuccessfully moved a Grand Jury amendment stating that this additional force was unwarranted. (Ibid., 9 Mar.1850.) Ker's agent understood the possible motives of his attackers: 'when more than a fourth of the population of... Ireland has really no interest in the country, what are we to expect but discontent, outrage, and revolutionary sentiments?' (Anketell, *Absenteeism*, p.37-38.)

25. Downshire considered that the county would be 'at best neutralised by [the return of] a Conservative and a Radical'. PRONI D/3324/G/1/163 Downshire to Maxwell 28 Mar.1852.

26. Robert Gordon accused Ker of betraying the conservative cause. Ditching Ker by denying him Hill second preferences remained on the Downshire agenda until three weeks before polling. PRONI D/3244/G/1/227 Gordon to Maxwell 16 June 1852.

27. PRONI D/3244/G/1/161 Londonderry to Maxwell 24 Apr. 1852.

28. We can see shades of 1805 in this reluctance. The formation of a junction with Downshire would have guaranteed Ker 1200 votes. PRONI D/3244/G/1/221 Bateson to Maxwell 5 June 1852.

29. PRONI D/3244/G/1/159 Price to Maxwell 15 Apr.1852.

30. PRONI MIC 22/3/26 Anna to Dufferin 31 May 1852. Anna arrived in May to discover that Crawford's canvassers 'been collecting votes & money' on the estate 'for these last five months'. This had been done without Dufferin's permission, which Anna considered to be a breach of electoral etiquette, an indication of the all pervasive extent

of landlord influence.

31. PRONI D3244/G/1/209 Hall to Maxwell late May 1852, *Downpatrick Recorder* 29 May 1852.

32. PRONI D/3324/G/1/224 Downshire to Maxwell 10 June 1852.

33. *Downpatrick Recorder* 1 May 1852.

34. *Downpatrick Recorder* 3 Apr., 14 Aug.1852. Thomas Jones of Moneyglass was another convert. He advised his thirty-six County Down voters to 'give one vote to the independent member, Mr. Ker', and allowed them 'full liberty to vote as they please' with the other. (Each voter had two votes.) *Downpatrick Recorder* 12 June 1852.

35. *Downpatrick Recorder* 24 Apr.1852.

36. PRONI D/671/O/2/6. The 1852 Downshire Poll Book reveals interesting differences in voting intentions within the Portavo estate, with Portavo, Ballyminetragh and the Copeland Islanders (Downshire's men made it all the way to the Copeland Islands, an indication of their thoroughness) promising to give their second votes to Lord Edwin, while all but one of Ballyfotherly's eight electors intended to give their second vote to Crawford.

37. PRONI D/3244/G/1/199 Blakiston-Houston to Maxwell 24 May 1852.

38. PRONI D/654/N2/31 Thomas Andrews to John Vandeleur Stewart 27 June 1852; *House of Commons Sessional Papers* 1852-53, vol.83, p.414.

39. Ibid.

40. *Downpatrick Recorder* 10 July 1852. Hardinge promptly bedded himself in by making £300 worth of charitable donations to local institutions.

41. *Downpatrick Recorder* 24 July 1852.

42. Ibid,

43. Ibid.

44. *Banner of Ulster* 23 July 1852.

45. The pro-Crawford *Banner of Ulster* estimated their number at 5,000. (*Banner of Ulster* 23 July 1852.) Very few will have been entitled to vote.

46. *Banner of Ulster* 23 July 1852. At least he could put a steak on it.

47. Ibid.; *Northern Whig* 24 July 1852.

48. *Downpatrick Recorder* 24 July 1852. The *Banner of Ulster* records two deaths.

49. *Banner of Ulster* 23 July 1852. The *Northern Whig* reported that 'forty men from Mr Ker's works, at Ballycarry… armed with poles cut out of the woods of Red-hall' arrived by boat 'to assault the peaceable electors at the polling booths of Newtownards'. (*Northern Whig* 22 July 1852.)

50. Electors had to vote in one of four towns: Ker's Downpatrick (the traditional electoral centre), Downshire's Hillsborough, Londonderry's Newtownards, and Needham's Newry.

51. *Banner of Ulster* 23 July 1852.

52. *House of Commons Sessional Papers* 1852-53, vol. 83, p.306. This list of expenses charged to and paid by candidates will have been but a fraction of their actual expenses.

53. *Northern Whig* 15 Jan.1853. This figure is of a piece with the fabulous sums reportedly spent in earlier contested elections. The Whig's objective in citing this figure was to impress its readers with the lengths landlordism had had to go to stop Crawford. (*Downpatrick Recorder* 4 April 1857.) Why did estates spend so much on elections? Clausewitz' description of politics as 'war by other means' is relevant here. Fighting elections, a form of madness the biggest landowners were particularly prone to, was the nearest thing that estates did to waging war. As well as being struggles between differing philosophies and interests, elections were virility contests, rumbles in the pride. Winning was all, and the huge sums spent on doing so can be equated with the open-ended amounts states spend when in conflict.

54. *Downpatrick Recorder* 31 July 1852.

55. Anna did not reply, convention did not permit it. Incongruously, the nine-year-old Alfred replied on her behalf. David then expressed his regret at this circumstance; and to much cheering and laughter reminded the audience that, yes, 'she exceeded all in canvassing, but he would tell them, that in his day, he canvassed her.' (Ibid.)

56. PRONI D/671/O/2/6. The Downshire electorate was the best managed in the county. This low figure suggests that Downshire also withheld support from his 'ally' or sought plumpers.

57. Andrew Angus, Thomas McBride, John McConnell, John McCutcheon and John Perry gave Ker plumpers. Willie Anderson, Alexander Angus and William Burrows voted for Ker and Hill, suggesting that the political mood of the townland was then centre-right.

58. Griffith, *Union of Newtownards*, p.104.

59. PRONI D/671/O/2/6. Forty of the Portavo estate's forty-two electors voted, and of these 39 (97%) voted for Ker, 23 (57%) of them exclusively.

60. The isolated and relatively recently acquired townland of Ballyalloly (near Comber) proved the most wayward. Three of its four electors plumped for Crawford.

61. As Hoppen remarked somewhat archly, electoral violence was so widespread that its absence and not its presence was newsworthy. (Hoppen, p.390.)

62. PRONI D/3244/G/1/214 Maxwell to John Vandeleur Stewart 4 June 1852.

63. *Downpatrick Recorder* 24 July 1852.

64. *Downpatrick Recorder* 14 Aug. 1852.

65. PRONI D/2223/21/11. Petition to parliament lodged by James Boyle of Rostrevor. The Martin & Henderson Papers include a printed copy of the petition, torn (no doubt illegally!) from the relevant volume of the 1852 House of Commons Sessional Papers (by Ker?). On it are some scribbled calculations, in a contemporary hand, respecting sums of £2,342 and £5,860. It would be ironic indeed, and cheeky beyond belief, if this page was used to rough out the estate's unadmitted and illegal electoral expenses.

66. County Down sent two county members ('Knights of the Shire'), and two borough members to Westminster. See Vol. 1, p.223.

67. *Downpatrick Recorder* 31 July 1852.

21 'A crow with a peacock's feather in his tail'

'The Times is furious'

1. PRONI D/2651/6/10 George John Langley to Anna Ker, 1846.

2. PRONI MIC 22/5/7 David to Dufferin 23 Jan 1855. Ker's London house was in Upper Grosvenor Street, Mayfair.

3. Conacher, p.14.

4. The government's somewhat petulant counterblast was the 1851 Ecclesiastical Titles Act, which was aimed at preventing the newly created Catholic dioceses from using existing Anglican names.

5. *Downpatrick Recorder* 18 & 25 Jan 1851.

6. Members included Ker's Uncle Maxwell, William Wallace his solicitor, and of course Johnston of Ballykilbeg.

7. *Downpatrick Recorder* 23 Feb.1856. The words were Johnston of Ballykilbeg's: 'All true Protestants were called bigots nowadays' he complained.

8. *Northern Whig* 22 Jan.1853.

9. *Banner of Ulster* 4 Apr.1857.

10. PRONI D2651/5/17 David & Anna to Richard Ker 10 Oct.1853.

Our man in St. Petersburg

1. Richard to Selina, St. Petersburg, 19 Sept.1851. (Letter held by the Ker family.)

2. Richard to David, St. Petersburg, 'February 18'. (Letter held by the Ker family.)

3.   Richard to Selina, St. Petersburg, 19 Sept.1851.
4.   Richard to David, St. Petersburg, 'February 18'; Gertrude Seymour to Lady Selina, St. Petersburg 'December 3rd'. (Letter held by the Ker family.)
5.   King-Hall, *Sea Saga*, p.298.
6.   Ibid.
7.   Paget, *Life*, p.223. This apparently still hung in the Embassy's throne room in the early 1920s. The Government Art Collection does not now include this work. (Alison Fuller, Asst. Curator, DCMS, London, letter to author, 23 Aug.2005.)
8.   King-Hall, *Sea Saga*, p.299.
9.   PRO Kew, FO 72/905/2. Richard Ker to the Earl of Clarendon 21 Feb.1856. The couple married at the British Embassy in Paris then honeymooned at Fontainebleau. (PRONI D/2651/5/20) Rose's father, the Rev. Nicholas Calvert, had restored and extended Quentin Castle in around 1850, 'at a cost of approximately £40,000'. (*Newtownards Chronicle* 17 Sept.1927.) His estate comprised the townlands of Ballymarter, Knockinelder, Dooey, Newcastle and Kearney, which were then worth £1,300 a year.
10.   Rose was 'very beautiful, with auburn hair'. (Richard Perceval-Maxwell, formerly of Inch Lodge, Downpatrick, pers. comm., 2005.) The only surviving likeness of her was destroyed in a fire in 1953.
11.   Paget, *Life*, p.222.
12.   PRO Kew Foreign Office List, 1858, p.70.
13.   King-Hall, *Sea Saga*, p.298-99.
14.   Rose brought £6,000, the income from which may have allowed Richard to think of again entering parliament
15.   On the hustings, Richard's diplomatic service earned him the title of 'the Rooshan' or 'the bear'. (*Banner of Ulster* 10 Feb.1857.)

'She shines by not seeking to shine': Anna

1.   PRONI MIC 22/3/13 Ker to Dufferin 26 Mar.1852.
2.   PRONI D2651/5/36. Whenever Anna wanted pork or wool for the use of the house she bought it from the farm, as on the 20th April 1854, when the Hon. Mrs Ker spent £132.14.0. on mutton for Montalto.
3.   *Downpatrick Recorder* 27 June 1857.
4.   PRONI D/2651/6/10 George John Langley to Anna Ker, 1846.
5.   The Ker womenfolk excelled in sewing and embroidery. McCullough credits the Misses Ker with introducing embroidery to Ballynahinch in the 1840s by giving instruction in a hotel room. (McCullough, *Heart*, p.116.) Did the males of the family manage in John Updike's words, to give this art 'its beautiful due'? Not if the following lines, found amongst the Ker Papers, are anything to go by:
> Our clothes are rent, and minus strings
> Our house is in disorder,
> And all because my lady wife
> Has taken to embroider.
(PRONI D/2651/6/10. From 'The Husband's Complaint', author unknown. Found among the Ker papers from this period.)
6.   *Downpatrick Recorder* 27 June 1857.
7.   Ibid.

The Porters last gambit

1.   See Part 1, p.218-21.
2.   H&WRO BA 3940/64, Anne Porter's Irish journal. They toured their lands at Navan, County Armagh, in a hired barouche, receiving presents of butter and eggs from their

tenants.

3.   Ibid. Anne Porter was godmother to David and Anna's second daughter Helen, but there is no kind word for Helen in the Journal. The Porters found little to admire at Montalto

4.   Ada Anketell, 1934 reminiscences in red, undeposited 'Madalena Guardi Notebook', held by Richard Perceval-Maxwell.

5.   H&WRO BA 3940/64, Anne Porter's Irish journal.

6.   PRONI D1255/3/28 Alexander Shannon, to Richard Ker, 14 Oct. 1873. One of Madalena's servants was allegedly offered money, presumably to concoct a story. He 'indignantly refused it'. In spite of this 'sharp practice', no grounds upon which the will could be contested emerged. (Ibid., Richard Ker to Wallace 24 Oct.1873.)

7.   Anne left most of her money to a Porter relative, her Ker relations received almost nothing.

'A crow with a peacock's feather in his tail'

1.   Guests included members of the nobility and gentry, civic dignitaries like the Mayor of Belfast and the President of Queens's College, and estate groupies like the former moderator of the Presbyterian Church in Ireland, the Rev. Henry Cooke, who liked nothing better than to have the ear of a man with 35,000 acres.

2.   Aynesworth Pilson 'A Downpatrick Diary', vol.1 26 July 1847. Pilson wrote these words in anger after Ker demolished a medieval tower, known as Castle Dorras, in the centre of Downpatrick. Cultured they might have been, antiquarians they were not.

3.   *Downpatrick Recorder* 18 April 1857.

22   The orphan townland

The orphan townland

1.   PRONI T/2610/3. The house may have been intended for Alfred, who would come of age in five years time. The apparent inclusion of only four family bedrooms may have been a caution against Alfred reproducing as prodigiously as his parents.

2.   PRONI T/2610/1.

3.   H&WRO BA 3940/64 Anne Porter's journal, 28 Sept.1850.

4.   In possession of David Ker, Aldworth.

5.   Its letting value fell from £876 in 1858 to £784 in 1867. (PRONI D/1255/3/31B, D/1255/3/20B).

6.   PRONI D/2651/5/32. *Belfast News Letter* cutting from c.1877.

The post-Famine recovery

1.   The 1858 letting value of the demesne is recorded at £876 against £198 for the rest of the townland.

2.   Aird Lowry, pers. comm. 1990. The ruins of the old farmhouse still stand.

3.   1850 Agricultural Return, p.190; 1851 & 1861 Censuses. Between 1851-61 Portavo's housing stock leapt from 20 to 26 dwellings. One of these was acquired via a change in the townland boundary. The remaining five were cottages, four built in a new row on the Warren Road.

4.   Savings nearly doubled during the 1850s. (Whyte, *Independent*, p.166.) This contrasts with farmers' circumstances during the 1830s when, 'capital among the farmers… is as hard to be discovered as the philosopher's stone.' (Anketell, *Absenteeism*, p.35.)

5.   Willie Bell, pers. comm. 1988; Harry Humphreys 2004.

6.   Willie Bell, pers. comm. 1988; Jimmy & Mina Muckle, pers. comm. 2000.

7.   Jimmy & Mina Muckle, pers. comm. 2000.
8.   Surveyed 1862, published 1863.

The 1860s townland
1.   This was self-built, and work proceeded slowly. PRONI VAL 2B/3/1C.
2.   Willie Bell. pers. comm. 1988, Jimmy & Mina Muckle, pers. comm. 1993.
3.   Arthur Davidson, pers. comm. 1998 (the story of the Maharrys).
4.   PRONI MIC/15C/2/10. Will of William Burrows, d. 12 Jan.1869.
5.   Aird Lowry, pers. comm. 1998.
6.   Griffith Valuation, 1863, Union of Newtown Ards, townlands of Orlock, Portavo and Ballywilliam.
7.   Groomsport Presbyterian Church, Registry of Baptisms 1841-1903. Six of the thirteen children Nelson had with his second wife Sarah Morrison died as unbaptised infants. It is interesting to contrast the level of infant mortality the Nelsons experienced with that of the Kers, all of whose twelve children reached maturity.
8.   Both John McConnell's sons, Alexander and John, had wanted to farm, so in the interests of fairness, McConnell set primogeniture aside, and divided the 28 acre family farm between them. A second house was built alongside the original homestead. (See also vol. 1, p.255.)
9.   Plus those of Madeline Magee, the widow Davis, and Fargie the miller.
10. Shore Street Presbyterian Church, Donaghadee, Marriage Register.

The flight from the land
1.   There are, however, Nelsons in Groomsport and Donaghadee, who may be descendants.
2.   Jimmy and Mina Muckle, pers. comm. 1998. Destination unknown. They were attracted by the prospect of cheap land.
3.   Aird Lowry, pers. comm. 1990.
4.   There is room for doubt. In 1841 the townland officially contained 19 dwellings, 20 households and 117 people. The First Six Inch Ordnance Survey map, understood in the light of Griffith (1863) and local knowledge, however, apparently shows 25 occupied dwellings in 1833.

23   'Ker and Independence!': the 1857 election

'Ker and Independence!'
1.   *Banner of Ulster* 7 Apr.1857. The term 'liberal conservative' was in 1857 widely used to mean Peelite or moderate Conservative.
2.   PRONI MIC 22/7/20 Ker to Dufferin 25 Mar.1857. The *Downpatrick Recorder* 'earnestly besought' Ker to withdraw his Liberal address. He refused, and explained himself as follows: 'After the fall of Lord Derby's and Lord Aberdeen's Government, there was no one to take the helm, although we were engaged in a doubtful European war [the Crimean War]. At last, Lord Palmerston came to the rescue. He conducted the country through the war, and restored peace to Europe. After accomplishing such objects successfully, I am not prepared to join with any party factiously to oppose the present government.' (*Downpatrick Recorder* 28 Mar.1857.) The *Downpatrick Recorder's* regard for Ker muted its criticism of his politics. However its gut Toryism continually asserted itself, as in its report of Ker's nomination speech, which omitted key passages from his address. (*Downpatrick Recorder* 11 Apr.1857.)
3.   Forde's candidacy came as a shock to Ker as Forde had privately assured him that he would not join with Downshire. (PRONI MIC 22/7/39 15 Apr.1857, Ker to Dufferin.)

Seasoned election watchers will have enjoyed the irony of Downshire's embracing of Forde. In 1830, Forde's uncle Matthew had, like Ker, contested the county in the independent interest, but had been crushed by the Downshire-Londonderry junction.

4. *Banner of Ulster* 4 Apr.1857.
5. Ibid.
6. *Banner of Ulster* 9 Apr.1857.
7. *Banner of Ulster* 7 Apr.1857.
8. *Downpatrick Recorder* 11 Apr.1857.
9. Tenant right and secondary issues like scriptural education and the Maynooth grant.
10. *Downpatrick Recorder* 11 Apr.1857; PRONI MIC 22/7 A.Rowan-Hamilton to Dufferin, undated.
11. *Downpatrick Recorder* 28 Mar.1857. Hill advocated protectionism (*Banner of Ulster* 9 Apr.1857.) Downshire had led the protectionist movement in County Down.
12. *Downpatrick Recorder* 4 Apr.1857. William's father Hugh had died in 1855.
13. MS in possession of David Ker, Aldworth.
14. *Banner of Ulster* 9 Apr.1857.
15. PRONI MIC 22/7 Rowan-Hamilton to Dufferin, April 1857. In some ways these conditions were well suited to a moderate candidacy like Ker's; however they were unlikely to generate tenant defections in the sort of numbers Ker needed if he was to win.
16. Ibid.
17. PRONI MIC 22/7/39 Ker to Dufferin 15 Apr.1857. The campaign lasted weeks, not months, so this time personal canvassing made less impact. No fey diplomat, Richard also did his bit. David writes that his brother, 'was at Newry shouting with Kirk [the borough's Liberal candidate] bearding Giants driving a bus to the poll'.
18. *Banner of Ulster* 9 Apr.1857

'Oh bother the electors of Downpatrick; sure my brother owns all them niggers.'
1. *Banner of Ulster* 4 Apr.1857.
2. Ibid. The borough then had 196 electors (PRONI D/2223/21/10).
3. Dufferin wrote to Johnston, urging him to back Ker. (PRONI MIC 22/7 A.Rowan Hamilton to Dufferin, undated.)

The county votes
1. This time a truce was agreed, and largely held to. (The violence could apparently be turned on and turned off at will.) Each side, for example, posted advertisements in the press assuring the other that they would not raise a mob at Newtownards. (*Banner of Ulster* 9 Apr.1857.)
2. *Downpatrick Recorder* 18 Apr.1857.
3. *Banner of Ulster* 7 Apr.1857.
4. *Downpatrick Recorder* 18 Apr.1857.
5. MIC 22/7 W.Anketell to Dufferin Apr.1857.
6. PRONI MIC 22/7/39 Ker to Dufferin 15 April 1857; *Downpatrick Recorder* 12 Oct.1878. In his nomination speech, Forde claimed that Ker had been doubtful about defending his seat due to 'ill-health and family circumstances'.
7. PRONI D/880/2/7 Ker joined Lodge 86 in 1849, and served as master from 1858-68. Lord Edwin Hill and Colonel Forde were also members. Entry was carefully controlled, 'one black bean shall exclude'.
8. All prospect of a return to the electoral arena was not abandoned. In March 1864 the estate was still collecting voter data. (PRONI D/1167/10/2.)
9. PRONI MIC7/7/39. Helen (?) Lady Dufferin to her son Frederick, Fifth Lord Dufferin, 16 April 1857.
10. PRONI D/671/O/2/7&8.

11. Of the 703 voters on Ker's County Down estates, 96% voted. Of these, 96% voted for Ker, 92% of them giving him his sought after plumpers. 5% voted for Lord Edwin and 3% voted for Forde. (PRONI D/671/O/2/7&8.)

12. Ibid.

13. PRONI MIC 22/7 W. Anketell to Dufferin Apr.1857.

14. *Banner of Ulster* 7 Apr.1857.

15. *Banner of Ulster* 11 Apr.1857.

16. This was paid for by tenant subscription, and held in a 'beautifully constructed canvas pavilion… brilliantly lighted by about 300 gas lustres' in Ballynahinch market square. The Rev. Henry Cooke delivered the eulogy. (*Downpatrick Recorder* 27 June 1857.)

17. Ibid. The vases said all that needed to be said. The main piece depicted the prostrate King Alexander of Scotland, his fallen steed beside him, about to be gored by a maddened stag, had not his faithful servant come to his rescue.

24 The great engine falters

1. Burke, p.671.

2. PRONI MIC 22/7 T.Woodward to Dufferin 13 Apr.1857.

3. PRONI MIC 22/7 Ker to Dufferin 19 July 1857. The adjective is Ker's.

4. PRONI D/1255/3/6B Estimate based on debts extant in 1867.

5. Advanced to Ker out of trust funds by the Duke of Bedford at 5%, reduced to 4½% in 1844.

6. The Downpatrick loan, and an unknown percentage of the £39,847.

7. PRONI D/1255/3/25, 1842 will of David Ker.

8. PRONI D/2223/2/20, 1842 marriage settlement.

9. PRONI D/1255/3/6B.

10. Most of the money was raised locally. Lenders included Hugh Feenan, a farmer from Saul (£250), the Rev. Alexander Orr (£750), Hugh Purdy, a coastguard officer living in Dundrum (£250), John Robert Moore, a clerk living in Rowallane Cottage, Saintfield (£500), William Russell, a ship-owner from Strangford (£350), and of course John Perry of Portavo (£300). Some of these men appear to have been investing life savings. Most estate borrowings were of the order of £1,000 or so, and with the exception of the Northern Banking Company, Ker did not borrow from institutions.

11. PRONI D/1255/3/32B.

12. Anthony Trollope, *The Last Chronicle of Barset*, ch.25, quoted in Maguire, *Downshire Estates*, p.106.

13. He adds that the debt's manageability would depend on how much of it was 'productive', and whether the estate was otherwise well run. (Maguire, *Downshire Estates*, p.83-84.) The 50% threshold was also significant. When it was crossed, creditors could seek recovery of their debt through the Encumbered Estates Court. (Maguire, *Economic History Review*, 2nd series, vol.29, no.4, p.572.)

14. PRONI D/1255/3/31B.

15. Estimated at 5%, the standard rate for an Irish landowner. An English landowner could have expected to borrow at 4% or less.

16. PRONI D/1255/3/6B. Lady Selina had a jointure of £1,384 per annum. £461 each went to David's surviving aunts, Madalena Maxwell and Frances Mahon, both in their seventies. Other personal allowances to the value of c. £975 p.a. were due out of the revenues from Red Hall. Allowances totalling over £2,300 p.a. were due to David Stewart Ker's brother Richard, and sisters Frances and Madalena Selina Anketell, a net c. £5,600.

17. PRONI D/1167/10/1 & 2.

18. Maguire, *Downshire Estates*, p.69. In his study of nine Irish estates (most of them smaller than the Ker estate) Vaughan (1994, p.110, p.277-78) found that administration costs averaged c. 6% of gross income. However, there is as much art in these assessments as science. As both authors readily acknowledge, differences in contemporary accounting practices, and differences amongst researchers as to what should be classified where, etc., mean that all such figures should be approached with a certain amount of caution.

19. These costs would have included agents' fees (at 4%) and legal expenses. Some administrative expenses, including the cost of staffing the estate offices in Ballynahinch and Downpatrick, were met by the agents. As the Ker estate was less litigious than many of its peers (including Downshire), its legal costs may have been lower. (*Portavo*, p.240.) Equally, if the legal costs of say, evicting, were recovered from the evicted person's estate (as was the case on the Ker estate), this could have made relatively little difference. This too is a grey area.

20. PRONI D/10/1, p.55-57, 239-40. Accounts for 1865-66, adjusted to remove payments made to Lady Selina Ker and the De Clifford estate, which in that year were entered amongst Ker's private expenses. The caveat applied to 'civic' expenditure also applies here.

21. PRONI D/1255/3/6B.

22. Only family charges can be deducted. After this, 'personal' and 'estate' borrowings cannot be distinguished.

23. D/1255/3/32B, Memorandum.

24. Ibid.

25. In order to give his son more financial freedom than he himself had enjoyed, David Ker had been careful not to bind this property by settlement in his will of 1842. The monumental settlement of 1810 governed all dealings on the 'settled estates' of Portavo, Clough, Ballynahinch and the Five Towns, and the other County Down townlands purchased between 1787-91.

26. Spring, Agricultural History, p.80-81.

27. National Archives, Dublin Q.R.O., rental 363, vol.30 (shelf 2A/2/53). The prospectus announced the sale of 3,339 acres, however Ouley and Carnalea were withdrawn. The County Antrim lands of Ballee (part of), Tullynewey, Tuftarney, and part of Killyree were sold at an average of thirty-eight times the annual rental. Killyree fared best fetching $44^1/_2$ years purchase. (D/2223/2/9) Ker's timing, if nothing else, was impeccable as land values were then high.

28. PRONI D/2223/2/22. See indenture no.64 (Ker-Harper) & others.

29. *Downpatrick Recorder* 24 Sept.1864. The illuminated address is one of its proudest possessions. Alfred (an introvert, who lacked his father's talent for public relations) 'modestly declined' the tenantry's offer of a banquet to celebrate his coming of age. (*Downpatrick Recorder* 22 Oct.1864, quoting *Northern Whig*.)

30. *Downpatrick Recorder* 22 Oct.1864, quoting the *Northern Whig*, which had retained a soft spot for Ker.

31. Ibid.

25 'The fact is David is a complete lunatic': collapse

'Poor Mrs Ker! What Horror!'

1. *Downpatrick Recorder* 8 Nov. 1862.

2. The addresses presented to Alfred in 1864 went out of their way to draw attention to 'her kindliness, liberality and charity on every occasion when her help was required' and to 'heartily lament' her passing. (*Downpatrick Recorder* 5 & 12 Nov.1864.)

3.   PRONI MIC 22/13 De Ros to Dufferin 2 Nov.1862.
4.   PRONI MIC 22/13/45 Ker to Dufferin 27 Oct.1862.
5.   There is no death certificate, as these did not begin to be issued until 1864. (General Registers Office, pers. comm., 2004.)
6.   In retrospect, Anna's driving about so soon after the birth of her seventh child, Henry, may have been not a symptom of health, but an act of defiance.

Oh rose, thou art sick
1.   PRONI MIC 22/13 Arthur Grantham to Dufferin
2.   PRONI D/1071/F/E2/2 Caroline Norton to Mrs Hamilton Ward 8 Jan.1863.
3.   These difficulties had been evident since at least 1855. A garbled apology to Dufferin, in which Ker blames bad spirits and 'obfuscated judgement' for a disastrous visit to Clandeboye, survives from that year. (PRONI MIC 22/5/7 Ker to Dufferin 23 Jan.1855.)
4.   Elizabeth Inglis-Jones, Unpublished Memoir.
5.   David to Richard 22 Dec.1857. (Ker family, Aldworth.)
6.   PRONI D/2651/2/69 David Ker to Richard Ker 4 May 1793; *Downpatrick Recorder* 29 Oct.1864; Ibid. 26 Nov.1864.

The gorgeous mask
1.   PRONI D/892/I/7. To the Dean of Connor, who leased the house and demesne for £200 p.a. in 1855.
2.   A contemporary source reported the loss of 'many thousands of the finest trees in Montalto demesne'. Carr, *Big Wind*, p.75.
3.   PRONI D/1167/10/1; D/2651/5/36.
4.   Ibid.
5.   Downpatrick Agricultural Society Medals were won for, amongst other things, the best bull and best stallion in 1864, and best ram in 1865, beating quality entries from farms at Castleward, Florida Manor, Finnebrogue and Seaforde.
6.   *Post Office Guide* 1870; *Downpatrick Recorder* 6 Sept.1862, p.2.
7.   Richard Ker, the sitting member, had put himself beyond the pale by voting for reform, and by implication the annihilation of the borough. Johnston of Ballykilbeg seized on this. Referring to the *Last of the Mohicans*, he asked, rhetorically, if Richard wanted to be remembered in a similar work as the last of Downpatrick's MPs. (*Downpatrick Recorder* 7 May 1859.)

La dolce vita: the Kers at the Palazzo Barbaro
1.   Paget, *Linings*, p.223.
2.   Ibid.
3.   King-Hall, *Sea Saga*, p.299. Lady Paget described the great novelist as, 'rough, heavy, persevering and rather vulgar, like his books, but interesting.' (Paget, *Embassies*, p.322.)
4.   Richard Perceval-Maxwell, pers comm. 2005.
5.   Richard to Jack Wilkins 'Jan.12th' D/2651/6/6.
6.   Paget, *Linings*, p.223. Whether he had emancipated himself or gone to seed must remain a matter of conjecture.
7.   King-Hall, *Sea Saga*, p.299; Paget, *Linings*, p.222. Richard was a dilettante in the best sense of the word, whose passions included middle-eastern languages, and in the 1860s, Anglo-Saxon Art. (D/1071/H/B/K/73/1 Richard to Dufferin 26 Oct.1871.)
8.   See part one, p.123-28.
9.   Paget, *Linings*, p.222-23.
10. D/2651/1/27 Frances E.K.Cordner, Pension Suisse, Venice, to her mother, 21 May

1880.
11. King-Hall, *Sea Saga*, p.299.
12. D1071/H/B/K/74/1 Rose to Dufferin 9 Dec.1880; /K/73/5 Richard to Dufferin 29 May 1883; /K/73/1 26 Oct.1871
13. King-Hall, *Sea Saga*, p.299.
14. King-Hall diaries 7 Dec.1931, 10 Feb.1931, Olga to her husband Admiral George King-Hall. Olga also remembers Browning complaining about Barrett of Wimpole Street and punning poor puns. (King-Hall, *Sea Saga*, p.299.)
15. Some of the more colourful sources describe the Dario as 'cursed'. The American comedian Woody Allen apparently considered buying it in 2002, but was put off by its daunting reputation.
16. Ariana Curtis, 26 June 1908, quoted in *Gondola Days*, p.68.
17. Foreword to James, *Barbaro*, by Leon Edel, p.17. This circle is celebrated in the excellent *Gondola Days*. Its one shortcoming is that it, inevitably, focuses on the celebrities and the names, thus distorting and unduly downplaying the position of the Kers in the early life of the circle and its milieu.
18. King-Hall, *Sea Saga*, p.298.
19. Byers, *JUAHS*, p.7; King-Hall, *Sea Saga*, p.299.

Landlordism's Indian summer
1. This not withstanding the fact that most of the tenantry now held on either an 'at will' or a yearly basis, and were in theory susceptible to an annual rent rise.
2. *Banner of Ulster* 4 Apr.1857; Ledgers, Kinelarty estate (Ballynahinch & district) 1850-61, 1861-72, 1872-87 in Brown McConnell Clark, estate agents, Rosemary Street, Belfast.
3. Vaughan and O'Grada, quoted by Kennedy (p.41, 60) in Kennedy & Ollerenshaw. The estate could have legitimately increased rents in order to maintain its share of the increased agricultural wealth, but chose not to. This protected tenants from the vagaries of the market. The shock that followed the withdrawal of this protection, as in Red Hall in 1870, when two Ker townlands were sold and the incoming landlord increased rents by 30%, can be imagined. (*Northern Whig* 18 Apr.1870.)
4. *Downpatrick Recorder* 27 June 1857.
5. From 1848 on. These were for use on dwelling houses only. By 1861 this scheme had apparently been replaced by one in which the estate paid half the cost of slating homes. D/1167/10/1, p.94.
6. *Downpatrick Recorder* 15 May 1852; D/1167/10/1, p.90-94; /2, p.100.
7. *Downpatrick Recorder* 15 May 1852. The decade 1845-55 saw large scale investment in drainage across the estate. By the mid 1860s drainage payments on the Clough and Downpatrick estates had fallen to under £30 p.a. (PRONI D/1167/10/1&2.)
8. *Newtownards Chronicle* 15 Sept.1883. Angus laid over four miles of drains on his 13 acre farm.
9. Many landlords and agents were hostile to tenant right, viewing it as an evil they had to live with. (Dowling, p.252.)
10. Dufferin quoted in Vaughan, p.60.
11. *Banner of Ulster* 4 Apr.1857.
12. Ibid.
13. Chelmsford Committee, Evidence of John Dinnen, Solicitor. *House of Commons Sessional Papers* 1872 vol.11, p.216-17. In 1870, tenant right on the Red Hall estate fetched £20 per Irish acre (*Northern Whig* 18 Apr.1870.) In 1881, twelve years after Ker sold it, Dun (p.108) wrote that 'no tenant right obtains' on the Red Hall estate, 'but the farmers manage successfully and as prosperously as their neighbours who enjoy the full privilege of the Ulster right.'

14. PRONI D/2223/2/2, p.124. The sums involved could be considerable. When the Widow Claney of Lower Balloo sold her farm in 1884 the estate reclaimed almost £70 in advances for improvements.

15. Dowling, p.225, 240. This policy was not and did not need to be forcibly pursued. The early nineteenth century tendency towards sub-division was replaced in the middle of the century by a tendency towards amalgamation, which usually occurred 'naturally' on the death of a tenant or the transfer of a farm, as the result of interest by neighbours.

16. Dowling p.250-51, quoting Maguire on the 1851 Civil Bills Courts Ireland Act. During the 1820s-30s David Ker (1779-1844) had largely replaced lease-holding with 'at will' tenancies. After 1851 the holders of these tenancies could be evicted relatively inexpensively by civil bill.

17. 1857 Address (given by the tenantry to Ker). *Downpatrick Recorder* 27 June 1857. This was not just the idiosyncratic expression of the tenants' view, it was a restatement of the basis of relations.

18. The 1857 declaration was subscribed to by at least 500 Ker tenants. It makes clear that, for this group at least, the social compact was working. (*Downpatrick Recorder* 27 June 1857.)

19. *Downpatrick Recorder* 27 June 1857, 12 Nov.1864, 10 Feb.1857, 9 Feb.1871, 20 Dec.1873.

20. See *Banner of Ulster* 9 Apr.1857 for a well publicised, and apparently characteristic example of the estate's approach.

21. Though the tenantry had no powers to compel the estate as such, they had formal and informal ways of calling it to account. They could go to law, have the estate's behaviour scrutinised in the press, and through representation, non-cooperation, boycott and indeed extra-legal methods, use their collective weight to subvert the will of the estate.

The 'dripping roast'

1. PRONI D/1255/3/31B; D/1255/3/20B. D/1255/3/20B records an 1867 gross rental of over £31,074 (all component rentals gross, except Red Hall). D/1255/3/6B records a gross rental of £32,788 in 1865.

2. Canavan, p.151. In the 1840s Downshire created a 'garden suburb' on the edge of Newry.

3. PRONI D/1255/3/32A. Lanyon to Ker, 12 Jan.1858. Lanyon's hopeful inclusion of districts which were convenient to 'existing or progressing Railways' is a powerful reminder of the part the railways played in opening up the county to development.

4. PRONI D/1255/3/32A Lanyon to Ker 12 Jan.1858.

5. These poor tenurial terms led to poor returns. In Ballymisert Ker let out building plots at £6-8 per acre. His neighbour Lord Ranfurly achieved £8-13 per acre for less advantaged sites let on perpetuity leases. (D/2223/2/20.)

6. PRONI D/1255/3/32A. Lanyon's report was prepared with this object in mind. (These events were carefully choreographed!) Although it had sought the power to grant 999 year or perpetuity leases, the estate was content with this result. The trustees were William Anketell, Robert Gordon, Richard Ker, Spencer Perceval and Hans Blackwood.

7. This increase seems to have owed relatively little to the arrival of the railway in 1858. Town populations mostly defied the overall population fall in the county between 1841-81, but the picture is mixed. (Clarkson, Table 15.8 in Proudfoot, p.399.)

8. Hugh Press (Alexander, Reid & Frazer), pers. comm. 1999.

9. Buchanan & Wilson, p.6-7.

10. The railway arrived in 1859. Ker's towns were well served by the Belfast & County Down Railway – not surprising perhaps, given that Anketell was its chairman. (Haines, p.123.)

11. From 4,651 to 3,621. *Census of Ireland* (1871), p.508.

12. Between 1841-1911 the largest population losses occurred in the middle of the county. By 1881 Downpatrick also had the dubious distinction of having the highest percentage of unmarried adults in the county, with over a quarter of the population remaining unmarried. (Clarkson in Proudfoot, p.385, table 15.11 p.400.)

13. In 1834, 1864 and 1873 the Downpatrick estate rental is cited as £7,537 per year. In 1857 the estate yielded an actual rental income of over £8,000. (*Downpatrick Recorder* 27 June 1857.) In 1871 Conway Pilson put the actual income from the estate at 'upwards of £10,000 a-year'. (*Downpatrick Recorder* 9 Dec.1871.) The 1861-72 Clough & Downpatrick Estate Cash Books (D/1167/1&2) would seem to confirm this higher figure. As rental income is jointly accounted, neither the Downpatrick Estate income nor the urban element of this income can be isolated, but it is the dynamic element in the figures. These vary enormously year-on-year (from £9,735 in 1862-63 to £14,602 in 1867-68), but when income is plotted using a three year moving average it can be seen to have risen from £10289 to £12,863 between 1863-71(av). The Clough input will have varied around c.£2,000 p.a.

14. A. Pilson, Diary, vol.3, 1852-54, 23 May 1853.

15. Hugh Press, (Alexander, Reid & Frazer) pers. comm. 1999.

16. David Good, Myra Castle, pers. comm. 2005.

17. Twelve of Anketell's and fourteen of Keown's tenements were held jointly. (1873 Downpatrick Estate Rental.)

Armageddon and beyond

1. Dick Ker, pers. comm. 1988.

2. Mrs Stone & Mrs Day, the Manor House, Donaghadee, pers. comm. 1988

3. Ibid.

4. D/1556/21/6 Ker to Perceval-Maxwell 2 June 1869.

5. Dick Ker, pers. comm. 1988.

6. PRONI D/1255/3/6B.

7. PRONI D3244/F/7/10 Maxwell to Ker 21 Jan.1868

8. PRONI D3244/F/7/9 Maxwell to Ker 16 Jan.1868. Shortly before Maxwell died, Johnston of Ballykilbeg passed the house after dark. The curtains had not been pulled and in his diaries Johnston records looking through the lighted window to see a weary Maxwell lying on a sofa in the parlour, a touching picture of the old man shortly before his death in 1869.

9. Ibid.

10. PRONI D/3244/F/7/11 Richard Ker to Maxwell 16 Feb.1868.

11. Dean, p.83-84.

12. PRONI D/1071//H/B//K/1 Alfred Ker to Dufferin 2 Sept.1868.

13. Under the terms of this indenture, dated 8 July 1868, the trustees were given the authority to manage the estate for a period of seven years. For this they received 4% of net income, out of which they were to meet their secretarial (etc.) fees, terms similar to those of Anketell's agency. Anketell became the effective manager of the trust, hence the estate.

14. Under the terms of the 1849 Encumbered Estates Act.

15. National Archives, Dublin, LEC 92. This represented almost twenty-five years purchase, a very good price.

16. It appears to have sold for £15,300, its purchase price. (D/1259/1/30.)

17. Caroline's grandfather and Augusta Gregory's grandfather were brothers. (Burke, p.591, p.559.)

18. Dick Ker, pers. comm. 1989; David Ker 1999. Elizabeth Inglis-Jones records that she was 'an intrepid horsewoman'. 'Nimrod', the *Northern Whig's* hunting correspondent, recalled hunting with her at Montalto.

19. David Ker, pers. comm. 1999.
20. David's mother, Lady Selina Juliana Ker, died in February 1871, aged 85.
21. PRONI D/1255/3/20B. The couple's creditors included hoteliers in London, brewers in Edinburgh, booksellers in Belfast and Dublin (nice to see that he was still reading), a Dublin jeweller, a Belfast hatter, and the architects Lanyon and Lanyon, whose invoice also languished in Anketell's in tray, as under the terms of the 1868 indenture, all bills went to the trustees for payment.
22. *Downpatrick Recorder* 16 Dec.1871.
23. Ibid. His stay was brief. Ker recollected that he 'had a friend in Dublin, and got a little boy to go out to him… and see what could be done.' The friend paid the £42 bill. (*Downpatrick Recorder* 16 Dec.1871.)
24. Ibid.
25. Ibid.
26. This quiescence could be explained less benignly. The proceedings of the Court were notoriously slow, and it could have taken until 1872 for creditors to have obtained a judgement.
27. A threatened default in 1869 had apparently been made good. (*Downpatrick Recorder* 16 Dec.1871.)
28. Both judgement and mortgage creditors (like the De Clifford trustees) had the power to petition the Court of Equity Exchequer to have a receiver appointed over the estate. (Maguire, *Lord Donegall*, p.353.)
29. *Downpatrick Recorder* 9 Dec.1871. Preparations to sell the estate were begun in September 1871, in response to a similar threat by the De Clifford trustees, issued after the first default, but not acted upon.
30. PRONI D/1071/H/B/K/1 Richard Ker to Dufferin December 1871.
31. David Ker, pers. comm. 1999; PRONI MIC 22/5/7 23 Jan.1855; D/1167/10/2, p.205.
32. Elizabeth Inglis Jones, Memoir.
33. PRONI D/2223/2/13.
34. Printed 'Statement of the Affairs of David Stewart Ker, Esq.', held by the Ker family. The property being the remaining 'unsettled' estates. The other £35,000 was due to 'simple contract creditors', many of whose claims, according to Wallace, Ker's solicitor, 'would not stand the test of investigation'. (PRONI D/1255/3/20B.)
35. This term needs read broadly as it included business, estate and personal debts incurred by both David and his father.

26 Renewal? Alfred Ker and the revival

1. PRONI D/2223/2/14.
2. *Downpatrick Recorder* 15 Dec.1877.
3. *Downpatrick Recorder* 15 Dec.1877; Dick Ker, pers. comm. 1988; D/2223/2/14. A possible parallel might be the Third Marquis of Downshire, who inherited huge debts, and 'made their liquidation a major object of his life'. Maguire, *Downshire*, p.7.
4. PRONI D/1255/3/18A. Conveyance of 21 Jan.1873.
5. PRONI D/1167/10/2. The Downpatrick and Clough estates generated an average gross annual income of £13,056 between 1866-71.
6. This replicated Ker's grandfather's approach to the development of Clough. The 1873 rental records that 'the greater portion of the Town is held by Fee Farm Tenants'.
7. PRONI D1255/3/6B; D2651/5/5.
8. Mulholland was a coming man. The Mulhollands had recently bought Ballywalter, on the Ards Peninsula, from Dufferin, and were then making the journey from trade to

land that the Kers had made had a century before.

9. *Downpatrick Recorder* 25 Jan.1873, 13 June 1868. He was welcomed amid hopes that Ker-era schemes like building a new town hall and extending the Quoile navigation, both shelved for lack of money, might be revived.

10. *Downpatrick Recorder* 20 Dec.1873.

11. A letter in possession of Sara Bennett, Ufton, Leamington Spa, shows Alfred being exhorted to be responsible from the age of five.

12. In 1875 for £240. The buyer, a Mr. F. Ricardo (to whom it had been loaned) got a bargain. Thirteen years later it changed hands for £1,000, having been 'quietly stalked' by its new purchaser for several years. It is now considered priceless. (*The Tuscan*, p.17; c.1888-89 newspaper article by H.R. Haweis, in possession of the Ker family.)

13. PRONI D/2223/2/14.

14. PRONI D/2223/2/5; D/2223/2/13. This debt, a loan of £76,000 from the Representative Church Body, secured on David Stewart Ker's life interest in the settled estates, had been reduced to £52,000 by 1878, and £41,000 by 1881.

15. PRONI D/1529/1/39.

16. *Downpatrick Recorder* 15 Dec.1877.

17. Calculated on the basis of their County Down holdings. Downshire (73,800 acres) Kilmorey (37,540 acres), Annesley (23,570 acres), and Londonderry (23,550 acres) had larger holdings than Ker. In terms of rental value, the Kers came third. (Proudfoot, 'Land ownership', p.209) (When lands held elsewhere are added, their respective positions are seventh and fifth.)

18. David continued to serve on the County Grand Jury, remained a member of his elite Masonic Lodge, and attended Down Hunt functions.

19. David Ker, pers. comm. 2005.

20. Bateson owned some 17,000 acres. His father had of course been one of the principal architects of Ker's father's electoral ruin in 1857. The settlement guaranteed the children a whopping £34,000 in the event of Alfred's death.

21. In a letter to his brother Hamilton. Elizabeth Inglis-Jones, Memoir.

22. David Ker, pers. comm. 1999.

23. Elizabeth Inglis-Jones, Memoir.

24. David Ker, pers. comm. 1999.

25. PRONI D/2223/2/14.

26. Dick Ker, pers. comm. Stories about Alfred which emanate from Richard's side of the family must be treated with caution. Alfred's and Richard's descendants fell out, and somewhere along the line each seems to have become as keen as possible to blacken the other's name.

27. Office of the Registrar General, Death Certificate, 18 Feb.1876, from an 'Effusion on brain.'

28. Office of the Registrar General, Death Certificate, 14 Sept.1876. Elizabeth Inglis-Jones (Alfred's grand-daughter), wrote that he 'was driven to blow his brains out at his lodging in Dublin.' This factual inaccuracy shows how completely discussion of the affair was suppressed within the family. Her words carry a clear imputation of family responsibility.

29. *Downpatrick Recorder* 15 Dec.1877.

30. PRONI D/1071/H/B/K/71/1 Richard William Blackwood Ker to Dufferin 13 Dec.1877.

31. PRONI D/1071/H/B/K/71/2 Eva Ker to Dufferin 2 Mar.1878; K/71/3 Eva Ker to Dufferin 7 Feb.1891.

32. Elizabeth Inglis-Jones, Memoir.

33. He died at Selina Perceval-Maxwell's home, Glen House, Crawfordsburn, after a

three month confinement.
34. Letter from Mooltan, Afghanistan, Nov.1878, quoted in letter to Dick Ker, 15 Oct.1970. (Ker family, Aldworth.)

27 The boy can't help it: the recovery founders

1. Dick Ker, pers. comm.1988. Richard was one of the boys taken out of Eton by his father. At Sandhurst he was known as Paddy Ker.
2. Hamilton, *Boy*, p.262-65, 286-87. His commission was probably purchased. (David Ker pers. comm. 2005.)
3. PRONI D/2223/2/7. Debt level 1880.
4. PRONI D/2223/2/1 p.184. The Wallaces were a successful professional family who were then working their way into the minor gentry. William Wallace married an Annesley, bought a castle to live in (Myra Castle, near Downpatrick), and became High Sheriff of County Down in 1891. He also became solicitor to the Belfast & County Down Railway Company, possibly through Anketell's influence.
5. PRONI D/2223/2/3 p.229. Their allowance was increased from £600 to £800 annually, leading Wallace to note caustically that, 'This is the sort of help he [Richard] gets from his friends'. Bateson was ennobled in 1885.
6.   PRONI D/2223/2/1 p.138. The 'Trust' estate comprised the Ballynahinch and Five Towns estates, minus Montalto House and demesne. The 'life' estate comprised the Portavo and Clough estates, Killinchy Woods, Ballymisert and Carnalea.
7. Ibid, p.62.
8. Ibid. p.138. Document of 21 May 1883. In May 1883 Richard was responsible for £1,300 of the £11,000 annual debt and family charge bill. By November 1886 he was responsible for £3,300 of the debt and charge bill of £12,100. Richard's personal debt overtook the inherited debt in the late 1880s.
9. Ibid. p.138. Document of 21 May 1883.
10. Interest payments on loans under negotiation would reduce this maximum by £700 to £3,400 during the incoming year.
11. PRONI D/2223/2/3 p.108.
12. PRONI D/2223/2/4 p.372, p.134, /3, p.119. *Force majeure* led Wallace to contemplate the art sale. He did so with reluctance, aware of the loss of stature that the sale would entail. The collection, however, had been acquired not so much to enhance the family's stature as to proclaim its taste, a meaning now lost on nearly all.
13. PRONI D/2223/2/1 p.62 (March 1883). The lying gale was the custom of collecting rents six months in arrears. Richard vetoed this suggestion. His grasp of the politics of land management was surer than Wallace's. The consequences of abolishing the lying gale in the immediate wake of the Land War could have been more far reaching than the diligent old solicitor imagined.
14. PRONI D/2223/2/4 p.286-87, p.12, p.117.
15. PRONI D/2223/2/1 p.138, document of 21 May 1883; D/2223/2/7, document of November 1886.
16. PRONI D/2223/2/1 p.122,138. In 1893 the estate considered accepting loans at 5%, rising to 6% and even 8% if not punctually paid. (/3 p.339).
17. In the family folklore, and some documentation, Richard's difficulties are ascribed to 'extensive transactions with Jews'. David Ker, pers. comm. 1999; PRONI unclassified box B42275, document of 1906.
18. PRONI D/2223/2/3 p.101.
19. PRONI D/2223/2/1 p.184.
20. Ibid.

21. David Ker, pers. comm. 1999.
22. Sheep, carts, pictures, statues, anything he could get a few pounds for.
23. PRONI D/2223/2/3 p.242.
24. PRONI D/2223/2/3 p.356.
25. Dick Ker pers. comm. 1991. This apparently happened quite often.
26. Quoted in Lyons *Culture and Anarchy*, p.34.
27. PRONI D/2223/2/7. Document of November 1886.
28. PRONI D/2223/2/1 p.170 (June 1883).
29. PRONI D/2223/2/4 p.279. Wallace used this phrase in 1892, but made the same assessment in the mid 1880s. He had difficulty in finding security for loans from as early as 1883. (D/2223/2/1, p.122.)
30. PRONI D/2223/2/1 May 1883. Caroline intended to leave Charley everything, but as the result of an error in the drafting of her will she left him only £1.
31. PRONI D/2223/2/1 p.171-83; D/2223/2/3 p.3. Ker used the policies in the way his grandfather David Ker (d.1844) used the unsettled estates – as a way of creating financial room to manoeuvre. They were generally used to raise short-term loans. In 1885, for example, borrowings secured on insurance policies amounted to a small fraction of the policies' £46,000 maturity value. These borrowings kept the estate liquid until the early 1890s.
32. PRONI D/2223/2/3 p.148. Edith his wife, a natural worrier, was unable to exert a moderating influence because she – apparently – knew nothing about the dire state of his affairs. The one enduring fruit of Ker's extravagance was his new house at Portavo, built not in the grand style of yesteryear, but as a summer retreat by the sea.
33. Ibid., p.163.
34. Ibid., p.122.
35. Ibid., p.159.
36. PRONI D/2223/2/3 p.181.
37. PRONI D/2223/2/3 p.265.
38. Ibid., p.310.
39. Ibid., p.414, 417.
40. Ibid., p.419.
41. Ibid., p.438.
42. Ibid., p.427.
43. PRONI unclassified box B42275.
44. *Newtownards Chronicle* 22 Jan.1898.
45. Dick Ker, pers. comm. 1991.

28 'The gallant Nimrod'

'All cucumber and hooves'

1. *Newtownards Chronicle* 21 Apr.1883.
2. In 1893 Wallace wrote that, 'It is perfectly ridiculous to think that a man on the edge of bankruptcy is to be keeping up these places'. (D/2223/2/4, p.308.) Wallace (unfairly) blamed Edith for wanting to keep up the two houses.
3. *Newtownards Chronicle* 29 Jan.1887.
4. Richard's younger brother Henry, who had been 'holed up' in the old house for some years, could not be shifted so lived with them until his untimely death in 1890, at the age of thirty-six. (General Register Office, Belfast.)
5. The Kers rented various houses in London, the most longstanding being 18 Jermyn Street, a brisk walk from Parliament.
6. *Downpatrick Recorder* 28 Nov.1885; David Campbell, County Down Staghounds,

pers. comm. 2004. If his hunt killed a lamb, it is said that Ker would call the next day asking, 'How much do I owe you?' (Arthur Davidson, pers, comm. 1998.)

7.   *Newtownards Chronicle* 29 Jan.1887.
8.   Ibid. Ker was quoting Adam Lindsay Gordon's *Ye Wearie Wayfarer, hys Ballad*. This plea for tolerance stole the show, upstaging Londonderry's speech.
9.   Ibid.
10. Ibid.
11. *Northern Whig* 13 Nov.1884.
12. Ibid.
13. David Ker, pers. comm., 2005.
14. David Ker, pers. comm., 1999.
15. The words are those Dylan Thomas used to describe Gossamer Benyon's fantasy lover in *Under Milk Wood*.
16. Dick Ker, pers. comm. 1988.
17. David Ker, pers. comm. 1999.
18. David Ker, pers. comm., 2002.
19. PRONI D/2846/2/28 Magdalen (Nini) Ker, Orangefield to Theresa, Lady Londonderry 6 Feb.1914.
20. *Chips: The Diaries of Sir Henry Channon* p.425. (London, 1993)
21. David Ker, pers. comm., 1999.

'The gallant Nimrod' sallies forth: the 1884 election
1.   *Northern Whig* 24 Nov.1884.
2.   By 1892 the position of Master had become so prestigious it was filled by the Marquis of Downshire.
3.   *Downpatrick Recorder* 22 Nov.1884.
4.   Ibid.
5.   Some named their children after him, others hung his picture on their walls. Carr, *Most unpretending*, p.151 & note 15, p.237.
6.   These were Colonel Forde and Colonel Waring. Waring was even good enough to propose Ker, admitting 'that CAPTAIN KER was not an Orange Tory like himself… but the Constitutional party was broad'. (*Northern Whig* 15 Nov.1884.) Wallace was unable to support Ker. (PRONI D/1889/9 /19A.) His candidacy also divided the Hunt. Wallace was asked to persuade Ker to withdraw. (/19B.)
7.   *Northern Whig* 17 Nov.1884. The paper claimed that Ker's candidacy 'has astonished the farmers in this district, [Downpatrick] where he is known from infancy, having been regarded by them always as a Liberal'.
8.   *Belfast News Letter* 26 Nov.1884.
9.   *Northern Whig* 15 & 17 Nov.1884.
10. *Northern Whig* 26 Nov.1884. This observation overlooks Ker's return to a pro-Tory stance two years later. David Stewart Ker sat as member for Downpatrick from 1859-68.
11. *Belfast News Letter* 25 Nov.1884.
12. Ibid.
13. The subject gave rise to endless humour. At a pro-Ker rally in Donaghadee the electors were asked not to part 'the poor old man (whose favourite reading was 'not unnaturally the nursery rhymes of his early childhood') from his old wife, for she would feel it worse than all – (laughter)'. (Ibid.)
14. *Northern Whig* 24 Nov.1884. Crawford himself remained unfailingly polite about Ker, describing his opponent's candidacy as 'the greatest compliment the Tory party could have paid to him.' (*Northern Whig* 22 Nov.1884.)
15. Barry, p.28.
16. PRONI D/2651/5/30 *Lines on the County Down Election* 1884 (Anon).

17. *Belfast News Letter* 24 Nov.1884.

18. Ibid. No Liberal meetings were held south of a line from Banbridge to Downpatrick, a line which could be seen as denoting the southern border of what Bew and Wright called 'inner Ulster', the Presbyterian pale, which rose in 1798 and by the early 1880s had become one of the last bastions of Irish Liberalism. (Bew & Wright, p.222.)

19. Thompson, *Liberal Ulster*, p.290.

20. *Northern Whig* 1 Dec.1884.

21. Walker, 'The Land Question', in Clark & Donnelly, p.232. Thomas Dickson, the Liberal victor in Tyrone, and one of the more far thinking of the country's Liberal parliamentarians, sought to win back that Catholic support by radicalising Liberal policy to recreate 'a liberal party composed of all creeds and classes'. (Walker, *Ulster Politics*, p.194.)

22. In Tyrone the Land League had fielded a spoiler candidate in an attempt to split the Liberal vote and let in the Tory. The tactic failed, hurting Protestant support for the League. At a by-election in County Londonderry later in 1881 a nationalist candidate was entered (with the same objective) but withdrawn, amidst confusion, on the eve of the poll. Though supporters of the Land League were advised to vote against the government, the Liberal candidate was elected. (Thompson, *Liberal Ulster*, p.277-79.)

23. Walker, *Ulster Politics*, p.173. They were also in the way, and this created stresses. In 1885 Salisbury called the Ulster Tories 'troublesome and unreliable allies' and Churchill wrote of 'those foul Ulster Tories who have always been the ruin of our party'. (Cooke, *PRIA* p.62-63.)

24. Three were hanged for the murder of a family at Maamtrasna, County Galway in 1882, amid claims of a miscarriage of justice.

25. *Northern Whig* 29 Nov.1884. The quid pro quo came at Home Rule Party meetings in Newry and Castlewellan, at which nationalist voters were advised to abstain. The Castlewellan gathering was chaired by a Ker tenant, a Mr Fitzpatrick, who told the meeting that he would back his landlord. (*Belfast News Letter* 24 & 26 Nov.1884.)

26. *Northern Whig* 26 Nov.1884.

27. Ibid.

28. *Northern Whig* 25 Nov.1884.

29. *Downpatrick Recorder* 15 Nov.1884. One of Ker's tenant farmers appeared on several platforms declaring that 'if he had fifty votes he would give them all to Mr. Ker.' (*Belfast News Letter* 25 Nov.1884.)

30. Ibid.

31. *Belfast News Letter* 24 Nov.1884. Lord Arthur Hill proposed a scheme under which tenants could buy out landlords at terms equivalent to less than their current rent, when both sides were agreeable to the arrangement. Though the Liberals scoffed, the Tories were serious about land purchase. In 1885 they introduced the 'Ashbourne Act' which allowed the tenant to buy his holding over 49 years at a charge that was generally below the current rent. Nearly a million acres were purchased under the Act.

32. *Northern Whig* 27 Nov.1884. On the day before the vote the Liberals published a Ker estate document which implied that Ker tenants did not enjoy free sale. (*Northern Whig* 26 Nov.1884.) The document was an 1873 rent receipt, which forbade sales by auction and required tenders to be sent to the agent, 'who will select the future tenant'. The Wallace letter books record that 'the custom on Mr Ker's estates has… been to allow the tenants to sell their holdings to the best advantage to a tenant to be approved of, an adjoining tenant or tenant's son to have the preference over an outsider', a passage which manages to both partly confirm and refute the charge. (PRONI D/2223/2/1 p.144, 1883.) The Tories were unable to reply before the poll.

33. *Belfast News Letter* 28 Nov.1884.

34. *Belfast News Letter* 29 Nov.1884.

35. *Northern Whig* 28 Nov.1884. See also Walker, *Ulster Politics*, p.141-42.

36. Ibid.

37. PRONI D/2651/5/30 *Lines on the County Down Election* 1884.

38. *Newtownards Chronicle* 29 Nov.1884.

39. Ibid. This verse, and this verse only, is cast in Ulster Scots, whether in tribute to Crawford or to ridicule him is not clear.

40. *Downpatrick Recorder* 29 Nov.1884. This was one of the campaign's better sound-bites. A 'grand display of fireworks' followed.

41. *Belfast News Letter* 29 Nov.1884. Three by-elections were held during this week. The Liberals won both of the others.

42. *Northern Whig* 1 Dec.1884. In an angry letter, W.T. McGrath, a Liberal and a Catholic, asked his co-religionists if they were proud of their conduct, 'I was wholly puzzled to know why the speeches of Lord Arthur Hill were so mild… Now I am wise. As many of the Roman Catholics as could be befooled were to be befooled, and the befooling process has been remarkably successful.'

43. *Northern Whig* 1 Dec.1884. These may indeed have been Ker as opposed to Tory votes. The percentage split in the Catholic vote is unclear. Liberals drew some comfort from the perception that 'The more respectable Roman Catholics generally remained true to their party allegiances and voted Liberal'. (*Northern Whig* 28 Nov.1884.)

44. *Northern Whig* 5 Dec.1884. The paper recorded the vote in each of the County's 26 polling districts. 52% of the county's electors were Presbyterian, and 25% Episcopalian. (Walker, 'The Land Question', in Clark & Donnelly, p.232.)

45. *Northern Whig* 1 Dec.1884.

46. *Northern Whig* 28 & 29 Nov., 5 Dec.1884.

47. Ibid., 24 Nov.1884; *Belfast News Letter* 25 Nov.1884.

48. *Downpatrick Recorder* 6 Dec.1884.

49. PRONI D/2223/2/3 p.40.

50. UCD Archives Dept., McCartan Letter Book, P11/B Michael McCartan to Timothy Harrington 12 Nov. 1885. This was part of a mooted deal that divided the representation in eleven seats between Conservatives, Liberals and Nationalists. The original proposal had involved seven seats, with 'Captain Kerr not to be opposed in East Down'. However, Churchill, Sir Thomas Bateson, Finnegan and Lord Arthur Hill felt that this gave the Tories an insufficient share of the spoils, and pressed for the more advantageous eleven seat deal. The wider deal collapsed, but this element seems to have survived.

51. Walker, *Elections*, p.342.

29 The world turned upside down

The miller's tale

1. The family date their arrival to 1882 (newspaper cutting from 1942-43). They moved from First Bangor to First Donaghadee in 1883. (First Donaghadee Presbyterian Church Session Book.)

2. John Boyd, pers. comm. 1999.

3. Willie Bell, pers. comm. 1988.

4. PRONI D/2223/2/2, p.21-22. Lisa lived in the last of the fisherman's cottages. She was an 'at will' tenant like 'those who went before her'. Jenny Wightman did not pay rent either. She held 'a free house and three acres of grazing at Orlock Meadow'. So much for the tyrannous Ker estate. In 1888, the going rate for a cottage was 6d per week. (D/2223/2/7 Wellwood memo, 11 July 1888.)

5. PRONI D/2223/2/1, p.143; /2, p.192.

6. PRONI D/2223/2/2, p.21-22.

7. PRONI D/2223/2/1, p.143.
8. PRONI D/2223/2/1, p.235.
9. Ibid., p.302.
10. D/2223/2/1 p.62 Mar.1883.
11. D/2223/2/1 p.236, 238, Aug.1883.
12. John Boyd, pers. comm. 1999; PRONI D/2223/2/2 p.21-22.
13. *Newtownards Chronicle* 25 Oct.1930.
14. This at least was the practice at Portavo Mill. (John Boyd, pers. comm. 1999 & 2001, Willie Bell, pers. comm. 1988, Aird Lowry, pers. comm. 1990.) The 'shews' or husks were used as bedding, and when the mill was eventually motorised, were used to feed the fire which powered the engine that drove the wheel.
15. Willie Bell, pers. comm. 1988. Sometimes they arrived with, 'Cold feet, oft blue with Winter's hoar, And dripping from the salty shore', from *The Old Schoolhouse at Ballywilliam* by C. Stewart. (*Newtownards Chronicle* 24 May 1924.) Aird Lowry recalled that when he was growing up, 'men never wore boots till they were about twenty'. (Aird Lowry, pers. comm. 1991.)
16. PRONI VAL/12B/23/14A, p.72. This comment was entered when the school was struck out of the valuation list in 1909.
17. *Newtownards Chronicle* 24 May 1924.
18. The PRONI ED and SCH catalogues appear to make no reference to it. It does not appear on the 1900 (03) Six-Inch Ordnance Survey.
19. Willie Bell, pers comm. 1988; Edwin Boyd 1987.
20. 1901 Census, PRONI MIC 354/3/64.
21. Ibid.
22. Jimmy & Mina Muckle, pers. comm. 2000. Though good workers, these exiles were perceived as having been changed or even coarsened by city life. Jimmy Muckle's description of them as 'a rum bunch' is typical of the comment they receive.

Two ghosts and a banshee
1. Aird Lowry, pers. comm. 1990; Jane Burrows was Aird's grandmother's sister. She saw the figure clearly.
2. Jimmy & Mina Muckle, pers. comm. 1998; Small's mother had her roots in the Ballycopeland district.
3. Fairy belief persisted here until the mid-twentieth century (see chapter 38.)
4. Jimmy & Mina Muckle, pers. comm. 2000.

The world turned upside down
1. 'Of course all the tenants will get reductions', Wallace advised Ker, preparing him for the worst. PRONI D/2223/2/1, p.147.
2. Clough estate. *Northern Whig* 2 Mar.1874
3. Portavo estate sample: 27 cases, heard 1883-88, excludes three cases on which there was no change. (PRONI FIN/23/3/3/4 Down; D1255/3/5; *Newtownards Chronicle* 15 Sept.1883.) Reductions averaged 15.5% on the Ballynahinch estate, where between 1882-86 a quarter of the tenantry took cases. Ballynahinch estate sample: 80 cases, townlands of Ballynahinch, Ballykine, Ballymaglave, Ballylone, Ballymacarn. (Ker estate ledger 1872-87, held by Brown, McConnell, Clark, Rosemary Street, Belfast.) Judicial rents were valid for fifteen years, after which they could be reviewed.
4. PRONI D2223/2/15.
5. D1255/3/5. Portavo estate, sample of twenty cases. John Perry's rent was cut to just under £49, McBride's to under £8, McCutcheon's to £10.10s and John Small's to just over £5.
6. Devon Committee Proceedings. *House of Commons Sessional Papers* 1836 vol.33,

p.76.
7.   Chelmsford Committee Proceedings. *House of Commons Sessional Papers* 1872 vol.11, p.146. Commenting on these business-like relations, James Murland, solicitor, of Downpatrick stated that he had, 'frequently had conversations with tenants... who have told me they sincerely wished that the Land Bill had never been passed.' (Ibid.)

The mooted 'invasion' of the Copelands
1.   Ibid. The 1894 rental shows everyone in the townland up to date with their rent, except Hugh Angus, who was a year behind.
2.   PRONI D/2223/2/4 p.316, 366. On the basis that Ker should be treated 'like any other tenant'.
3.   PRONI D/2223/2/1, p.243 Aug.1883.
4.   Ibid.
5.   D2223/2/7. In Nov.1885 the estate went to court to get £234 in backrent from the Airds.
6.   PRONI D/2223/2/2, p.35 Oct.1883.
7.   *Newtownards Chronicle* 22 Aug.1925.
8.   PRONI D/2223/2/3, p.60 Nov.1885. Emerson applied under the terms of the 1885 Ashbourne Act. This advanced tenants the purchase price of their farm, which they repaid over forty-nine years at 4% interest. The islanders might have been remote, but they were up to date, and ready to take advantage of the latest legislation.
9.   PRONI D/2223/2/3, p.275-79 May-June 1886.
10. Bar that of Richard Clegg 'who is not to be turned out'. Clegg was the only islander not to amass large debts; and is the only islander known to have taken his case to the Land Commission, which reduced his rent by a third. The islanders were to sign their tenant right over to the estate, which would accept it in lieu of rent, and seek new tenants. (D/2223/2/3, p.385.)
11. The island had been successfully let on the same terms as any other part of the estate.
12. As a stop-gap, and by way of a show of determination, the estate put in a caretaker and let out the vacant land for grazing. (D/2223/2/15)

Primus inter pares
1.   PRONI D2223/2/15.
2.   PRONI D/2223/2/3 p.188, 195, 419.
3.   Ibid., p.440. Ker was then in London, ignoring Wallace's letters.
4.   Ibid., p.473. The trees were not Richard's to cut. They belonged to the creditors. Though Wallace threatened Ker with an injunction, Ker was too quick for him. The trees were last seen 'on Donaghadee Quay' awaiting the boat. (Ibid., p.481.)
5.   Horses and deer (which ran 'over the whole country and ate the people's turnips' for the use of the Stag Hounds became the only livestock kept there. (Jimmy & Mina Muckle, pers. comm. 1988.)
6.   D2223/2/4, p.303, 1893.
7.   Montalto cost at least £500 a year to run. (D/2223/2/12 Rose to Fox 13 Mar.1901.)
8.   D/2223/2/4 p.382.
9.   Dick Ker, pers. comm., 1988.
10. The contents were returned to Montalto. The speed and relish with which the Pattersons were sacked suggests that they were probably Edith's protégées.
11. D/2223/2/4 p.307. Wallace could be mean with Edith. In 1893 he refused to advance her money for seeds for the garden. (Ibid., p.308.)

The circle widens
1.   Nor did the family die out. The Andersons were a young couple who had just had a

daughter. (Shore Street Baptismal Register.)
2.   Jim & Sarah George, the Cotton, pers. comm. 1990.
3.   First Donaghadee Session Book. These were the Perrys, McCutcheons, McBrides, and latterly the Boyds, who had been admitted to the congregation in 1883 on production of a 'certificate' issued by their previous minister stating that Boyd was a communicant member of the church, in effect a certificate of good character.
4.   Both John Perry and Thomas McBride (d.1908) were trustees of the church and represented it at General Assemblies. The Perrys were tantamount to hereditary elders.
5.   PRONI, 1901 Census, MIC 354/3/64.
6.   Six of the men and boys who classified themselves as labourers were farmer's sons and nephews, and as such not so much labourers as farmers-in-waiting.
7.   PRONI MIC 354/3/64; John Boyd, pers. comm. 1999.
8.   Ethel Petersen (nee Boyd), Ontario, pers. comm., 2004.
9.   Boyd family tree (Ethel Petersen); the cottage was re-thatched in 1895 with £2.10s of straw from McCutcheon's (D/2223/2/15 9 Mar.1895); Taylor, p.147.
10.   The Commissioners of Irish Lights website, Mew Island.
11.   D/2223/2/12 Fox to Rose 7 Apr.1899.
12.   Ibid..

30 Going, going, gone!

Going, going, gone! – the estates are sold
1.   His relatively inactive co-trustee was Baron Monkswell. Rose owned 14,000 acres in Warwickshire and was a man of some substance. (David Ker, pers. comm. 2005.)
2.   D/1889/4/1/3. Boer War Diary.
3.   Robert Hugh Wallace (1860-1929) of Myra Castle near Downpatrick, was educated at Harrow & Oxford, and called to the bar in 1886. He ended the Boer War as a Lt. Colonel commanding 5th Battalion Royal Irish Rifles. His duties included detaining the beaten Boer General de Wet, who later thanked him for his kindness to himself and his family. Always highly clubbable, Wallace was a freemason and an Orangeman, in which capacity he rose to become County Grand Master of Belfast 1903-21, Grand Secretary of the Grand Orange Lodge of Ireland 1903-10, and Grand President of the Grand Orange Council of the World 1909-12. In 1921 he declined Craig's offer of a baronetcy and a place in the senate.
4.   David Ker, pers. comm. 2005.
5.   PRONI D/2223/2/12 Rose to Fox 27 Sept.1900.
6.   Miss Mitchell, High Bangor Road, Ballyfotherly, pers. comm. 1992.
7.   PRONI D/2223/2/12 Edith Ker to Robert Fox 5 Mar.1901.
8.   PRONI D/1255/3/5; Edith to Fox 5 Mar.1901. Rose (1905) felt that the previous regime had not been tough enough: 'they ought to have paid the old creditors *in full* long ago with the money they have had from the Estate and it is disgraceful that they have not done so.'
9.   PRONI D/1529/1/39. Gross rental 1879, £18,183.
10.   Mrs Stone & Mrs Day, pers. comm. 1988; Dick Ker, pers. comm. 1988.
11.   At Sandhurst, David had excelled at boxing. On one occasion, Ker's carriage is said to have met another gentleman's on the road. The track was narrow and neither carriage could pass the other, and neither man would give way. The question of who should yield became a matter of honour, which they decided to settle with their fists. Ker gave his unknown opponent a thrashing, leading the defeated party to exclaim, 'You must either be the devil or Captain Ker'. (Dick Ker pers. comm. 1999.)
12.   PRONI D/2223/2/12 Rose to Fox 11 Mar.1901.

13. Ibid 13 Mar.1901.

14. PRONI D/1255/3/24B. Edith to Wallace 'Sunday' 1905.

15. By 1906, 586 of the Ballynahinch estate's 601 tenants had signed provisional purchase agreements. (PRONI Unclassified Box B42274.)

16. D/1255/3/24B. Wallace to Rev. Hamilton Ker, 30 Aug.1907.

17. D/1255/3/24B. Moorhead & Wood to Wallace, 1 Sept.1905.

18. Ibid., 23 Feb.1906.

19. Mew Island had been sold to the Irish Lights in 1890 for £625. (D2223/2/12 Letter of June 1896.)

20. Unclassified Box B42274. The House and its 460 acre demesne (which straddled Portavo, Ballyminetragh, Balloo Lower and Orlock) accounted for £7,726 of the total. Under the terms of the Act, Ker had to sell the house and demesne to the Irish Land Commission and buy it back at the same price. As a bankrupt he could not do this, so the house was re-purchased by two of his brothers. They were to buy it as proxies, but thanks to a faulty contract ended up as its outright owners. They were too principled to keep it, and this heaven-sent opportunity to oust Richard passed.

21. This comprised Ballymisert and Carnalea on the shores of Belfast Lough, the Portavo demesne, parts of the Copelands, lands at the Spa, and various properties and pieces of land in and around Ballynahinch town.

22. £2,000 of this £7,500 p.a. went to Eva, Alfred's widow, £3,300 went on insurance and mortgage repayments.

23. Wallace received 2½% of the purchase money and 2% of the bonus, a total of nearly £7,000, for handling the sale.

24. PRONI D/1255/3/24A Edith to Wallace 'Sat' 1912.

25. D2223/2/12 Fox to Rose 1900; Ibid., Wallace to Fox 21 Sept.1900; D1255/3/24A Florinda Ker to Wallace 10 Sept.1912.

26. When she was not crying on Wallace's shoulder, she was berating him, or complaining to her brother that he was neglecting their affairs. In 1912 this charge probably had some basis. Wallace was then so 'overburdened with political matters' his handling of estate business may have suffered. (D/1255/3/24A.)

27. PRONI D/1255/3/24B, Rose to Wallace 11 Sept.1907.

28. *The King-Hall Diaries*, 9 Jan.1904, 21,26 Dec.1904, with thanks to Richard Perceval-Maxwell. She lived with her brother in Wales for at least a year.

29. Ibid., David Ker to Wallace 28 Oct.1910.

30. Ibid.; Edward Ker to Wallace, c. April 1912. The sale of Montalto aroused strong emotion. Edward likened his dilemma to being ordered to kill his mother, or forfeit his own life if he refused.

31. Brett, *Mid Down*, p.37.

32. Incredible as it seems, they haggled over the contents of the greenhouse. Clanwilliam, a keen gardener, asked the Kers to throw the greenhouse plants into the bargain. Edith refused. (D/1255/3/24A Edith to Wallace 19 April 1912.) The £20,000 went to the trustees, who – ironically – gave most of it to Alfred's daughters, who were due to receive £34,000 out of the estate under the terms of the settlement of 1871.

33. Shades of David Ker's 'Shovel-Land' letter from Rome, see p.152. Florinda did not tell Edith as, 'she worries so, & does not set ab^t a thing quietly' (D/1255/3/24A Florinda Ker to Wallace 10 Sept.1912.) According to the folklore, Ker lost Montalto in a card game, an inaccurate but telling comment on his lifestyle. (Derek Tughan, pers. comm. 1997.)

34. D/1255/3/24A, Rose to Wallace 4 April 1912. There was even talk of restoring the 1819 mansion.

35. Ibid., Wallace to Edith 17 June 1912.

36. And somewhere to put their furniture. The Brownlows mentioned their ballroom, but

the offer came to nothing, so the furniture went into storage, with Richard and Edith begrudging every penny.

37. Ibid., Edith to Wallace 28 March 1912.
38. Ibid., Wallace to Edith 17 June 1912. Ballywhite was 'dog cheap & easily kept', but these are hardly compelling reasons for buying a house.
39. David Ker, pers. comm. 1999.
40. Though Olga is known to have played ouija with Trollope's niece in Florence, her mother Rose and sister Nini are much more likely to have been the room's creators. (Richard Perceval-Maxwell, pers. comm. 2005.)
41. PRONI D/2846/2/24 Magdalen (Nini) Ker, Quentin Castle to Lady Londonderry 'May 20th'.
42. D/2846/2/20 Magdalen (Nini) Ker, Orangefield, to Lady Londonderry 6 Feb.1914.
43. D/1255/3/24A Edith to Wallace, Dec.1912 & Jan 1913. The house had gaslight.
44. D/1255/3/24B Edith to Wallace 20 Jan.1914.

31   Guns & freedom 1900–1914

Smiths and smugglers
1. 1901 Census, PRONI MIC 354/3/64; 1911 Census, National Archives, Dublin, Down 112/22.
2. John McCoubrey, pers. comm. 1998; Sammy McCully, Ballyminetragh, 1989.
3. 1901 Census, ibid.; 1911 Census, ibid.
4. 1901 Census, ibid.
5. 1911 Census, ibid.
6. 1901 Census, ibid.; 1911 Census, ibid.
7. Hugh Andrews, Balloo Lower, pers. comm. 1989. The pony was called 'Charlie'. No record of any mitigating circumstance has survived to spoil the tale.
8. James McCully remembers him as a 'wicked man… very fond of cheese and could put a spittle across the road.' (James McCully, pers. comm. 2001.)
9. Aird Lowry, pers. comm. 1990.
10. James McCully, pers. comm. 2001; Aird Lowry 1990. Here too, lights were flashed to show that the coast was clear.
11. Willie Bell, pers. comm. 1988.
12. Ibid.

Hanging by a thread: the Copelands
1. Aird Lowry, pers. comm. 1991.
2. The islands may have annulled the taboo on occupying evicted men's farms by filling the vacant Emerson farms from within with Cleggs and Andersons, who, through James Anderson's wife Mary, were related to the Emersons. (1901 Census, National Archives, Dublin, Down 19-27C; Shore Street Presbyterian Church, Baptismal Record.)
3. *Newtownards Chronicle* 20 Sept.1913.
4. James Clegg (b.1897), Memoir, written mostly between 1913-23, held by his daughter Kitty Strain, transcribed by Harry Allen. Clegg used the present tense. The island was then (just about) a going concern.
5. There were occasional disasters. James Clegg remembers the rabbits laying waste a large corn field, after burrowing under its fences. (James Clegg, Memoir; Aird Lowry, pers. comm. 1991.)
6. 1911 Census. At its recorded peak in the 1830s the island had seven households.
7. HMSO, *Census Summaries*, County Down 1926.
8. As on the mainland, each emigrant got a bonfire: 'It is the custom on the Island, when

the ship passes by bearing overseas anyone belonging to… the Isle, to light a huge bonfire on the high ground, to show the exiles that their friends' thoughts go with them'. (Campbell, p.59-60.)

9.   Aird Lowry, pers. comm. 1991.

10.   James Clegg, Memoir.

11.   Ibid. The service was performed by the minister of Shore Street. No collection was gathered, a particular the islanders found 'very satisfactory'.

12.   Aird Lowry, pers. comm. 1991.

13.   Ibid. Aird Lowry described the islanders as leathery-skinned and a bit odd, adding that they 'got a lot of stick' from mainlanders.

14.   PRONI D/1255/3/12. Belfast people greatly enjoyed these trips. As Sam McAughtry wrote, 'for us city kids the mile journey across Copeland Sound was every bit as exciting as a world cruise'. For a sub-*Gape Row* style impression of a day trip to the Copelands, see the *Newtownards Chronicle* 20 Sept.1913 27.

15.   PRONI D/1255/3/12, 1 April 1914.

The farmers lose their awe

1.   D/1255/3/12 11 Sept.1913. Though subsequently sold to the tenants, the island's initial position seems to have been anomalous. (*Belfast Telegraph* 10 Mar.1947, with thanks to Tom Brown.)

2.   PRONI Unclassified Box B42274 Wallace to Ker Nov.1903, Kinnaird to Wallace 6 Feb.1904.

3.   PRONI D/1255/3/5. Portavo estate rents included a weighing that took account of the tenant's right to 'take seaweed from the landlord's foreshore'. Where this right was abandoned (as with a farm in Ballyminetragh) the rent was reduced.

4.   Undeterred, Willie McCutcheon and John Small had a go in 1902. The results were again disappointing. Small won a further cut of just 8d, which was hardly worth putting on his Sunday suit for, and McCutcheon had his rent *increased*.

5.   PRONI Unclassified Box B42274. Alexander Kinnaird, secretary, Ballyminetragh, to Wallace 6 Feb.1904.

6.   PRONI Unclassified Box B42274. Alexander Kinnaird, secretary, Ballyminetragh, to Wallace 5 Jan.1904. The letters show the Association to have been tough and courteous in its dealings with the estate.

7.   Bence-Jones, p.116-17.

8.   Tom Brown of Brown McConnell Clark, pers. comm. 2004; *150 Years Young*; Bardon, *Belfast*, p.172, 140, 164.

9.   1911 Census, ibid. Somerset's five-storey warehouse off the Dublin Road in Belfast, is believed to have been the first reinforced concrete building in Ireland. In 1916-17 Somerset (later Sir Thomas) built 'The Weir' on the Malone ridge, overlooking Shaw's Bridge, Belfast. Earlier tenants included Alexander Macdonald Maclean (-1903) and Robert Parsons (1903-06). (Brown McConnell Clark leases.)

10.   Alex Martin, High Bangor Road, pers. comm. 1997.

11.   Hugh Andrews, Lower Balloo, pers. comm. 1988.

12.   Mrs Stone, the Manor House, Donaghadee, pers. comm. 1988.

13.   Alex Martin, pers. comm. 1997.

14.   PRONI D/1255/3/24A Rose to Wallace 4 April 1911.

15.   Ker admired the dignity of the Boers. In one letter he wrote, 'The third day of drive we got 80 Boers on our flank who surrendered there were some splendid looking men among them huge, boney men & they just sat on their ponies & stared at one as if to say: "Well you have got us at last, you have been long enough about it, you professional Roinecks."' (David to Edith 17 Apr.1901, Ker family.)

16.   Public Record Office, Kew WO 39341. David Ker's Army Service Record, kindly

supplied by Gloria Siggins.

17. D1255/3/24A David to Wallace 18 Oct.1910. Between 1904-06, David Ker served as Master of the County Down Staghounds. His father frequently talked of giving him responsibilities, but did nothing.

18. David Ker, pers. comm. 1999.

19. Gordon Moore, pers. comm. 2001. The hare coursing at Montalto was described as 'a very cruel business altogether'. (D/1255/3/24A.)

20. Ibid. Rose to Wallace 2 Sept.1911.

21. Ibid. Rose to Wallace 3 Apr.1911. Edith's protests cut little ice as Rose knew that Richard had by then received an advance of £250 for the timber.

22. Ibid.; 9 Apr.1912 Edith Ker to Wallace.

23. David had marked 808 'old and failing trees'. Scott, one of the timber men, marked the remainder, which included some of the best in the demesne. (D/1255/3/24A David Ker to Wallace 8 April 1912.)

24. PRONI D/1255/3/24A Wallace to Hartley 6 Dec.1912.

25. Ibid., Richard to Wallace 27 Feb.1912. This clampdown was not aimed at stopping legitimate personal use of sand and gravel, but at stopping its commercial exploitation.

26. The farmers had the right to take seaweed but not sand or gravel. The foreshore belonged to the Crown. The estate could have bought it for a nominal sum around 1913. Rose advised buying, but Wallace decided not to. (D1255/3/24/B.)

27. D1255/3/24/B Edith to Wallace 9 Apr.1912.

'We live in Wonderful Times': the Home Rule crisis

1. From Rudyard Kipling, *Ulster 1912*.

2. Colvin, p.82-83; Stewart, p.91; Montgomery-Hyde p. 292-93, 298-99, 304, 320-21. Montgomery-Hyde credits Wallace with turning the Ulster Volunteer Force into 'a single coherent organisation on a territorial basis'. (Ibid., p.298.) Wallace went on to command its East Down regiment. (PRONI D/1263/5.)

3. Stewart, p.63. The *Irish News* claimed that the standard was a fake. (Bryan, p.55.)

4. Ulster Covenant, PRONI. The known signatories were Willie & Nellie Angus, Lizzie Bell, Minnie Burrows, Robert, Thomas & William Boyd, Willie John Boyd, Sarah Campbell, Mary McConnell, Mr & Jane McKeag, Maggie & Henry Moderate, John Muckle, John & Mary Perry. Their ages ranged from fourteen to seventy-one.

5. D/1255/3/24A Richard to Wallace 3 Mar.1914.

6. Mrs Stone, Manor House, Donaghadee, pers. comm. 1988. Ker was not a member of the Ulster Volunteer Force, but it was nonetheless considered proper that he be in residence on the night. Word could equally have come from Wallace, one of the select band of twelve who had full knowledge of the arms importation plan.

7. Wallace was by then completely shattered. April-May 1914 found him in Switzerland taking 'a complete rest', on his doctor's orders. (D/1889/1/2/3/363.) Craig bought the freehold of his home, Craigavon, from the estate in 1905 for £7,849. (D/2223/2/9.)

8. PRONI D/2846/2/28 Magdalen (Nini) Ker to Lady Londonderry 6 Feb.1914.

9. Mrs Stone and Mrs Day, pers. comm. 1988; Stewart, *Ulster Crisis*, p.245; Aird Lowry 1991; Dick Ker, 1991. The attempt to distract the coastguards was unsuccessful. The Donaghadee station was linked by submarine cable to Coastguard Headquarters at Kingstown (Dun Laoghaire). Donaghadee informed Dublin that something was afoot. Dublin contacted Belfast, but the message apparently arrived too late to be of use. One coastguard died, apparently of a heart attack, in Lieutenant Ducat's garden, in the act of bringing the news to his commander.

32 'Past talking about': World War One

1. Mina Muckle, pers. comm. 2000.
2. Aird Lowry, pers. comm. 1991. Between 1910-18, in the wake of compulsory tillage, the ploughed area within the six counties of what would become Northern Ireland increased by a third. (Johnston in Kennedy & Ollerenshaw, p.186.)
3. D2223/2/unclassified Wellwood to Hartley July 1921.
4. Willie Bell, pers. comm. 1988.
5. *Newtownards Chronicle* 27 Nov.1915. As well as being about duty, commitment and patriotism, this recruiting poem is also about sinners getting saved. Big Andy and his unnamed friend see the light and decide to stop shooting rabbits (bad) and start shooting Germans (good), and so find redemption. It appeared beside a report on a recruiting march in Donaghadee, led by a military band.
6. 1911 Census & local knowledge. In 1914, seventeen males would have been eligible for service (aged 16-40). Six of these were from farming families. Two of the four recruits had a service background (Sammy Boyd and David Ker). The other two, Thomas and William John Boyd (brothers aged 16 and 18 respectively in 1914) were among the youngest eligible males in the townland. No married men enlisted.
7. The Portavo evidence suggests that there may have been some basis to the charge, levied in a recruiting article in the *Newtownards Chronicle* (27 Nov.1915) that 'the labourers [have] responded and shamed the farmers' sons'.
8. John Boyd, pers. comm. 1999. He worked with the ships guns. Johnny Aird's nephew George Batten was at Jutland too, on the battlecruiser *H.M.S. Tiger*. (Aird Lowry, pers. comm. 1990.)
9. John Boyd (William Boyd's brother), pers. comm. 2004.
10. John Boyd, pers. comm. 2000.
11. Eye-witness account quoted in Oakeshott, *Blindfold*, p.61.
12. Crewman's recollection quoted in Bennett, *Jutland*, p.111.
13. David Ker, pers. comm. 2005.
14. After a month spent kicking his heels in barracks. David to Edith, undated, 1914. (David Ker's war letters, Ker family.)
15. He declined *The Tatler*, as he could borrow that from any number of friends. Hopeful of taking on Portavo after the war, he begged Edith for *Farm & Home*, 'it is only 1d per week & wont break you'. (David to Edith New Year's Day 1915, 2 Feb.1915.)
16. David to Edith, GHQ, 14 Nov.1914.
17. David to Edith 5 Nov.1914.
18. David Ker, pers. comm. 2005.
19. David to Edith 28 Oct.1914.
20. David to Edith, GHQ 14 Nov.1914; David to Edith, GHQ 2 Nov.1914. David 'found a Russian's purse & money on one [of the dead Germans] so he had evidently been over the Russian side & back again'. (David to Edith, GHQ 14 Nov.1914.)
21. David to Edith, GHQ 14 Oct.1914.
22. David to Edith, GHQ 20 & 28 Oct.1914.
23. D/1255/3/24B Edith to Wallace 23 Jan.1914. David urged his mother not to communicate with the Pollocks: 'I *beg* of you not to write… to Mrs Pollock or any one, as I know for a *fact* that once you get your rag out on paper you say things you *don't* mean "Nuff said." (David to Edith New Year's Day 1915.) Edith
24. D/2846/2/28/18 Magdalen (Nini) Ker to Theresa, Lady Londonderry (undated).
25. David to Edith 'Sunday, Mountainstown, Navan'.
26. Verse in family scrapbook (Ker family).
27. David to Edith 13 Jan.1915, GHQ. Anna had 'a great horror of a War wedding'.

28. A post to which he was perfectly suited. Gloria Siggins adds that after his 1915 promotion Ker was given instructional posts with the 2nd Divisional Cavalry School and then the First Army, for duties connected with Artillery Horse Lines. (It is interesting to speculate on whether he owed these 'safer' postings to his skill as a horseman, or to his connections and his recent marriage.)

29. David told Anna that what he had seen in Flanders would haunt him for the rest of his life. (David Ker, pers. comm. 2005.)

30. Dick Ker, pers. comm. 1988; Glendinning, p.26-27. It is said within the family that David was court-martialled, however no court-martial evidence appears to have survived. This memory could be a blurred recollection of the Belgian arrest.

31. Robin Glendinning, Island Reagh, pers. comm. 2005.

32. D2846/2/28/23 Magdalen Ker to Theresa, Lady Londonderry 22 Jan.1916.

33. Ibid.

34. Ibid. In the last months of the war Nini set up a home for convalescent officers in Quentin Castle. (*King Hall Diaries* 9 &12 Apr.1918.)

35. Ibid.

36. Hugh Andrews, Lower Balloo, pers. comm. 1987.

37. Sammy McCully, pers. comm. 1995.

38. These had leather uppers and iron tips, and were reportedly very comfortable to wear. (Willie Bell, pers. comm. 1988; Dick Ker 1991, Aird Lowry 1990.)

39. Extract from *Bangor Spectator*, Nov.1916, with thanks to Ian Wilson.

40. David to Edith 2 Feb.1915.

41. Sammy McCully, pers. comm. 1995. The air ships were based in Ballycarry. (Michael McCaughan, Ulster Folk & Transport Museum, pers. comm. 2005.)

42. Ibid.

43. *Newtownards Chronicle* 29 Aug.1914.

44. Sammy McCully, pers. comm. 1995.

45. Ibid.

46. The six counties of what would become Northern Ireland lost c.24,000 men, or 12.6% of males aged 18-40 at the time of the 1911 Census. (Johnston in Kennedy & Ollerenshaw, p.184.)

47. James Muckle, pers. comm. 1998.

48. Carr, *Unpretending*, p.176.

33   Through a golden glow - the 20s & 30s

1. John Boyd, pers. comm. 1999.

2. Ibid.

3. Ibid.

4. Ibid.

5. Willie Bell, pers. comm. 1988.

6. Aird Lowry, pers. comm. 1990; Sammy McCully 1995.

7. Willie Bell, pers. comm. 1988; John Boyd 1999.

8. Ibid. In *Prejudice and Tolerance*, Rosemary Harris mentions farms in Tyrone having a dishcloth used as a communal handkerchief hanging on the back of the kitchen door in the 1950s (with thanks to Jonathan Bell for bringing this to my attention). John was too polite to remark on this, and so never learned the secret.

9. John Boyd, pers. comm. 1999.

10. Aird Lowry, pers. comm. 1990.

11. Cattle were herded along the Warren Road until the 1930s. (John Boyd, pers. comm. 2001.) James McCully remembers sitting on Shore Hill for most of the day in the early

1920s, and counting three cars pass on the Warren Road. (James McCully 2001.)

12. In 1924 Edith nearly died when her horse fell on a winter's morning, tipping her gig. She put the fall down to smoother road surfaces, and changes in road maintenance that were designed to facilitate the car. (*Newtownards Chronicle* 27 Dec.1924.) Wallace loved cars. Rose couldn't abide them. He didn't even like them on his estate, but magnanimously promised not to chase Wallace if his poor besotted friend turned up in one.

13. The farm was near Ballinalee. Harry Humphreys, pers. comm. 2004.

14. *Newtownards Chronicle* 5 July 1924. The 55 acre farm was purchased for £3,000. The Arnolds moved to Canada, amid fears for their well-being, as John Arnold had grown fond of the bottle.

15. Willie Bell, pers. comm. 1988, John Boyd 2001. The cottages got their water, as they always had, from an uncovered well by the roadside: 'They weren't fussy in those days'. (John Boyd 1999.)

16. John Boyd, pers. comm. 1999.

17. John Bell, pers. comm. 1988, John Boyd 1999, 2001; David Donaldson 1989; Aird Lowry 1991.

18. For this sum they carried the clubs, teed up balls from sandholes (there were no golf tees then, not even wooden ones) and cleaned up everything after the game. (Willie Bell, pers. comm. 1988.)

19. John Boyd and Willie Bell knew a 'double hole' on Portavo Point where they were sure to catch not one but two crabs at low tide. (John Boyd, pers. comm. 2001.)

20. John Boyd, pers. comm. 1999. They practiced on one of Willie Donaldson's fields, on the field where the remains of the saw mill now stand, and under what is now Stockbridge Park. The team ran for about four years in the late 1920s, and went through one glorious season unbeaten.

21. Harry Humphreys, pers. comm. 2004, Alec Martin 1997.

22. Ian Kinnaird, pers. comm. 2005.

23. Harry Humphreys, pers. comm. 2004.

24. David Donaldson, pers. comm. 1989, John Bell 1988, John Boyd 1999, Aird Lowry 1990, John McCoubrey 1998, Martin & Isobel Boyd 2001.

25. Martin Boyd, letter to author, Sept.2005.

26. Martin and Isobel Boyd, pers. comm. 2001.

27. John McCoubrey, pers. comm. 1998.

28. David Donaldson, pers. comm. 1989, John Bell 1988, John Boyd 1999, Aird Lowry 1990, Gilbert McCutcheon, 2002; undeposited Valuation & Lands Agency Second Revaluation list maintenance records, townland of Portavoe. The Valuation Office assessed his living area as eight square yards.

29. John McCoubrey, pers. comm. 1998, John Boyd 1999.

30. Ibid.

31. The Griffith Valuation (surveyed 1862) does not name them, but the Portavo McKeags appear on the Shore Street Presbyterian Church communicant records in 1859, and on the marriage and baptismal registers in 1866. Griffith may have omitted them as theirs was an unrecognised tenancy on a subdivided farm.

32. Sammy McCully, pers. comm. 1995.

33. Aird Lowry, pers. comm. 1990.

34. In her study of mental illness in the rural west of Ireland Nancy Scheper-Hughes identifies, 'drinking patterns among the stay-at-home class of bachelor farmers, and the general disinterest of the local populace in sexuality, marriage, and procreation [as] signs of cultural stagnation'. (Scheper-Hughes, *Saints*, p.4.) The correlation between 'characters' and womenless households is also too clear to be ignored.

35. John Bell, pers. comm. 1988, John Boyd 1999, Edwin Boyd 1997, Roy Neill 1994,

David Donaldson 1989, John McCoubrey 1998, James & Mina Muckle 1998.

36. John Boyd, pers. comm. 1999, David Donaldson 1989.

37. Willie Bell, pers. comm. 1988, Roy Neill 1994, David Donaldson 2001, Fred McCutcheon 2002, Harry Humphreys 2004. Frank Humphreys (Harry Humphreys 2004. Frank Humphreys (Harry Humphreys' father) led the collecting.

38. Terry Donaldson, Newtownards, pers. comm. 2001, James McCully 2001. Ellen Boyd was an Aiken, whose brother 'built half of Bangor'.

39. Terry Donaldson, pers. comm. 2001, James McCully 2001, Martin & Isobel Boyd 2001.

40. Harry Humphreys, pers. comm. 2004, Martin & Isobel Boyd 2001.

41. Edwin Boyd, pers. comm. 1997, John Boyd 2001, Willie Bell 1988.

42. Alec Martin, pers. comm. 1997.

43. The Muckles, who gardened for the Kers, applied their expertise on their own small holding. Strawberry jam was the favourite. When strawberries were short, Millars reputedly added stewed gooseberries, to little apparent ill effect, as their jam was said to be 'as good as Hartleys'. (James & Mina Muckle, pers. comm. 2000.)

44. *Newtownards Chronicle* 5 July 1924.

45. Harry Humphreys, pers. comm. 2004, David Donaldson 1989. The Donaldsons bought the 55 acre farm for £3,000.

46. David Donaldson, pers. comm. 1989.

47. John McCoubrey, pers. comm. 1998, Aird Lowry 1990, Willie Bell 1988, Sammy McCully 1995.

48. A haggis made with a pig's bladder rather than a sheep's stomach. Willie Bell, pers. comm. 1988, Aird Lowry 1990; with thanks to Jonathan Bell, Ulster Folk & Transport Museum.

49. Alec Martin, pers. comm. 1997, Sammy McCully 1995. Both men smoked non-stop. In the house 'you wouldn't have seen which other for smoke'. (Sammy McCully 1995.)

50. Aird Lowry, pers. comm. 1990, John McCoubrey 1998.

51. Rudnitsky, MS Ch.2.

52. Ibid.

53. Ibid.

54. David Donaldson, pers. comm. 1989, Aird Lowry 1990, John McCoubrey 1998.

55. Their brother John, who wore a hard hat and carried a rolled up brolly – clothing that proclaimed him the success of the family – had gone to Dublin, and (although he had the same teetotal convictions as his brother and sister) become a manager in Gilby's gin distillery. (Fred McCutcheon 2002.)

56. Fred McCutcheon, pers. comm. 2002.

57. They walked to First Donaghadee every Sunday, morning and evening, 'hail rain or shine'. (Fred McCutcheon, formerly of Ballyminetragh, pers. comm. 2002.)

58. Ibid.

34 'Bankrupt to the hilt & knee deep in bills'

1. PRONI D/1255/3/24B Letter of 2 August 1917.

2. Ibid; David Ker, pers. comm. 2001. Many items were stored in outhouses.

3. D/1255/3/24B Ker to Fox 17 Nov.1917.

4. John McRobert, Murland & Co., Downpatrick, pers. comm. 1998.

5. Income rose from c.£4,000 p.a. in 1915 to £6,600 p.a. in 1927. A third of this derived from land (the non-agricultural rump of the estate). Two-thirds came from investments. A £30,000 trust fund was created for David and Anna's children.

6. D/1255/3/24C Anon to James Gracey 1928.

7.   Letter to Anna, 'Dec.17th', held by David Ker, Aldworth.
8.   Sara Bennett, pers. comm. 1999. The visitor was her uncle, Roderick Inglis-Jones.
9.   Dick Ker, pers. comm. 1987; Gavin Perceval-Maxwell, letter to author 11 Sept.2000.
10. Gavin Perceval Maxwell, ibid.; Dick Ker pers. comm. 1987; Joe Clarke 2000.
11. David Ker, pers. comm. 1999; *Newtownards Chronicle* 13 Oct.1977. The King-Hall diaries make no mention of this.
12. D1255/3/24A Edith to Wallace 28 Jan.1913.
13. D/1255/3/24C Letter to Fox 17 Nov. 1929; D/1255/3/24B Richard to Fox 17 Nov.1917; Sammy McCully, pers. comm. 1995.
14. James McCully, pers. comm. 2001.
15. D/2223/2/10 Martin & Henderson to Macintosh 18 Feb.1931; Unclassified Box B42290, 1923.
16. Nellie Mitchell, pers. comm. 1992.
17. Roy Neill, pers. comm. 1994.
18. D/2223/2/12 Richard to Fox 17 Nov. 1917.
19. Sammy McCully, pers. comm. 1995.
20. Ibid.
21. *Newtownards Chronicle* 27 Nov.1915.
22. Dick Ker, pers. comm. 1988.
23. David Ker, pers. comm. 2002.
24. Dick Ker, pers. comm. 1988.
25. Dick Ker, pers. comm. 1987; King-Hall Diaries, 14 July 1922. Their cook, a Catholic, spent the attack under the kitchen table reciting the rosary. (David Ker, pers. comm. 2005.) In 1926 Colonel Forde achieved what the IRA had been unable to. He would not fix the property's drains, so the Kers moved, fearing typhoid.
26. King-Hall Diaries, May-June 1922.
27. 'Old Jock Perceval-Maxwell' had a Lewis gun set up at some vantage point in the house. A ferocious exchange of fire is said to have ensued. (David Ker, pers. comm. 2005.)
28. Ibid., 14 July 1922.
29. George L. Delacherois to his sister Madeline 15 Aug.1933. (Manor House, Donaghadee.)
30. Dick Ker, pers. comm.; Gavin Perceval-Maxwell, letter to author, 11 Sept.2000.
31. Alec Martin, pers. comm. 1997.
32. Lawlor, *International Fibres & Fabrics Journal*, vol.. 8, no. 2 (1942), p.45.
33. David Ker, pers. comm. 1999.
34. Dick Ker, pers. comm. 1991, Nellie Mitchell 1994, John Boyd 2001, Willie Bell 1988.
35. Joe Clarke, pers. comm. 2000, Dick Ker 1991, John Boyd 2001, Jimmy & Mina Muckle 1998.
36. Jimmy & Mina Muckle, pers. comm. 1998, Honor Rudnitsky 2001, John Boyd 1999, David Ker 1991. John Boyd's brother Sydney manned the van.
37. David Ker, pers. comm. 2001. 'She brought her Mountainstown ways with her'.
38. In 1932, 'rabbits, hawks, woodcock, snipe and a few wild pheasants' were shot at Portavo. (*Newtownards Chronicle* 6. Feb.1932.)
39. Arthur Davidson, pers. comm. 1998, John McRobert 1998. Illegal cockfights also took place in Downpatrick and the Mournes.
40. 'Outdoors with C. Douglas Deane', *Belfast News Letter* cutting dated 'spring-summer' 1979; John Moore, Milecross, pers. comm. 2001.
41. John Moore, pers. comm. 2001.
42. Dick Ker, pers. comm. 1991, 97; Alec Martin 1997; Outdoors with C. Douglas

Deane, ibid.; John Boyd 1999.
43. John McCoubrey, pers. comm. 1998; Sammy McCully 1995, John Boyd 2001.

35 Toffs and tourists

Toffs and tourists
1. *County Down Spectator*, 22 June 1935.
2. The Donaldsons and the McCullys could be found here on a Sunday afternoon. Willie Bell, pers. comm. 1988, John Boyd 1999, David Donaldson 1989, Aird Lowry 1990, Sammy McCully 1995, Aird Lowry 1990, Willie Bell 1988, Honor Rudnitsky 2001, *County Down Spectator*, 22 June & 20 July 1935.
3. Aird Lowry, pers. comm. 1990.
4. The case went to court. Dunn argued that he had invested his savings only because he had received an assurance from the now deceased Johnny Aird that his lease would be renewed. 'With regret', the judge found in favour of the Airds, saying that he could not go behind the words of the written agreement. He did not award the Airds costs, either for this case, or for any appeal. (*County Down Spectator*, 20 July 1935.)
5. Her home was of course Glenburnie. Willie Bell, pers. comm. 1988, Honor Rudnitsky 2001.
6. Honor Rudnitsky, pers. comm. 2001.
7. John Boyd, pers. comm. 2004.
8. During the First World War, Smiles fought in Belgium, the Middle East, and Russia. He was wounded twice, mentioned in despatches, and decorated by Russia, Rumania and the government of the United Kingdom, which awarded him the DSO with Bar. Two of his brothers died in the war, serving with the 36th (Ulster) Division. He was knighted in 1930.
9. PRONI D/1255/3/24C Nov. 1928.
10. Johnston represented Armagh in the Northern Ireland House of Commons from 1929-45. He was knighted on his retirement. He was chairman of Johnston, Allen & co., and W.B.F. Baird & Co. of Lurgan, a director of the Brookfield Spinning Company in Belfast, and a director of the Milltown Bleaching Company in Donacloney. (Central Library, Belfast, cuttings file.)
11. Aird Lowry, pers. comm. 1991. The architect was Dennis O'D. Hanna.
12. This iconic potential was exploited in the 1980s, when Volvo featured the Stone House in a television advert. Many local people describe the Stone House as their 'favourite house', and the owners are 'always getting pestered by people who want to use the place for something'. (Betty Thompson, the Stone House, pers. comm. 2005.)
13. Ibid. The staff included a chauffeur, with Rolls Royce. Johnston's spinster daughters, Dorothy and Anne, sold the house around 1957, when its upkeep became too much for them. It was bought by Colin and Denise Anderson, of Anderson & McAuley in Belfast. In 1962 the house was sold to its current owners, the Thompson family.
14. David Donaldson, pers. comm. 1989.
15. Ethel Petersen (nee Boyd), letter to author, 1995; John Boyd 1999.
16. UAHS, *Donaghadee & Portpatrick*, p.29.
17. Ibid.
18. The Donaghadee lifeboat was named the Sir Samuel Kelly in his honour. In January 1953 this boat put to sea in an attempt to save the passengers on the *Princess Victoria*. These included Kelly's neighbour, Sir Walter Smiles, who went down with the ship.
19. Willie Bell, pers. comm. 1988.
20. Edwin Boyd, pers. comm. 1987.

21. Betty Thompson, pers. comm. 2005.

22. In 1858 it had a collection of cottages, two ample gentleman's residences, a couple of small 'Bathing Houses', two National Schools, a coal yard at Portavo and a couple of 'old Salt Pans' on the site of the original Warren.

23. Clarkson in Proudfoot, p.387, 399.

Water, water everywhere…

1. *Newtownards Chronicle* 23 May 1931, 28 Oct.1933. It was claimed that the shortage was crippling the development of Donaghadee, and that the town's name had become 'synonymous with no water and discomfort'.

2. *Newtownards Chronicle* 11 Oct.1931.

3. This was the second ringing endorsement that the site had received. In 1909 another report by a different expert had come to the same conclusion. *Newtownards Chronicle* 11 Oct.1930

4. *Newtownards Chronicle* 6 Feb.1932; D/2223/2/10. Everyone put in an inflated claim. Johnny Aird claimed £333 for 2½ acres but took £85 for one. The Ker estate, in possibly the most ingenious piece of accounting ever known to man, claimed £7,939. It accepted £2,200.

5. A low interest, 75% government loan towards labour costs was secured.

6. *Newtownards Chronicle* 21 Oct.1933. 'C.C.S' of Donaghadee wrote a poem, celebrating (?) the beauty of the new lake, 'Portavoe Waterworks, seen from an uncommon angle'.

7. John McCoubrey, pers. comm. 1998.

8. D/2223/2/10, care of a 1½ inch pipe.

9. Roy Neill, pers. comm. 1994.

10. Martin Boyd, pers. comm. 1995.

11. *Newtownards Chronicle* 8 Aug.1931. This thoughtful contribution came from a former councillor.

12. 'There was no water in Donaghadee or Portavo'. Martin Boyd, pers. comm. 1995, Roy Neill 1994.

13 Roy Neill, pers. comm. 1994, Hugh Andrews 1987.

14. 1930 Report, by Binnie & Deacon of London, quoted in *Newtownards Chronicle* 23 May 1931.

15. John McCoubrey, pers. comm. 1998.

16. Roy Neill, pers. comm. 1994.

17. Ibid.

18. In winter it supports some five hundred wildfowl, including rare species of duck and swan such as Goldeneye and Whooper. (*County Down Spectator*, 22 June 1995.)

Farewell to the island

1. *As luck would have it*, by M.H. Campbell. The Campbells may have been related to the Wellwoods, Philips's younger brother being a William Wellwood Campbell.

2. Ibid., p.27. Freddie Clegg's sisters appear only once, pushing and 'hup, hupping' a pair of their cows onto the island's leaky, sod-patched cattle boat, *The Four Brothers* (p.44).

3. Ibid., p.30.

4. *Belfast News Letter* 24 Aug.1944; *Belfast Telegraph* 24 Aug.1944.

5. *Belfast News Letter* 24 Aug.1944; Hugh Andrews, pers. comm. 1987.

6. O'Crohan, p.244.

7. Aird Lowry, pers. comm. 1991.

36   World War Two

1.   Barton, p.21.
2.   Ibid., p.20.
3.   Alec Martin, pers. comm. 1997.
4.   Ibid.
5.   Ibid.
6.   Others (equally implausibly!) said that the bombers had followed the railway line to Donaghadee, and on seeing her lights had mistaken the adjacent Ballyfotherly halt for an important railway station. (William Pollock, Ballyfotherly, pers. comm. 2001.)
7.   William Pollock, pers. comm. 2001.
8.   James & Mina Muckle, pers. comm. 2000.
9.   James McCully, pers. comm., 2001.
10.   Harry Humphreys, Ballyfotherly, pers. comm. 2004.
11.   Jimmy & Mina Muckle, pers. comm. 2000.
12.   There were 'two or three round the Six Road Ends', four or five on the Gamble's land, and one on McCoubreys. (Alec Martin, pers. comm. 1997.)
13.   David Ker, pers. comm. 2001.
14.   Alec Martin, pers. comm. 2001.
15.   Ibid.
16.   David Donaldson, pers. comm. 1989.
17.   Ibid.
18.   Edwin Boyd, pers. comm. 1987.
19.   Blake, p.202 note, p.204. It was manned by the Auxiliary Territorial Service. The battery is chiefly and not very kindly remembered for letting off practice rounds at 2am in the morning, thus waking the whole neighbourhood. These guns 'had some thump off them'. When they went off, windows shook two miles away in Ballyfotherly. (Harry Humphreys, pers. comm. 2004.)
20.   David Ker, pers. comm. 1997.
21.   Aird Lowry, pers. comm. 1997.
22.   Alec Martin, pers. comm. 1997.
23.   James McCully, pers. comm. 2001.
24.   Jim & Mina Muckle, pers. comm. 1998.
25.   Alec Martin, pers. comm. 1997.
26.   Blake, p.409, 411.
27.   David Donaldson, pers. comm. 2001.
28.   James McCully, pers. comm. 2001.
29.   Martin & Isobel Boyd, pers. comm. 2001.
30.   Alec Martin, pers. comm. 1997.
31.   Willie Bell, pers. comm. 1988, Honor Rudnitsky 2001.
32.   Jimmy & Mina Muckle, pers. comm. 1998.
33.   Honor Rudnitsky, pers. comm. 2001.
34.   John Boyd, pers. comm. 2001. His letters home were laced with sweat, which for his family conjured up the heat of the desert better than any words could.
35.   His demobbed rank was captain, which became the title he was known by.
36.   *Daily Telegraph* 23 July 1977.
37.   He recuperated in 'a looney-bin-cum-hospital' in the Midlands.
38.   Dick Ker, pers. comm. 1995.

37 The new brooms

1.   Lubbock was a remarkable man. The 1871 Bank Holiday Act was the first of many pieces of progressive legislation the former governor of the Bank of England and naturalist (who studied with Darwin) initiated. Acts to preserve public open spaces, protect wild birds, encourage public libraries, and limit the hours of shop workers under eighteen to 74 per week (considered a major breakthrough at the time) followed.

2.   David Ker, pers. comm. 2002.

3.   Virginia Ker, pers. comm. 2001.

4.   Ibid.

5.   Joe Clarke, pers. comm. 2000.

6.   David Ker, pers. comm. 1999; Dick Ker 1991.

7.   David Ker, pers. comm. 1999.

8.   Clem Parkinson killed 2-3,000 rabbits a year for the first four or five years of Dick Ker's tenure. (David Ker, pers. comm. 1999.)

9.   Joe Clarke, pers. comm. 2000.

10. Alec Martin, pers. comm. 1997. 'Not a stick' of local wood was cut here. The estate's trees belonged to the trustees, for whom tree felling was still a sensitive subject, so the timber that was cut in this sawmill came from everywhere but Portavo.

11. David Ker, pers. comm. 2002. The mill employed eight or nine, and in a revealing instance of the way in which the old estate ethos still influenced Ker's thinking, a terrace of three houses was built alongside to house some of its workers.

12. Geoff Cannon, pers. comm. 2002.

13. Joe Clarke, pers. comm. 2000.

14. Ibid.

15. Joe Clarke, pers. comm. 2000; Dick Ker 1987.

16. David Ker pers. comm. 2001, 1999; Dick Ker 1987, *Daily Telegraph* 23 July 1997.

17. Dick Ker, pers. comm. 1991.

18. Dick Ker, pers. comm. 1991. Ker explained May's extraordinary outburst as a misplaced attempt to tell his culchie audience what he thought they wanted to hear.

19. *Daily Telegraph*, 23 July 1997.

20. Merged with the Irish Thoroughbred Breeders' Association in 1981.

21. David Ker, pers. comm. 2001.

22. Vida Woodhouse, pers. comm. 2001.

23. Joe Clarke, pers. comm. 2000.

24. Ibid.

25. Dick Ker, pers comm. 1991; Joe Clarke 2000.

26. Freda Jamison, pers. comm. 2001.

27. Jimmy & Mina Muckle, pers. comm. 1998.

28. Vida Woodhouse, pers. comm. 2001. These were trained by George Dunwoody, father of Richard Dunwoody, whom Ker helped place with a stable at the beginning of what would become an illustrious career. (David Ker, pers. comm. 2005.)

29. Ibid.

30. *Daily Telegraph* 23 July 1997.

31. Ibid.

32. Alec Martin, pers. comm. 1997.

33. David Ker, pers. comm. 2002.

34. Vida Woodhouse, pers. comm. 2001, David Ker 2001.

35. Joe Clarke, pers. comm. 2000, Vida Woodhouse 2001, Alec Martin 1997.

36. Freda Jamison, pers. comm. 2001.

37. David Ker, pers. comm. 2001.
38. David Ker, pers. comm. 2001, Vida Woodhouse 2001.

38 Farmers, fairies and the 'Karpet King'

1.   This took the life of a man named Knox near the Six Road Ends. (John Bell, pers. comm. 1988)
2.   David Donaldson, pers. comm. 2001.
3.   Newspaper cutting held by Terry Donaldson, Newtownards.
4.   Edwin Boyd, pers. comm. 1987. The farm cost £7,000.
5.   Martin & Isobel Boyd, pers. comm. 2001; Terry Donaldson 2001. Both combines paid for themselves through contract work.
6.   John Boyd, pers. comm. 1999, James McCully 2001.
7.   Terry Donaldson, pers. comm. 2001.
8.   James McCully, pers. comm. 2001.
9.   Frank Humphreys was the district's electrical pioneer. He wired and lit Donaghadee in 1927. (Harry Humphreys, pers. comm. 2004.)
10. Fred McCutcheon, pers. comm. 2002.

The death of the little farms
1.   Aird Lowry, pers. comm. 1990; David Donaldson 1989.
2.   David Donaldson, pers. comm. 2001.
3.   Ibid.; Isobel & Martin Boyd 2001.
4.   Isobel & Martin Boyd, pers. comm. 2001.

Frights and fairies
1.   Aird Lowry, pers. comm. 1990.
2.   Gilbert McCutcheon, pers. comm. 2002, Harry Humphreys 2004. McCutcheon paid £250 per acre for McConnell's, a price that was 'the talk of the country'.
3.   Martin & Isobel Boyd, pers. comm. 2001.
4.   John McCoubrey, pers. comm. 1998.
5.   John Boyd, pers. comm. 1999.
6.   Ibid.
7.   John Boyd, pers. comm. 1999; Willie Bell 1988, Joe Clarke 2000.
8.   Folklorist Anthony Buckley has written about the persistence of fairy belief in this part of Down. He recounts a story, collected in 1976-77, in which a young man's black hair turned white overnight after cutting down a fairy thorn 'about half a mile' from Cyril Lord's factory in Donaghadee. (Buckley in Proudfoot, p.547-565.) The links between fairy belief & rural alcoholism might make an interesting study.
9.   Martin & Isobel Boyd, pers. comm. 2001; Willie Bell 1988.
10. John Boyd, pers. comm. 1999; Joe Clarke 2000.

Suburbanisation
1.   Ker fought to save it, but heritage considerations then counted for little.
2.   Roy Neill, pers. comm., 1994; Dick Ker 1991.
3.   Sir Ivan Neill, pers. comm. 2000.

'Keep the old trap shut': the Smiles
1.   Sir Walter Smiles was High Sheriff of County Down in 1943, and from 1945 on, President of the Belfast Chamber of Commerce.

2.   In India, Smiles became a member of Assam's State Legislative Council. He led the group which addressed the Simon Committee on Indian self government, becoming the only European in India to do so. Upon his return he became a loyal Conservative, breaking with the party only over its plans for the Indian sub-continent, a breach which led Churchill to describe Smiles as 'that rascal who opposed me over India'. (D/3437/C/8/2&3.)

3.   Smiles, who did not enjoy good health was then living out of homes in Portavo, Lancashire and London.

4.   D/3437/D//6/1, D/3437/C/8/2. As was his Unionist running mate J.M. Blakiston-Houston. County Down in 1945 was once again a two seat constituency.

5.   In 1945 Blackburn, also a two seat constituency, elected two Labour MPs.

6.   PRONI D/3437/C/8/2&3.

7.   From an address presented to Smiles when he left the chair of the Assam Provincial Committee in 1929. (PRONI D/3437/D/6/1.) Cutting from *The Times* 7 Feb.1953.

8.   Central Library, Belfast, cuttings file CB31, p.227; D3437/C/7/3; Pollock, *Last Message*, p.40.

9.   Harry Humphreys, pers. comm. 2004.

10.   Aird Lowry, pers. comm., 1991. It is estimated that the *Princess Victoria* sank about five miles NNE of Mew Island. (Pollock, *Last Message*, p.40.)

11.   Patricia Ford also became the darling of the gossip and society columns, which rather obscured the fact that she was also a hardworking MP.

12.   David Ker, pers. comm. 2002. As Chairman of the North Down Imperial Unionist Association, the job fell to Ker.

13.   David Ker, pers. comm. 2004.

The 'Karpet King'

1.   PRONI VAL/4C/1/2/7/21. The rating valuer described the house as 'modern and garish… There is nothing quite like this place in Northern Ireland'. The lavish interior, on which 'no expense [had been] spared to provide every convenience and comfort', also made a big impression.

2.   Aird Lowry, pers. comm. 1990; *Belfast Telegraph* 30 May 1978.

3.   *Belfast News Letter* 25 March 1982, *Belfast Telegraph* 30 May 1978, Carrington Viyella unpublished factory history, Sir Ivan Neill pers. comm. 2000, David Donaldson 1989, Aird Lowry 1990, Alec Martin 1997, VAL4C/1/2/7/21, Margaret McCully 2002.

4.   On one occasion, when Patton needed something in Newtownards, Lord took him there by helicopter to get it. (Willie Bell, pers. comm. 1988.)

5.   Alec Martin, pers. comm. 1997, Aird Lowry 1990, Percy Donaghy 2002, Harry Humphreys 2004, *Belfast News Letter* 25 Mar.1982.

6.   Central Library, Belfast, cuttings book 41, p.99. 103; book 42, p.77; *Belfast Telegraph* 30 May 1978.

7.   *Belfast News Letter* 29 Nov. 1972, *Irish Times* 5 June 1984, *Belfast News Letter* 25 Mar.1982.

8.   *Belfast News Letter* 25 Mar.1982, *Belfast Telegraph* 30 May 1978, Margaret McCully, pers. comm. 2002.

39   'This auld place wouldn't be for sale, would it?'

'This auld place wouldn't be for sale, would it?'
1. Best, *Bubbly*, p.94.
2. The men were found things to do. Jimmy Morrow spent his time cleaning ditches, others were put to work in the woods. (David Ker, pers. comm. 1999.)
3. Ibid., 2002.
4. Ibid., 2002.
5. Ibid., 2002.
6. Vida's husband Alfie spent his time in the walled garden, 'pulling up the wrong plants'. Frank's wife Maggie helped Vida in the kitchen. (David Ker, pers. comm. 2002.)
7. David Ker, pers. comm. 2002, Willie Bell 1987.
8. Where she had been looking after Brian Faulkner's brother's children. (David Ker, pers. comm. 1999, Freda Jamison 2001.)
9. Freda Jamison, pers. comm. 2001.
10. David Ker, pers. comm. 2002.
11. Ibid.
12. The dogs had the run of the house, 'You needed to be careful where you stood', Twinks remembers. (Alexandra Watson, pers. comm. 2003.)
13. Ibid.
14. David Ker, pers. comm. 2002.
15. Joe Clarke, pers. comm. 2000.
16. Osborne King & Megran, sale catalogue. Auctioned items included everything from paintings by Teniers and Carraci, through Persian rugs and rosewood tables, to postage stamps and fishing tackle.
17. Osborne King & Megran, Sale brochure, Freda Jamison, pers. comm. 2001, Joe Clarke 2000.
18. Derek Tughan, pers. comm. 2002. Fred Tughan, who rarely talked about his father's death, was instrumental in founding Action Mental Health, a charity which helps rehabilitate people with mental difficulties, and went on to become its Life President.
19. Bishop James Moore, pers. comm. 1999.
20. Tina Tughan, pers. comm. 2002
21. Geoff Cannon, pers. comm. 2002. Initially they had settled on an almost blighted farm on the edge of Carrickfergus.
22. From time to time these got blown everywhere, and were 'often seen doing their shopping in Groomsport'. (Robert Crofts, pers. comm. 2002.)
23. Ibid. These were Joe Clarke, and Michael Strain.
24. Ibid.
25. Geoff Cannon, pers. comm. 2002.

The song of the earth
1. *Northern Ireland Agricultural Census*, p.31. In 2001 there were just 4,700 dairy farms in the province.
2. David Donaldson, pers. comm. 2002.
3. Alec Martin, pers. comm. 2002, David Donaldson 2002, Gilbert McCutcheon 2002, Alan Hops, Greenmount College 2002.
4. Alec Martin, pers. comm. 2002, Geoff Cannon 2002.
5. Gilbert & Nessa McCutcheon, pers. comm. 2002.
6. Ibid.
7. Martin & Isobel Boyd, pers. comm. 2002.
8. Sammy McCully, pers. comm. 1995.

9.   In 1901 twelve of Portavo's twenty-one households earned their living directly from agriculture. Three more earned their living from farming-related activity. In 2001 just two of the townland's 78 households (or four of its 182 people) lived primarily off the land. (Census Office, 2001 Census.)

Thesis, antithesis, synthesis
1.   Sir Ivan Neill, pers. comm. 2000.
2.   The division used to be between houses on the sea-side and the landward-side of the Warren Road.
3.   Royal Mail, p.53.
4.   Full and part time. Diana Gass, pers. comm. 2003.
5.   Mina Muckle, pers. comm. 2003.
6.   David Ker, pers. comm. 2005.
7.   *Daily Telegraph*, undated cutting held by Ker family.
8.   For the last ten years she has been working on a series of paintings based on the Mysteries of the Rosary.

Bibliography (vol. II)

Abbreviations
EHR: Economic History Review
HMSO: Her Majesty's Stationery Office
H&WRO: Hereford & Worcester Record Office
IB: The Irish Builder
IE: Ireland's Equestrian
IESH: Irish Economic & Social History
IIFFJ: Irish & International Fibres & Fabrics Journal
JUAHS: Journal of the Upper Ards Historical Society
NAI: National Archives of Ireland
NIHGI: Northern Ireland Heritage Gardens Inventory,
PRIA: Proceedings of the Royal Irish Academy
PRO: Public Record Office
PRONI: Public Record Office of Northern Ireland
QUB: Queens University Belfast
UAHS: Ulster Architectural Heritage Society
UCD: University College Dublin

Books
Anon. *A Short History of the Ancketill or Anketell Family, compiled by One of its Members* (Belfast, 1901)
Ball, Len & Rainey, Desmond *A taste of old Comber: the town & its history* (Dundonald, 2002)
Bardon, Jonathan *Belfast: an Illustrated History* (Belfast, 1982)
A History of Ulster (Belfast, 1992)
Barton, Brian *Northern Ireland in the Second World War* (Belfast, 1995)
Barry, John *Hillsborough* (Belfast, 1962)
Beckett, J.C. *The Making of modern Ireland 1603-1923* (London, 1966)
Bence-Jones, Mark *Twilight of the Ascendancy* (London, 1987)
Best, George (with Ross Benson) *The Good, the Bad and the Bubbly* (London, 1991)
Bennett, Geoffrey *The Battle of Jutland* (London, 1964)
Black, R.D.Collison *Economic Thought and the Irish Question 1817-70*

(Cambridge, 1960)

Blake, John W. *Northern Ireland in the Second World War* (Belfast, 1956)

Brady, Ciaran; O'Dowd, Mary & Walker, Brian (eds.) *Ulster: an Illustrated History* (London, 1989)

Brett, C.E.B. *Buildings of North County Down* (UAHS, 2002)

Historic Buildings in Mid Down (UAHS, 1974)

Bryan, Dominic *Orange parades: the Politics of Ritual, Tradition and Control* (London, 2000)

Buchanan, R.H. & Wilson, Anthony *Irish Historical Towns Atlas, no.8, Downpatrick* (Dublin, 1997)

Burke, J.P. *Dictionary of the Landed Gentry* (London, 1843)

Burke's Irish Family Records (London, 1976)

Campbell, M.H. *As luck would have it* (Dundalk, 1948)

Canavan, Tony *Frontier Town: an illustrated history of Newry* (Belfast, 1989)

Carr, Peter *The Most Unpretending of Places: a history of Dundonald, County Down* (Dundonald, 1987)

Carr, Peter *The Night of the Big Wind* (Dundonald, 1993)

Census of Ireland (1871) vol. 3, Ulster (Dublin, 1875)

Clark, Samuel & Donnelly, James S. *Irish Peasants: Violence & Political Unrest 1780-1914* (Manchester, 1983)

Colvin, Ian *The Life of Lord Carson* (London, 1934)

Connolly, S.J. (ed) *The Oxford Companion to Irish History* (Oxford, 2002)

Costello, John & Hughes, Terry *Jutland 1916* (London, 1976)

Crossman, Virginia *Local Government in Nineteenth-century Ireland* (Belfast, 1994)

Daly, Mary E. *The Famine in Ireland* (Dundalk, 1986)

Day, Angelique & McWilliams, Patrick *Ordnance Survey Memoirs of Ireland* (Belfast, 1990-92)

Dean, J.A.K. *The Gate Lodges of Ulster* (Belfast, 1994)

Dixon, Hugh (with Kenneth Kenmuir & Jill Kennett) *Historic Buildings in Donaghadee & Portpatrick* (Belfast, 1986)

Doherty, J.E. & Hickey, D.J. *A Chronology of Irish History since 1500* (Dublin, 1989)

Dowling Martin W. *Tenant Right & Agrarian Society in Ulster 1600-1870* (Dublin,1999)

Dun, Finlay *Landlords & Tenants in Ireland* (London, 1881)

Farrell, Michael *Arming the Protestants: The Ulster Special Constabulary 1920-27* (Dingle & London, 1983)

Gailey, Alan *Rural Houses of the North of Ireland* (Edinburgh, 1984)

Gray, John & McCann, Wesley *An Uncommon Bookman: Essays in Memory of J.R.R. Adams* (Belfast, 1996)

Hamilton, Gen. Sir Ian *When I was a Boy* (London, 1939)

Healy, John *The Death of an Irish Town* (Cork, 1968)

House of Commons Sessional Papers 1836, vol.31, 33, 34; 1847, vol.17, 50, 52; 1872, vol.11 (London, various)

HMSO *Census Summaries 1901-26, County Down* (Belfast, 1928)

Jackson, Terry *Friends and Acquaintances of Henry Cooke* (Unknown, 1985)

James, Henry *Letters from the Palazzo Barbaro* (London, 1998)

Killen, John (ed) *The Famine Decade: Contemporary Accounts 1841-51* (Belfast, 1995)

Kinealy, Christine *This Great Calamity: The Irish Famine 1845-52* (Dublin, 1994)

Kinealy, Christine & Parkhill, Trevor (eds) *The Famine in Ulster* (Belfast, 1997)

King-Hall, Louise *Sea Saga* (London, 1935)

Knox, R. Buick *A History of Congregations in the Presbyterian Church in Ireland* (Belfast, 1982)

Lyons, F.S.L. *Culture and Anarchy in Ireland 1890-1939* (Oxford, 1979)

Lyons, May Cecelia *Illustrated Encumbered Estates 1850-1905* (Whitegate, 1993)

McCauley, Elizabeth Anne; Chong, Alan; Zorzi, Rosella Mamoli & Lingner, Richard *Gondola Days: Isabella Stewart Gardner and the Palazzo Barbaro Circle* (Boston, 2004)

McCavery, Trevor *Newtown: a history of Newtownards* (Dundonald, 1994)

Montgomery-Hyde, Harford *The Life of Sir Edward Carson* (London, 1953)

Northern Ireland Agricultural Census, Results for June 2001 (Belfast, 2001)

O'Crohan, Tomas *The Islandman* (Oxford, 1992)

O'Grada, Cormac *Black '47 and Beyond: the Great Irish Famine in History, Economy, and Memory* (Princeton, 1999)

Oakeshott, Ewart *The Blindfold Game: the Day at Jutland* (London, 1969)

Paget, Walburga, Lady *The Linings of Life* (London, 1928)

Patterson, Edward M. *The Belfast & County Down Railway* (London, 1982)

Pederson, J.P. (ed) *The International Directory of Company Histories, vol.22* (Detroit, 1998)

Pollock, W.G. *Six Miles from Bangor: The story of Donaghadee* (Belfast, 1975)

Pollock, W.G. *Last Message 13.58, the Death of the Princess Victoria* (Belfast, 1990)

Proudfoot, Lindsay (ed) *Down: History & Society* (Dublin, 1997)

Royal Mail *The Postal Address Book 1995-96 Northern Ireland* (Gateshead, 1995)

Rudnitsky, Honor *An old wife's tale* (MS now pub)

Scheper-Hughes, Nancy *Saints, Scholars and Schizophrenics: Mental Illness in Rural Ireland* (Los Angeles, 1979)

Shirley, E.P. *History of the County of Monaghan* (London, 1879)

Stewart, A.T.Q. *The Ulster Crisis: Resistance to Home Rule 1912-14* (London, 1967)

Taylor, Richard M. *The Lighthouses of Ireland: a Personal History* (Cork, 2004)

Thompson, Frank *The End of Liberal Ulster* (Belfast, 2001)

Vaughan, W.E. *Landlords & Tenants in Mid-Victorian Ireland* (Oxford, 1994)

Walker, Brian M. (ed) *Parliamentary election results in Ireland 1801-1922* (Dublin, 1978)

Ulster Politics: the Formative Years 1868-86 (Belfast, 1989)

Wallace, Robert Hugh (ed. Cecil Kilpatrick) *The Formation of the Orange Order 1795-98* (Belfast, 1994)

Whyte, J.H. *The Independent Irish Party 1850-59* (Oxford, 1958)

Williams, Jeremy *Architecture in Ireland 1837-1921* (Dublin, 1994)
Wilson, Catherine Anne *A new lease on life: landlords, tenants and immigrants in Ireland and Canada* (Montreal, 1994)

Articles
Anon. 'Villas, Donaghadee, County Down', in *IB*, vol.36, 1894.
Byers, Thomas 'Quintin Castle', in the *JUAHS*, no.6, 1982.
Conacher, J.B. 'The Politics of the "Papal Aggression" Crisis 1850-51', in *CCHA* Report, 26 (1959).
Cooke, A.B. 'A Conservative party leader in Ulster: Sir Stafford Northcote's diary of a visit to the province, October 1883', in *PRIA*, vol.75, section C, p.61-84.
Glendinning, Lorna 'Off to war on horseback', in *IE*, vol.1, no.1.
Lawlor, H.C. 'Rise of the Linen Merchants in the 18th century', *IIFFJ*, vol.8, no.2, 1942.
Maguire, W.A. 'Lord Donegall and the sale of Belfast: a case history from the Encumbered Estates Court', *EHR*, 2nd series, vol.29, no.4.
Proudfoot, Lindsay 'The management of a great estate; patronage, income and expenditure on the Duke of Devonshire's Irish property c.1816-1891', in *IESH*, vol.13 (1986), p32-55.

Pamphlets
Anketell, W.R. *The conduct of the resident landlords of Ireland contrasted with that of the absentees, and taxation as a remedy for absenteeism, demonstrated to be necessary, just and constitutional.* (London, 1844)
Anketell, W.R. *The effects of absenteeism briefly considered in the following pages, which are respectfully dedicated to the resident proprietors of Ireland, as a trifling but sincere tribute of respect, and addressed to the absentees as a short expostulation.* (London, 1843)
Anon. *The Tuscan, A Short Account of a Violin by Stradivari* (London, 1891)
Anon. *150 Years Young: Brown, McConnell, Clark 1854-2004* (Belfast, 2004)
Bailie, Rev. W.D. *Bi-centenary History of Edengrove Presbyterian Church 1774-1974* (Ballynahinch, 1974)
Barkley, J.M. *Francis Hutcheson (1694-1746) Professor of Moral Philosophy, University of Glasgow* (Belfast, 1985)
Christie & Manson, *Sale Catalogue of May 1848* (London, 1848)
Coastguard Service *The History of HM Coastguard* (Southampton, 1995)
Mulholland, Brian, Baron Dunleath *Ballywalter Park* (Ballywalter, 2003)
Pollock, William *Donaghadee Golf Club: 100 Years in the Making* (Donaghadee, 1999)
Reid, Horace *Ballynahinch Guide* (Downpatrick, 1998)

Websites
www.bromley.gov.uk (for Sir John Lubbock)
www.dardni.gov.uk/econs/stats (for farm incomes)
www.ehsni.gov.uk (for Belinda Jupp, NIHGI, 1992)
www.firstworldwar.com/battles/ypres1
www.king-hallconnections.com

www.proni.gov.uk/ulstercovenantsearch
www.worldwar1.co.uk

Unpublished
Carpets International (U.K) Ltd. 'Cyril Lord Carpets'
Clegg, James 'The Copeland Islands' (1913-23, 1936-37)
Customs Records, PRO Kew
Delacherois Papers, PRONI
Downshire Papers, PRONI.
Dufferin Papers, PRONI
First Bangor Presbyterian Church, Baptismal Record 1852-87; Marriage
Register 1810-1864.
First Donaghadee Presbyterian Church, Baptismal Record 1799-1873;
Committee Book 1824 on; Marriage Register 1805-45 (discontinuous); Session
Book 1824-1912 (discontinuous); Sick Book 1841.
Frey, Joseph, 'An analysis of rural settlement change in the Barony of
Kinelarty during the nineteenth century' B.A. thesis, Dept. of Geography,
QUB, 1979.
Groomsport Presbyterian Church, Baptismal Register 1841-1903; Marriage
Register 1842-1942.
Inglis-Jones, Elizabeth A Family Memoir
Kennedy, Brian A., 'Sharman Crawford 1780-1861 A political biography' D.Lit
thesis, QUB, 1953.
Ker papers: Brown McConnell Clark, Belfast; PRONI; Aldworth, Reading,
reproduced with the kind permission of Humphrey Ker.
Landed Estates Court records, NAI
Londonderry Papers, PRONI.
McCartan Letter Book, UCD
Maxwell Papers, PRONI.
Newtownards Workhouse, Board of Guardians Minute Book, PRONI
Perceval-Maxwell Papers, PRONI.
Pilson, Aynesworth A Downpatrick Diary, vol.1, 1799-1849, PRONI & Linen
Hall Library
'Historical and Topographical Illustrations of the County of Down', 1936
(originally published in instalments in the *Downpatrick Recorder* 1850-53).
Perceval-Maxwell, Richard, (ed) 'The King-Hall Diaries'.
Porter Papers, Hereford & Worcester Record Office, Worcester.
Relief Commission Papers (County Down), NAI
Shore Street Presbyterian Church, Baptismal Register 1849-84; Committee
Book 1851 on; Communicants 1857-1920s; Marriage Register 1850-1947.
Smiles Papers, PRONI
Ulster Unionist Council Archive, PRONI

Interviewees
Hugh Andrews of Balloo Lower; Moore Anketell of Portballintrae; Willie Bell
of the Close, Portavo; Edwin Boyd, formerly of Ballywilliam; John Herron
Boyd, formerly of Portavo; Martin & Isobel Boyd of the Hill, Portavo; Geoff
Cannon of Ballyminetragh; Joe Clarke of Portavo; Robert Crofts of Portavo;

Arthur Davidson of the Spa, Ballynahinch; David Donaldson, formerly of Stockbridge House, Portavo; Terry Donaldson, Newtownards; Jim & Sarah George of the Cotton; Freda Jamison, formerly of Portavo; David, Dick & Virginia Ker, formerly of Portavo; Ian Kinnaird of Ballyminetragh; Aird Lowry of Orlock; John McClintock of Red Hall; John McCoubrey of Ballyfotherly; James McCully formerly of Ballyminetragh; Sammy McCully of Crows Hill, Ballyminetragh; Fred McCutcheon of Groomsport; Gilbert McCutcheon of Portavo; Alec Martin formerly of Moor Farm, Ballyminetragh; Miss Mitchell of Ballyfotherly; Gordon Moore of Milecross; Jimmy & Mina Muckle of Portavo; Sir Ivan Neill of Ballywilliam; Roy Neill of Portavo; Dr. John Nelson of Ballycarry; Richard Perceval-Maxwell of Marlborough; Billy Pollock of Ballyfotherly; Mrs Stone & Mrs Day of the Manor House, Donaghadee; Derek & Tina Tughan of Portavo; Vida Woodhouse, formerly of Portavo.

Newspapers
Bangor Spectator, Banner of Ulster, Belfast News Letter, Belfast Telegraph, Downpatrick Recorder, Irish News, Newtownards Chronicle, Northern Whig

Index (vols.1&2)